PROGRESS IN
BEHAVIOR THERAPY
WITH DELINQUENTS

PROGRESS IN BEHAVIOR THERAPY WITH DELINQUENTS

Compiled and Edited by

JEROME S. STUMPHAUZER, Ph.D.

School of Medicine
University of Southern California
Los Angeles, California

C H A R L E S C T H O M A S · P U B L I S H E R

Springfield · *Illinois* · *U.S.A.*

Published and Distributed Throughout the World by
CHARLES C THOMAS • PUBLISHER
BANNERSTONE HOUSE
301-327 East Lawrence Avenue, Springfield, Illinois, U.S.A.

© *1979, by* CHARLES C THOMAS • PUBLISHER
ISBN 0-398-03733-7 cloth
ISBN 0-398-03738-8 paper
Library of Congress Catalog Card Number: 77-15604

Printed in the United States of America
N-1

Library of Congress Cataloging in Publication Data

Main entry under title:

Progress in behavior therapy with delinquents.

    Includes indexes.
    1. Juvenile delinquency—Addresses, essays, lectures. 2. Behavior ther-
apy—Addresses, essays, lectures.
I. Stumphauzer, Jerome S.
RJ506.J88P76   616.8'914   77-15604
ISBN 0-398-03733-7
ISBN 0-398-03738-8 pbk.

Dedicated to
the Youth of
East Los Angeles

CONTRIBUTORS

THOMAS W. AIKEN, University of Southern California

TOM S. ALLISON, Stockton State Hospital, Stockton, California

JANE F. BECKER-HAVEN, Stanford University

MICHAEL W. BEHLES, Hathaway Home for Children, Lakeview Terrace, California

GASTON E. BLOM, Michigan State University

CURTIS J. BRAUKMANN, University of Kansas

JOHN D. BURCHARD, University of Vermont

BARRY R. BURKHART, Auburn University

BONNIE W. CAMP, University of Colorado School of Medicine

KENT CANDELORA, Center For Living, South Pasadena, California

WILLIAM S. DAVIDSON II, Michigan State University

D. STANLEY EITZEN, Colorado State University, Fort Collins, Colorado

JAMES FILIPCZAK, Institute for Behavioral Research, Silver Spring, Maryland

DEAN L. FIXSEN, Father Flanagan's Boys Home, Omaha, Nebraska

WALTER S.O. FO, Behavior Therapy Clinic, Honolulu, Hawaii

ROBERT M. FRIEDMAN, Florida Mental Health Institute, Tampa, Florida

ELOISE J. FULLER, University of Vermont

WILLIAM G. HAVEN, Learning House, Palo Alto, California

FREDERICK HEBERT, University of Colorado School of Medicine

CARL F. JESNESS, California Youth Authority

SHIELA KENDALL, Solano County Juvenile Hall, California

KATHRYN A. KIRIGIN, University of Kansas

STANLEY B. KLEIN, Learning House, Palo Alto, California

MARK F. LEFEBVRE, University of Vermont

MICHAEL J. MAHONEY, Pennsylvania State University

CAROLYN M. MILLS, Bowling Green State University, Bowling Green, Ohio

CLIFFORD R. O'DONNELL, University of Hawaii

ELERY L. PHILLIPS, Father Flanagan's Boys Home, Omaha, Nebraska

SANDRA C. REESE, Institute for Behavioral Research, Silver Spring, Maryland

MICHAEL J. ROBINSON, Kentfields Rehabilitation Program, Grand Rapids, Michigan

DOUGLAS SLOANE, Solano County Juvenile Hall, California

MARTIN E. SHOEMAKER, Assertion Training Institute, North Hollywood, California; Cox Pain Center, Cambia, California

JOHN R. STAHL, Regional Educational Assessment & Diagnostic Services, Lakeville, Massachusetts

JEROME S. STUMPHAUZER, University of Southern California School of Medicine

CARL E. THORESEN, Stanford University

KATHERINE E. THORESEN, Learning House, Palo Alto, California

WILLIAM J. VAN DOORNINCK, University of Colorado School of Medicine

ESTEBAN V. VELOZ, El Centro, East Los Angeles, California

HENRY B. VENEMA, Pembroke General Hospital, Pembroke, Ontario

TIMOTHY L. WALTER, Rhode Island College

CURTIS S. WILBUR, National Heart, Lung and Blood Institute

MONTROSE M. WOLF, University of Kansas

BRIAN T. YATES, The American University

PREFACE

I⊤ HAS BEEN nearly five years since *Behavior Therapy With Delinquents* was published in 1973. Perhaps the primary question from readers is "has there been progress over these years?" There has indeed, and there has been enough sustained interest in delinquency and behavior therapy to warrant a second volume on the topic.

Again, the editor's task has been to bring some organization to the area, to underscore noteworthy trends, to guide the reader to related work, and to provide a reference volume for those many struggling with understanding, treating, and preventing delinquent behavior: probation officers, sociologists, psychologists, psychiatrists, institutional staff, educators, juvenile court personnel, police agencies, community agencies, and students. This book may serve as a text or supplementary text for courses in juvenile delinquency, criminology, police science, and behavior modification. Although it deals specifically with young offenders, the principles and programs might well be applied with children and adolescents with other problems, as well as with adults.

The same material is *not* covered both in *Behavior Therapy With Delinquents* and in this volume. Although the present volume can stand on its own and requires no particular requisite background, *Behavior Therapy With Delinquents* does contain several classic, pioneering programs that will continue to be of interest to those actively involved in developing delinquency programs today. In that volume the editor had introduced the reader to a list of basic principles which has recently been expanded and published as a brief, programmed introduction and training manual: *Behavior Modification Principles* (Stumphauzer, 1977; *Behaviordelia*).

These twenty chapters, of course, do not represent all of the progress in this field, but rather represent the editor's choices of innovative developments that are seen as important trends in recent years. Many are "firsts." Several other programs are referenced by individual authors and in the editorial comments. The reader will be interested to note that nine of the twenty chapters are *original* papers prepared expressly for this volume.

The book begins with three introductory chapters: a review of history and trends, an important chapter discussing cognitive issues, and a related, innovative project for developing cognitive self-control in young, aggressive boys. The remaining seventeen chapters are presentations of treatment, training, or preventative programs which the editor has ordered along a continuum—from institutional or *closed* settings in which membership is required, to community or *open* settings in which membership is voluntary: *Institution* (Chapters 4, 5, & 6), *Group Home* (Chapters 7, 8, 9, & 10), *Probation* (Chapters 11 & 12), *School* (Chapter 13), *Clinic* (Chapter 14), *Court/Community Program* (Chapters 15, 16, & 17), *Open Community Program* (Chapters 18, 19, & 20). The direction of this continuum reflects the editor's interest in underscoring and adding whatever delayed reinforcement comes with publication to wide-scale community and preventative programs *in the natural environment.* In four instances two related chapters on the same program are represented (Achievement Place, Learning House, probation training, and East Side Story).

Rather than providing a general introduction to the book, a goal in part accomplished by Chapter One, the editor has prepared comments to introduce each chapter; underscoring that chapter's importance, noting related work, and pointing out the need for further systematic replication and extension.

The editor wishes to express his gratitude to each of the authors, journals, and publishers who graciously granted permission to reproduce articles here; they are acknowledged individually at the beginning of each chapter. In addition the editor would like to thank the following authors who prepared chapters exclusively for this volume: Michael J. Mahoney, Tom S. Allison, Shiela Kendall, Douglas Sloane, Martin E. Shoemaker, Kathryn A. Kirigin, Montrose M. Wolf, Curtis J. Braukmann, Dean L.

Fixsen, Elery L. Phillips, Katherine E. Thoresen, Carl E. Thoresen, Stanley B. Klein, Curtis S. Wilbur, Jane F. Becker-Haven, William G. Haven, Brian T. Yates, James Filipczak, Robert M. Friedman, Sandra C. Reese, Carolyn M. Mills, Timothy L. Walter, J. R. Stahl, Eloise J. Fuller, Mark F. Lefebvre, and John D. Burchard.

JEROME S. STUMPHAUZER

CONTENTS

Page

Preface xi

Chapter

1. MODIFYING DELINQUENT BEHAVIOR: BEGINNINGS AND CURRENT
PRACTICES—*Jerome S. Stumphauzer* 3

2. COGNITIVE ISSUES IN THE TREATMENT OF DELINQUENCY—
Michael J. Mahoney 22

3. "THINK ALOUD:" A PROGRAM FOR DEVELOPING SELF-CONTROL
IN YOUNG AGGRESSIVE BOYS—*Bonnie W. Camp, Gaston E.
Blom, Frederick Hebert, and William J. van Doorninck* 34

4. THE YOUTH CENTER PROJECT: TRANSACTIONAL ANALYSIS AND
BEHAVIOR MODIFICATION PROGRAMS FOR DELINQUENTS—
Carl F. Jesness 56

5. NEW DIRECTIONS IN A JUVENILE HALL SETTING—*Tom S.
Allison, Shiela Kendall, and Douglas Sloane* 73

6. GROUP ASSERTION TRAINING FOR INSTITUTIONALIZED MALE
DELINQUENTS—*Martin E. Shoemaker* 91

7. ACHIEVEMENT PLACE: A PRELIMINARY OUTCOME EVALUATION
—*Kathryn A. Kirigin, Montrose M. Wolf, Curtis J. Braukmann, Dean L. Fixsen, and Elery L. Phillips* 118

8. THE EFFECTS OF BEHAVIOR MODIFICATION ON THE ATTITUDES
OF DELINQUENTS—*D. Stanley Eitzen* 146

9. LEARNING HOUSE: HELPING TROUBLED CHILDREN AND THEIR
PARENTS CHANGE THEMSELVES—*Katherine E. Thoresen,
Carl E. Thoresen, Stanley B. Klein, Curtis S. Wilbur,
Jane F. Becker-Haven, and William G. Haven* 156

10. COST-EFFECTIVENESS ANALYSES AT LEARNING HOUSE: HOW
MUCH CHANGE FOR HOW MUCH MONEY?—*Brian T. Yates,
William G. Haven, and Carl E. Thoresen* 186

11. TRAINING JUVENILE PROBATION OFFICERS IN BEHAVIOR MODI-

Chapter   *Page*

    FICATION: KNOWLEDGE, ATTITUDE CHANGE, OR BEHAVIORAL
    COMPETENCE?—*Barry R. Burkhart, Michael W. Behles,
    and Jerome S. Stumphauzer* 223

12. A FOLLOW-UP OF PROBATION OFFICERS TRAINED IN BEHAVIOR
    MODIFICATION—*Jerome S. Stumphauzer, Kent Candelora,
    and Henry B. Venema* 233

13. PREP: EDUCATIONAL PROGRAMMING TO PREVENT JUVENILE
    PROBLEMS—*James Filipczak, Robert M. Friedman, and
    Sandra C. Reese* 236

14. ELIMINATION OF STEALING BY SELF-REINFORCEMENT OF AL-
    TERNATIVE BEHAVIOR AND FAMILY CONTRACTING—*Jerome S.
    Stumphauzer* 259

15. COMMUNITY PSYCHOLOGY AND BEHAVIOR MODIFICATION: A
    COMMUNITY-BASED PROGRAM FOR THE PREVENTION OF DE-
    LINQUENCY—*William S. Davidson II and Michael J.
    Robinson* 266

16. REDUCING JUVENILE DELINQUENCY: A BEHAVIORAL-EMPLOY-
    MENT INTERVENTION PROGRAM—*Carolyn M. Mills and
    Timothy L. Walter* 287

17. THE BUDDY SYSTEM: RELATIONSHIP AND CONTINGENCY CON-
    DITIONS IN A COMMUNITY INTERVENTION PROGRAM FOR
    YOUTH WITH NONPROFESSIONALS AS BEHAVIOR CHANGE
    AGENTS—*Walter S. O. Fo and Clifford R. O'Donnell* 302

18. THE TOKEN ECONOMY COMMUNITY YOUTH CENTER: A MODEL
    FOR PROGRAMMING PEER REINFORCEMENT—*J. R. Stahl,
    Eloise J. Fuller, Mark F. Lefebvre, and John D. Burchard* 317

19. EAST SIDE STORY: BEHAVIORAL ANALYSIS OF A HIGH JUVENILE
    CRIME COMMUNITY—*Jerome S. Stumphauzer, Thomas W.
    Aiken, and Esteban V. Veloz* 345

20. BEHAVIORAL ANALYSIS OF NONDELINQUENT BROTHERS IN A
    HIGH JUVENILE CRIME COMMUNITY—*Thomas W. Aiken,
    Jerome S. Stumphauzer, and Esteban V. Veloz* 362

Author Index 383
Subject Index 389

PROGRESS IN
BEHAVIOR THERAPY
WITH DELINQUENTS

CHAPTER 1

MODIFYING DELINQUENT BEHAVIOR: BEGINNINGS AND CURRENT PRACTICES*

JEROME S. STUMPHAUZER

EDITORIAL COMMENTS

This first paper serves as an introduction to the volume. It covers four of the major beginnings of behavior therapy with delinquents—case studies, a symposium in England in 1964, subject-experimenter psychotherapy, projects in the national training school—and then explores more recent progress in institutions and in clinics, and major trends toward modification directly in communities since **Behavior Therapy With Delinquents** was published in 1973.

The reader should note that several of the programs reviewed in this first selection are represented as chapters in the book. The large California Youth Authority project comparing a token economy in one institution with transactional analysis in another is presented by Jesness in Chapter 4. Shoemaker's group assertion training with delinquents appears in Chapter 6. The probation training program of Burkhart, Behles, and Stumphauzer is found in Chapter 11. Both an outcome evaluation of Achievement Place (Chap. 7) and a study of changes in attitudes of Achievement Place youth (Chap. 8) appear elsewhere in the book. To a large extent, the remaining chapters in this book exemplify trends noted in this review and are recent and ongoing projects of which the editor has become aware since the first selection was written. The major trend noted, toward intervention directly in the natural environment of delinquent and nondelinquent behavior—the community—will only be underscored further by the remainder of this

---

*Reprinted with permission from *Adolescence,* 1976, 11, 13-28. (Libra Publishers, Inc.)

book.

A few other important reviews of behavior modification and delinquency have appeared in recent years and should be consulted as well (Braukmann & Fixsen, 1975; Burchard & Harig, 1976; Davidson & Seidman, 1974; Stephens, 1974; Stumphauzer, 1974).

ABSTRACT

THE BEGINNINGS of behavior therapy with delinquents are traced to the early 1960s when a number of case studies and demonstration projects were first presented. Current practices are reviewed in more detail. In institutions for delinquents, many token economies have gradually developed; their shortcomings and results are discussed. In clinic settings, several individual and group techniques are reviewed as they are currently practiced. A major trend is seen as being away from institutional and traditional clinic behavior therapy. Direct community intervention is seen as the most parsimonious mode for modifying and preventing delinquent behavior, and several model programs are described.

INTRODUCTION

Behavior therapy or behavior modification may be defined simply as the systematic application of the psychological principles of learning in the modification of human deviant behavior. Behavior therapy with delinquents in particular now seems a logical development. On the one hand, behavior therapists have developed a series of techniques and experimental methods with demonstrable effectiveness. On the other hand, delinquents represent a most perplexing and difficult population, and, as Krasner (1971) clearly underscores, behavior therapists have been quick to pick up such challenges. The attitude has been "give me your most difficult patient, and I will show you that behavior therapy works." This has been true with chronic schizophrenics, the retarded, and also with adult criminals and juvenile delinquents.

Behavior therapy has experienced a phenomenal growth in the last few years, and this can be seen as due to both the demonstration of effectiveness and to the gradual disenchantment with traditional methods (Bandura, 1969). A small but consistent literature has related delinquency and behavior therapy. My recent book, *Behavior Therapy with Delinquents,* presents a thorough introduction, along with the major reports of such work (Stumphauzer, 1973). Here instead, I will explore a few of the key beginning developments of behavior therapy with delinquents in the 1960s, and present what I see as major current practices and trends. This paper is meant in no way to present a static picture as there is a rapid, yet almost deliberate evolution taking place.

THE BEGINNINGS

Case Studies

Like most new therapies, behavior therapy first presented itself through many varied and sometimes loose case demonstrations. Patterson (1971) has called this the "whoopie" developmental phase of behavior therapy, where therapists say "Hey, look at me," and he also saw it as a period when the law of effect—that behavior can be controlled by its consequences—was demonstrated over and over again with every conceivable kind of patient and a multitude of behaviors. So, too, with the behavior of delinquents. Wetzel (1966), for example, was able to show that the "compulsive stealing" of a 10 year old could be controlled by the withdrawal of attention. Tyler (1967) used tokens to radically improve the academic performance of one delinquent in an institution. Case studies do have their place as perhaps a first proving ground, but as Patterson said, we are beyond that hit-and-miss stage now and should focus on total, more sophisticated programs and on generalization. Some therapies are tied to the case study technique because of their limited methods which do not allow for measurement or clear demonstration of cause, effect, and generalization; this need not be the case with behavior therapy.

1964 Symposium

Behavior therapy with delinquents was also launched by a symposium in London, England (Jones, Gelder, & Holden, 1965). Jones reviewed behavior modification techniques in general and suggested aversive conditioning as potentially relevant to the treatment of delinquents. For most of the specific techniques that he reviewed, Jones doubted the direct applicability to delinquency. Instead, new approaches might be designed for treatment of this group of individuals. Gelder concluded on a halfhearted note that behavior therapy may find a small but important place in treatment, and results are not so bad that the approach should be discarded altogether. He cited one research study, that of Tyler (1967). Holden, a psychiatrist, responded to these "dangerous goods" on ethical grounds, terming aversion therapy a "highly refined form of torture." He went on to warn us of the horrors of *1984* and *Brave New World.* Holden found it too short a step from "pocket do-it-yourself super-egos" to "Thought Police." Finally, Holden chose not to accept the "dangerous gift" of behavior therapy, and excluded it from "medical matters" and even from the title "therapy." This symposium brought many of the issues of behavior therapy with delinquents into the open. Although some have responded to these issues, these very complaints and criticisms are still discussed today (Krasner, 1964; London, 1969; Rogers & Skinner, 1956; Schwitzgebel, 1970; Skinner, 1971).

Subject-Experimenter Psychotherapy

A third beginning may be traced to Subject-Experimenter Psychotherapy which was developed at Harvard University in the early 1960s by C.W. Slack and his students, Ralph and Robert Schwitzgebel. Much of this surprisingly current approach is covered in Ralph Schwitzgebel's (1964) book, *Street Corner Research.* They started first by modifying one major problem behavior for delinquents (for therapists?) —attendance at therapy sessions. They simply paid delinquents two dollars to come in for each session, and it worked. Later, they took the innovative steps of recruiting delinquents from the street and set up their project in an old storefront in a high-crime area. In short, they were doing behavior therapy with delinquents directly *in the community,* a major development to which we have only recently again directed our efforts as the most plausible approach to youthful law breaking in the community. They were the first to point the way to contingency contracting with delinquents in their natural environment, and this has become a major thrust in practice today (Schwitzgebel, 1969). Further, they experienced generalization phenomena—the delinquents became "attached" to the research facility, began to meet there on their own, began to imitate the experimenters, to seek their approval, and to improve their behavior elsewhere. It was much later that we would refocus directly on his modeling, imitation, and generalization as such.

National Training School

A "final" beginning may be found in the many demonstration projects to come out of the old National Training School for Boys in Washington, D.C. These were the beginnings of token economies in institutions for delinquents. Harold Cohen et al. (1966) demonstrated that the education of institutionalized delinquents can be brought under reinforcement control in a programmed environment. A little later they converted an old cottage at the National Training School into a "24-hour learning environment" for 41 delinquents. Over the year that they participated in the project, significant increases were found in academic progress, and a significant mean gain of over 12 IQ points on the Revised Beta was found as well. In addition, social and attitudinal changes were found. There was a new pride of ownership in personal belongings and in living quarters. Discipline became no more than a minor problem; officers were even removed during the day shift. The authors stressed their philosophy as being of major importance. Rather than the usual penal code of "do what we say or be punished," they applied a positive reinforcement approach which did not force the inmates to do anything. This first large-scale token economy for delinquents, together with Burchard's (1967) early work, became the cornerstone for the modern practice of token economies with delinquents, which will be explored next.

TRENDS AND CURRENT PRACTICES

In Institutions

The picture shows a boy with a gun in his hand and the caption reads, "prison isn't a waste of time, a lot of kids come out learning a trade." This provocative advertisement for the National Council on Crime and Delinquency (*Time,* June 15, 1970) points to one of the major criticisms of institutions for delinquents—they represent *a place to learn more delinquent behavior*. While the youth is supposedly being punished (confined) he is exposed to hundreds of other delinquents, and a large part of their existence is spent swapping stories and skills. Rehabilitation? *Correctional* institution? Hardly. There is some research suggesting that, in fact, delinquent peers in institutions run quite a sophisticated behavior modification program for shaping *anti*social, delinquent behavior, while the institutional staff exert a much less consistent counterinfluence (Buehler, Patterson, & Furniss, 1966).

The token economy has now come of age. First developed fully by Ayllon, Azrin (1968), and their colleagues within wards of chronic schizophrenics, the token economy is widely practiced in hospitals, schools, and in many institutions for delinquents. We may accept Cohen's description of a token economy as a "24-hour learning environment;" not an hour of therapy, or six hours of school, or eight hours of work, but 24 hours of programmed environment planned to promote prosocial development and to minimize antisocial behavior. Token economies are attractive for many reasons. There is tight structure, stress on measurement, and an inherent accountability in their design that funding agencies are increasingly looking for (Stumphauzer, 1972b, 1974). They work, and this *can* be demonstrated clearly. There are several large token economies for delinquents, and I will describe two.

The new federal Robert F. Kennedy Youth Center (KYC) in Morgantown, West Virginia is largely a token economy (Karacki & Levinson, 1970). Its programs grew, in part, from the many token economy demonstration projects at the old National Training School for Boys, which it replaced. At the KYC, the three hundred students (as they are called) basically earn points for good behavior. The points can be converted to money to purchase goods or privileges. There is a class level system at KYC, and potential earnings vary with level: "trainee" to "apprentice" to "honor student." All, however, earn points from school for productive academic and social behavior, from the cottage largely for prosocial behavior, and from chore detail for good work and social development. Points can be saved, spent for room rental, spent on fines for misconduct, used in the commissary or snack bar, or used for recreation. The effectiveness of token economies with academic behavior has been demonstrated many times elsewhere (O'Leary & O'Leary, 1972), and at KYC this is also the case. One of the KYC token economies (they have gradually developed into a number of more or less separate programs) has focused on the most difficult kind of delinquent, the unsocialized sociopathic type. This particular token economy included very individualized programs, short-term (six to eight weeks) performance goals, and a generalized tangible reinforcement system (Wotkiewicz, 1972). After nine months in the token economy, great educational gains were made for the group of 15 students studied—gains 58 percent greater than the rate of progression for community public schools—and this is for a group of students who usually do very poorly in school. Strides in job training and elimination of assaultive and disruptive behaviors are reported as well.

Another series of large-scale token economies for delinquents is being developed by the California Youth Authority. Jesness and De Risi (1973) thoroughly describe techniques of contingency management in one large school for boys. What makes this project so interesting, in addition, is that this token economy is being compared with a sister institution whose programs are based on transactional analysis. Their design is experimentally sound with randomized assignment of delinquents, comparable training, with adequate measures and follow-ups. Preliminary results are not altogether surprising and do point to one of the major problems still facing token economies and, for that matter, all therapies. Grossly summarizing some of the findings, gains were made in both institutions: those with the token economy programs improved their behavior, and those in the transactional analysis program developed more favorable feelings about themselves and others! The really critical findings would be expected in the follow-up measures, but here they were both only somewhat better than previous institutional results, each with about 30 percent failing parole at twelve months (still too sizable a percentage) as compared to the usual 40 percent. But I believe the problem here is that *both* programs ceased when the delinquents were released back to the community, to parole, and so did most of their treatment effect. There was little generalization, and having learned our lesson from other token economies with longer histories, there should be no reason to expect it.

Generalization is becoming the problem of the 1970s, and remains a key issue which behavior therapists are actively and quite deliberately pursuing (Baer, 1973). That is, what variables control the degree of generalization, from, say a token economy with delinquents, to behavior once they are released to the community? The most obvious alternative is that they probably should not be removed from the community in the first place, but rather should be treated in the natural environment—as will be discussed later. Yet it seems that institutionalization will continue for some time, and token economies are still on the increase. How can we *maintain* their effects? How can we keep the youth out of trouble? The only answer is to extend the token economy into the community after release in order to maximize generalization. One way is the use of "halfway houses" where the tight control of the token economy is only gradually turned over to natural community controls (self-control, parents, schools, friends, jobs, etc.). For example, a youth may live in a community token economy halfway house, but go out to the community school, or work for a paycheck rather than for points. Now recognizing this need, the California Youth Authority is working with the parole personnel that will follow the youth once he is released to help them *complete* the behavior modification and prosocial adaptation back at the community level. Of course the largest task is still in seriously examining and changing the neighborhood or environment which teaches and maintains delinquent behavior. A new issue facing behavior therapy in institutions is the recent notoriety of abuses and misuses of behavior therapy in prisons and the (consequent?) withdrawal of much of the federal support for behavior therapy programs in prisons. True, the "dirty water" of abuses may have been thrown out, but so too were the "clean babies" of humane progress like those projects previously mentioned. Partially in response to this, the American Psychological Association has recently appointed a blue ribbon panel to explore limits and ethical codes for behavior therapy (*APA Monitor,* April, 1974) .

In Clinics

Individual behavior therapy and group behavior therapy are the most obvious counterparts of traditional psychotherapy in clinics. They are based on a professional-client model and on a "once or a few sessions a week" format. This is in direct contrast to 24-hour token economies and to the community models that will be discussed later. Both individual and group behavior therapy *are* flourishing, and a number of techniques have been developed in treating delinquents (Stumphauzer, 1974) . Yet, as I see trends away from institutions, I also see trends away from "clinic behavior therapy" as it too is a limited model. It relies on one-to-one contacts of too few professionals and too many delinquents, on treatment long after the youth has been in trouble, has been arrested, and now perhaps is on probation or parole in the same environment which originally spawned his delinquent behavior. These techniques will continue to grow in sophistication but cannot hope to solve the social problem of delinquency; the dent may be noticed here in the literature but not on the streets. There *are* some important functions of clinic behavior therapies: they allow for the development of techniques, they do help a (curiously) chosen few who find their way to clinics and private practices, and they might add enough to our knowledge to point out areas of needed social change. Still, the practicing clinician today does need to know what techniques have been developed that do work.

Behavioral family therapy immediately comes to mind as a shining example. In this kind of behavior therapy the whole family is seen, and after a careful behavioral analysis is begun (with close scrutiny of behaviors and possible controls on behavior) , the therapist becomes a negotiating agent and teacher, helps set up contingency contracts, and gradually transfers these skills to the family (Patterson, 1971, Alvord; 1971). Stuart (1971),

Liberman (1972), and Stumphauzer (1974) have shown this clearly with delinquents. This technique is becoming very widely used in general. We are now extending this technique by training indigenous paraprofessionals to do behavioral family therapy directly in the homes of alcohol-abusing adolescents (Teicher, Sinay, & Stumphauzer, 1976). This is a good example of taking a solid, proven clinic technique and extending it into the community.

While aversion therapy has been used widely with alcoholics and sexual disorders, and remains a controversial yet often applied technique, only very limited aversion therapy has been attempted with delinquents. MacCulloch, Williams, and Birtles (1971) successfully treated a 12-year-old exhibitionist with anticipatory avoidance aversion therapy, pairing mildly painful electric shock with pictures of the kind of older women that the youth exposed himself to, and paired shock avoidance with the pictures of "age appropriate" girls. At five-months follow-up the boy ceased his exhibitionism and had a 13-year-old girlfriend. Similarly, covert sensitization has been reported as being successful with some very difficult delinquent problems—car stealing, breaking and entering, and drug abuse. In covert sensitization, the aversive conditioning is carried out in the patient's imagination or *covertly* by pairing images of antisocial approach behavior (e.g., a stealing scene) and repulsive images such as throwing up (Cautela, 1967).

In group techniques, modeling, the all important yet neglected peer reinforcement, and tangible rewards may be used (Stumphauzer, 1972a, 1972c). In my Behavioral Psychodrama (Stumphauzer, 1974), we follow a ten-step technique which includes: (1) discussion or symbolic modeling of a particular problem situation (e.g., getting into a fight), (2) actual demonstration of the problem situation with the delinquent making it as real as possible, (3) some kind of punishment or disapproval for that poor way of handling it, (4) discussion or symbolic modeling by group members or leaders of better alternative ways of handling the situation, (5) an actual demonstration or modeling of the better way, (6) reinforcement of modeling the better way (since models who are reinforced, tend to be imitated), (7) practice by the youth in role-playing the better way, demonstrating that he or she *has* in fact learned it, (8) social and perhaps tangible reinforcement, even applause, for the new behavior, (9) suggestion that they practice this new behavior during the week, and (10) reinforcement of this practice or *generalization* the following week, and perhaps going further in working on the problem or beginning another behavior psychodrama with someone else. Children and adolescents seem to enjoy this kind of work and that is an added attraction of this behavior therapy over a traditional group where they sit around talking about problems (only the *first* step in this scheme!). Shoemaker (1974) has used group assertive training techniques with delinquents. True, delinquents may be assertive in an aggressive sense, but in these sessions they learn socially appropriate assertiveness (talking, standing up for their legitimate rights *without* fighting, etc.).

One difficulty in seeing delinquents as outpatients is that they do not want to come in, but another is that their delinquent behavior occurs in the community and is not apparent during clinic appointments. A few behavior therapy techniques allow us an approximation to "bringing the behavior in"—behavioral family therapy is one, behavioral psychodrama and assertive training are others. Yet they are all very limited glimpses of the real outside world beyond our office doors, and only approximate the reality of delinquent behavior in the natural environment.

In The Community

Increasingly, behavior therapy is being practiced directly in the community. By this I do not mean in a community clinic or in a mental health center, but rather the principles are being applied directly *in vivo,* in the natural environment (Tharp & Wetzel, 1969; Buehler, 1973; Fo & O'Donnell, 1974). This is not a traditional psychotherapy model but is more closely related to a community mental health model. I hasten to add that it is not a traditional behavior therapy model either, except that finally we are heeding our own dictum that *environment controls behavior,* and are doing something *in* that environment. What is developing, then, and is pointed to as *the* future practice, is a behavioral

community mental health model. Current practice takes the form
of either the development of specific community-based programs
or a more general behavioral community consultation.

The concept of consultation, of an outside expert helping a
program or community develop, is now well represented in behavior therapy. This is perhaps most evident in school programs,
and to a lesser extent in behavior therapy with delinquents.
Probation departments, for example, respond well to behavioral
consultation. Traditional probation may be viewed as a series
of loose behavioral contingencies which are usually not at all
clear to delinquents. If you ask what probation means or what
will happen if you do such and such, you will get responses either
like "stay out of trouble or else. . ." or "I don't know." The behavioral consultant can help probation officers learn the principles
of behavior therapy and then how to negotiate clear, meaningful
contingency contracts with the probationers and their families.
In my work with one teenage child molester his understanding of
probation was "he told me to stay out of trouble and to mind my
grandmother or I would get into more trouble." I asked him
what behaviors were permitted, which were not, and what did
"mind your grandmother" mean. He did not know. And the
consequences, what would really happen if he molested another
child? He wasn't sure. The probation officer was sure, but he had
not spelled it out clearly for the boy or his grandmother. With
consultation, the probation contingency was made very clear: "If
you molest another child, you will be taken out of your home and
placed in juvenile hall." The behavior was clearly delineated
and so were the consequences. The probation was now clear.
But most probation is based on threat of punishment, an exceedingly poor behavior therapy regime. We went further and outlined some contingencies with the grandmother and probation
officer that focused on the specific *positive* behaviors that were
wanted (e.g., "be in by 9:00 every week night") and what the
positive consequences would be ("and you can stay out to 11:00
on one weekend night"). We have just completed a training
consultation program with juvenile probation officers and were
able to demonstrate that officers can learn to do behavioral an-

alyses and to set up behavioral probation programs with only six weekly two-hour training sessions (Burkhart, Behles, & Stumphauzer, in press). In summary, probation is often a series of loose negative contingencies or threats. Behavior therapy principles suggest clearer contingencies and a focus on positive behavior and positive reinforcement. This can form the basis for behavioral consultation with probation.

Community self-help groups are developing in many cities. For example, a church or a school may develop an adolescent drug abuse program in their own neighborhood and may ask an "expert" for help. Twenty such programs were recently presented in Los Angeles, many of them making use of behavioral principles and consultation (Los Angeles Federation of Community Coordinating Councils, 1973). They blatantly rejected traditional models of hospital and clinic treatment with the feeling that it had been tried for years and didn't work or was available only to the rich and/or white. There was considerable anger at the medical establishment and over the millions being squandered without any effect in *their own* neighborhoods. They'd rather do it themselves. A few of them only reluctantly accepted behavioral consultation because it was different and "made common sense" since it focused on current behavior and on community control of behavior. One group, for example, was functioning as "big brothers" in an all black school system. They had some promising success in keeping youths in school and off drugs. They were using their attention as social reinforcement and, in some cases they used tangible rewards. They were helping "their own" and this *is* different from "there's something wrong with you and you must go see the doctor to get treated." In one of our projects, we are helping already functioning paraprofessionals in such agencies to do behavioral contracting directly in the homes of alcohol-abusing adolescents—combining their knowledge and close touch with the community culture with our behavior therapy skills (Teicher, Sinay, & Stumphauzer, 1976).

Can a group home for delinquents in the community, based on behavior therapy principles, serve as a viable *alternative* to traditional delinquency institutions? The results of Achievement

Place continually provide answers in the affirmative (Phillips, 1968; Phillips et al., 1973) . This series of exemplary projects was begun about eight years ago by an innovative group at the University of Kansas and is continuing to proliferate. It began with a set of foster teaching-parents trained in behavior modification, a modest house in the suburbs, and nine court-referred delinquents. Using convincing baseline or experimental analysis designs, they have clearly demonstrated improvement in social behavior, self-care, self-government, leadership, and perhaps most remarkably have been able to improve delinquent and academic behavior in the school *from the home*. They have developed a program for training other sets of teaching-parents (Phillips et al., in press) , and have even written a novel which gives a close account of one boy's experience with Achievement Place and a look inside a community-based token economy (Allen et al., in press). This is a brief excerpt near the beginning, while the boy and his new "family" were finishing lunch on the first day. Note the behavior, the contingency, the social and token reinforcement, the measurement, and the importance of peer attention:

> I finished off the sandwich and chips in a hurry and got up. The wife was still eating, but she looked up at me, everybody else did too, like I did some terrible thing.
>
> "Would you please carry your dishes to the sink, Paul?"
>
> Man, oh man, oh man, I felt like telling her, I ain't no damned waitress, lady, but I kept quiet. I looked at the warden, and he nodded his head, meaning I had to do what she said.
>
> "But that's woman's work," I said louder than I planned. My voice sounded weird to me, cause I'd hardly said nothing out loud since I left the courthouse. All the guys looked around at each other, rolling their eyes and grinning, and I thought, these sons of bitches, ain't nobody going to laugh at me, you'll see.
>
> "We all do things here you'll probably call 'women's work'," the warden said. "Elaine couldn't possibly do everything for all of us, and there's no reason why she should. We want you to learn how to do things for yourself while you're here. Now please carry your dishes to the sink."
>
> He said that all pretty nice, not grouchy or like he lost his temper. I took the damn dishes over to the sink, since I didn't figure that he'd let me out of there until I did.

"Good Paul, that's fine, thank you, give yourself 500 points."

This guy was like a broken record. But I wrote down 500 points for "carrying dishes to sink," and the warden put a big "L" by it but he erased the "S" and put "M" and said it was for maintenance or something. The guys were being quiet, watching again.

Police are probably the most active and yet overlooked and mistrusted community workers (Snibbe & Snibbe, 1973). They in turn tend to view traditional mental health practice with at least skepticism and probably disrespect. Together with probation they are developing a quite promising community program: delinquency diversion. They are diverting young people *out of* the traditional system (arrest, juvenile hall, court, probation, etc.) and are attempting to intervene very early in the development of delinquency, making some kind of environmental intervention. Delinquents usually reach us long after they have been in a great deal of trouble and are perhaps forced into treatment by probation. Behavior therapy is completely consistent with a policy of delinquency diversion and I believe we will see an increased blending of the two. There has already been considerable behavior therapy work with "predelinquents." What is needed is rapid environmental intervention, following the principles of behavior therapy, when trends toward delinquent behavior are *first* noted by police, teachers, and parents—not as an afterthought, or as punishment much later when there is less chance for effecting a change, but at the beginning.

Again, the innovative group at the University of Kansas has led the way with another form of direct behavioral community consultation. Todd Risley (1972) reports Juniper Gardens as a fairly typical government housing project that began as a beautiful, well-planned community, but after a number of years had deteriorated into a community with many problems: delinquency, vandalism, litter, abandoned cars, fighting, loud parties, etc. Risley took the innovative step and began attending a monthly tenants association meetings, listening to the community's concerns, and finally offering his help as a consultant for them to help themselves. Using the principles of behavior therapy they have begun controlling many of their problems. They have been able to change their community, their own environmental controls on their behavior, and with only limited behavioral consultation. This is a far cry from "doctor" treating "patient." It is a model program to watch, one that warrants imitation and replication elsewhere—in other communities with other problems.

In summary, a wide variety of behavior therapy techniques have developed and are currently practiced, and a philosophy of preventive intervention is gradually developing. At this time I see trends away from traditional institutional treatment, and even clinic treatment, and toward intervention directly in the natural environment of delinquent and non-delinquent behavior—the community.

REFERENCES

Editorial Comments

Braukmann, C.J., & Fixsen, D.L. Behavior modification with delinquents. In M. Hersen, R.M. Eisler, and P.M. Miller (Eds.) *Progress in behavior modification*. New York: Academic Press, 1975.

Burchard, J.D., & Harig, P.T. Behavior modification and juvenile delinquency. In H. Leitenberg (Ed.) *Handbook of behavior modification and therapy*. Englewood Cliffs, N.J.: Prentice Hall, 1976.

Davidson, W.S., & Seidman, E. Studies of behavior modification and juvenile delinquency: A review, methodological critique, and social perspective. *Psychological Bulletin,* 1974, 81, 998-1011.

Stephens, T.M. Using reinforcement and social modeling with delinquent youth. *Review of Educational Research,* 1974, 43, 323-340.

Stumphauzer, J.S. *Six techniques of modifying delinquent behavior.* Teaneck, NJ: Behavioral Sciences Tape Library, 1974.

Text

Allen, J.D., Phillips, E.L., Phillips, E., Fixsen, D.L., and Wolf, M.M. *Achievement Place: A Novel.* Champaign, Illinois: Research Press. In press.

Alvord, J.R. "The Home Token Economy: A Motivational System for the Home," *Corrective Psychiatry and Journal of Social Therapy,* 1971, 17, 6-13.

Ayllon, T., and Azrin, N. *The Token Economy.* New York: Appleton, 1968.

Baer, D.M. "Methods for Generalizing Experimentally Produced Behavior Changes," Paper presented at the Fifth Annual Southern California Conference on Behavior Modification, Los Angeles, October 28, 1973.

Bandura, A. *Principles of Behavior Modification.* New York: Holt, 1969.

Buehler, R.E., Patterson, G.R., and Furniss, J.M. "The Reinforcement of Behavior in Institutional Settings," *Behavior Research and Therapy,* 1966, 4, 157-167.

Buehler, R.E. "Social Reinforcement Experimentation in Open Social Systems," in J.S. Stumphauzer (Ed.), *Behavior Therapy with Delinquents.* Springfield, Illinois: Thomas, 1973, 250-262.

Burchard, J.D. "Systematic Socialization: A Programmed Environment for the Habilitation of Antisocial Retardates," *Psychological Record,* 1967, 11, 461-476.

Burkhart, B.R., Behles, M., and Stumphauzer, J.S. "Training Juvenile Probation Officers in Behavior Modification: Knowledge, Attitude Change, or Behavioral Competence?", *Behavior Therapy,* In press.

Cautela, J.R. "Covert sensitization," *Psychological Reports,* 1967, 20, 459-468.

Cohen, H.L., Filipczak, J.A., Bis, J.S., and Cohen, J.E. "Contingencies Applicable to Special Education of Delinquents," U.S. Dept. of H.E.W., 1966.

Fo, W.S., and O'Donnell, C.R. "The Buddy System: Relationship and Contingency Conditions in a Community Intervention Program for Youth with Nonprofessionals as Behavior Change Agents," *Journal of Consulting and Clinical Psychology,* 1974, 42, 163-169.

Jesness, C.F., and DeRisi, W.J. "Some Variations in Techniques of Contingency Management in a School for Delinquents," in J.S. Stumphauzer (Ed.), *Behavior Therapy with Delinquents.* Springfield, Illinois: Thomas, 1973, 196-235.

Jones, H.G., Gelder, M., and Holden, H.M. "Symposium on Behavior and Aversion Therapy in the Treatment of Delinquency," *British Journal of Criminology,* 1965, 5, 355-387.

Karacki, L. and Levinson, R.B. "A Token Economy in a Correctional Institution for Youthful Offenders," *The Howard Journal of Penology and Crime Prevention,* 1970, 13, 20-30.

Krasner, L. "Behavior Control and Social Responsibility," *American Psychologist,* 1969, 17, 199-204.

Krasner, L. "Behavior Therapy," *Annual Review of Psychology,* 1971, 22, 483-532.

Liberman, R., and Weathers, L. "Contingency Contracting with Adolescent Drug Abusers," Fourth Annual Southern California Conference on Behavior Modification, Los Angeles, October 28, 1972.

London, P. *Behavior Control.* New York: Harper & Row, 1969.

Los Angeles Federation of Community, Coordinating Councils: The community acts for delinquency prevention. 40th annual meeting Los Angeles, April 27, 1973.

MacCulloch, M.J., Williams, C., and Birtles, C.J. "The Successful Application of Aversion Therapy with an Adolescent Exhibitionist," *Journal of Behavior Therapy and Experimental Psychiatry,* 1971, 2, 61-66.

O'Leary, K.D., and O'Leary, S.G. *Classroom Management: The Successful Use of Behavior Modification.* Elmsford, New York: Pergammon Press, 1972.

Patterson, G.R. "Recent Trends in Behavior Modification with Children," Western Psychological Association Convention, San Francisco, April 23, 1971.

Patterson, G.R. *Families: Application of Social Learning to Family Life.* Champaign, Illinois: Research Press, 1971.

Phillips, E.L. "Achievement Place; Token Reinforcement Procedure in a Home Style Rehabilitation Setting for Predelinquent Boys," *Journal of Applied Behavior Analysis,* 1968, 1, 213-223.

Philips, E.L., Philips, E., Fixsen, D.L., and Wolf, M.M. "Achievement Place: Behavior Shaping Works for Delinquents," *Psychology Today,* June, 1973.

Phillips, E.L., Phillips, E., Fixsen, D.L., and Wolf, M.M. *The Teaching Family Handbook.* Champaign, Illinois: Research Press. In press.

Risley, T. "Juniper Gardens," American Psychological Association Convention, Honolulu, September, 1972.

Rogers, C.M., and Skinner, B.F. "Some Issues Concerning the Control of Human Behavior: A Symposium," *Science,* 1956, 124, 1057-1066.

Snibbe, J., and Snibbe, H. (Eds.). *The Urban Policeman In Transition.* Springfield, Illinois: Charles C Thomas, 1973.

Schwitzgebel, R.L. "A Belt from Big Brother," *Psychology Today,* 1969, 2, 45-47, 65.

Schwitzgebel, R.K. *Street Corner Research: An Experimental Approach to the Juvenile Delinquent.* Cambridge: Harvard University Press, 1964.

Schwitzgebel, R.K. "Ethical and Legal Aspect of Behavioral Instrumentation," *Behavior Therapy,* 1970, 1, 498-509.

Shoemaker, M.E. "Group Assertiveness Training for Institutionalized Delinquents," Fuller Graduate School of Psychology, Unpublished dissertation, 1974.

Skinner, B.F. *Beyond Freedom and Dignity.* New York: Knopf, 1971.

Stuart, R.B. "Behavioral Contracting with the Families of Delinquents," *Journal of Behavior Therapy and Experimental Psychiatry,* 1971, 2, 1-11.

Stumphauzer, J.S. "Increased Delay of Gratification in Young Prison Inmates through Imitation of High-delay Peer Models," *Journal of Personality and Social Psychology,* 1972, 21, 10-17. (a)

Stumphauzer, J.S. *Daily Behavior Graph Manual.* Box 1168, Venice, California: Behaviormetrics Publishing Co., 1972. (b)

Stumphauzer, J.S. "Training in Social Manipulation: The Use of Behavior Therapy," *Crime & Delinquency,* 1972, 18, 112-113. (c)

Stumphauzer, J.S. (Ed.). *Behavior Therapy with Delinquents.* Springfield,

Illinois: Charles C Thomas, 1973.

Stumphauzer, J.S. *Six Techniques of Modifying Delinquent Behavior.* Leonia, New Jersey: Behavioral Sciences Tape Library, 1974.

Teicher, J.D., Sinay, R.D., and Stumphauzer, J.S. "Training Community-Based Paraprofessionals as Behavior Therapists with Families of Alcohol-Abusing Adolescents," *American Journal of Psychiatry,* 1976, 133, 847-850.

Tharp, R.G., and Wetzel, R.J. *Behavior Modification in the Natural Environment.* New York: Academic Press, 1969.

Tyler, V.O. "Application of Operant Token Reinforcement to the Academic Performance of an Institutionalized Delinquent," *Psychological Reports,* 1967, 21, 249-260.

Wetzel, R. "The Use of Behavioral Techniques in a Case of Compulsive Stealing," *Journal of Consulting Psychology,* 1966, 30, 367-374.

Wotkiewicz, H. "Operant Strategies with Delinquents at Kennedy Youth Center," Unpublished manuscript, West Virginia University, 1972.

CHAPTER 2

COGNITIVE ISSUES IN THE TREAT-
MENT OF DELINQUENCY

MICHAEL J. MAHONEY

EDITORIAL COMMENTS

John B. Watson rather neatly did away with cognitions, or perhaps more precisely with scientific attention given to them, with his "radical behaviorism" of the 1920s. Well, cognitions, it would seem, are in fact not only alive and well (and living in Waterloo, Palo Alto, and University Park?), but also are receiving a great deal of attention today from many behavior therapists. This recent trend is perhaps best represented in the work and writing of Donald Meichenbaum (1974, 1977), Albert Bandura (1969, 1977), and Michael Mahoney (1974, 1977). A new journal, "Cognitive Therapy and Research" (Plenum) has just made its appearance, with Mahoney as editor.

In this original chapter prolific Mahoney focuses his attention on cognitive issues as they relate specifically to our topic here — the treatment of delinquents. His discussion of stimulus control, iatrogenic labeling, choice, counter-control, perceived contingencies, and personal problem-solving skills should provide considerable stimulation for those of us struggling with the intricacies of understanding, modifying, and preventing delinquent behavior.

The reader should note that some of these very perspectives are taken up by Camp et al. in the following chapter with her "Think Aloud" program for developing self-control in young aggressive boys.

THERE ARE numerous signs that a more mediational breed of behavior therapy has taken hold in some quarters—a breed which has been variously termed *covert conditioning, cognitive behavior modification,* and *social learning theory* (cf. Mahoney, 1974, 1977; Bandura, 1977; Meichenbaum, 1977). The basic tenets of this cognitive-behavioral hybrid include a greater emphasis on mediating processes in human learning. The individual is viewed as a complex product of personal, biological, and environmental forces, and the processes by which a person learns are said to be more adequately viewed as cognitive rather than peripheral conditioning. Dedication to empirical scrutiny and methodological rigor remain, and many of the techniques of more orthodox behavior modification are employed. Indeed, although emphasizing the role of cognitive *processes* in human learning, Bandura (1977) notes that behavioral *procedures* seem to be among the most powerful contemporary means of activating those processes.

If the procedures employed by the cognitive and noncognitive behavior therapist are similar, this might imply that their only real difference is an esoteric one—namely, the nature of learning (information processing versus conditioning). While this is probably their most fundamental disagreement, there are other areas of practical divergence between these two perspectives. Since cognitive factors are thought to influence behavior and emotion, for example, the more mediational therapist will tend to devote more time and therapeutic attention to the assessment of "private events"—thoughts, perceptions, values, beliefs, and so on. This "private environment" is not viewed in exclusion to its more public counterpart, but it is given a significant role in assessment. Moreover, the cognitive therapist believes that appropriate assessment and interpretation of a person's private experiences can substantially facilitate the selection and refinement of therapeutic techniques. Where a more orthodox counselor might base treatment strategy on publicly observable aspects of a client's external environment, the cognitive therapist will more often focus on the environment (and contingencies) as they are *perceived* by the client. These two approaches often lead to very different treatment strategies, particularly when the problem is formulated as one of misperceived (rather than misprogrammed) contingencies.

Although few areas have managed to escape the recent expansion of cognitive-behavioral strategies, the treatment of deviant juveniles seems to have been at least partially delinquent in this regard. There are, of course, several notable exceptions, and many of the chapters in the present volume reflect an increasing endorsement of a cognitive-behavioral perspective. Nevertheless, there are numerous relevancies of cognitive social learning theory which have yet to be adequately explored. In the present chapter I shall take the liberty of speculating on some of those potential relevancies. I use the word *"liberty"* intentionally, since I am sorely aware of the difference between armchair psychologizing and day-to-day survival in the sober world of delinquency treatment. Mark Twain aptly noted that one of the most fascinating aspects of scientists was their ability to offer "wholesale returns of conjecture from a trifling investment of fact." In my own defense, I would hope that some of the issues briefly discussed here might offer some potential guidelines for needed research. Thus, our conjectures need not be so shameful as long as they breed something other than still more conjecture.

In the interest of brevity, I shall not discuss some of the more obvious and familiar implications of social learning theory for delinquency treatment. This has already been done most ably in Bandura's (1973) excellent analysis of aggression. Thus, the influence of the mass media and the importance of nondelinquent role models will not be here reiterated. Likewise, patterns of child rearing and family interaction will be topics left to other chapters. My main concern will be examination of issues which might, in my opinion, afford more adequate understanding and treatment of delinquent patterns.

Stimulus Control

Stimulus control may seem like a strange topic with which to initiate a discussion of cognitive issues, but it is used here in a sense which is a bit broader than its more typical orthodox meaning. While behaviorists are usually aware of the continuum that separates the delinquent from the nondelinquent, this is more apparent in their theoretical debates than in their treatment programs. In the latter, one often gets the impression that the delinquent is one of "them"—a discrete and distinguishable member of an antisocial species. It is assumed that the delinquent often needs reculturization to prosocial values when, in fact, it is likely that at least some of those "delinquents" already endorse said values. In these situations—which are probably not rare—it may be the case that the delinquent does not need moralizing therapy so much as some pointers on stimulus control—i.e. how to "get by with" harmless mischief without getting caught. If the reader had an adolescence anything like that of this author, he would probably confess to a multitude of misdemeanors which could have gotten him "booked" had he not had the ingenuity to know how, when, and where to be "delinquent."

I am not, incidentally, advocating criminal apprenticeships in which we refine the delinquent's antisocial skills—such opportunities are already too available in many of our correctional institutions. What I am advocating is a more relativistic and realistic perspective. If current statistics are accurate, most young people will commit more than a few minor "crimes" against society before they are adults. The difference between the "real" and "pseudo–" delinquent—if one can defend such a distinction —may be whether these crimes accelerate (in frequency or magnitude) toward a lifestyle. However, this would still leave us with the rare pseudodelinquent who may be receiving moralizing therapy when his crime was indiscrimination. Without an analysis of the individual's beliefs about social responsibility, the waywardness of this treatment might go undetected. Thus, it may sometimes be the case that an adjudicated youth has been antisocial in behavior but prosocial in attitudes. We need to explore the possibility that very different skills may be needed in the treatment of different "types" of delinquents.

Assessment of socially relevant beliefs need not, incidentally, take the form of traditional psychometric measurement. It is all too evident that our conventional paper-and-pencil measures of "personality traits" have shown poor predictive utility (Mischel, 1968; Stuart, 1970). On the other hand, there is ample evidence suggesting that individuals are often accurate in predicting their own behavior—partly on the basis of their personal beliefs (Bandura, 1977, in press). Thus, from a cognitive-behavioral perspective, one must assess such things as the individual's perception of the contingencies which are in effect, his or her actual ability to perform the desired response, his or her *perceived* ability to perform that response, and his or her motivation to satisfy the contingency in question. These are issues which can only be adequately addressed when intrapersonal factors are taken into account.

Iatrogenic Labeling

The second area with which we are concerned is the effects of being labeling *delinquent*. There are now a number of studies suggesting that psychiatric classification may be an iatrogenic (harmful) practice (Goffman, 1963; Stuart, 1970; Scheff, 1975; Farina, 1976; Mahoney, in press). Persons who have been labeled "mentally ill" are perceived and treated very differently from their unlabeled peers. They are seen as untrustworthy, frightening, and even unpredictable. Moreover, no matter how normal their behavior, they do not seem to be able to shake the label (Rosenhan, 1973). This is vividly illustrated by headlines that emphasize a felon's status as an "ex-mental patient." When was the last time you read "ex-mechanic stabs wife?"

The extent to which a label can influence perceptions of a person's behavior was dramatically shown in a study reported by Temerlin (1968). He hired a professional actor to play the part of a self-confident, happily married man in a videotaped interview which was engineered to approximate the epitome of mental health. Psychologists and psychiatrists were then asked to view this tape and were told that it was either an employment interview or a psychiatric interview. To examine the perceptual biases induced by a label, some of the professionals were told that the man was exceptionally normal; others were led to believe he was psychotic. When the psychologists and psychiatrists were asked to rate the man's psychological adjustment, their judgments were dramatically influenced by the previous labels assigned to the actor. Despite the fact that he showed no apparent signs of psychopathology, when he had been labeled *psychotic* 60 percent of the psychiatrists agreed with this diagnosis! As a matter of fact, when the abnormal label was present, almost 90 percent of the mental health specialists saw him as neurotic or psychotic. Their evaluations were much more positive in the absence of that label.

Thus, the delinquent may come to be perceived as more deviant in part because of the evaluative label he has received. But this only refers to other people's perceptions of the delinquent. If he accepts the label, then self-perceptions must be added as a supplementary factor which may influence his future behavior. Intentionally or otherwise, he may begin to act out the role which has been cast for him—that of the deviant (Ullmann & Krasner, 1969; Scheff, 1966). Thus, one of the primary concerns of a cognitive therapist would be whether the delinquent "sees" himself as an antisocial deviant. This cannot be ascertained by the simple question, "Are you a delinquent?" More informative questions might be: "What is a delinquent?" "How do you feel about delinquents?" "According to your own definition, are you a delinquent?" Answers to questions such as these may inform the counselor of important self-perceptions on the part of a youth —perceptions which may help to form future patterns of behavior.

Choice, Counter Contol, and Perceived Contingencies

I have elsewhere discussed some of my hunches about the phenomenon of *counter-control* and its apparent elevated frequency in delinquent populations (Mahoney, 1974). Briefly, counter-control is exhibited when a person responds in a manner which is intentionally opposite to the prevailing contingencies. The "intentionality" of this oppositional behavior can usually be inferred from overt revelations of strategy, e.g. "Screw you, fella—you're not going to control me!". They can also be suspected when a person consistently partakes of a reinforcer except when it is contingent; or alternatively, when he avoids an aversive stimulus except when it is part of an artificially programmed punishment contingency. In my own work with predelinquents (Mahoney & Mahoney, 1973), we had ample instances of this apparent "misbehavior of organisms." One child seemed to delight in earning time-out; another refused to accept sweets if they were presented as reinforcers. A third liked to flaunt his counter-control—belittling the privileges he had lost and arguing that none of our "stupid rules" would make him change. Other examples from the delinquency literature are not hard to find.

One of the intriguing aspects of counter-control is the fact that it is apparently difficult to generate (and therefore study) in non-delinquent populations. For example, I have now made no less than eight attempts to produce counter-control in the laboratory so that we could study some of its parameters. Despite the aid and collaboration of several capable colleagues, I have not been very successful. Our sophomoric subjects have been frustratingly compliant. In one study we tried to insult the intelligence and sensitivities of our subjects by rewarding them with pennies for performing a meaningless and boring task. Despite various and sundry impersonal insults—and an obnoxious monologue that compared them to overgrown rats—they were obedient. Similarly negative results were obtained in a thesis project designed to produce counter-control in the laboratory (Kennedy, 1974).

While counter-control has been elusive in our laboratory, it has been infrequent but hardly rare in research dealing with deviant populations and applied settings (Davison, 1973; Mahoney, 1974). Some of the situational parameters which seem to be positively correlated with counter-control are the following:

1. A task or contingency which is devalued by the subject;
2. A situation in which the subject has little, if any, control over the contingencies;
3. A situation wherein oppositional behavior may be poorly detected (anonymous) or its responsibility dissipated across a group;
4. A situation where the experimenter's (or counselor's) efforts to "manipulate" the subject are relatively conspicuous;
5. A situation where counter-control has been modeled;
6. A situation where counter-control is likely to earn some form of personally meaningful reinforcement (social recognition, self-respect, a "rep");
7. Situations involving punishment (rather than reinforcement);
8. Situations where the relationship between the subject and

experimenter are "hostile" or negative; and

9. Situations where the subject-experimenter interaction is temporary and trivial (such that the subject does not feel that he will be at the future mercy of the experimenter).

Unfortunately, much of the extant evidence on counter-control is anecdotal and/or unreplicated. Investigators have not set out to produce it; rather, they have lamented its occurrence. Thus, the foregoing list must be viewed as a loose collection of apparent correlates—not a roster of demonstrated influences. The potential significance of controlled research on these and other potential variables need hardly be emphasized.

One of the more intriguing parameter candidates is *choice*— the extent to which an individual has options with regard to (a) the responses which will satisfy a contingency, and (b) the contingencies with which he must cope. This introduces the concept of the *perceived* contingency, which may be very different from that which has been programmed by society or a counselor. The oft-noted problems of "miscommunication" and "generation gaps" may partially relate to different perceptions on the part of delinquents and authority figures. The problem is not that they "misbehave," but that they behave in accordance with contingencies other than those endorsed by society. When a counselor or correctional officer tries to alter the delinquent's behavior, the latter often perceives this as an imposition of arbitrary contingencies. A "me against them" dichotomy is not uncommon, and atmospheres of cooperative goal seeking are rare. Cognitive social learning theory would predict very poor therapeutic outcome when the delinquent is forced to comply with contingencies which are *perceived* as conflicting with those valued personally. More positive results would be expected when there is (a) clarification of the actual degree of conflict between contingencies, and (b) perception of compromise and choice such that the delinquent feels that he has been given an active and legitimate voice in selecting the contingencies which will guide his behavior. The delinquent who does not feel manipulated by an arbitrary and alien set of rules will be more likely to take an active and constructive role in his own adjustment.

The foregoing remarks do not imply that we should assume a permissive stance and allow delinquents to follow their idiosyncratic perceptions of how to survive. What is needed, however, is research on the effects of client involvement in the selection and implementation of prosocial contingencies. Peer-mediated contingencies—such as those used at Achievement Place—should help to avoid the cognitive dichotomy between "me, the oppressed" and "them, the oppressors." Likewise, to the extent that the delinquent has been given a nontrivial role in the selection of realistic contingencies, one would expect greater compliance to those contingencies. In my own work with delinquents this collaborative philosophy has also been an educational one for me. I often had trouble defending the rationality of society's laws and frequently wrestled with the ethics of endorsing a social system which sometimes violates my own values. The experience was sometimes painful, but it increased my appreciation for the inanity and inequity of some of the social contingencies which my delinquent clients perceived all too accurately. The adjudicated youth is not always an "irresponsible rebel;" many of today's delinquents can offer sad and accurate commentary on a system of "justice" that pardons the rich and persecutes the poor. From a value perspective, it is, in my opinion, the counselor's right and obligation to help a "deviant" client refine his perception of a societal contingency and, should he object to that contingency, help him to develop skills which will allow him to work constructively toward its repeal. We are not servants of the *status quo* and, in fact, are fulfilling our professional roles much more responsibly when we teach our clients *how* to think rather than *what* to think.

Personal Problem-Solving Skills

One final area of relevance has to do with recent research suggesting that personal skills in problem solving may play an important role in adjustment. In a series of interesting studies with a wide range of populations, George Spivack and his colleagues have offered some potentially dramatic insights into adjustment processes (cf. Spivack & Shure, 1974; Spivack, Platt, & Shure,

1976). These researchers have found that the problem-solving skills of many people who are labeled "maladjusted" (emotionally disturbed, delinquent, mentally ill, etc.) differ from the skills of those of us who have not yet been caught. A recent study with prison inmates at Penn State yielded results consistent with those of Spivack and his colleagues. When prisoners were given hypothetical real-life problems and asked how they would resolve them, they tended to show less proficiency than an unincarcerated control group. According to Spivack et al., maladjusted persons often show deficiencies in their ability to perceive problem solutions. In addition to a lower quantity of perceived solutions, they also tend to suggest less socially appropriate options, e.g. physical aggression. Likewise, when asked to anticipate the probable consequences of their preferred solution, many maladjusted people seem to have unrealistic expectations about outcome.

Differences between intact groups do not, of course, demonstrate anything; they can only be suggestive. In this case, the suggestion and its treatment implications are clear. Perhaps one of the factors responsible for "deviant" and "antisocial" behaviors is a skill deficiency which restricts the individual's perception and implementation of socially condoned methods of conflict resolution. If so, effective training in real-life problem solving might help to alleviate said patterns of deviance. These implications have begun to receive empirical scrutiny, and with preliminary success. Studies in which delinquents and other "deviant" subjects have been given interpersonal problem-solving training suggest that this experience may indeed ameliorate some adjustment problems (cf. Spivack, Platt, & Shure, 1976; Mahoney & Arnkoff, in press). The research has hardly begun, however, and there is more than ample reason for caution. Given the refractory nature of antisocial patterns, however, we are well advised to energetically examine anything that even hints of enduring improvement.

Conclusion

I have briefly sketched the armchair speculations of an aging delinquent from the perspective of cognitive social learning theory. Aside from affording me the opportunity to take part in what I think is a valuable book in the area, my goal has been to selectively examine some of the more salient implications of a cognitive perspective for delinquency researchers. As will have been very apparent to those readers who are familiar with recent developments in cognitive behavior modification, my survey has been short and superficial. It will have served its purpose, however, if it has sparked any lingering interest in those readers who may not have been familiar with this emerging perspective. It may turn out that the cognitive-behavioral hybrid will offer little to our refinement of therapeutic methods. At the present time, however, such a verdict is both premature and inconsistent with at least some preliminary data returns (Mahoney, 1977). While cognitive-behavioral approaches face several conceptual and methodological challenges, they have also demonstrated enough suggestive promise to warrant our continued attention. That attention could hardly find a more urgent or challenging expression than in the area of delinquency.

REFERENCES

Editorial Comments

Bandura, A. *Principles of behavior modification.* New York: Holt, 1969.

Bandura, A. *Social learning theory.* New York: Wiley, 1977.

Mahoney, M.J. *Cognition and behavior modification.* Cambridge, Mass.: Ballinger, 1974.

Mahoney, M.J. Reflections on the cognitive-learning trend in psychotherapy. *American Psychologist,* 1977, *32,* 5-13.

Meichenbaum, D.M. *Cognitive behavior modification.* Morristown, NJ: General Learning Press, 1974.

Meichenbaum, D.M. *Cognitive behavior modification: an integrative approach.* New York: Plenum, 1977.

Text

Bandura, A. *Aggresion: A social learning analysis.* Englewood Cliffs, NJ: Prentice-Hall, 1973.

Bandura, A. *Social learning theory.* Englewood Cliffs, NJ: Prentice-Hall, 1977.

Bandura, A. Self-efficacy: Toward a unifying theory of behavior change. *Psychological Review,* in press.

Davison, G.C. Counter-control in behavior modification. In L.A. Hamerlynck, L.D. Handy & E.J. Mash (Eds.), *Behavior change: Methodology, concepts, and practice.* Champaign, IL: Research Press, 1973, 153-167.

Farina, A. *Abnormal psychology.* Englewood Cliffs, NJ: Prentice-Hall, 1976.

Goffman, E. *Stigma.* Englewood Cliffs, NJ: Prentice-Hall, 1963.

Kennedy, R.E. Counter-control: An attempt to create a laboratory paradigm. Unpublished master's thesis, The Pennsylvania State University, 1974.

Mahoney, M.J. *Cognition and behavior modification.* Cambridge, MA: Ballinger, 1974.

Mahoney, M.J. Reflections on the cognitive learning trend in psychotherapy. *American Psychologist,* 1977, *32,* 5-13.

Mahoney, M.J. *Human variance: Abnormal behavior and clinical science.* Philadelphia: J.B. Lippincott, in press.

Mahoney, M.J., & Arnkoff, D.B. Cognitive and self-control therapies. In S.L. Garfield & A.E. Bergin (Eds.), *Handbook of Psychotherapy and behavior change.* 2nd ed. New York: Wiley, in press.

Mahoney, M.J., & Mahoney, F.E. A residential program in behavior modification. In R.D. Rubin, J.P. Brady, & J.D. Henderson (Eds.), *Advances in behavior therapy.* Vol. 4, New York: Academic Press, 1973, 93-102.

Meichenbaum, D. *Cognitive-behavior modification.* New York: Plenum, 1977.

Mischel, W. *Personality and assessment.* New York: Wiley, 1968.

Rosenhan, D.L. On being sane in insane places. *Science,* 1973, *179,* 250-258.

Scheff, T.J. *Being mentally ill: A sociological theory.* Chicago: Aldine, 1966.

Scheff, T.J. (Ed.), *Labeling madness.* Englewood Cliffs, NJ: Prentice-Hall, 1975.

Schur, E.M. *Labeling deviant behavior.* New York: Harper & Row, 1971.

Spivack, G., Platt, J., & Shure, M.B. *The problem solving approach to adjustment.* San Francisco: Jossey-Bass, 1976.

Spivack, G., & Shure, M.B. *Social adjustment of young children: A cognitive approach to solving real-life problems.* San Fransisco: Jossey-Bass, 1974.

Stuart, R.B. *Trick or treatment: How and when psychotherapy fails.* Champaign, IL: Research Press, 1970.

Temerlin, M.K. Suggestion effects in psychiatric diagnosis. *Journal of Nervous and Mental Diseases,* 1968, *147,* 349-353.

Ullmann, L.P., & Krasner, L. *A psychological approach to abnormal behavior.* Englewood Cliffs, NJ: Prentice-Hall, 1969.

CHAPTER 3

"THINK ALOUD": A PROGRAM FOR DEVELOPING SELF-CONTROL IN YOUNG AGGRESSIVE BOYS*†

BONNIE W. CAMP, GASTON E. BLOM, FREDER.CK HEBERT, AND WILLIIAM J. VAN DOORNINCK

EDITORIAL COMMENTS

In the preceeding chapter Mahoney stressed the importance of cognitive issues in delinquency. Bonnie Camp (Camp 1976) has shown that aggressive boys fail to utilize verbal mediation in achieving functional control over their behavior. In this chapter Camp, Blom, Hebert, and van Doorninck take us a step further by presenting a project focusing on the development of **cognitive** self-control of aggression in young boys. The editor selected this paper because of the new ground it breaks with regard to understanding, treating, and preventing aggression. True, the subjects are not delinquents, but rather are second-grade boys who were viewed as aggressive by their teachers. However, many implications are readily seen for implementing and evaluating such programs with adolescent and adult offenders.

While this "Think Aloud" program was effective in producing changes in some of the measures, it was not in others. Camp et al. explore several

*This investigation was supported in part by a Research Scientist Award No. MK3-47 356 from the National Institute of Mental Health and by Grant No. NEG 003-0029 from the National Institute of Education. We are grateful to Mary Ann Bash and Margaret Simmons for their assistance in carrying out the program and to the Denver Public Schools for their continued cooperation.

†Reprinted with permission from *Journal of Abnormal Child Psychology*, 1977, *5*, 167-169 (Plenum Publishing Corporation).

shortcomings and suggest some possible refinements. Systematic replications of this kind of project are needed, as are, for our central topic here, extensions in which such programs could be developed and evaluated with aggressive delinquents as well as adult offenders. In fact, the editor has had the good fortune to help steer a student in this direction in his doctoral dissertation, evaluating verbal mediation and social skills training with institutionalized young male offenders (Atrops, in progress).

The reader is also referred to Bandura's **Aggression: A Social Learning Analysis** (1973) and to Patterson, Reid, Jones, and Congers **A Social Learning Approach To Family Intervention: Families With Aggressive Children** (1975).

ABSTRACT

"THINK ALOUD" WAS DESIGNED as a training program to improve self- control in 6- to 8-year-old boys. It involved modeling and verbalization of cognitive activity to foster use of verbal mediation skills in dealing with both cognitive and interpersonal problems. It was hypothesized that this training would lead to improvement in test performance and teacher ratings of classroom behavior in hyperaggressive boys. Twelve Aggressive, second-grade boys participated in daily, 30-minute, individual sessions for 6 weeks. Normal and Aggressive control subjects received no intervention. Teachers rated both trained and untrained Aggressive boys as improving in Aggressive behaviors but they rated the experimental group as showing improvement on a significantly larger number of prosocial behaviors. The pattern of performance on cognitive tests also changed significantly in the experimental group. On pretest, their pattern differed from Normals and resembled the Aggressive control group while on posttest, their pattern resembled Normals and differed from Aggressive controls. Suggestions were made concerning additional refinements needed in the program, but overall results indicated potential value in the present approach for providing assistance to aggressive boys in the early grades.

"THINK ALOUD": A PROGRAM FOR DEVELOPING SELF-CONTROL IN YOUNG AGGRESSIVE BOYS

Impulsivity and difficulty maintaining sustained response inhibition are characteristics which may contribute both to poor achievement and behavior problems in children (Achenbach, 1970; Kagan, 1966; Koegh & Donlon, 1972). Previous studies have also shown that these are distinguishing features of test performance in young aggressive boys (Camp, 1976) whose progressive decline in achievement with increasing age is also well documented (Feldhusen, Thursten & Benning, 1970). A program which could decrease impulsivity and increase capacity for sustained attention in this group could be potentially useful in counteracting both achievement and behavior problems. This would be particularly true if the program were designed for use by educational personnel to assist children in developing control of their own behavior.

Several previous programs have demonstrated that impulsivity during test performance can be decreased with training in verbalization of problem-solving strategies (Bem, 1967; Meichenbaum & Goodman, 1971; Palkes, Stewart & Kahana, 1968). With the exception of Meichenbaum and Goodman, who selected children from an "opportunity remedial class," children in these previous studies have been selected on the basis of test performance only and not on the basis of deviant behavior. Although impulsivity in hyperaggressive boys would be expected to yield similar results to those obtained in previous studies, this needs to be verified empirically.

Not only are there questions concerning whether similar results can be obtained in deviant children but there are questions regarding whether training may be expected to affect behavior outside the training or testing situation. Of the three studies mentioned, only Meichenbaum and Goodman attempted to measure effects of the program on classroom behavior. They found no significant differences between children in their training and an attention-control group. Though disappointing, their results were readily understandable. Their program was brief, consisting of four sessions over two weeks; they selected children on the basis of assignment to the remedial class rather than on behavioral criteria; and their training program consisted entirely of visual materials and impersonal tasks. In addition, it was not clear what rationale guided their selection of classroom behavior to be examined.

Thus despite the apparent promise of cognitive behavior modification as a method for improving behavior and test performance in aggressive children, several alterations seem indicated to increase the likelihood of effects with this group. The present study reports on development of such a program along with results of initial trials with hyperaggressive, second-grade boys. The specific purpose was to determine whether test performance in hyperaggressive boys could be altered by cognitive behavior modification training procedures and whether evidence of impact on behavior outside the training sessions could be demonstrated.

Method

Subjects

As part of a larger study, 85 regular first– and second-grade classroom teachers in the Denver Public Schools rated all boys in their classes on Miller's (1971) School Behavior Checklist (SBCL) between October 1974 and January 1975. This scale was selected because of the extensive background information available on it (Miller, 1971; Ross, Lacy & Parton, 1965) which indicated a high degree of stability in ratings performed by one person at different times and comparable findings between parent and teacher ratings (Miller, Hampe, Barnett & Noble, 1971). Furthermore, our own work (Camp & Zimet, 1974) showed significant correlations between ratings on the prosocial scale (Low Need Achievement Scale) and classroom observations of on-task behavior performed by independent observers. Significant correlations were also obtained on the Aggressive Scale between checklists completed by teachers a year apart (Camp, 1976).

The scores on the SBCL are based on the total number of items checked on each scale. Miller reported that most children have some "deviant" behaviors but very few children have a large number and his norms provide standard T scores (mean $= 50$, standard deviation $= 10$) based on the number of items checked in each of 7 factorially derived scales. Scales used in the present study consisted of the Aggressive Scale (37 items) and the Low Need Achievement (23 items).

Using Miller's norms, a T score of 70 ($+ 2$ SD above the mean) was used as the basis for identifying Aggressive boys. Out of 832 teacher ratings, there were 115 boys with a $T \geq 70$ on the Aggressive scale. Parent permission for testing was obtained on 52. All second-grade boys in this group ($n = 24$) were selected for participation in the present study.

At the beginning of this project, there were 23 Aggressive second-grade boys from 15 schools still living in the project area. They were randomly assigned to an experimental group (Agg-Exp) of 12 and a control group (Agg-Con) of 11. Before group assignment was announced, one child in the Agg-Con group was eliminated from further participation by the school social worker who felt that too much service was being provided. This resulted in an Agg-Con group of 10.

The Normal group consisted of boys who had no SBCL scale with a *T* score of 60 or higher, i.e. no more than 1 standard deviation above the mean. In the larger study, a total of 375 boys were so identified and parent permission for initial testing was received on 193. As each Aggressive boy was selected for the larger study, a Normal boy was selected randomly from those Normal subjects in the same age group and census tract of residence. This resulted in a total of 24 second-grade boys who received initial testing. Twelve of these were selected at random from schools where Agg-Exp boys were located to participate as Normal controls (Norm-Con) for follow-up with no treatment other than regular classroom instruction.

Tests Administered

The complete battery of tests administered within 2 months prior to initiating the program is described in a previous paper (Camp, 1977). For purposes of pretest-posttest comparisons in the present study, the following tests were repeated within 3 weeks after the program ended: Block Designs, Object Assembly and Maze subtest from the Weschler Intelligence Scale for Children—Revised (WISC-R) along with recording of private speech[1]; the reading test from the Wide Range Achievement Test (WRAT); Auditory Reception from the Illinois Test of Psycholinguistic Abilities; Kagan's Matching Familiar Figures Test (MFF). These tests were selected because previous studies had shown that they

---

[1]Recording and scoring of speech during the testing session is described more fully in Camp (1977). Word play and Outer-directed, nonsocial speech were scored as Immature; Inner-directed, self-guiding speech and inaudible muttering were scored as Mature; comments directed toward the examiner and tension-releasing verbalizations were scored Social.

contributed to a pattern of differences between aggressive and normal boys (Camp, 1977) or because they had been used by Meichenbaum and Goodman (1971).

In addition to the above tests on which both pre– and posttest scores were available, an abbreviated version of the Preschool Interpersonal Problem-solving test (PIPS) (Shure and Spivack, unpublished) was administered as a posttest only. This was selected because it was expected to be influenced by the social training dialogues included in the treatment program.

Teacher Ratings

As described previously, only the Aggressive scale of the SBCL (Miller, 1971) was used in identifying boys as Aggressive while scores on all scales were used to identify Normal boys. If social behavior in Aggressive boys was altered by the training program, it was expected that these effects would be demonstrated in a reduction in teachers' reports of aggressive behavior.

Several considerations also led us to anticipate that the Low Need Achievement Scale (LNA) might be equally or more sensitive to effects of the program. The LNA scale consists of 23 items dealing primarily with prosocial behavior such as "Is helpful," "Volunteers to recite," and "Completes assignments." High scores on LNA result from large numbers of negative answers to such questions. Only one item ("seems unconcerned when misbehaves") overlaps with the Aggressive scale and items on these two scales represent the two most important factors identified from the total pool of 96 items which comprise the SBCL (van Doorninck & Camp, unpublished).

The LNA scale has also been described as less stable over a year's time period (Camp, 1976) and more related to achievement (Camp & Zimet, 1974) than the Aggressive scale. In addition, scores on LNA have also been related in first graders to classroom observations of on-task behavior which in turn was related to achievement (Camp & Zimet, 1975). These considerations suggested that LNA might be more sensitive to any program that would affect behavior through altering cognitive strategies and that this could be independent of changes in aggressive behavior.

Improvement on LNA behaviors could also be viewed as the positive effects expected from increased self-control. Thus, improvement on the Aggressive scale could be expected as a result of a decrease in undesirable behavior while improvement on LNA would represent an increase in desirable behavior. Since the behaviors tapped by these two scales were not necessarily mutually exclusive or incompatible, changes could be observed on either alone or both. Consequently, both the aggressive scale items and the LNA scale items were selected for inclusion in the postratings to be performed by teachers.

The complete SBCL was originally obtained, as noted previously, in the fall of 1974. This complete checklist was obtained again on children in the present study just prior to spring vacation in 1975. Correlations between T scores on these two checklists were .84 for the Aggressive scale and .82 for the LNA scale.

At the end of the training program, teacher checklists were obtained again using only the items for the LNA and Aggressive scales. In addition to completing the checklist in the usual fashion, teachers were also asked to indicate for each item whether the child was "worse," "no change" or "improved" since spring vacation. Items on the two scales were presented in the order in which they were included on the original SBCL. Teachers were unaware that two scales were involved, and no mention was made of how or whether the items were to be separated.

Program

For this study, a training program entitled "Think Aloud"[2] was designed for use with children in daily, 30-minute, individual sessions extending over 6 weeks. This particular schedule was adopted for the following reasons. The most obvious shortcoming of the Meichenbaum and Goodman program was its brevity. Although Bornstein and Quevillon (1976) have subsequently reported significant effects on classroom behavior of even briefer treatment of three preschool children, few would expect significant, sustained improvement in less than a month or two. The Shure and Spivack (1974) kindergarten program, from which the social training lessons were adapted, involves approximately 30 lessons. Experience with the tutorial program for children with severe reading problems (Camp, 1971; Camp & van Doorninck, 1971) has suggested that significant gains may not be expected with fewer than 40 lessons and the impact seems to be improved if these are daily.

The procedures used in training were very similar to those described by Meichenbaum and Goodman (1971) in placing heavy emphasis on modeling of cognitive strategies and concentration on developing answers to the following four basic questions: What is my problem, What is my plan, Am I using my plan and How did I do? (See Meichenbaum & Goodman, 1971 for a rationale regarding the choice of this group of questions.) To engage the child in reacting to all features of modeling (speech and action), the program begins by using the "copy cat" game. During "copy cat," the teacher used cognitive modeling while performing a simple task, e.g. coloring a circle, to introduce the child to the above four basic steps in dealing with the problem. As the child and teacher worked through additional problems (copying designs, puzzles), "copy cat" was gradually faded and the child encouraged to verbalize his strategy.

With increasingly difficult cognitive tasks (Raven Progressive Matrices, PMA perceptual speed materials), the child was encouraged to verbalize to himself while working independently and eventually to fade the problem analysis and strategy planning to a covert level.

Problem-solving content included both cognitive, impersonal problems such as used by Meichenbaum and Goodman (1971) and interpersonal problem-solving games as described by Shure and Spivack (1974). Meichenbaum and Goodman used primarily visual materials such as the perceptual speed tasks from the Primary Mental Abilities Test, the Raven Progressive Matrices and Porteus Mazes. We also considered the possibility that results of the Meichenbaum and Goodman program might have been limited by this restriction of tasks to visual material. Some problems in sequential processing and reasoning about auditory information tended to characterize the high aggressive boys in our studies (Camp, 1977; Camp, Zimet, van Doorninck & Dahlem,

1977). "Doesn't follow directions" and "doesn't listen" are common complaints from teachers in describing impulsive children. It is also evident that children may respond impulsively to verbal questions rather than reason through to an answer. Achenbach (1970), for example, demonstrated that the tendencies to give associations to verbal analogies rather than reasoning to a solution relate to impulsivity. The fact that impulsive children have difficulty with inductive reasoning (Kagan, Pearson & Welch, 1966) may be another manifestation of the same problem. These considerations led us to concentrate on adding auditory-verbal tasks to the visual tasks used by Meichenbaum and Goodman, particularly ones which would require blocking the first impulsive association and reasoning to a solution. This was accomplished in part by devising complex forms of the "Simon Says" game, use of riddles, verbal justification of answers and following complex instructions in a semantic conditioning task.

Concern for generalization to the classroom also influenced selection of the content and procedures. Meichenbaum and Goodman relied entirely on impersonal tasks for self-instructional training. To increase the likelihood that techniques developed in the training sessions would generalize to interpersonal situations, it seemed important to introduce techniques for dealing with interpersonal problems.

The training program designed by Shure and Spivack (1974) for kindergarten children seemed ideally suitable for this purpose, if adapted for a slightly older child. Their program was designed to assist kindergarten teachers in helping young children increase their interpersonal problem-solving abilities and, as a result, their subsequent behavioral adjustment. The program itself consists of a carefully sequenced series of games in which small groups of children can participate. Forty-two preliminary games deal with developing specific language and attentive skills, identifying emotions, thinking about how people have different likes and dislikes and learning to gather information about other people. These preliminary games were collapsed into a series of seven preparatory games dealing with exercises in identifying emotions, determining antecedents to an emotion, considering what might happen next in various situations and evaluating fairness of outcomes.

Following these preliminary games, the final games from the Shure and Spivack program were used as described by them with modifications to include content more appropriate for older children. These games pose the problem of finding several alternative solutions to interpersonal situations, anticipating consequences and evaluating outcomes. In addition to formal games and dialogues, Shure and Spivack presented a general problem-solving approach which could be incorporated into conversations in problem situations as they arose naturally. This approach, especially as it dealt with encouraging development of several alternative plans, solutions and possible outcomes, was incorporated into the cognitive portion of the program as well.

The program introduced easy cognitive problems first, then preliminary social games beginning with the fifth day. Thereafter, cognitive and social problems were intermixed.

Procedure

A manual and script[2] were prepared which incorporated the previously described material and procedures into a 6-week curriculum. The procedures were rehearsed by the two teachers who were assigned to work with the children. Preliminary role-playing, observation and coaching during trial runs with nonproject children also served to standardize program delivery. In addition, tape recordings were made of each session with each child in the project. These were reviewed regularly by the senior author and served as a basis for monitoring and supervising conduct of the program. Although no formal ratings of fidelity to the program were made, these procedures produced as much homogeneity in program delivery as seemed feasible.

The 12 boys in the Agg-Exp group were divided into two groups based on geographical location in the city. Two teachers were randomly assigned to work with children in each group beginning the week after spring vacation. Children were intro-

---

[2]For information concerning availability of the manual for the "Think Aloud" Program, contact the senior author.

duced to the program by being asked to figure out what game the teacher was playing as they walked down the hall. The teacher began copying the child's words and actions until he recognized what she was doing. After switching roles and further play, she explained that they were going to use the "copy cat" game to learn how to "Think Aloud" so it could help them solve problems. At the end of the first session she explained to the child that they would be getting together every day at the same time to learn more about how to use "Think Aloud."

At various opportune times during the 6 weeks, the teacher suggested that thinking out loud could help in the classroom and asked the child to think of ways he could use thinking out loud in doing his schoolwork or in getting along with others.

At the end of the 6-week training period, posttesting was completed by graduate students otherwise uninvolved in the subject and teacher checklists were obtained again with the modifications described previously.

Results

Test Data

One objective of the present study was to determine whether participation in the "Think Aloud" program would alter test performance in treated, aggressive (Agg-Exp) boys so that their pattern of scores would resemble normal boys (Norm-Con) rather than untreated, aggressive boys (Agg-Con). Information pertinent to this question was obtained in two ways. One was through analysis of data collected in a pretest, posttest design and one through data collected in a posttest only design. In addition, analysis of pretest-posttest data was performed in two ways, one through univariate analysis of covariance on individual test scores and one through analysis of discriminant scores derived from discriminant function of analysis.

In the univariate analyses of covariance, two a priori, planned comparisons were performed as recommended by Winer (1971). One comparison involved examining the differences between the Agg-Exp group and the Agg-Con group. The second comparison examined differences between the Agg-Exp and the Norm-Con group. Table 3-I presents unadjusted means of each group for pre– and posttest scores on each variable. In addition, this table contains F values for the previously mentioned comparisons based on adjusted means obtained from the analysis of covariance (Winer, 1971, p. 772).

Tests on which the Agg-Exp group was significantly different from Agg-Con included Maze scores, reaction time on the MFF and Salkind's[3] Impulsivity score from the MFF. Reading achievement, prorated Performance IQ and scores for Immature and Social Speech showed a trend toward the predicted differences. Tests on which the Agg-Exp group remained similar to the Agg-Con group and different from the Normal-Controls were Object Assembly and Relevant and Other Speech on the MFF. The Agg-Exp group also showed a trend toward significantly greater Inefficiency than Normals.

When several dependent variables are available on different groups of subjects, it is often of interest to determine whether the pattern of test scores in the two groups differs irrespective of differences on individual tests. Discriminant function analysis has been employed in this fashion to derive a variable which is a linearly weighted combination of the several dependent variables. The resulting discriminant score is standardized to a mean of 0 and a standard deviation of 1. Since this score permits assessment of the pattern based on the relationship among dependent variables, it is possible to obtain a significant multivariate discrimination without significant univariate test analyses (McCall, 1970). This technique was employed in the present study to evaluate the overall pattern of similarity between aggressive treated, aggressive untreated and normal boys.

Data from all first– and second-grade subjects who participated in the larger study ($n = 93$) were utilized to derive a discriminant function score for pretest data. However, the discriminant func-

---

[3]Salkind (1975) has described a method for deriving an Impulsivity and an Efficiency score from the MFF. Average reaction time and total errors are first converted to z scores. The Impulsivity score (positive values represent more impulsivity) is derived by the formula $\frac{z\text{error} - z\text{time}}{2}$. The Efficiency score (positive values represent inefficiency) is derived by the formula $\frac{z\text{error} + z\text{time}}{2}$.

TABLE 3-I

PRE- AND POSTTEST MEANS AND *F* VALUES FOR PLANNED NONORTHOGONAL CONTRASTS ON ADJUSTED MEANS

Tests	Pretest Group A-E n = 12	A-C n = 10	N-C n = 12	Posttest Group A-E n = 12	A-C n = 10	N-C n = 12	F Contrasts A (A-Exp vs. A-Con)	B A-Exp vs. N-Con)
SBCL-AGG	71.0	75.2	46.0	69.2	74.2	47.3	ns	6.54*
SBCL-LNA	58.9	57.7	42.4	57.6	57.1	41.4	ns	ns
WISC-R Tests								
Block Design	7.9	9.2	9.0	9.2	9.7	9.7	ns	ns
Object Assembly	9.3	9.2	10.3	10.0	10.4	12.1	ns	ns
Mazes	8.7	10.0	10.3	13.0	10.0	11.3	6.96*	5.77*
PIQ	90.7	95.8	98.6	104.6	99.7	106.3	3.51	ns
ITPA								
Auditory Reception	29.0	34.7	38.7	32.6	35.8	33.7	ns	ns
WRAT	2.1	2.6	2.7	2.5	2.7	3.3	4.08	ns
WISC-R Private Speech								
Immature	3.8	12.7	4.8	5.2	3.1	1.9	3.89	ns
Mature	30.7	30.2	18.4	8.1	8.0	8.0	ns	ns
Social	10.8	9.5	7.3	3.4	5.7	1.8	2.99	ns
MFF								
Inner Speech	1.3	.5	.6	.6	.8	1.2	ns	ns
Other Speech	2.9	1.9	.4	13.0	11.0	3.9	ns	5.76*
Relevant Speech	2.5	1.9	.8	7.2	6.7	2.7	ns	4.72*
Irrelevant Speech	.5	.7	.2	.6	1.0	.3	ns	ns
Time (AVERAGE)	10.1	9.7	11.5	17.1	10.6	11.2	6.39*	5.89*
Errors (TOTAL)	18.7	19.3	14.9	12.6	14.2	11.2	ns	ns
Impulsivity	.43	.58	-.36	-.31	.35	.05	4.69*	ns
Efficiency	.03	.04	-.23	.30	-.05	-.25	ns	3.86

Note: F values with p > .10 are reported as ns

*p < .05
**p < .01

tion analysis used only those test variables on which both pre– and posttest measures were available. Coefficients derived from this analysis of pretest scores were then applied to posttest data available on subjects in the present study. In this fashion, each subject in the present study received both a pretest discriminant score and posttest discriminant score. Table 3-II presents the standardized discriminant function coefficients for variables used in the present study in order of importance. In this table, the larger the value the greater the weight placed on this score, irrespective of

TABLE 3-II

STANDARDIZED DISCRIMINANT FUNCTION COEFFICIENTS DERIVED FROM ANALYSIS OF TEST PATTERNS IN AGGRESSIVE AND NORMAL BOYS

Measure	Coefficient
MFF – IRREL SPEECH	.46
MFF – Average Response Time	-.44
WISC – IMM SPEECH	.40
WISC – Mazes	-.36
ITPA – Auditory Reception	-.32
MFF – Errors	.30
WISC – Object Assembly	-.15
WRAT – Reading grade	-.15
WISC – Social Speech	-.09
WISC – Mature Speech	-.05
MFF – Revelant Speech	.05
WISC – Block Design	-.02
Centroid	
Aggressive	.49
Normal	-.49

the sign. The positive and negative signs associated with the centroids indicate whether the sign associated with each discriminant score results in weighting toward the Aggressive or Normal group.

A repeated measured analysis of variance was used to evaluate hypotheses regarding change in the pattern of test scores. The hypothesized treatment effects were expected to result in a significant interaction between time of discriminant score and treatment group with the Agg-Exp and Agg-Con groups differing from Normals on pretest and Agg-Con differing from Agg-Exp and Normals on posttest. The pre– and posttest centroids for subjects in the present study were .60 and −.69 for Agg-Exp, .42 and −.03 for Agg-Con and −.58 and −.73 for Norm-Con. These are presented graphically in Figure 3-1.

Results of the analysis of variance confirmed all hypotheses. Significant differences were observed for pre– versus postdiscriminant scores, F (1,30) = 14.47, $p < .001$, for treatment group, F (2,30) = 3.80, $p < .05$, and the discriminant score × treatment group interaction, F (2,30) = 4.29, $p < .05$. Linear contrasts within the interaction showed a significant difference on pretest between Norm-Con and the Aggressive groups combined, F (1,30) = 21.74, $p < .001$, and nonsignificant differences between the two aggressive groups. On posttest, significant differences were observed between Agg-Con and the combination of Agg-Exp and Norm-Con, F (1,30) = 7.33, $p < .05$, while differences between Agg-Exp and Norm-Con were nonsignificant.

The PIPS test was given as a posttest only. According to Shure and Spivack, emotionally and behaviorally disturbed children tend to offer fewer different solutions to the problems while engaging in more repetitive talk, irrelevant answers, etc. Group means for these different scores are present along with results of a one-way analysis of variance in Table 3-III.

Agg-Exp boys gave significantly more solutions than either Agg-Con or Normal-Con boys and they showed a trend toward surpassing Agg-Con in the proportion of solutions to total output. However, whatever advantage they may have had in this regard was probably offset by the fact that it appears to have been gained

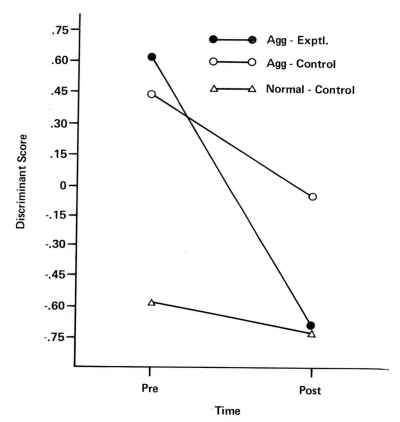

Figure 3-1. Pre- and Postdiscriminant scores for Aggressive-Experimental, Aggressive-Control and Normal-Control Groups.

through their use of a higher proportion of aggressive solutions than either Agg-Control or Normal Controls. Thus, the training program seems to have loosened their tongues but failed to assist them toward developing enough constructive alternatives.

Teacher Ratings

A second objective in the present study was to determine whether teacher ratings would indicate significant improvement in the Agg-Exp boys. These ratings were analyzed both in terms

TABLE 3-III

COMPARISON OF POSTTREATMENT PIPS SCORES IN THREE GROUPS

Category	Group Means			F Contrasts	
				A	B
	A - E	A - C	N - C	(A - E vs. A - C)	(A - E vs. N - c)
	n = 12	n = 10	n = 13		
Total solutions	8.8	7.2	6.4	5.66**	14.55***
Total other talk	5.5	7.6	5.5	ns	ns
SOL/SOL + TALK	.659	.509	.551	3.65*	ns
AGG SOL/Tot Sol	.241	.057	.038	8.26***	11.50***

*$p < .10$
**$p < .05$
***$p < .01$

of T scores on the LNA and Aggressive scales of the SBCL and ratings of change on individual items. Pre– and post–T scores on the LNA and Aggressive scales are included in Table 3-I. Analysis of covariance on the posttest scores showed no significant differences between Agg-Exp and Agg-Con while Agg-Exp and Normals differed only on the Aggressive Scale. This amount of stability is not surprising since these scores are fairly gross measures and the checklist was not prepared as a dependent measure.

Teacher ratings of improvement, on the other hand, should be more sensitive to smaller degrees of change than would be required to alter a T score. Groups were therefore compared on the average number of items improved on the LNA and Aggressive scales. It was predicted that Agg-Exp would improve more than either Agg-Con or Norm-Con on both of these scales. In this instance, however, it was also of interest to determine whether Agg-Con showed more or less Improvement than Norm-Con as it was to compare Agg-Exp results with the other two groups. The Tukey test recommended by Winer (1971) was used to evaluate differences between all pairs of means. On the Aggressive scale, the average number of items improved was 9.7 for Agg-Exp, 10.9 for Agg-Con and .75 for Normal-Control. For the Tukey Test, a difference of 4.87 was necessary to reject the hypothesis of no difference between these means at $p < .05$. By this criterion, the two Agg groups did not differ from each other but did differ significantly from the Normal-Controls.

On the LNA scale, however, the Agg-Exp group showed significantly more improvement than the Agg-Control group which in turn did not differ significantly from the Normal-Control group in number of items improved. Here the mean number of items improved was 10.3, 3.9 and 1.7 for the Agg-Exp, Agg-Control and Normal-Control groups respectively. A difference of 4.57 was required for rejecting the null hypothesis at the .05 level of confidence.

Discussion

The purpose of the present study was to evaluate the impact of 6 weeks with the "Think Aloud" program on test performance and teacher ratings of behavior in young aggressive boys. Specifically, it was hypothesized that the treated boys would show changes in the direction of becoming more like normal boys and less like untreated aggressive controls. This hypothesis was most clearly supported by results of the teacher ratings of improvement in prosocial behavior and by changes in the pattern of performance on a battery of cognitive tests.

The pre-posttest findings are consistent with the results reported by Meichenbaum and Goodman (1971) following a similar brief program for boys selected only on the basis of test impulsivity. Although some of the tests contributing to the discriminant score involved activities similar to those used in the training program (WISC-R Mazes, Matching Familiar Figures), others did not (WRAT Reading). Furthermore, the private speech measures obtained during testing could be considered measures of spontaneous generalization from the training program to the testing situation.

The demonstration of improved prosocial behavior in the classroom is encouraging, even though the treated group did not differ significantly from the untreated group in reduction of aggressive behavior. However, serious questions could be raised about the validity of teacher ratings both as a measure of change and as a measure of treatment effect in the present study.

Although some have questioned whether teacher ratings accurately reflect the behavior they are purportedly measuring, others have found them to be useful in evaluating effects of treatment in disturbed children (Conners, 1972; Werry & Sprague, 1970, 1974). Furthermore, teacher reports are a form of data which is important in its own right. In contrast to the limited time samples often involved in obtaining observational data, teachers have the advantage of prolonged daily contact which provides a large time sample on which to base their report, particularly in regard to infrequent behaviors. In addition, there are significant correlations between independent behavior observations and teacher report $(r = -.38)$ when it involves frequent behaviors readily observed by both teachers and observers as in the case of items of the LNA scale (Camp & Zimet, 1974) versus observations of off-task behavior.

In the present study, a more serious question concerns the validity of the teacher ratings as a measure of change. Since teachers knew whether the child being rated was in the program or not, one could propose that the expectation of behavioral change with the program could result in general ratings of improvement. The fact that there is a difference in results of their ratings on the two scales argues against this explanation.

The possibility that unreliability in the scale influenced results must also be considered. Though reliability has not been established for the rating form in which teachers rated improvement, there is no reason to believe that unreliability would be greater for one group of aggressive boys than another. Unreliability in the measures would have tended to decrease the likelihood of finding significant differences. Yet the magnitude of differences on the Aggressive scale was so small it is difficult to believe that the two groups actually differed on this scale. Differences on the prosocial scale were large enough to be significant despite possible unreliability.

It therefore seems reasonable to conclude that the "Think Aloud" program was powerful enough to produce significant improvement in both test performance and classroom behavior in aggressive boys. At the same time, the program failed to produce changes in all areas examined and in some instances may have had a negative effect. The points where the program seemed to fail were in channeling the voluminous verbal output of aggressive boys and in improving efficiency. In designing the program we failed to recognize the extent to which chatter, silliness and inappropriate verbal activity might actually interfere with goals of the program. These were handled by ignoring them rather than by trying to attack them directly. Similarly, aggressive solutions to interpersonal problems were considered along with non-aggressive solutions, and no effort was made to consider these categorically "bad." Rather, they were evaluated in light of the consequences along with other kinds of solutions.

Apparently this approach was not enough, given the current program. It is of course possible that more time with the program as it stands could have brought the children to a more appropriate level of functioning with regard to quality of verbal output, efficiency and social appropriateness of their thinking. Another approach, however, would be to structure the program differently so that silliness, for example, is attacked directly and the negative consequences of aggressive solutions are emphasized more.

And finally, even if one accepts the teacher ratings as valid, the present design does not allow us to determine whether the observed results, especially the ratings of improved classroom behavior, are attributable to the type of program or to increased individual attention. At this point in our research, however, it was felt that the first priority was to determine whether any alteration in behavior or test performance could be demonstrated in hyperaggressive boys. Further research should help to clarify the specific aspects of the program which are most responsible for the observed changes and to offer less questionable data in support of the "real life" changes. Results of the present study are nevertheless encouraging and suggest that further efforts to develop this approach for use by school personnel may be quite fruitful.

REFERENCES

Editorial Comments

Atrops, M. *Cognitive mediation and social skills training with institutionalized young male offenders for the self-regulation of an aggressive response in the moment of provocation.* Doctoral dissertation, Fuller Graduate School of Psychology, in progress.

Bandura, A. *Aggression: a social learning analysis.* New York: Prentice-Hall, 1973.

Camp, B.W. Verbal mediation in young aggressive boys. *Journal of Abnormal Psychology,* 1976, *86,* 145-153.

Patterson, G.R., Reid, J.B., Jones, R.R., & Conger, R.E. *A social learning approach to family intervention: Families with aggressive children.* Eugene, OR: Castalia, 1975.

Text

Achenbach, T.M. Standardization of a research instrument for identifying associative respondings in children. *Developmental Psychology,* 1970, *2,* 283-291.

Bem, S.L. Verbal self-control: The establishment of effective self-instruction. *Journal of Experimental Psychology,* 1967, *74,* 485-491.

Bornstein, P.H. & Quevillon, R.P. The effects of a self-instructional package with overactive pre-school boys. *Journal of Applied Behavior Analysis,* in press.

Camp, B.W. Remedial reading in a pediatric clinic. *Clinical Pediatrics,* 1971, *10,* 36-42.

Camp, B.W. Stability of behavior ratings. *Perceptual and Motor Skills,* 1976, *43,* 1065-1066.

Camp, B.W. Verbal Mediation in young aggressive boys. *Journal of Abnormal Psychology,* 1976, *86,* 145-153.

Camp, B.W., & van Doorninck, W.J. Assessment of "motivated" reading therapy with elementary school children. *Behavior Therapy,* 1971, *2,* 214-222.

Camp, B.W., & Zimet, S.G. The relationship of teacher rating scales to behavior observations and reading achievement of first-grade children. *Journal of Special Education,* 1974, *8,* 353-359.

Camp, B.W., & Zimet, S. G. Classroom behavior during reading instruction. *Exceptional Children,* 1975, *2,* 109-110.

Camp, B.W., Zimet, S.G., van Doorninck, W.J., & Dahlem, N.W. Verbal abilities in young aggressive boys. *Journal of Educational Psychology,* 1977, *69,* 129-135.

Conners, C.K. Pharmacotherapy of psychopathology in children. In H.C. Quay & J.S. Werry (Eds.) *Psychopathological Disorders of Childhood.* New York: Wiley, 1972.

Kagan, J., Pearson, L., & Welch, L. Conceptual impulsivity and inductive reasoning. *Child Development,* 1966, *37,* 583-594.

Kenny, D.A. A quasi-experimental approach to assessing treatment effects in the nonequivalent control group design. *Psychological Bulletin,* 1975, *82,* 345-362.

McCall, R.B. Addendum: The use of multivariate procedures in developmental psychology. In P.H. Mussen (ed.) *Carmichael's Manual of Child Psychology.* New York: Wiley & Sons, 1970.

Meichenbaum, D.H., & Goodman, J. Training impulsive children to talk to themselves: A means of developing self-control. *Journal of Abnormal Psychology,* 1971, *77,* 115-126.

Miller, L.C. School Behavior Check List: An inventory of deviant behavior for elementary school children. *Journal of Consulting and Clinical Psychology,* 1972, *38,* 134-144.

Miller, L.C., Hampe, E., Barrett, C.L., & Noble, H. Children's deviant behavior within the general population. *Journal of Consulting and Clinical Psychology,* 1971, *37,* 16-22.

Palkes, H., Stewart, M., & Kahana, B. Porteus maze performance of hyperactive boys after training in self-directed verbal commands. *Child Development,* 1968, *39,* 817-826.

Salkind, N.J. *Errors and Latency on the MFFT: A Reassessment of Classification Strategies.* Paper presented at the Society for Research in Child Development, Denver, Colorado, April 1975.

Shure, M.B., & Spivack, G. *The PIPS Test Manual.* Unpublished manuscript, Hahnemann Medical College and Hospital, Philadelphia, Pennsylvania.

Shure, M.B., & Spivack, G. *A Mental Health Program for Kindergarten Children: A Cognitive Approach to solving Interpersonal Problems.* Philadelphia, Pennsylvania: Community Mental Health/Mental Retardation Center, Department of Mental Health Sciences, Hahnemann Medical College and Hospital, 1974.

van Doorninck, W.J., & Camp, B.W. *Factor Analysis of the School Behavior Check List.* Unpublished manuscript, 1975.

Werry, J.S., & Sprague, R.L. Hyperactivity. In C.G. Costello (Ed.) *Symptoms of Psychopathology: A Handbook.* New York: Wiley, 1970.

Werry, J.S., & Sprague, R.L. Methylphenidate in children—effect of dosage. *Australia and New Zealand Journal of Psychiatry,* 1974, *8,* 9-19.

White, S.H. Evidence for a hierarchical arrangement of learning progresses. In L.P. Lipsitt and C.C. Spiker (Eds.) *Advances in Child Development and Behavior* (Vol. 2). New York: Academic Press, 1965.

White, S.H. Some general outlines of the matrix of developmental changes between five and seven years. *Bulletin of the Orton Society,* 1970, *20,* 41-57.

Winer, B.J. *Statistical Principles in Experimental Design.* New York: McGraw-Hill Book Company, 1971.

THE YOUTH CENTER PROJECT: TRANSACTIONAL ANALYSIS AND BEHAVIOR MODIFICATION PROGRAMS FOR DELINQUENTS*†

CARL F. JESNESS

EDITORIAL COMMENTS

The editor's comment in **Behavior Therapy With Delinquents** in 1973 that there is every indication that our society will continue to institutionalize juvenile criminals still holds true. In that book Jesness and DeRisi presented the details of their contingency management program which was, and continues to be, part of a large-scale project in the California Youth Authority (CYA).

The Youth Center Project, here summarized in Chapter 4 by Jesness, is tremendous in scope. The staffs of two large institutions for boys in northern California were trained — one in transactional analysis and the other in behavior modification. Those subsequently assigned to the Youth Authority were randomly assigned to one or the other institution. These two treatments have now been compared to each other as well as to other CYA institutions which continued with their "usual" treatment — an admirable design rarely seen in corrections research. Jesness's typologies,

*The Youth Center Research Project was supported by PHS Grant No. MH 14411 NIMH (Center for Studies of Crime and Delinquency). The grant was made to the American Justice Institute which worked closely with the California Youth Authority in the development and implementation of the project.

†Reprinted with permission from *Behavioral Disorders,* 1976, 1, 27-36 (Council for Children with Behavioral Disorders).

multiple measures of behavior and attitude, as well as parole and follow-up measures were also incorporated in the program. Data have now been collected on hundreds of youths. Voluminous results are summarized in this chapter and in other works (Jesness, 1975).

The major finding — that results of the two programs do not greatly differ — is probably quite a disappointment to those who were mainly interested in the "contest" nature of the study. **Both** programs were more successful than previous and current comparison institutions with regard to recidivism, but they did not differ from each other. Also, it should come as no surprise that each treatment had some specific treatment effects: transactional analysis resulted in significant attitude changes and behavior modification in improved behavior ratings! There are plenty of data to bolster arguments for either approach.

While results for both were significantly better than "usual" programs (42% recidivism), postrelease arrest records for these two programs still averaged 33 percent at twelve months, indicating considerable room for improvement. One suggestion (which should have been learned from experience with token economies elsewhere) is that aftercare programs need to be implemented to continue the program after release and return to the community in order to help insure generalization of effects. Jesnes' final suggestion (blending the strengths of each program) has yet to be tried.

T HIS PAPER BRIEFLY DESCRIBES the Youth Center Research Project, a four-year research and evaluation project that compared the effectiveness of behavior modification and transactional analysis in the rehabilitation of institutionalized juvenile delinquents. The feasibility of applying these two approaches to the treatment of an institution's entire population was evaluated, as well as the relative effectiveness of the treatment strategies in modifying the behavior of different types of delinquents. Additional details of the study are reported in Jesness (1975).

The two treatment approaches implemented were widely accepted as tenable. At one institution, the treatment strategies were based on the psychodynamic principles and group therapy methods of transactional analysis (TA). The primary sources on TA were Berne (1961, 1966, 1967). At the other institution, the treatment program was based on the principles of behavior modification (BMod). Extensive descriptions and bibliographies on

BMod can be found in a variety of sources (e.g., Bandura, 1969; Krasner & Ullman, 1967; Ullman & Krasner, 1969).

METHOD

Settings

The Youth Center Research Project was located at two adjacent institutions, O.H. Close School and Karl Holton School. Close and Holton were alike in their organizational structure, staffing patterns, and physical layout. Each was designed to house approximately 400 male youths in eight 50-bed living halls.

Each youth spent from 8 a.m. to 3 p.m. in a school program, five days a week. Classroom buildings were near but apart from the living halls. Each hall's "treatment team" included its own three teachers (two for academic and one for shop courses) so that a youth attended class with others from his own hall. Because classes were small, averaging 15 to 17 students, individual attention was the rule rather than the exception. Additionally, there were facilities, equipment, and coaching for an extensive physical education program, and a music specialist taught instrumental and choral music.

Recreation in the living units included television viewing, record playing, ping-pong, pool table games, and reading. Movement to and from school and to activities outside of the hall was relatively free and unregimented, although the wards said they were almost always aware they were being watched, and that they were locked in.

There was a theatre for weekly movies and occasional live shows. There were Catholic and Protestant chapels for Sunday services, and full-time chaplains.

Youths' work assignments were not heavy. They included kitchen duties, housekeeping, and a little outside work on the grounds; most of the plant maintenance was done by hired personnel.

Six weeks after arrival most youths were permitted to go off-grounds with their parents on "day passes." Toward the end of his stay the youth went home once or twice for week-long "furloughs" in preparation for his release on parole. Young people and adults from the outside community came to the school almost daily for volunteer, student, or subsidized work with the youths in tutoring, recreation, arts and crafts, etc.   Staff occasionally took groups of youths out for picnics, snow trips, movies, fishing, camping, and other diversions.   The living units hosted occasional dances, talent shows, or parties, to which groups of girls were invited from community organizations or clubs.

Subjects

Subjects included all youths from 15 to 17 years of age assigned to the two institutions by the California Youth Authority Board during the 19-month period from August, 1969 through March, 1971.   First offenders, those with prior institutionalization, and those transferred in from other institutions for disciplinary purposes were all included in a common pool of experimental subjects, provided they remained in the program at least three months and spent more than half their stay in the institution after the experimental programs were fully operational.   The specific institution into which a youth was placed was determined on a random basis, 589 youths were assigned to Close, 541 to Holton. Of 1,130 potentially eligible subjects, 988 were available for parole follow-up and essentially complete test data were available for 904.

The median age of the subjects was 16.6 years.   They had been committed for offenses ranging from murder to incorrigibility; burglary and auto theft were the most common.   Thirty-three percent had been convicted previously and almost all had fairly extensive arrest records.   Only 5 percent were committed for drug offenses, although 60 percent had some drug use history. The sample was 56 percent white, 13 percent Mexican-American, 28 percent black, and 2 percent other.

Generally subjects had backgrounds of serious difficulty in school.   Average reading ability was at eighth-grade level (Gates-MacGinitie test) ; arithmetic was at sixth-grade level (Comprehensive Test of Basic Skills).   Seventy-two percent of the youths had been suspended from school on at least two occasions and 40 percent had been sent to the principal's office for misbehavior 10 or more times.

TA Procedures: Close Supervision

STAFF TRAINING.   Training and supervision of Close (TA) and Holton (BMod) staff in their respective treatment method were given high priority throughout the first three years of the project. At Close, the project's TA specialist scheduled a 16-hour introductory course in TA for all staff.   A unique feature of the on-going training was the participation of treatment staff as clients in the modality they were to use as counselors.   Over a period of several months following the introductory course, almost all management and treatment staff voluntarily attended, in twos and threes, a 3-day TA treatment marathon, held away from Close at an institute for TA therapy.

Teachers also completed the introductory TA course, and most attended at least one 3-day marathon.   Although project staff devoted most of their training and supervision time to social workers and counselors, the educational staff regularly participated in weekly training sessions and case conferences.   Project staff developed special manuals to assist teachers in using TA principles in their everyday transactions with students. A few teachers offered a basic course in TA for their students and sat in as cotherapists in small-group sessions.

YOUTH TREATMENT.   Although TA is primarily a group treatment method, its principles are applicable in every part of an institutional program.   Therefore, staff at Close were encouraged to use their knowledge of TA in small-group therapy sessions, group "community meetings," everyday management problems, and all other transactions with the youths and with each other.   Group treatment guidelines and a "Youth Counselor's Handbook" were available to guide staff implementation of TA treatment.

The TA treatment was intended to take advantage of a youth's expectation, however slight, that he would accomplish something for himself.   He generally had eight or nine months in which to do so.   Immediately upon arrival at Close, the youth was assigned to the load of a caseworker on his living hall; case loads averaged eight.   The caseworker functioned as TA therapist in twice-weekly small-group meetings of this case load.

The caseworker negotiated verbal treatment contracts with

each of his youths so that both youth and staff knew precisely what treatment goals the youth had set for himself. Treatment contracts were of three kinds: (a) "academic," (b) "small group," and (c) "social behavior." The most important was usually the small-group contract, its goal being a "life-script redecision." Goals of the social behavior contract involved correction of unsatisfactory staff and peer relationships. Academic goals were specific achievements in the school program.

All goals had to be agreed to by both youth and staff, and all had to be achievable while the youth was at Close. The criteria for having reached goals were described in the contracts. For example, "quitting drugs" was accepted as a good decision but not a small-group treatment goal, because neither the youth nor the therapist could see that he had quit until after he left. On the other hand, "stop setting myself up for punishment" could be a small-group treatment goal, because criteria for achieving this goal could be observed in the institution and described in the contract.

Five weeks after a youth's arrival, he prepared for an initial case conference with the treatment team. In order to best present his own case, the youth and his caseworker reviewed exactly what the youth's goals were and specified how his observable behavior would indicate, to both himself and the treatment team, that he had reached these goals. In the case conference, instead of asking the team how he was doing in the program, the youth told them. If the treatment team and the youth disagreed on the appropriateness of his goals, or on the degree to which he was accomplishing them, they sought to resolve the differences in conference.

As therapists, staff were to have no expectations of any youth except those that he set for himself, a concept very foreign to most of the youths. Appropriate goals—goals that included converting from an offender to a nonoffender—were encouraged, but the youth was required to name them. The life-script interview, administered early in his stay, encouraged the youth to specify acceptable goals rather than facetious or inappropriate ones such as, "I want to become a better burglar."

A community meeting was an assembly of the youths and staff in a living hall. These were held one to three times weekly for about 45-60 minutes. Community meetings were not particularly intended or suited for TA therapy; but youths and staff had the opportunity to bring up a wide range of matters. The meetings could be as relaxed as spending a pleasant social hour together, or as serious as deciding what to do about interracial conflicts. Often, community contracts—deciding specific courses of action toward explicit goals—were negotiated. Community contracts were two sided: both youths and staff made clear what their commitments were. Frequently, difficulties that threatened orderly living in the hall were discussed. For example, if the matter at issue was youth's reluctance to follow rules, but all agreed that community life required rules, the youths might decide that they would more willingly abide by the rules if they had a hand in making them. Staff could agree to this condition, and both sides could democrat- ically decide their course of action. Community meetings were sometimes followed by a 15-minute "critique," attended only by staff, or by staff and a youth representative or two. Most staff be- lieved that the meetings were necessary for the treatment team to stay on top of problems which may have interfered with the overall treatment program.

BMod Procedures: Holton

STAFF TRAINING. The BMod program at Holton was devel- oped as a collaborative effort of project and institution staff. The project BMod specialist trained management (superintendent and administrative personnel) and treatment team staff (youth coun- selors, social workers, and teachers) in the basic principles and terminology of BMod and contingency management. Management completed an 80-hour basic course, and all treatment staff com- pleted a 40-hour course that required mastering the content of the programmed text, *The Analysis of Behavior* (Holland & Skinner, 1961). After this initial training was completed, the first institu- tion-wide BMod program was designed and implemented. There- after, two hours per week of on-the-job consultation were pro- vided to each treatment team. A Holton program manual, which described all program elements in detail, was available to guide treatment.

YOUTH TREATMENT.   The setting and some general program aspects at Holton were similar to those at Close.   There was somewhat greater emphasis placed on vocational education, but less on large- and small-group meetings.

The BMod youth treatment program influenced many aspects of the youth's activities at Holton, especially in the classrooms and living halls.   Two partially overlapping token systems operated concurrently at Holton.   One was geared to a recommendation for release, the other affected a youth's access to more immediately desired comforts, materials, services, and recreational opportunities.

TARGET BEHAVIORS.   Three different kinds of behaviors were identified and managed in the Holton program.   These were "academic," "convenience," and "critical behavior deficiency" behaviors.

Academic behaviors referred to educational achievements and skills.   Classroom teaching materials and methods were developed or adapted to conform to principles of BMod.   Most teaching materials were locally or commercially developed programmed materials.   Each student's school program was individualized and based on an educational prescription that outlined his strengths and weaknesses.   An important feature of each prescription was a set of behavioral objectives written by the teacher.   The student's entire educational experience was then directed toward achieving these objectives.   The Holton educational program is further described in Jesness and DeRisi (1973).

Convenience behaviors were those that made it easier for staff and youth to live and work together: getting up on time, dressing properly, keeping the hall neat and clean, being courteous and cooperative with peers and staff, adhering to hall rules, and other everyday routines of social living.   Convenience behaviors were not always crucial to the youth's becoming a nondelinquent, but were important to the youth's social and work adjustment, as well as to the efficient, orderly functioning of the institution.   Convenience behaviors were rated continuously throughout the day by the youth counselor, on a check sheet.

Critical behavior deficiencies were behaviors deemed most likely to increase the chance of a youth's failing parole (in many instances these happened to be convenience behaviors). A youth's first step in the BMod program ordinarily involved specification of critical behavior deficiencies and formulation of a corresponding list of appropriate terminal behaviors. For some youths, deficiencies were obvious; for others, locating specific deficiencies was quite difficult. Three information sources were available to help the caseworker: the Jesness Behavior Checklist (Jesness, 1971), other direct behavior observation, and youth's records.

The Jesness Behavior Checklist produced systematic self- and observer-ratings for the youth's behavior patterns. It produced profiles which indicated critical behavior deficiencies, often establishing agreement between the youth and the treatment team on deficiencies. A major objective of the Holton program was, in effect, transforming profile "valleys" to "peaks."

Critical behavior deficiencies could also be identified through other systematic or informal observation of behavior in the classroom and living hall. Some staff were taught time sampling and frequency recording procedures, but most used informal, more subjective observation as the basis for their evaluation. Regular shortcomings on the convenience behavior check sheet were also indications of critical behavior deficiencies. Additionally, caseworkers read the main file of each youth assigned to them. However, since it was usually found that most of the material did not refer to observable behaviors, the caseworker had to evaluate the data carefully.

After identifying a youth's critical behavior deficiencies, he and his caseworker negotiated their correction. The general strategy for achieving this was "contingency management" contracting. This is a motivational technique in which access to resources or activities desired by the youth was contingent on his performance of caseworker-determined behavior objectives designed to correct critical behavior deficiencies. Ideally, these objectives involved behavior that the youth also appraised on the self-rating form of the Behavior Checklist as being in need of improvement.

After determining target behavior objectives, the next step in contracting required stating how these were to be measured. In order to maintain and improve the quality of contingency contracting, contracting progress checks were completed by the treatment team supervisor. The final step in writing a contract was specification of the benefits to the youth of achieving objectives agreed on. In order to ensure reliability and consistency in contracts, a brief set of characteristics of good contingency contracting was developed as a guideline for the rater.

To aid staff who contracted with youths, a contract package was developed that eventually contained more than 100 sample contracts. Designed to correct particular behavior deficiencies, contracts were arranged in incremental steps so that each behavioral objective was easily within the capabilities of the youth, and each subsequent objective was a successive approximation to the terminal goal. The packaged contracts were not the only ones a counselor could use. They were a series of contracts that had been tested in practice, and saved the caseworker from repeatedly having to rediscover effective procedures for certain common deficiencies.

TOKEN SYSTEMS. All youth were required to earn the right to be referred to the Youth Authority Board for release on parole. This was earned through the accumulation of "Behavior Change Units" (Units). The number of Units each youth needed to earn referral was partially based on the sentence imposed by the Board (the average youth remained at Holton about seven months). The Board accepted recommendations of Holton staff in more than 80 percent of cases, but youths were aware that earning the required units guaranteed referral to the Board, not release.

It was required that youth earn 45 percent of Units in the area of convenience behaviors, 28 percent by academic behaviors, and 27 percent by the correction of critical behavior deficiencies. The proportions were established arbitrarily, no doubt reflecting staff's necessary preoccupation with management.

A simultaneous token system governed availability of certain "extras"—playing pool, bringing in personal clothing to wear, renting a private room, etc.—to the youth. These goods and services were exchanged for "Karl Holton Dollars" (Dollars), and were listed on "reinforcement menus" in each living hall. Each Unit earned toward release also earned one Dollar for the youth.

The BMod program emphasized the necessity of providing frequent, immediate, and clear-cut consequences for appropriate and inappropriate youth behavior. Units and Dollars were available to youth through contracting to correct critical behavior deficiencies, and in other ways. Appropriate youth behavior was also reinforced by staff praise or approval, immediate Dollar bonuses, and written commendations which documented a youth's prosocial behavior.

Consequences for inappropriate behavior were also programmed. A clear statement of Dollar fines for certain behaviors was posted in the living halls. Some inappropriate behavior resulted in a timeout, usually consisting of a brief period of isolation in a bland, well-lighted place.

In some cases, a youth could be prohibited from participating in desirable institutional events until the completion of a series of contracts related to the inappropriate behavior. For serious incidents, such as participation in a riot, serious injury, escape, etc., written reports were placed in the youth's permanent records. More Units could be added to the youth's Unit requirement for referral to the Board, particularly when the incident indicated a critical behavioral deficiency that would require more time for correction than remained in the youth's program.

RESULTS

Besides the differential treatment program variables, youths who served as subjects in the research project were classified as to level of personality maturity on the basis of tests and an interview. This permitted a finer analysis of changes in dependent variables; this aspect of the project is described in Jesness (1975).

Numerous dependent variables associated with changes in youths, staff, and the programs were measured. The present paper reports major findings in brief; extensive results are available in Jesness (1975).

YOUTH EVALUATION. The parole performance of project parolees was clearly superior to that of preexperimental subjects at both Close and Holton. Table 4-I shows the parole violation rates of Close and Holton parole release cohorts for the 2-year baseline period (1968-69) prior to the full implementation of the Youth

TABLE 4-I

PAROLE VIOLATORS IN HOLTON AND CLOSE RELEASE COHORTS
AT 12 MONTHS PAROLE EXPOSURE

Year Released	Number Released	Parole Violators	Percentage of Violators
1968[a]			
Close	253	124	49.0
Holton	232	99	42.7
1969[a]			
Close	407	189	46.4
Holton	267	109	40.8
1971[b]			
Close	233	80	34.3
Holton	187	58	31.0
1970[b]			
Close	220	69	31.4
Holton	211	71	33.6

[a] Includes only youths aged 15, 16, or 17 at entry.
[b] Includes project youths only.

Center Research Project, and the rates for project subjects (1970-71). The differences from preexperimental period are significantly lower for both Close and Holton (χ^2 for Holton = 8.09, p < .01; χ^2 for Close = 23.32, p < .001). There were no differences between the revocation rates of youths from the two schools at any parole exposure period. At 12 months after parole release, 32 percent of Close (TA) subjects and 32 percent of Holton (BMod) youths had been returned to an institution; at 24 months, 48 percent of Close and 48 percent of Holton subjects had been returned.

Recidivism rates for youths released from two comparison California Youth Authority institutions, Nelles and Paso Robles (to which youths of approximately the same age were assigned) were compared to rates for Close and Holton. As shown in Table 4-II, the failure rate for project youths released from Close and Holton (33.1%) was significantly lower (p. < .001) than failure rates at either Nelles (42.5%) or Paso Robles (42.8%).

The treatment programs at Close and Holton did not reduce the frequency of major breeches of discipline and other serious

TABLE 4-II

PAROLE VIOLATORS IN COMBINED CLOSE-HOLTON, NELLES AND
PASO ROBLES 1970-71 RELEASE COHORTS AT 12 MONTHS
PAROLE EXPOSURE

Institution	Number Released	Parole Violators[a]	Percentage of Violators
Close-Holton	842	279	33.1
Nelles	835	355	42.5
Paso Robles	710	304	42.8

[a] Prorated on the basis of proportion of youths at each age (unprorated data produced similar results).

incidents, but staff reaction to them was modified. The number of youths sent to detention was reduced by over 60% at both Close and Holton. Staff reported that when detention was used, it was used differently that is, for briefer periods, and for promoting change in behavior rather than for retribution.

Achievement testing revealed interesting patterns of gains in school subject achievement. The TA and BMod programs differentially affected achievement of youths, according to their level of personality maturity (see Jesness, 1975a).

Using an Observer Behavior Checklist instrument, treatment teams rated each youth's behavior in several situations early in his stay and again just before release. Although youths in both programs improved on these ratings, Close (TA) youths improved most on "Insight," while Holton (BMod) youths improved most on "Independence," "Ability to Communicate," and "Calmness."

Each youth completed a Self Behavior Checklist instrument early and late in his stay. Close (TA) youths showed greater gains, especially in the area of "Enthusiasm" and "Sociability." Additionally, personality testing revealed that Close youths improved more than Holton youths on numerous subscales related to personal adjustment.

STAFF EVALUATION. Youths' opinions about the treatment staff members at their institution were surveyed. Significantly more Close (TA) than Holton (BMod) youths reported that staff usually said positive rather than negative things to them, and that staff treated all youths equally and fairly. Significantly fewer Close youths reported that staff insulted them, made them feel inferior, and did not respect them.

Other results showed that Close (TA) staff was perceived as more involved and understanding. Holton (BMod) caseworkers were perceived as more strict and less willing to allow youths to participate in rule making. Significantly more youths at Close made positive evaluations of their academic teachers, but Holton youths saw their teachers as more demanding of performance in the classroom.

Clearly, the Close (TA) program promoted much more positive regard for staff. Further analysis of the importance of a good caseworker-youth relationship showed that, for youths at either Close or Holton, positive regard for staff was correlated with (a) greater improvement on attitudinal and self-behavioral gains, and (b) slightly improved (but significant) parole outcomes. The data suggested that the specific effects generated by both programs were further enhanced if the residents perceived staff as treating them with respect, as more often emphasizing their positive rather than negative behaviors, and as treating residents fairly.

INSTITUTION EVALUATION. The Correctional Institutional Environment Scale (Moos, 1970) provides measures on 10 subscales which are combined into four major dimensions—relationship, treatment, systems maintenance, and aggression. Pre- and posttesting of staff and youths on this instrument indicated changes in both staff's and youths' perceptions of the social climates of Close and Holton.

The greatest shifts were apparent in the perceptions of the youths at Holton (BMod), who saw their institution in a poorer light on all four scales, in comparison both to their own pretests and to Close youths' tests.

Responses to five questions, designed to determine the extent to which anti-institutional "delinquent" subcultures existed, showed that the TA program was more effective than the BMod program in developing pro-institutional attitudes among residents. Other measurement suggested that the TA program was more effective in improving youths' self-concepts, increasing the youths' certainty that they would not again break the law, and convincing the youths that they, not external circumstances, controlled their own lives.

DISCUSSION

The implications of the Youth Center Research Project are unusually favorable. Institutions can be run so that most of the youths change for the better. A high proportion of the youths became more socialized, friendly, and responsible. They achieved scholastically at a high rate, showed improvement in self-concept, and became more optimistic about their future.

Parole data showed that the two programs were equally effective in reducing recidivism. Whether youths from both institutions would continue to do equally well, after being away from the institutions for a longer time, remained to be seen. In theory, those who showed the greatest gains in the TA program might be expected to maintain themselves longer in the community, because that program helped the youths improve their self-image and may have altered the direction of their destructive life-scripts. It is possible, on the other hand, that behavior changes such as those made at Holton do in fact alter the environment. A boy behaving in a better way on returning to his home will elicit different responses from those in his immediate environment. If his constructive behaviors are reinforced, he will maintain them. If, however, he returns to precisely the same environment that generated his problems in the first place, and only his previous behaviors are reinforced, it would be only a matter of time until his new behaviors are extinguished and the old behaviors reinstated.

At this project's end, both Close and Holton were establishing greater contact with the community, promoting continuity in their treatment programs. Parole staff from the field were visiting the institutions and participating in case planning. They were becoming acquainted with the youths prior to release on parole and were establishing themselves as persons to whom the youths could turn for support when they returned to the streets. These may prove to be ways to maintain behavior changes made by youths in effective institutional programs.

Perhaps the most important finding of the study was that each program generated specific treatment effects. The BMod program resulted in greater gains on the observer ratings, and the TA program yielded greater gains on attitudinal and self-report dimensions. Both the attitudinal and the behavioral gains were relevant intermediate objectives, in that both the behavior checklist post-test ratings and the posttest attitudinal variables correlated with parole performance criteria.

Another important finding was that a nonspecific factor, client positive regard for staff, potentiated specific treatment effects. The data suggested that in a behavior modification program where specific overt behaviors are targeted, greater changes can be made if the client feels positively toward staff; in a transactional analysis program, greater changes on attitudinal and self-report measures can be obtained if good relationships exist. Good interpersonal relations and counseling skills are probably necessary ingredients of any educational or treatment enterprise.

The most promising direction is toward a blending of the obvious strengths of each program. BMod treatment specified small units of behavior as contract goals; TA called for establishing global, lifetime goals. Persons who work to accomplish short-term objectives as steps toward broader goals may do better than those who concentrate on only immediate, unrelated behaviors. Neither system need be restricted to setting only one type of goal; each system is based on learning theory, and each uses reinforcement (by self and others) as the motivational system. Both are contractual, and both, in the long run, promote self-management. The advantages of integrating two such ostensibly different approaches may be considerable.

REFERENCES

Editorial Comments

Jesness, C.F. Comparative effectiveness of behavior modification and transactional analysis programs for delinquents. *Journal of Consulting and Clinical Psychology,* 1975, *43,* 758-779.

Jesness, C.F., & DeRisi W. Some variations in techniques of contingency management in a school for delinquents. In J.S. Stumphauzer (Ed.) *Behavior Therapy with Delinquents.* Springfield, IL: Thomas, 1973, 196-235.

Text

Bandura, A. *Principles of Behavior Modification.* New York: Holt, Rinehart and Winston, 1969.

Berne, E. *Transactional Analysis in Psychotherapy.* New York: Grove Press, 1961.

Berne, E. *Games People Play.* New York: Grove Press, 1967.

Holland, J.G., & Skinner, B.F. *The Analysis of Behavior.* New York: Mc-Graw-Hill, 1961.

Jesness, C. F. *Jesness Behavior Checklist: Manual.* Palo Alto: Consulting Psychologists Press, 1971.

Jesness, C.F. Comparative effectiveness of behavior modification and transactional analysis programs for delinquents. *Journal of Consulting and Clinical Psychology,* 1975, *43,* 758-779.

Jesness, C.F., & De Risi, W. Some variations in techniques of contingency management in a school for delinquents. In J.S. Stumphauzer (Ed.), *Behavior Therapy with Delinquents.* Springfield, IL: Thomas, 1973.

Krasner, L., & Ullmann, L.P. *Research in Behavior Modification: New Developments and Implications.* New York: Holt, Rinehart and Winston, 1967.

Moos, R. Differential effects of the social climates of correctional institutions. *Journal of Research in Crime and Delinquency.* 1970, 7, 71-82.

Ullman, P., & Krasner, L. *A Psychological Approach to Abnormal Behavior.* Englewood Cliffs, NJ: Prentice-Hall, 1969.

CHAPTER 5

NEW DIRECTIONS IN A JUVENILE HALL SETTING*†

TOM S. ALLISON, SHIELA KENDALL, AND DOUGLAS SLOANE

EDITORIAL COMMENTS

There are a large number of juvenile halls in the United States. They are usually attached to juvenile courts and probation departments and often are simply "holding stations" or detention facilities where youths are waiting for court, waiting after court, waiting for placement elsewhere; waiting. At times they are also used by protective services departments as temporary placement for children who are abused or abandoned by parents. Too often these are overcrowded facilities in which all of the above are thrown together — at times with disastrous results for the relatively naive youngster who all too quickly "learns the ropes." Treatment and program evaluation are often forsaken for the more demanding, immediate needs of temporary housing and control for large numbers of young people. The short-term nature and limited funding of juvenile halls are the biggest problems facing investigators trying to develop or evaluate such programs.

*The authors gratefully acknowledge the support and assistance of the staff and administrators of the Solano County Juvenile Probation Department and Juvenile Hall, during the present study. Special thanks are due to Richard Grable, Chief Deputy Probation Officer, and Anthony Bukwich, Superintendent of the Juvenile Hall, whose commitments to the improvement of treatment services for young offenders led to the development of the New Directions program. Portions of this paper were presented at the annual meeting of the Western Psychological Association, Los Angles, California, April, 1976.

†Portions of the present study were conducted while the first author was serving as a Research Specialist with the Cooperative Behavior Demonstration Project (Carl F. Jesness, Director), Division of Research, California Youth Authority.

As a result, very little research literature is available. Yet, juvenile halls obviously represent an important link between juvenile justice and intervention or treatment.

In this original chapter, Allison, Kendall, and Sloane evaluate a behavioral "New Directions" program which provides short-term treatment beyond usual juvenile hall "holding," but a less severe step than long-term placement. The authors differentiate between a token or point economy program and a contingency contracting system; they utilize both and compare their effectiveness. The authors discuss the overall superiority of the phase level contracting system as well as several limitations in their research design.

A cost analysis of the program revealed that while "New Directions" costs a little more **per day** than long-term placements, the overall cost was substantially less because the average stay was much more brief (see Chap. 10 for a more thorough discussion of cost-effectiveness). Data on subsequent recidivism rates were not yet available at this point, but are being assessed. The need for further evaluation of various juvenile hall programs should be underscored.

ABSTRACT

A BEHAVIORALLY ORIENTED delinquency treatment program, called *New Directions,* was created in the Solano County (California) Juvenile Hall to provide a short-term treatment setting beyond the usual probation services, but short of commitment to long-term or out-of-county facilities. During the course of program operation, the effectiveness of an in-house contingency management strategy based on a contingency contracting model was compared with a point economy system. The data indicated that in-house behavior management objectives were more reliably achieved during the period of the contingency contracting-based system than during the point system period. Counselors initially reported that the contracting-based system was easier to learn and implement than the point system and ameliorated several problems associated with point system operation. The program was found to be less costly to the county than placement in other residential care facilities.

INTRODUCTION

The usual purpose of a juvenile hall is to provide short-term detention of young persons who must be temporarily removed from the community because of a lack of parental or other supervision or because of legally defined behavioral problems. Juvenile hall "treatment" programs are, therefore, usually directed toward maintenance of good order and discipline within the hall and collaboration with the detained youths, families, or guardians, and court or court agents in arranging further disposition of cases. The actual rehabilitative responsibilities are usually assigned to other persons or agencies such as family, foster parents, probation or mental health caseworkers, county "camps" or "ranches" for delinquents, or state or private institutions, etc. Juvenile halls have not generated a *treatment effectiveness* literature of their own, probably because of the usual brevity of their involvement with the youths they serve.

The Solano County (California) Juvenile Hall delinquency treatment program, called *New Directions,* was created to demonstrate the efficacy of providing treatment for juvenile offenders in a juvenile hall setting as contrasted with long-term, out-of-community placement. The projected primary advantages of the program were (1) retaining clients closer to their homes so that families or guardians could be more involved in the treatment effort, (2) increased collaboration of probation officers or other community caseworkers in the in-house phase of treatment, and (3) reduced cost to the families and/or county for treatment services. Treatment effectiveness was expected to at least equal that produced by other available placements. The present study examines (a) the cost-effectiveness of the program and (b) the effectiveness of a contingency contracting-based, in-house treatment program as compared with a point economy system.

PROGRAM

Clients

The clients were adjudicated male and female delinquents assigned to the program by the juvenile court. They ranged in age from 12 to 18, with a mean of 14.6 years. Socioeconomic backgrounds of clients ranged from lower to middle class. The client group was of mixed ethnic composition, including blacks, Caucasians, and Mexican-Americans. All of the clients were chronic "status" offenders (runaway, truancy, beyond control), and a few had records of more serious offenses such as car theft and drug abuse or sale.

Setting

The treatment program operated in one living unit of the Solano County Juvenile Hall in Fairfield, California. The twenty-bed unit included a lounge area with a piano, T.V., table tennis, chairs and end tables, and the counselors' communications station. A kitchenette was separated from the lounge by a partition, with access through a single doorway. An outside, walled patio recreation area was accessible through a side door. There were private rooms for each client, with a bed, chest of drawers, toilet, and a wash basin. A shower room was located adjacent to the kitchenette. School classroom facilities, indoor and outdoor recreation areas, food service, and dining facilities were available in the hall. New Directions clients used the latter facilities separately from detention unit clients.

Staff

Counselors assigned to the New Directions program were selected from permanent duty staff who voluntarily committed themselves to involvement in the program by written request. They were committed to full-shift coverage without assistance from other juvenile hall staff. Each counselor agreed to use the principles of Applied Behavior Analysis and to maintain control of the unit with a minimum of punitive reactions. The counselors' primary function was to maintain control of the clients as mandated by the juvenile court, providing individual and group counseling and as near a homelike atmosphere as the physical plant and circumstances would permit.

The initial counselors had received forty hours of training in basic principles and techniques of Applied Behavior Analysis prior to the start of the program. Subsequent consultation was provided by the first author.

Goal

The general goal of the in-house program was to assist clients in practicing behaviors that would be expected of them after their return to their own homes, schools, and the community in general. It was hypothesized that this practice would improve their chances of avoiding further contacts with and penetration into the juvenile justice system.

Objectives

The behavior change objectives of the in-house program were, for the most part, identical to those of the community follow-up program. They represented performances expected of the clients by the juvenile court as conditions of probation. The objectives are described below.

OBJECTIVE 1: Each client will maintain an average of 80 percent or more in school performance during each week of his/her stay in the program.

OBJECTIVE 2: Each client will obey general rules of the program during an average of 95 percent of the one-hour periods of each week during his/her stay in the program.

OBJECTIVE 3: Each client will obey the major rules of the program during 95 percent of the one-hour periods of each week during his/her stay in the program.

OBJECTIVE 4: Each client will obey the dining hall conduct standards of the program during 80 percent of the mealtimes each week during his/her stay in the program.

OBJECTIVE 5: Each client will meet the program's standards of grooming and dress at 80 percent of the premealtime inspections each week during his/her stay in the program.

OBJECTIVE 6: Each client will obtain 80 percent of the marks for cleaning and care of his/her own room during each week of his/her stay in the program.

PROCEDURES

Point System

Applied Behavior Analysis was selected as the primary treatment strategy in the New Directions program because of the existing evidence of success of that modality in the treatment of delinquency (Jesness, DeRisi, McCormick, and Wedge, 1972; Phillips, Bailey, and Wolf, 1969; Stuart, 1970; Stumphauzer, 1973; Tharp and Wetzel, 1969). The initial strategy used (May, 1973 to December, 1974) was a point system similar to that described by Phillips (1968) and Phillips, Bailey, and Wolf (1969). Clients were awarded points for achieving behavioral objectives and could exchange the points for various privileges and commodities. Earned points were recorded in a client's point record book at the end of each day and were available for spending the next day.

By achieving a specified percentage of total available points each week, a client could advance through a series of program *phases* or *steps*. Each step afforded more privileges than the one preceding, including greater access to the community. Clients in Phase Level I were eligible only for activities in the hall. Phase Level II clients were eligible for out-of-hall activities and brief home visits (no overnights). Phase Level III clients were eligible for outside activities and overnight and weekend home visits. Phase Level IV was the follow-up period, supervised by a probation officer. Phase Level IV clients lived in their own or foster homes.

Transition Period

The requirements for phase level advancement were modified after the first year of program operation. A client was required to earn a specified percentage criterion in each of the program performance areas, rather than an overall percentage of points, to advance in phase level. This procedural change was introduced in an effort to discourage clients from maximizing their point earnings in a few behavioral areas while ignoring other more important areas. The twenty-one-week period of time during which this procedural variation was in effect is referred to in this paper as the *Transition Period* because of its inclusion of elements common to both the point system period and the contingency contract-based system.

Phase Level System

This procedural modification in the in-house program was introduced in an effort to reduce training and administrative problems associated with the point system strategy. The main problem to be reduced was the complication of differential adjustments in point awards and prices frequently required to maintain the economy in balance. The way in which the phase level system reduced that problem is described later.

Another problem that the phase level system was intended to reduce was the extreme lack of similarity between the point system and the reinforcement systems in the community. In the point system each targeted client behavior is consequated. In the natural community system the amount and/or quality of rewards are, for the most part, determined by an individual's "position" or "status," which is usually obtained and maintained by achievement of multiple behavior objectives (including omission of certain proscribed behaviors) over time. The phase level system was designed to more closely approximate the community reward system, but with greater consistency of consequation. It was hypothesized that generalization of the clients in-house behavior changes to the community would be enhanced. It was also hypothesized that this system would seem more familiar and acceptable to parents, guardians, and others who would be involved in community follow-up programs with the clients.

The adoption of the phase level system was also intended to reduce staff's and resident's concentration on point earnings rather than achievement of behavior change objectives. The significance of this variable to the issue of behavior change is equivocal, but at the time the counselors, administrators, and consultant "felt" good about the potential change in concentration.

In the phase level system period, clients entered the program in Phase Level I and earned their way to successively higher levels by meeting prespecified weekly criteria in each of the six performance areas of the program (described in this chapter). The program thus operated as a standing contingency contract (Stuart, 1970; Tharp and Wetzel, 1969) specifying that "if the client meets the specified weekly criterion in each program performance area, then he/she will be promoted to a higher phase level, or given time credit toward promotion if more than one successful week is required for promotion." Two successive weeks of criterion performance were required for promotion from Phase Level I to II, and II to III. Four successive weeks were required for advancement from Phase Level III to IV.

Points were retained as the medium of exchange during the phase level period, but were awarded as a lump sum at the end of each week. The amount awarded was determined by phase level status for each client. Adjustments in the balance of the point economy were made by raising or lowering the salaries associated with each phase level. It was not necessary to adjust differential point awards for target behavior or point prices, or for counselors to memorize new point values after each change.

The standing contract also included sanctions. Clients could be demoted in phase level for failure to meet specified minimum criterion levels in the program or for major rule infractions.

Behavior Definitions and Data Collection

All of the behavioral data collected were of the occurrence-nonoccurrence variety and were summarized as percentages by dividing occurrences by occurrences plus nonoccurrences and multiplying the result by 100. These summaries, and determination of each client's eligibility for phase level promotion or demotion, were carried out each week by a designated counselor on the Thursday night shift. Promotions and demotions took effect on Friday so that weekend privileges were immediately affected by the client's performance during the preceding week.

OBJECTIVE 1: Teachers in the juvenile hall school evaluated each student daily in terms of instructional objectives achieved and observance of school rules. Instructional objectives were individualized for each student and typically related to completion of specific tasks in programmed academic materials. School rules involved avoidance of the following behaviors:

1. Out of seat without permission
2. Talking without permission
3. Use of obscene language
4. Smoking
5. Physical fighting
6. Use of phone or teacher's desk
7. Physical contact other than hand-holding with member of opposite sex

The daily evaluations represented a consensus of the subjective opinions of two teachers and the school director. They were reported to the living unit counselors in terms of point earnings on a 100-point scale. Clients were required to have earned 80 percent of the school points available to them during the week to be eligible for advancement or for time credit toward advancement in Phase Level. Demotion occurred for earning less than 50 percent of the weekly points.

OBJECTIVES 2 AND 3: The general rules of the program specified eighteen behaviors to be omitted by clients. Five of those (indicated by asterisks below) were designated "major" rules by consensus of clients, counselors, and juvenile hall administrators. The following behaviors were to be omitted:

1. Use of obscene language
2. Failure to carry out reasonable requests and commands from counselors
3. Horseplay
4. Putting feet on walls or furniture
5. Breaking into the conversations of others without permission
*6. Theft
*7. Physical fighting
*8. Running away
9. Directing obscene language at another person
10. Verbal threats of physical harm to another person
11. "Necking" or "petting" in public
12. Two or more persons in the bathroom together
13. Smoking or being in possession of smoking materials
14. Being thrown out of school
*15. Removal from school or unit to detention
16. Marking or carving on self
17. Entering room of members of opposite sex
*18. Possession of drugs

Rules observance was measured with a pseudo-time-sample procedure. Client's names were listed on a data collection form with vertical columns representing hours of the day (excluding hours when the residents were in school or in bed). When a counselor observed a rule infraction by a resident, he/she placed a check mark on the data form in the cell corresponding to the intersection of the line on which the resident's name was written and the column representing the hour of the day during which the infraction occurred. If the infraction involved a major rule, the check mark was circled. The data, therefore, showed the number of hourly intervals in which each resident emitted or omitted general and major rule infractions. The exact frequency of infractions was not summarized but usually corresponded closely with the interval data.

Clients were required to avoid general and major rule infractions during a minimum of 95 percent of the measured intervals each week to earn promotion or time credit toward promotion. Demotion occurred for less than 50 percent performance in avoiding general infractions, and for less than 70 percent in major infractions.

OBJECTIVE 4: In the dining room, residents were expected to omit the behaviors listed on the general rules list, and also (1) gesturing or verbal interaction with wards from detention units and (2) throwing food, condiments, utensils, etc. The clients were expected to (1) make polite requests to have items passed to them, (2) move in a quiet and orderly manner to the dining area and through the food line, and (3) engage in socially acceptable table conversation.

Counselors marked a data collection form after each meal to indicate clients who had achieved all of the expected dining room performances. The promotion criterion for dining hall conduct was 80 percent, and the demotion criterion was less than 50 percent achievement.

OBJECTIVE 5: The clients' rooms were inspected daily. Their beds were to be made neatly, floors clear of debris and swept, toilet and sink clean, and personal items stored neatly on shelf or desk. Clients received credit for each room care area separately. The criterion for promotion was 80 percent of all credits for the week, and less than 50 percent constituted demotion.

OBJECTIVE 6: Clients were inspected for grooming and proper dress before each meal. They were expected to be dressed in clean clothes in good repair, wearing shoes, not wearing coats, hats, see-through blouses or halter tops (girls) or tank tops (boys). (Dress standards were not this strict on the unit, only for off-unit activities.) Clients were required to pass 80 percent of the dress and grooming inspections to earn promotion and were demoted for less than 50 percent achievement.

EVALUATION

Point System vs Phase Level

DATA RELIABILITY: Interobserver reliability of the New Directions data collection system was assessed only for room care data. Ten room care checks were carried out by independent observers during a two-week period in April, 1975. Those checks yielded reliabilities ranging from 71 percent to 100 percent and averaging 89 percent. Interobserver reliability checks were attempted for each of the other behavior areas, but were not completed because of administrative problems related to staffing. The data must, therefore, be interpreted with caution.

OBJECTIVE 1: SCHOOL PERFORMANCE. Figure 5-1 shows the percentage of clients who achieved the 80 percent performance criterion during successive weeks of program operation. Two weeks of data are missing for the transition period between point system and phase level, and one for the phase level period, because of school holidays. The program objective for school performance was achieved more often during the transition period (12 out of 18 weeks, or 67%) than during the point system period (4 out of 11 weeks, or 36%). The objective was achieved even more often during the phase level period (27 out of 35 weeks, or 77%).

OBJECTIVES 2 AND 3: RULES OBSERVANCE. Figure 5-2 shows the percentage of clients who achieved the 95 percent criterion in general rules observance during successive weeks. That criterion was achieved by all clients during one out of eleven weeks (09%) during the period of the point system for which data were available, five out of twenty-one weeks (24%) during the transition period,

OBJECTIVE 1: SCHOOL PERFORMANCE

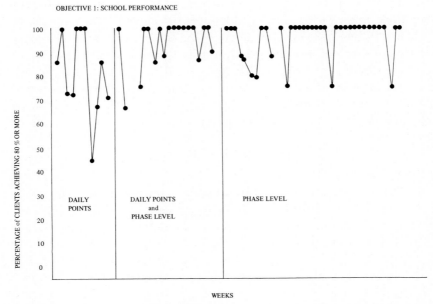

Figure 5-1. Percentage of clients achieving the 80 percent criterion level in school performance during successive weeks of the program, under each treatment condition.

and nineteen out of thirty-seven weeks (51%) during the phase level period. The difference favors the phase level period, but may not be significant.

Data for major rules observance are not depicted graphically because performance in that area did not show much variation between conditions. The 95 percent criterion was met by all clients during ten out of eleven weeks (91%) during the point system period for which data were available, twenty out of twenty-one weeks (95%) during the transition period, and thirty-two out of thirty-six weeks (89%) during the phase level system period. The difference favors the transition period, but is probably not significant.

OBJECTIVE 4: DINING HALL CONDUCT. Figure 5-3 shows the data for dining hall conduct during successive weeks of the program. The 80 percent performance level was achieved by all clients during three out of eleven weeks (27%) during the period

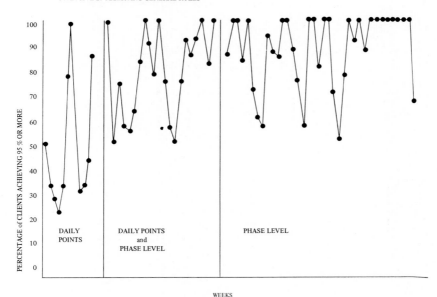

Figure 5-2. Percentage of clients achieving the 95 percent level in observance of general rules during successive weeks of the program, under each treatment condition.

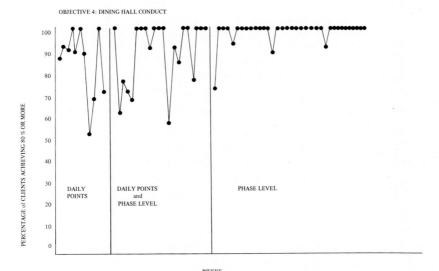

Figure 5-3. Percentage of clients achieving the 80 percent criterion in dining room conduct during successive weeks of the program, under each treatment condition.

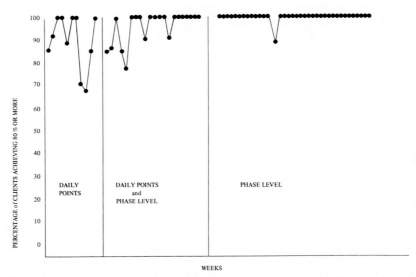

Figure 5-4. Percentage of clients achieving the 80 percent criterion in grooming and dress during successive weeks of the program, under each treatment condition.

of the point system for which data are available, twelve out of twenty-one weeks of the transition period (57%), and twenty-eight out of thirty-seven weeks (76%) during the phase level period. Again, the difference favors the phase level period.

OBJECTIVE 5: GROOMING AND DRESS. Figure 5-4 shows that the 80 percent criterion in grooming and dress was achieved by all clients during five out of the eleven point system weeks (45%) shown, nine out of twenty-one transition period weeks (71%), and thirty-six out of thirty-seven phase level weeks (97%).

OBJECTIVE 6: ROOM CARE. Figure 5-5 shows the percentage of clients achieving the 80 percent criterion in room care during successive weeks of the program. The objective of all clients achieving the 80 percent weekly criterion was never achieved during the point system period shown. The criterion was achieved during nine out of twenty-one weeks (43%) of the transition period and thirty-three out of thirty-six weeks (92%) of the phase level system.

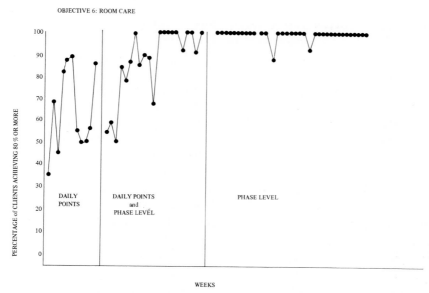

OBJECTIVE 6: ROOM CARE

Figure 5-5. Percentage of clients achieving the 80 percent criterion in room care during successive weeks of the program, under each treatment condition.

DISCUSSION

Point System vs. Phase Level

The conclusions that may be drawn from the data used in the comparisons above must be tempered somewhat because of the absence of precise assessments of the reliability of the data collection systems across conditions. The measured behaviors were, however, sufficiently well specified that at least moderate levels of interobserver reliability might be expected. It is likely, therefore, that the indicated superiority in the relative frequency of achievement of objectives 1, 2, 4, 5, and 6 during the transition and phase level treatment periods in the present study is true effect rather than an artifact of data. The small difference in relative frequency of achievement of objective 3 across conditions is equally likely to be a true datum.

The findings of the present study are consistent with the notion that the phase level system was more effective than the point system and transition period procedures in achieving the in-house behavior management objectives of the program. The design of the study does not, however, rule out other alternative explanations of the differences in effects between conditions. Staff, client, management, and policy changes all occurred during the course of the study and may have differentially affected the outcomes. Further investigations of contingency management systems such as the phase level system described here, in settings affording better control of potentially confounding variables, are needed to determine the specific effects of the system itself.

The adoption of the phase level system did appear to reduce the training and administrative problems it was intended to reduce. Counselors initially reported satisfaction with the ease of adjusting the economy, the simplicity of explaining the system to parents, guardians, or others, the emphasis on behavior changes rather than point earnings, and the impact on achievement of in-house behavior change objectives. After the senior author terminated his consulting services to the program, however, a revised point system was adopted in place of the phase level system. Greater immediacy of consequation of behaviors in the point system as contrasted with the phase level system was cited as a major reason for the change. Effectiveness evaluation has not yet been carried out.

Cost Analysis

Clients were usually referred to New Directions by the juvenile court as an alternative to other out-of-community placements such as county "ranches" and private or state institutions. Evaluation of the effect of New Directions on client recidivism, as contrasted with alternative out-of-community placements, proved unfeasible during the time period considered in this paper. Cost-comparison data were however, obtained. The average cost for treating a young person in New Directions during the first year of operation was $26.77 per day. The average cost for other treatment placements was $21.30 per day. The average stay in the New Directions program was 60 to 120 days, as contrasted with an average stay of 6 to 12 months in other placements. The average cost of completing the New Directions program was, therefore, between $1606.20 and $3212.40 per client, as contrasted with $3834.00 to $7668.00 for other placements. These figures do not take into account the additional costs of visits by parents to young persons in placements other than New Directions.

General Discussion

Solano County's initial experience with New Directions demonstrated the feasibility and cost advantages of operating a delinquency treatment program in their juvenile hall setting. Many other juvenile probation departments would probably find similar feasibility and cost advantages over out-of-community placements such as county or private "ranches," "camps," or state institutions.

New Directions also demonstrated that juvenile hall staff and settings have the flexibility necessary to conduct evaluation of alternative behavior change treatment modalities such as that reported here. It is worth noting that the New Directions staff and administrators have planned and implemented changes in their program since those reported here. Systematic data are being collected for the purpose of evaluating those modifications. The contingency contracting-based phase level system is currently being evaluated in an institution for developmentally disabled young adults. The behavior problems and objectives for these clients are very similar to those in New Directions. Initial data suggest that the combination of a point system with phase level system was accompanied by a marked increase in clients' achievement of behavior objectives, including omission of dangerous aggressive behaviors. A more detailed and systematic evaluation is to be reported later.

REFERENCES

Text

Jesness, C.F., DeRisi, W.C., McCormick, P.M., and Wedge, R.F., The Youth Center Project. The California Youth Authority, Sacramento, California, 1972.

Phillips, E.L., Achievement Place: Token Reinforcement Procedures in a Home Style Rehabilitation Setting for Pre-Delinquent Boys. *Journal of Applied Behavior Analysis,* 1968, *1,* 213-223.

Phillips, E.L., Bailey, J., and Wolfe, M.M., Achievement Place: "A Token Economy in a Homestyle Rehabilitation Program for Juvenile Offenders." Presented at the American Psychological Association Convention, Washington, D.C., 1969.

Stuart, R.B., Behavioral Contracting within the Families of Delinquents. *Journal of Behavior Therapy and Experimental Psychiatry,* 1971, *2,* 1-11.

Stumphauser, J.S., (ed.), *Behavior Therapy with Delinquents,* Springfield, Ill.: Charles C Thomas, 1973.

Tharp, R.G. and Wetzel, R.J., *Behavior Modification in the Natural Environment.* New York: Academic Press, 1969.

CHAPTER 6

GROUP ASSERTION TRAINING FOR INSTITUTIONALIZED MALE DELINQUENTS

MARTIN E. SHOEMAKER

EDITORIAL COMMENTS

Teach delinquents to be **more** assertive? Surely this is the last thing we need! The apparent incongruity disappears when **assertive** behavior is differentiated from **aggressive** behavior if aggression is viewed as "intentional harm to others" and assertion as "standing up for one's personal rights without harming others" (Stumphauzer, 1977, Chap. 11).

Anyone who has worked with overly aggressive adolescents has observed that those youths have a very limited behavioral repertoire. There is a high probability of aggressive response. In addition, the aggression often "pays off" (in the short run) with a variety of reinforcements. In the longer run the adolescent may get into trouble (delayed punishment?), but no new behavior is learned in this process. Also, there are the **un**assertive, withdrawn, or otherwise socially "inadequate" adolescents (who commit crimes) who could benefit from such training (Stumphauzer, 1972.) Assertion training, as shown here by Shoemaker in this original chapter, does teach new behavior — it **expands** the behavioral repertoire of the adolescent, and with techniques apparently attractive to young people, e.g. "Mental Kung Fu."

In the last few years there has been an explosion of articles and books on assertion training, much of it reaching the general public as "self-help" books from "The Assertive Woman" (Phelps & Austin, 1975) to "Stand Up, Speak Out, Talk Back!" (Alberti & Emmons, 1975). In this chapter Shoemaker introduces the concept of broad-spectrum assertion training and then goes on to describe a series of three studies implementing such programs with delinquents and predelinquents in a home for boys. These programs provide a viable alternative to other forms of group counseling. Social skills are being taught which should prove to be adaptive when the boys return to the community. Of course, this is an empirical question, and follow-up data are needed to support this contention.

A natural extension of Shoemaker's approach would be to utilize assertion training with groups of adolescents in the community: youth on probation, those in diversion programs, and perhaps in public schools as a preventative program.

ASSERTION TRAINING (AT), particularly in a group context, has become one of the most popular treatment approaches of this decade. From its humble beginnings, in the "nonhumble" writings and psychology of Andrew Salter (1949) and later Joseph Wolpe and Arnold Lazarus (1966), AT has grown both professionally and popularly in the 1970s in a way somewhat reminiscent of the "sensitivity training" movement or "T-group" phenomenon of the 1960s.

Although a thorough description or definition of AT has been attempted elsewhere (Shoemaker and Satterfield, in press) and is not the central task of this paper, before detailing this author's experiences in using AT with delinquent populations, a brief overview of the philosophy and goals of AT seems appropriate.

Graphically, broad-spectrum AT can be depicted as a trilevel inverted pyramid (see Fig. 6-1).

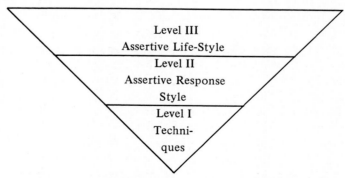

Figure 6-1.   Trilevel model of broad-spectrum AT.

The very bottom level of the model, *assertion techniques,* represents all of the interpersonal stratagems, or what Wolpe calls "gamemanship," that various assertion trainers have originated and perpetuated through their workshops and writings. The best example of the technique approach to AT is in the writings of Smith (1975) and can be supplemented by a summary article by Flowers and Booraem (1975). Some of the more popular techniques would include *Broken-Record, Negative Inquiry, Free Information, Process-Content Shift,* and *Fogging,* to name a few. Several of these techniques, as they were used in the delinquent groups, are discussed in this chapter.

The pure *technique approach* appears to have had very little to do with the original formation of AT by the early behavior therapists but has subsequently been incorporated into the procedures as a way of countering various manipulations, critical remarks, and potentially high-anxiety, interpersonal situations. Most nonassertive people either withdraw or become impulsively aggressive when confronted by troublesome interpersonal conflicts; therefore, these canned or nonspontaneous response "tricks" can be beneficial if properly taught and assimilated in the context of broad-spectrum AT (Paulson, Shoemaker, and Landau, in press).

The middle level of the model (Level II) represents a more basic training component of AT than the techniques mentioned previously. One cannot always use preset ways of talking or acting, and the complexity of interpersonal events necessitates a set of principles or covert models that can be generalized to a number of situations. This has been developed in the best-seller by Alberti and Emmons (1970) *Your Perfect Right* and is an integral part of most AT procedures. The model is a tripartite discrimination of interpersonal verbal responses into assertive, aggressive, and nonassertive (withdrawing or passive) categories.

At this level, AT is characterized by the development of an *interpersonal response style* that is an open expression of one's rights, needs, thoughts, and feelings. The target behavior is principally verbal behavior, e.g. talking to one's employer about a raise, but has grown to include specific nonverbal behaviors that give a more self-confident and congruent message, e.g. posture and eye contact (Eisler, Hersen and Agras, 1973; Serber, 1972). Of extreme importance in the development of the assertive response style is the comparison of the assertive type of expression to one that is aggressive (violates or abuses another's rights) or passive and withdrawing (backing away from one's own needs). Essential to the comparison are both the short— and long-term consequences of a certain type of response for oneself and others.

The strategies used to teach the difference between styles vary greatly among assertion trainers but usually contain some form of modeling, role-play or rehearsal, and systematic feedback (Shoemaker and Satterfield, in press). The way in which these were specifically used in the delinquent group is discussed later in the method sections.

Theoretically, the second level, or the acquisition of the assertive response style, systematically attempts to develop operant or voluntary verbal responses which inhibit and weaken the bonds between various interpersonal situations eliciting anxiety, anger, or fear (Wolpe, 1958). For example, being assertive and expressing dislike about the way you are treated by a friend would inhibit long-term irritation or resentment. Clinical experience seems to demonstrate that being assertive may not immediately reduce stress in a relationship, because it often leads to a confrontation, but in the long run more peaceful and open relationships are developed.

Similarly, assertive responses are conceptualized as incompatible to either aggressive or withdrawing responses, thereby replacing the latter in the individual behavior repertoire. An example from the delinquent population was the author's teaching of a "reversal" or socially unexpected response to a boy who was continually being provoked to fight at school. The goal was to substitute the new assertive response for his usual "talking shit" which took up the challenge and ended in a scuffle and disciplinary action. However, these new incompatible responses must be satisfactory and have some reinforcement value to the subject or they will not be generalized to settings away from the group.

The third and highest dimension of AT is entitled the *asser-*

tive life-style and represents a somewhat new conceptualization for assertion trainers or other professionals who are not familiar with the growing edge of some AT and behavior therapy procedures in general. This dimension deals substantially with less observable intrapersonal types of behavior, e.g. self-talk and less operationalized constructs such as self-control and personal value clarification. It theoretically and clinically joins hands with more traditionally "humanistic" approaches and attempts to deal with areas previously forbidden to behaviorists, such as thoughts and other "mental habits."

The technology for this upper level is still very formative, but serious attempts have been made by the emerging breed of cognitive-behavioral assertion trainers led by Arnold Lazarus (1975), Lange and Jakubowski (1976) and Paulson, Shoemaker, and Landau (in press). The assertive life-style holds an important interest to this author and will be dealt with in a paper now in production. These procedures did not play an active role in the groups to be discussed but remain an essential element of the broad-spectrum model of AT.

PROJECT HISTORY AND RATIONALE

In November of 1973, this author was contacted following a convention presentation on AT by one of the cottage social workers from a large boys' home in Southern California (Pacific Lodge Home for Boys, Woodland Hills, California). The initial discussion centered on the feasibility of incorporating an AT approach within the rehabilitative plan of the home. Of special interest to this worker and other staff members was the existence of a class of boys within the home who were basically very withdrawn and nonverbal, often giving up too soon. Some of these boys were seen by peers and staff as "pushovers" and as being too passive in their general responses to interpersonal conflicts. AT, as presented (Levels I and II), seemed somewhat appropriate for this group of boys even though the general idea of AT with delinquents was somewhat humorous, bordering on ridiculous at times. Admittedly, if the caricature of the "incorrigible roughneck" delinquent often held by most mental health professionals was true, then what was needed was "acquiescence Training" (aT) rather than AT.

Although encouraged by the promise that a population of passive boys, or what Quay calls the disturbed-neurotic delinquent (Quay, 1966), could be referred or selected, the absence from psychological literature of a similar project was temporarily discouraging. If one substituted the words, *socially appropriate behaviors* for *assertive,* then a few reports and research projects with delinquent population appeared (Sarason, 1968; Sarason and Ganzer, 1969). However, as the project unfolded in early 1974, there existed no real precedent to be followed although more reports of the application of behavior therapy to the problems of delinquency, in particular, token economies, were being published (see Stumphauzer, Chap. 1).

Actually, in theory and in practice, the rationale for using AT with delinquents is quite good. Theoretically, AT is especially geared for any passive youngster who has developed a high probability of *avoidance responses* or is overly timid. In contrast to these boys, AT even with the more aggressive fellows seemed plausible if developing *incompatible* assertive responses could be actualized to replace their more violent, impulsive actions. The key to our success lay in adopting the responses to fit their needs and not merely leaving them to temporarily swallow and regurgitate middle class *smackery*. *Smackery* is a general label this author adopted from the word *smack* which was used negatively by the group members to define a peer who exhibited any behavior that appeared to embrace establishment values, language, or regulations such as asking assistance from a counselor in a fight or in recovering a stolen article.

Learning to stand up for one's rights fits quite nicely into the delinquent subculture value system, but learning to do so without violating someone else's rights *smacks* heavily into their constant need to name-call, provoke, defend, and use other aggressive habits.

Practically speaking, AT seemed to meet several other institutional requirements for rehabilitative efforts. First, AT is usually done in groups, which requires less time and personnel. Second, since each boy's mean stay was about six months, a ten– to twelve-week AT group seemed to be short enough to allow completion. Third, most of the boys seemed to be quite resistant to the more "revealing," insight-oriented approaches which were not active and required spontaneous involvement to open-ended questions and nebulous expectations. Lastly, the possibility of evaluation seemed feasible since the targets were more explicit and observable than current or previous treatment approaches. Similarly, the group procedures as presented to the staff seemed reduplicatable with a minimum of training and exposure to the group methods and principles.

PROJECT DESCRIPTION

Pacific Lodge Home for Boys is a nonprofit, charitable institution which is licensed to provide residency, general supervision, and treatment to delinquent adolescent males. There are approximately eighty residents at any one time, ranging in age from thirteen to eighteen. Most of the boys are involuntary or court-ordered placements referred by the Los Angeles Probation Department and Department of Public Social Services. The average length of stay is six months. About 60 percent of the boys are Caucasian with the remaining 40 percent divided between other racial and ethnic groups. Ninety-five percent come from lower socioeconomic environments.

The author was hired as a part-time consultant early in 1974 while finishing his degree in clinical psychology. Three AT groups of varying procedures have been run thus far in the project, and plans for a fourth group were underway for the autumn of 1976. A report of these three group experiences plus varied evaluation procedures follows.

Group One: Mixed Cottages—Voluntary Participants

The first AT group conducted at the cottage was part of a broader, controlled research project designed to evaluate and measure the outcome of AT with male delinquents (Shoemaker, 1974). As this was primarily a research project attempting to isolate the effects of the AT, the staff was not aware of who was being treated by which method; therefore, some of the group's efficiency was reduced to maintain unbiased staff ratings and provide a semblance of scientific rigor.

Methods

Thirty group members were selected out of a pool of sixty-six residents on the basis of several measures of nonassertiveness. The pretests were given to boys who were between the ages of thirteen and sixteen and residents for at least one month. These measures consisted of the Adolescent Assertiveness Discrimination Test (AADT, Shoemaker, 1974) especially developed for this research, and staff-peer rating sheets. The rating sheets were filled out by both cottage counselors and every cottage member by listing the top five boys and the bottom five boys in their cottage on assertiveness variables. These scores were then collated into a final ranking, and the bottom thirty boys were randomly assigned to one of three groups: assertion training (AT), minimum treatment (MT), and no treatment (NT).

After signing contracts to voluntarily participate in the study, the groups met for fifty minutes each week. The AT and MT group met for twelve weeks and the NT group for only four weeks, sessions 1 and 2 and 11 and 12. Each boy was paid a basic wage of 1 cent per minute of attendance, in addition to which members of the MT group were given random bonuses as the author (group leader) saw fit. These noncontingent earnings were given to match the AT group's token reward system. At the third session, the AT group changed its focus from nondirective discussion format to an assertion training group by means of a carefully planned introduction and didactic material by the author. The boys were told they could earn extra money for appropriate verbal statements which received token feedback. The white tokens were given only for assertive statements or reports of assertive behavior, examples of which would include the following:

Feeling talk—"I get uptight when . . .," or "I feel very angry . . .," or "That makes me feel very happy . . ."

Thinking talk—stating likes and dislikes, agreeing or disagreeing, giving compliments.

Problem talk—talking about problems, giving suggestions about how to solve problems.

Practicing in-group role-playing or rehearsing how to handle difficult problems.

The didactic material and behavioral focusing consisted of telling the AT group members that this was going to be an opportunity for them to learn some ways of becoming more "gutsy" in handling people who intrude on their rights (Level II). A distinction was carefully drawn between *claim jumping* (aggressive behavior), *swallowing your claim* (withdrawn behavior), and *claiming a right* (assertive behavior) and the consequences of using these respective approaches in interpersonal situations.

Throughout the eight-week training session, various spontaneous *claims* were discussed and occasionally rehearsed or role-played. At the end of each session, *claim cards* were passed out which were to be filled out for the next week. The cards were to report an attempted assertion during the week. Eighteen cards were turned in for the eight weeks, and bonuses were given for these cards and successful claims.

During the above training period the MT met for informal discussion of any subject matter, this discussion being led also by the author. The NT group did not meet during the treatment phase (3-10). All groups were paid at the end of each session, and all returned to the discussion format for the last two sessions (11-12). Observers recorded all assertive and nonassertive (withdrawing and aggressive) target verbalizations for all groups throughout the study. Interrater reliability checks were taken every other week and were satisfactory.

At the end of training, all paper and pencil tests were administered as a posttest, and a special nonobtrusive test was constructed to measure generalized assertive behavior. This later test consisted of a staged interview between a prospective new staff member and each group member. A series of three situations was scored as either *pass* or *fail,* within a certain response class and time limit.

During the twelve weeks, attendance was excellent, but only

twenty-two of the original thirty remained for the entire project, eight in the MT, seven in the NT, and seven in the AT group. All the boys who completed the groups without an unexcused absence were taken to dinner as a special reward.

Results

Various statistical analyses were performed on all paper and pencil measures and all in-group behavior data in order to objectively evaluate the treatment procedures. The research project was concerned with evaluating the development and recognition of assertive behavior by the treated group members, plus changes in nonassertive behavior. Of primary concern were any changes in general behavior, and generalized assertive behavior outside the group setting.

ASSERTIVE BEHAVIOR. Both in-group observation and staff reports support the project's attempts to increase assertive behavior in the AT group members. Statistically significant increases (p < .05) were observed both between the AT group and MT-NT (control groups), and within *Ss* in the AT group across sessions.

Staff ratings support these in-group observations in that cottage counselors reported the AT group members as significantly (p < .05) more improved in assertive behavior compared to the other boys in their cottage than either the MT or NT (control groups). Peer rankings showed an increase in all groups but no significant changes between groups. These latter results moderately support the conclusion that assertive behavior demonstrated in the group generalized from the group setting to other counselor-observed settings. This finding was somewhat encouraging but was not clearly supported by other data produced in a nonobtrusive testing (false interview) done after training. Statistical analyses performed comparing frequencies of various assertive situations passed or failed between groups were not significant even though the AT group passed 81 percent of the tests compared to 66 percent by the two control groups.

One of the goals of the project was to teach the group members in the AT group to increase their recognition of the difference between assertive and nonassertive behavior. Most of the boys appeared to learn this discrimination in the AT group, but objective measures of recognition (AADT) did not show significant differences between groups. This was a definite area of concern for the groups that followed.

NONASSERTIVE BEHAVIOR. In the review of research on assertiveness training there is limited support for the idea that assertive behavior is incompatible with aggressive and withdrawing behavior; therefore, it was hoped that decreases would be found in the treated S's nonassertive responses. To the disappointment of the staff, statistically significant decreases were not found either between groups or within subjects of the AT across sessions. However, the AT group moved in the hypothesized direction on every measure. In other words, the AT members always reported or were observed to have decreases in nonassertive responses even when the other groups slightly increased in nonassertiveness. This interaction effect was observed not only in the group but was also reported on several paper and pencil tests. However, any positive conclusion about the substitution of assertive behavior for aggressive or withdrawing responses must be held with extreme caution in that statistical significance was never achieved.

Discussion

The general conclusion of this first study regarding the effectiveness of short-term training for increasing assertive behavior in male delinquents is consistent with previous findings in other population groups (Booraem & Flowers, 1972; Eisler, Hersen, & Miller, 1973; Hedquist & Weinhold, 1970; Paulson, 1974; Rathus, 1972; Shoemaker & Paulson, 1976). The in-group increases seem better than or consistent with that reported in a number of studies using operant token procedures with children's groups (Clement, Fazzone, & Goldstein, 1970; Clement & Milne, 1967; Stedman, Peterson, & Cardarelle, 1973) and more specifically with adolescent groups (Abuddabeh, Prendoni, & Jensen, 1972; Hauserman, Zweback, & Plotkin, 1972).

Of extreme importance to all behavior modifiers and procedural researchers is the generalization of treatment effects into the natural environment. The first group project found moderate support for stimulus generalization of assertive behavior by the AT group. This result is consistent with clinical reports from Gittleman (1965) and Lazarus (1966) and research findings of McFall and Twentyman (1973). The support for transfer of learning in the present investigation is somewhat encouraging compared to group research results reported by Goldstein, Heller, and Sechrest (1966); Clement and Milne (1967); Clement, Fazzone, & Goldstein (1970).

The inability of the AT group procedures to increase recognition of the difference between response styles may partially explain why no decrease in the nonassertive categories was observed. Subsequent groups run by the author made specific improvements in both of these areas.

Meetings with staff members of the home further clarified other improvements such as (1) more involvement of cottage workers in the training, particularly outside of group, (2) not mixing cottages, but running a group made up entirely of referrals from one living unit, (3) increasing the length of each session, (4) replacing the concrete reward system with more social rewards (fun activities with staff, e.g. going to a movie). Most of these suggestions were incorporated into the second group, which was more treatment oriented and free from the constraints of the research requirements imposed on the previous group study.

About six months following the completion of the first AT group, a follow-up investigation was initiated to determine if the recorded changes in the AT group would be maintained. Unfortunately, only a few of the boys in the original study were still residing at the lodge, and phone calls to the new residences were generally unfruitful in both locating or gaining access to the boys again.

Group Two: Single Cottage—Voluntary Participants

Based on the experience of the previous group, a second group was planned for the fall of 1975 and incorporated most of the suggestions mentioned above. The major changes outside of the group included increased staff involvement in the form of weekly meetings, training, a weekly cottage reporting system and a resident-counselor sponsorship program. Only one cottage was involved. The following in-group procedural changes were included: (1) session time was increased to one and one-half hours; (2) there was more structure in the group session (more use of Level I techniques); (3) group members were allowed to give token feedback to other members; (4) red and blue chips were added to help discriminate between aggressive and withdrawing responses, respectively; (5) videotape feedback was added; and (6) the entire group program was organized on a martial arts theme called *Mental Kung-Fu.* This theme was carried throughout the cottage and engendered a lot of cottage support, cohesion, and continuity not observed in the first project.

Methods

Before the second group was started, the author spent close to twenty hours preparing the staff of the chosen cottage on the basic rationale and procedures of AT and setting up the theme of *Mental Kung-Fu.* Central to this preparation was having each counselor select two boys whom he felt could benefit from AT and sponsor those boys in the program. Sponsorship basically entailed (1) explaining the idea to the boys, along with the author, and obtaining a voluntary commitment to the group, (2) general liaison between the group leader and the boys designed to handle problems such as attendance, questions on assignments, and turning in reports of "critical incidents" to the group leader, and (3) most importantly, being an assertive model by suggesting "on-the-spot" assertions to their boys when appropriate situations arose at the lodge between group meetings. Sponsors were asked to meet with the author one hour before each group session for the duration of the group meetings (12 weeks).

Mental Kung-Fu was adopted as a theme because of its catchiness and the immense popularity of the martial arts among the boys. The concept was developed to include three principles which in reality are only peripherally related to any martial arts or Oriental philosophy. The first principle for the group was to *Stand Tall,* which calls for acting assertive and claiming one's rights; taking active responsibility to change any violations of one's own rights or violation inflicted on others.   The second principle was to *Think Smart,* a principle which calls for thinking about one's own destiny and the consequences of one's actions with an "enlightened self-interest."   In other words, ultimately one must look out for oneself and make choices that take into account short-term versus long-term advantages.   The group's third principle was to *Be Self-Controlled,* a concept which calls for being the initiator of one's own responses, feeling in control and not just a reflex-response to someone else's behavior.   Self-control, as defined here, is not a moralistic principle, but more a locus-of-control issue which attempts to develop and use self-directed behavior as opposed to reacting like a puppet on someone else's string.   This last principle also was an attempt to develop "new thinking" or covert responses to break up old, reflexive habits (Level III).

This theme was used through group meetings as a criteria for evaluating behavior both in an out of the group A point system was developed which enabled the boys to earn home trips or various social reinforcers from their sponsor or other cottage personnel.   Through an accumulation of total points, each group member advanced through stages starting at *green belt* through to *black belt* or master level.   Points were earned in three ways: (1) in-group tokens for assertive behavior, role-playing, and correct answers on items role-played from the AADT, (2) for turning in claim cards and having them judged "successful" by the group, and finally (3) points were awarded by cottage staff for "critical incidents" that were observed to be handled assertively. When a group member reached the halfway point (orange belt) and correctly identified 75 percent of the assertive responses for 20 items of the AADT, he was given a box of tokens at the beginning of the group session and became part of the token feedback procedure.   If he continued to advance, upon reaching the black belt level he could then "self-discriminate" and reinforce his own in-group responses by giving himself tokens.   Only one member reached this level out of the twelve participants; seven reached the middle level.

Before the results of this group are discussed, three other

procedural changes should be mentioned. First, more of the techniques from Level I were incorporated into the training. This was done for several reasons. The changeover to more social rewards, and a longer delay between behavior and reinforcement, prompted the author to use interesting and entertaining content to "hook" the boys into coming on a permanent basis. Spontaneous material from the group members was at times slow in coming, particularly in the first group, and role-playing techniques, such as mentioned in the beginning of this paper, were a good attention-getter and built a feeling of reciprocity between the author and the group members. Space will not permit a detailed description of all these techniques, but two examples are given below.

Saving face—this was a popular technique among the boys which combined admission or owning a problem (thinking smart) plus assertion (standing tall). An illustration of *saving face* occurred when one of the boys was on the verge of being terminated from school for fighting. Whenever he was questioned about the matter he became so defensive that any attempts at reconciliation with the school seemed impossible. Using the *saving face* technique, we role-played the following situation:

High School advisor "Well, Mr. _____, are you going to get your act together and stop acting like a hood around here, or do you want to stay out of this school forever?"

John: "I know that I got into a hassle and I'm partly to blame, but I really don't like dudes bugging me, and Bill's been hassling me all year."

High School advisor: "However, young man, that's not an excuse, you're not an angel and this isn't an isolated incident."

John: "I know and I'm responsible for my action, but I still don't like to be hassled."

High School advisor:—"I don't know what to do with knotheads like you . . . you totally disregard authority."

John: "I have a hard time with authority, I don't like being told what to do, but I want to come back to school so I can graduate."

The technique is a compromise between a totally *smack* position of apology and *kissing-up* and a hardnosed attitude of, "it's never my fault . . . get off my back." The former is unacceptable to the delinquent, and the latter is unacceptable to most authority figures. *Saving face* can be adapted to many situations as a compromise between the two conflicting parties.

Fogging — This is a very controversial technique discussed by Smith (1975). It is designed to counteract nagging and was taught in the AT group as a way to handle a parent who was hassling in an irrational, highly repetitive way. These boys often live with parents or guardians who are very authority conscious and defensive and become enraged if any independence is demonstrated. *Fogging* was role-played with one boy as a possible response to his more-often-than-not intoxicated father who constantly nagged him on home trips.

Father: "Dammit, Joe when are you going to stop looking like a freak hippie, and get your hair cut and stop fooling around with all that street dope and shit."

Joe: "You're probably right, Dad, I ought to get my hair cut and stop smoking dope."

Father: "You're damn right, I'm right, and don't forget it."

Joe: "Dad, you're probably right a lot of the time."

Fogging is a technique that tries to disengage from an irrational or irritating demand by not defending, but by temporarily or partially agreeing, but making *no* commitment to change. In the above context, it was felt that *fogging* was a better alternative for Joe than the "blow outs" he and his father usually had, particularly when the father was drunk. Obviously, such a technique must be used sparingly and taught within a broader understanding of authentic assertive behavior (Level II).

The remaining two procedural changes include the addition of two colors to the token giving and the use of videotape feedback. Red tokens were used for aggressive responses and blue for withdrawing. A brief description of these two categories and examples follows:

Red is for talking or acting aggressively, claim jumping, not respecting the rights and feelings of others.

Examples:

(1) *Threats,* "If you touch me I'll blow your head off."
(2) *Insults,* "You look like a jerk," or any general putdowns that make the other person feel defensive or stupid.
(3) *Interrupting* another speaker.
(4) *Provoking* fights or destroying the things of other people.

Blue is for talking or acting small, withdrawing or running away from a problem, forgetting to look out for yourself and your rights.

Examples:

(1) *bad apologies,* especially when you are not to blame.
(2) *swallowing your claims* or feelings, withdrawing from group.
(3) *self-criticism* when the facts do not support it.
(4) *taking abuse* when you can try to stop it without fighting.
(5) *not looking out for your needs* . . . being someone else's puppet.

Videotaping was done throughout the group as a means of modeling a good response or technique example. Taping also followed role-plays or rehearsal as a means of feedback and showing members what they looked like. Nonverbal behaviors were particularly amenable to change when videotaping was used. Most of the boys responded very positively to being videotaped, and it was often used as a strong positive reinforcer.

In contrast to the first project, the second group was primarily treatment oriented, and rigorous or comprehensive evaluation was not attempted. However, the AADT was administered as a pre– and posttest measure to all of the members of the AT group who completed the group and to a control group which consisted of boys from a neighboring cottage matched as close as possible on age, race, and referral needs. This control group only participated in the regular rehabilitative experiences designed by the cottage counselors. The AADT was used as a self-report measure of both actual assertiveness of the group members and their ability to recognize assertive alternatives to typical conflict situations. The posttest was actually given almost two months after completing the group, therefore it really approaches a short followup procedure rather than a true posttest.

Results

ASSERTIVE BEHAVIOR. Significant increases were found between the (AT) group and controls on both the self-report measure of assertive behavior (p < .05) and the recognition of assertive behavior (p. < .01).

NONASSERTIVE BEHAVIOR. Complementing the significant increases in assertive behavior as reported on the AADT, statistically significant decreases in both aggressive (p < .05) and withdrawing behavior (p < .01) were found between the AT group and controls at posttesting. Again the control group reported a slight increase in nonassertiveness from pre– to posttesting while the AT group decreased. This finding was encouraging considering the statistically nonsignificant results reported on the AADT in the first project.

Of the original nine boys who were sponsored for the group, three dropped out for various reasons, e.g. termination, schedule conflict, etc., and three others were sponsored to replace these boys. There was 88 percent attendance by all group members with no special incentive being given for coming. A very pleasant result was the threefold increase of *claim cards* turned into the second group compared to the first group (Group 1 = 18, Group 2 = 61). The out-of-group procedures and assistance of the sponsors definitely effected this effort. Many of the boys are so illiterate that having to fill out the card was too difficult or embarassing, and having sponsors help here reduced this problem.

Discussion

Unhesitatingly, this author found the second group to be an immense improvement over the first. Having the entire cottage staff involved in the project and developing the *Mental Kung-Fu* theme brought the boys together and increased the group effectiveness. Occasionally, when strolling through the dorm, the author could hear talk about the group and plans being developed by participants to spend some of their points. Because so many procedural changes were made, it is impossible to isolate which variables caused both the self-report of assertiveness, and its recognition, to increase. Complementing the increase in assertive behavior, the self-report of decreased nonassertiveness is probably a result of many mixed variables. It appears that increased didactic role-playing in the group plus the sponsorship system and more involvement by staff in discrimination training outside of the group were tremendous assets. A general weakness of the second project was the absence of any systematic behavioral measures to support the results reported on the AADT.

Before turning to the last group design, one final observation needs to be pointed out. It is extremely important that accurate records of point acquisition and spending be kept. Some of the few negative situations that arose were disputes between the boys and the staff member assigned to keep the point tallies. The natural competition between the group members during the advancement to difficult belt levels occasionally led to squabbles about an individual's true point total. Also, when points were spent, they were not always correctly reported to the record keeper, which resulted in the emission of a considerable amount of "assertive" behavior. Constant confusion in this area could effectively destroy a well-conceived treatment plan.

Group Three: Single Cottage—Involuntary Participants

These recently completed AT groups represent a marked change in procedures from the first two reported. After finishing the *Mental Kung-Fu* group, the author was invited to conduct an AT group for a different cottage, but temporary resistance by this cottage's staff to a strong contingency management approach, e.g. using points, tokens, etc., necessitated a different tact. After several weeks of consultation and mutual sharing, a satisfactory design was developed.

Methods

Three central procedures constitute the core of this design: (1) the development of a *critical incidents* videotape served as the basis for most of the group's discussion and role-playing, (2) the sponsorship system was replaced by the natural small-group structure already in existence using the leaders as co-trainers, and (3) pre– and posttest behavioral evaluation was built into the video-taping procedures.

CRITICAL INCIDENTS TAPE. The first stage of the program was the development of a series of high-probability problem situations that the boys and counselors knew resulted in either anxiety or aggressive and/or withdrawing behavior. Each small-group leader was assigned the task of finding out which situations were frequently a problem to his boys by means of an openended questionnaire developed by the author. The stimulus questions read as follows:

1. What situations tend to make you feel real uptight, like you want to puke or break out in a cold sweat?
2. What do you tend to withdraw from, like want to split, kick-back or give up on?
3. What are the situations in which you blow up, get into a fight or mouth-off to hurt someone?

The answers to these questions were then collated, and out of over 140 responses, 30 items were selected by the staff based on frequency and criticalness basic to the boys' adjustment. These 30 situations were then role-played for taping, using cottage personnel and the residents themselves. The tape was produced to portray the problem situation and then, at a crucial point, cut off to allow for a response to be added later. The items ranged in complexity from refusing to give some cigarettes to being arrested on the sidewalk. The last item was a more dramatic item in that two local Los Angeles policemen were used. Needless to say, this produced a lot of excitement around the filming site. Making the tape also created considerable interest in the cottage and the groups that were to follow. The author was constantly being "bugged" to show the tape.

SMALL-GROUP TREATMENT. The rationale for the use of the existing small-group (about 4-5 boys were in each group) structure was based upon the desire to use the existing cohesion and relationships between leaders and group members. The plan was to run the tape and AT procedures in each group using the leader as a co-trainer along with the author. The only problem seemed to be that attendance in the small group was mandatory and that the voluntary status of the preceding groups would be lost.

The major procedures used were similar to aspects of the discrimination training of the previous group except that no tokens were used and the *Mental Kung-Fu* point system was dropped. After a pregroup assessment (baseline), the first group was instructed similarly to the previous group through role-playing items from the AADT. Later they were presented the three principles of *Stand Tall, Think Smart,* and *Be Self-Controlled.* Following this, ten items from the tape were discussed, and hypothetical responses were analyzed and noted. The "best" response was then voted on and role-played and recorded on tape. The groups averaged about eight weeks before the ten-item tape was finished.

BEHAVIORAL MEASURES. The baseline and postgroup assessment consisted of videotaping each group member's responses to ten items taken from the tape. Only half (5) of the items were discussed as a part of the treatment phase and half (5) were not. This division was intentional as a means of assessing generalization to situations not specifically practiced in the group. No control group data were collected as this project was not designed to explain differences between groups as was the case in the first two designs reported. The behavioral data collected were designed to study differences in response rates within subjects as a result of the experimental or AT procedures from baseline to postgroup assessment. The criterion for minimally successful intervention was a 50 percent change from the original baseline rate in each of the three target behaviors: assertive, aggressive, and withdrawing. Again, trained raters were used to score the subjects responses after reliability was satisfactorily established.

Results

Five subjects took part in the first group, and the videotaped data and scoring represent five separate studies for comparison, although a multiple baseline design or the traditional ABAB procedure was not used. Since only two observations across time were taken, these data must be judged somewhat cautiously until a more involved design is implemented.

All scores are given as percentages of change and are limited to a maximum of 100 percent using the following formulas to compute percentage of improvement: *assertive responses* = (obtained score minus baseline score) ÷ (the distance from the baseline score to the ceiling) ; *aggressive and withdrawing responses* = (baseline score minus obtained score) ÷ (the distance from the baseline score to the floor). The ceiling of the scoring system was ten, which equalled the number of videotaped trials, and the floor was zero.

ASSERTIVE BEHAVIOR. All five boys increased in their assertive behavior with the percentage of change ranging from 33.3 percent to 66.6 percent. Three of the subjects reached a significant level with an increase of assertive behavior of 50 percent or more. Four of the five boys reached the criterion level on the trained items, while two reached significance on the untrained or novel items used as a measure of stimulus generalization.

AGGRESSIVE BEHAVIOR. Four of the subjects reduced their aggressive responses to the taped situations; two reached the 50 percent reduction level. The range of percentage scores was 0 percent to 66.6 percent. The trained items showed the greatest percentage of change, with three boys exceeding the significance level. However, only one subject decreased 50 percent or more in his aggressive responses on the untrained items, with subject number 4 actually increasing his aggressive responses by 50 percent. He was the only subject to move in the opposite direction from the treatment projection on any of the measures.

WITHDRAWING BEHAVIOR. No real discriminating trends can be reasonably established from these data because only one subject had a frequency greater than one during the baseline observations. This was in part due to the heterogenous mixture of subjects in the third design. Early studies had selected passive boys for the group training. This was not the case in the last project. However, the one subject with the highest percentage did show a 50 percent reduction of his withdrawing behavior at the postgroup assessment.

Discussion

The previously reported behavioral data seem to support the conclusion that male delinquents can learn to become more assertive in key situations, particularly when they have had previous role-playing and discussion of the particular social context or problem area and an opportunity to practice alternative responses. Generalization of the class of assertive behavior seems to occur with some of the boys to novel situations, but over half the subjects assessed showed little or no increase. Even though only a moderate trend toward generalization was demonstrated, this is encouraging and supports other data previously reported.

Similarly, these last data offer support for the boys self-report of nonassertive behavior decreases reported in the second project. Delinquents are often prone to "fake" paper and pencil tests, and seeing that behavioral data at least show a reduction in aggressive responses gives some support to the use of self-report and is encouraging. Of course, being videotaped is a laboratory measure and not without its own obtrusiveness.

Not too surprising was the absence of significant decreases in aggressive responses to the novel situation. It appears that the reflex of impetuous, aggressive verbalizations is difficult to break in a short-term training procedure, at least as defined here. Most of the gains in assertive behavior appear to occur in situations where the male delinquent is usually passive or specifically trained to deal with potentially counteraggressive stimuli. Overall, however, the development of incompatible assertive responses to problem nonassertive response situations was positively substantiated.

PROJECT CONCLUSIONS

Looking back over the past two and a half years of doing AT with the residents of Pacific Lodge, several general conclusions can be reached both from the data collected and the clinical impressions of this consultation.

1. Increasing assertive behavior in male delinquents between the ages of thirteen and sixteen in a residential treatment home can be accomplished. Both stimulus and response generalization of the in-group behaviors appear to occur for at least several

months following the group. Recognition of what truly is assertive versus aggressive and withdrawing behavior can be taught if procedures similar to project numbers II and III are used.

2. Reduction of nonassertive responses (aggression and withdrawing) can also occur, but the magnitude of change is not as great as the former. To facilitate this reduction, staff members need to be involved in follow-up programs in the cottage environment, and "acceptable," incompatible assertions need to be demonstrated and practiced continually in the group and by staff models.

3. A cottagewide sponsorship system, which involves staff along with some form of contingency management or token system as was developed in the second project, appears to produce highly desirable results and maintain a high quality of voluntary participation by the group members.

4. Using videotape equipment can be highly advantageous as a means of teaching, assessing, and reinforcing target behavior. If possible, having a group member or technician run the equipment seems to be best and frees the group leader to do other tasks.

5. Eight to twelve weeks seems to be the minimum range of time needed to produce change. Group sessions should be between one and one and one-half hours in length, once per week.

6. Leading an AT group is not easy and often requires hours of pretraining and preparation for staff. The actual group training seems to take some limited knowledge of Assertion Training, group dynamics, behavior modification, and subcultural delinquent values. More importantly, a leader probably needs to possess "a little flair" or the freedom to "ham it up" when role-playing and presenting the crucial ideas. Traditional therapy or educational styles seem to quickly bore the group members.

AT seems to present an opportunity for the counselor or residential treatment staff to develop some "cultural assimilation" and learning without suppressing the important individual values of the male delinquent. Currently this author is engaged in some informal research using similar AT procedures within a residential treatment setting for young women to determine effectiveness with this population.

REFERENCES

Editorial Comments

Alberti, R.E. and Emmons, M.L. *Stand Up, Speak Out, Talk Back!* New York: Pocket Books, 1975.

Phelps, S. and Austin, N. *The Assertive Woman.* San Luis Obispo, CA: Impact, 1975.

Stumphauzer, J.S. Training in social manipulation: the use of behavior therapy. *Crime and Delinquency,* 1972, *18*, 112-113.

Stumphauzer, J.S. *Behavior Modification Principles.* Kalamazoo, MI: Behaviordelia, 1977, 82-88.

Text

Abudabbeh, N., Predoni, J.R., & Jensen, D.E. Application of behavioral principles to group therapy techniques with juvenile delinquents. *Psychological Reports,* 1972, *31*, 375-380.

Alberti, R.E., & Emmons, M.L. *Your perfect right: A guide to assertive behavior.* San Luis Obispo: Impact Press, 1970.

Booraem, C.D., & Flowers, J.V. Reduction of anxiety and personal space as a function of assertion training with severely disturbed neuropsychiatric inpatients. *Psychological Reports,* 1972, *30*, 923-929.

Clement, P.W., Fazzone, R., & Goldstein, B. Tangible reinforcers and child group therapy. *Journal of the American Academy of Child Psychiatry,* 1970, *9*, 409-427.

Clement, P., & Milne, P. Group play therapy and tangible reinforcers used to modify the behavior of 8-year-old boys. *Behavior Research and Therapy,* 1967, *5*, 301-312.

Eisler, R.M., Hersen, M., & Miller, P.M. Effects of modeling on components of assertive behavior. *Journal of Behavior Therapy and Experimental Psychiatry,* 1973, *4*, 1-6.

Eisler, R.M., Hersen, M & Agras, W.S. Videotape: A method for the controlled observation of non-verbal interpersonal behavior. *Behavior Therapy,* 1973, *4*, 420-425.

Flowers, J.V., & Booraem, C.D. Assertion training: The training of trainers. *Counseling Psychologist,* 1975, *5*(4), 29-36.

Gittleman, M. Behavioral rehearsal as a technique in child treatment. *Journal of Child Psychology and Psychiatry,* 1965, *6*, 251-255.

Goldstein, A.P., Heller, K., & Sechrest, L.B. *Psychotherapy and the psychology of behavior change.* New York: Wiley, 1966.

Hauserman, N., Zweback, S., & Plotkin, A. Use of concrete reinforcement to facilitate verbal initiations in adolescent group therapy. *Journal of Con-*

sulting and Clinical Psychology, 1972, *38,* 90-96.

Hedquist, F.J., & Weinhold, B.K.   Behavioral group counseling with socially anxious and unassertive college students.   *Journal of Counseling
Psychology,* 1970, *17,* 237-242.

Lange, A.J., & Jakubowski, P.   *Responsible assertive behavior.*   Champaign,
IL.: Research Press, 1976.

Lazarus, A. & Fay, A.   *I can if I want to.*   New York: William Morrow &
Co., 1975.

Lazarus, A.A.   Behavioral rehearsal vs. non-directive therapy vs. advice in effecting behavior change.   *Behavior Research and Therapy,* 1966, *4,* 209-
212.

McFall, R.M., & Twentyman, C.T.   Four experiments on the relative contributions of rehearsal, modeling, and coaching to assertion training.
Journal of Abnormal Psychology, 1973, *81,* 199-218.

Paulson, T.L.   *The differential use of self-administered and group administered token reinforcement in group assertion training for college students.*
Unpublished doctoral dissertation, Fuller Theological Seminary, 1974.

Paulson, T.L., Shoemaker, M.E., & Landau, P.   *Assert yourself, you deserve it.*
Unpublished manual, Assertion Training Institute, North Hollywood, Ca.

Quay, H.C.   Personality patterns in pre-adolescent delinquent boys.   *Educational and Psychological Measurement,* 1966, *26,* 99-110.

Rathus, S.A.   An experimental investigation of assertive training in a group
setting.   *Journal of Behavior Therapy and Experimental Psychiatry,* 1972,
3, 81-86.

Salter, A.   *Conditioned reflex therapy.*   New York: Farrar, Straus, and
Gireaux, 1949.   (Republished, New York: Capricorn, 1961.)

Sarason, I.G.   Verbal learning, modeling, and juvenile delinquency.   *American Psychologist,* 1968, *23,* 254-266.

Sarason, I.G., & Ganzer, V.J.   Developing appropriate social behavior of juvenile delinquents.   In Krumboltz, J.D. & Thoresen, C.E. (Eds.), *Behavioral
counseling: Cases and techniques.*   New York: Holt, Rinehart, and
Winston, 1969.

Serber, M.   Teaching nonverbal components of assertive training.   *Journal
of Behavior Therapy & Experimental Psychiatry,* 1972, *3,* 178-183.

Shoemaker, M.E.   *Group assertiveness training for institutionalized delinquents.*   Unpublished doctoral dissertation.   Fuller Graduate School of
Psychology, 1974.

Shoemaker, M.E., & Satterfield, D.O.   "Assertion training: An identity crisis
'that's coming on strong.'"   In Alberti, R.E. (Ed.), *Assertiveness: Inno-
vations, applications, issues.*   San Luis Obispo, CA: Impact Press, In
Press.

Shoemaker, M.E., & Paulson, T.L.   Group assertion training for mothers: A
family intervention strategy.   In Mash, Eric J., Handy, Lee C. & Hamerlynck, Leo A. (Eds.), *Behavior Modification Approaches to Parenting.*

New York: Brunner/Mazel, Inc., 1976.

Smith, M.J. *When I say no, I feel guilty.* New York: Dial Press, 1975.

Stedman, J.M., Peterson, T.L., & Cardarelle, J. Application of a token system in a pre-adolescent boys' group. In Stedman, J.M., Patton, W.F., & Walton, K.F. (Eds.), *Clinical studies in behavior therapy with children, adolescents, and their families.* Springfield, Illinois: Charles C Thomas, 1973.

Wolpe, J. *Psychotherapy by reciprocal inhibition.* Stanford: Stanford University Press, 1958.

Wolpe, J., & Lazarus, A.A. *Behavior therapy techniques.* Oxford : Pergamon Press, 1966.

CHAPTER 7

ACHIEVEMENT PLACE: A PRELIMINARY OUTCOME EVALUATION*

KATHRYN A. KIRIGIN, MONTROSE M. WOLF, CURTIS J. BRAUKMANN, DEAN L. FIXSEN, AND ELERY L. PHILLIPS

EDITORIAL COMMENTS

Achievement Place represents a decade of exemplary work as a behaviorally oriented group home for delinquents. It is perhaps the best example of continued **progress** in behavior therapy with delinquents. Over the last ten years there has been a steady flow of treatment, expansion, research, and evaluation. Achievement Place has become a standard to which other programs are compared. The investigators have done well in disseminating their model program.

In this original chapter, Kirigin, Wolf, Braukmann, Fixsen, and Phillips take a long and hard look at the "big picture," an overall program evaluation of Achievement Place. They differentiate between **component evaluation,** in which several different treatment components have been assessed, and **program evaluation,** in which overall results are assessed. Program evaluation is the focus of this chapter and should be welcome reading for those many who have followed with interest the "component" research. Systematic comparisons are made with institutions for boys.

Traditional measures of program success are amply documented with regard to recidivism, behavior improvement, and school achievement. In addition, **consumer evaluations** by the boys themselves here and in institutions show that Achievement Place was more appealing on several

*The research and development activities described in this paper were supported by grants MH20030 and MH13644 from the Center for Studies in Crime and Delinquency (NIMH) to the Bureau of Child Research and Department of Human Development, University of Kansas.

118

counts. Finally, the clincher: per boy, Achievement Place cost about one-third as much as the institutions — fifteen dollars a day per boy as compared to forty-four dollars a day! What stronger case can be made: Achievement Place works better and costs less.

Achievement Place has been replicated in California (Liberman et al., 1975) and is being evaluated in another country as well — Holland (Arnold Bartels, personal communication, April 13, 1977). Chapter 8 presents an examination by an independent investigator of attitude changes in Achievement Place youth.

F OR THE LAST DECADE, community-based services for delinquent and predelinquent youths have experienced a period of rapid development and expansion. The rate of expansion of community programs in many areas has been accelerated by the discouraging reports of the failure and substantial costs of institutional treatment (President's Commission, 1967), the debilitating effects of confinement (James, 1971; Wolfensberger, 1970; Sheridan, 1967), and the inhumane treatment conditions often associated with institutional care (*Morales v. Turman*, 1973). In recent years, many states including Florida, Massachusetts, California, North Carolina, Connecticut, Washington, and Kansas have begun to deinstitutionalize their correctional programs for delinquent youths and to implement a variety of community-based alternatives.

One important direction of the community-based treatment movement has been the development of group homes for delinquent youths. These programs, designed to provide services for youths requiring more supervision than probation, provide an alternative to and a diversion from institutional programs (Empey, 1967; Keller & Alper, 1970). Many of the states that are attempting to deinstitutionalize their programs for delinquents are establishing group homes as one of the alternatives.

Since 1967, we have attempted to develop Achievement Place as one model of group home treatment. The goals of the program have been to develop a community-based group home program that would be effective, responsive to the needs of its consumers, economical, and replicable in other communities. Since its inception, the model has gone through various stages of development, evaluation, and refinement leading to national dissemination (Braukmann, Kirigin, & Wolf, 1975).

Achievement Place is a *community-based, family-style,* group home treatment program for six to eight delinquent or predelinquent youths from twelve through fifteen years old. The program is directed by a board of directors composed of members of the community. The board is responsible for the financial, personnel, and the policy aspects of the program. The treatment program is administered by a couple whom we refer to as *teaching-parents.* The title *teaching-parents* is given to distinguish them from more traditional, untrained, custodial house-parents or foster-parents. In the Achievement Place Teaching-Family Model, the teaching-parents are given a year's professional training which includes classroom instruction, supervised practicum experience, and formal evaluation by the social service agencies in their community, as well as by a community board of directors, the court, the schools, the youths, and the parents of the youths.

The function of the Achievement Place program is to help youths who are in danger of institutionalization remain in their communities. Our assumption is that these youths are at risk because of the reaction to the youths' disturbing behavior by the parents, schools, court, and social welfare personnel. Thus, the role of the teaching-parents is twofold: (1) to develop positive personal teaching relationships with their youths, enabling them to teach the behavioral skills likely to produce positive community reaction and (2) to assume responsibility for the youths and become their advocates in the community.

The behavioral skill training component is based on a *behavior deficiency* model of deviant behavior. The youths' behavior problems are viewed as being due to their lack of essential skills. These behavioral deficiencies are considered to be a result of inadequate histories of reinforcement and instruction rather than internal psychopathology. The goal of the behavioral treatment program, therefore, is to establish through reinforcement, modeling, and instruction, the important behavioral competencies in social (including interpersonal relationship skills), academic, prevocational, and self-care skills that the youths have not acquired. The assumption is that after learning these skills the youths will be more successful in their homes and schools, the natural reinforcement from this success will maintain the new appropriate behaviors, and these will lead to greater acceptance by the parents and the community.

The Achievement Place behavioral skills training program has four main elements: a motivation system (token economy), a self-government system, a comprehensive behavioral skill training curriculum, and the development of a reciprocally reinforcing relationship between the youths and the teaching-parents (such a relationship enhances the reinforcing effect of the teaching-parents' social interaction and allows them to fade the more artificial token reinforcement).

The advocacy role of the teaching-parents is carried out in the community. The teaching-parents are responsible for establishing and maintaining good working relationships with various community agencies, such as the juvenile court, the schools, the police, the social welfare department, and the mental health center. By establishing relationships with the agencies and with the parents of the youths, the teaching-parents can almost assure that when the parents or a member of these agencies has a complaint about a youth, the teaching-parents will be contacted and given an opportunity to solve the problem. This is a diversionary function in that the parents and agency personnel who have the services of a teaching-parent are less dependent upon the formal juvenile justice system.

DESCRIPTION OF THE ACHIEVEMENT PLACE PROGRAM

Teaching-parents utilize a flexible motivation system to enhance their effectiveness as teachers. When a youth first enters the program he is introduced to the point system (token economy) which is devised to help him learn more appropriate behavior. Through that motivation system, a youth earns points for learning and engaging in appropriate, adaptive behaviors and loses points for inappropriate, maladaptive behaviors. The earned points are exchanged by the youth at first on a daily, and later on a weekly, basis for privileges such as allowance and returning to his or her natural home on the weekend. Success on the motivation system advances a youth to the merit system in which points are no longer required for privileges. If the youth maintains his appropriate behavior while on the merit system, he begins to spend more and more time with his natural or foster family before being released from the program.

The youths participate in the direction and operation of the Teaching-Family Model treatment programs through self-government. The youths exercise self-government through the daily family conference, which usually occurs after dinner. At that meeting, the family members democratically establish and review their guidelines for appropriate behavior, decide whether any behaviors that day were particularly appropriate or inappropriate, and determine the consequences of any such behaviors (Fixsen, Phillips, & Wolf, 1973). At the family conference, the teaching-parents teach the skills involved in constructive criticism, problem solving, and negotiation. At the conference, the performance of any youth who is on the merit system is reviewed. In addition, the youths participate in the daily review and democratic election of a peer manager who oversees and teachs routine social and self-help skills (Phillips, Phillips, Wolf, & Fixsen, 1973).

The community-based aspect of the Teaching-Family Model permits youths to return to their homes on weekends and to continue to attend their local schools, thus enabling the teaching-parents to assist them in learning to deal with their problems in those settings. Being community based also allows the teaching-parents to continue to monitor, advocate for, and, if necessary, to provide additional treatment for the youths after they graduate from the program.

A typical day begins with breakfast and housecleaning chores or last-minute homework preparation. Before leaving for school, the boys pick up their daily report cards. The daily cards permit the teaching-parents to work closely with the school teachers and administrators to solve the boys' school problems. Teachers provide systematic feedback for each youth by filling out a report card each day. The teacher can quickly answer a series of questions about the youth's behavior (Did he follow the teacher's rules today? Did he make good use of his class time? Did he complete his assignment at an acceptable level of accuracy?) by checking *yes* or *no* on his card. The youth then earns or loses points at Achievement Place depending on the teacher's judgement about his performance.

When the boys return to the home after school, they typically review their school report with the teaching-parents before having snacks and starting their homework or other point-earning activities. In the late afternoon, one or two boys usually help with dinner preparation for which they earn points.

Following dinner and family conference the youths and teaching-parents usually engage in family activities such as watching television or pursue special interests. During the evening there are often counseling sessions with individual youths who are having serious problems at school, in the group home, or in the natural home. In the counseling session the teaching-parent can express his/her regard and concern for the youth, help the youth explore the various alternative solutions and their possible consequences as well as teach specific skills in which the youth may have demonstrated a deficiency during the day.

Throughout the day the youths receive feedback and encouragement from the teaching-parents regarding their interpersonal social skills since this is an area in which many of the youths often need extensive help.

Criteria for Admission to Achievement Place

Candidates are selected for the program by a selection committee made up of personnel from the court, welfare, and school as well as one of the teaching-parents. These selection criteria are as follows:

Inclusion

1. Age—the youth usually must be between twelve and sixteen years old (specified by the licensing requirements).

2. IQ—the youth should have an IQ of at least 70.

3. Locale—the youth must reside within the county.

4. Presenting Problem—the youth's behavior problems and his status with the court, school, and his family are such that the youth is in danger of institutionalization in the opinion of the selection committee.
5. Court Adjudication—the youth's problems are so serious that the court has or is about to adjudicate the youth.
6. Failure of less Restrictive or Structured Forms of Intervention—the youth typically will have failed to respond favorably to probation or counseling services available in the community.
7. Family—the youth must have a family in the community (parents, relatives, or foster parents) to return to with the assistance of the program staff.

Exclusion

1. Certain Violent Offenses—a youth who has committed murder, forcible rape, or armed robbery would be excluded from consideration as a candidate for the program. The rationale for this is that the community often is not willing to tolerate the continued presence of a youth in the community after he has committed such a serious offense.
2. Drug Addiction—youths who show a serious physiological dependence on dangerous narcotics, e.g. heroin or barbituates, as judged by a physician would be temporarily excluded because of the lack of appropriate medical supervision in the Achievement Place facility.
3. Serious Physical Disabilities—a youth with a major physical handicap, e.g. blindness or confinement to a wheel chair, which would not permit normal mobility within the group home, school, or community would be excluded.

Characteristics of Achievement Place Youths

The first forty-one youths who were admitted to the Achievement Place for Boys program in Lawrence, Kansas, ranged in age from ten to sixteen (average age, approximately 14 years). Of the youths 61 percent were white, 29 percent were black, 7 percent were American Indian, and 2 percent were Mexican American. Two thirds of the youths came from families in which at least one parent was absent from the natural home. Sixty percent of the youths came from families whose annual income was below seven thousand dollars; 53 percent of the families were on welfare.

The tested IQs of the youths ranged from 73 to 113 with an average of 97. Of the youths, 41 percent were labeled by the schools as slow learners, 12 percent as retarded, and 12 percent as brain damaged (a youth could have more than one label). Although their average grade level in school was the seventh grade (range: third through tenth), achievement test scores placed them at the fifth-grade level on the average, range: first through tenth). Thirty percent of the youths were in special education programs and 57 percent had failed one or more grade levels. The youths' average grade in the classes one year prior to entering the program was a D minus (0.6 on a 4.0 scale).

In addition to their academic deficiencies, the youths had a number of other problems related to school. They missed an average of 40 days (range: 3 to 180 days) out of a possible 180 days of school during the year prior to entering Achievement Place. Sixty-five percent of the youths were suspended from school at the time they were admitted to the program. The schools labeled most of the youths as behavior problems (80%) and as emotionally disturbed (53%).

All forty-one youths had been court adjudicated prior to admission. Of the youths, 52 percent allegedly had been involved in delinquent acts (felonies), 45 percent in drug abuse, and 94 percent in other offenses. Their first police contact occurred at an average age of 12.6 years and their first adjudication occurred at an average age of 13.7 years. The average number of police and court contacts was about three per youth.

Of the youths 68 percent had spent some time in jail and 43 percent had been in some type of residential care or treatment before coming to Achievement Place. Almost all of the youths had received previous nonresidential treatment (for example, 95% had received probation services or psychology clinic services).

The youths had received various diagnostic labels by professionals. These labels included cultural deprivation, adolescent adjustment reaction, unsocialized aggression, childhood schizophrenia, psychopathic personality, retardation, psychotic sexual deviation, pyromania, suicidal tendency, and autism.

Evaluation of the Achievement Place Program

Procedural Evaluation

Our evaluation of the effectiveness of the Achievement Place program has had two dimensions: component evaluation and program evaluation (Wolf, Phillips, & Fixsen, 1974). The component evaluation has assessed the effects of and preferences of the youths for several of the individual treatment components of the program that have been designed to train a variety of social, academic, prevocational, and self-care skills. The feedback provided by these evaluations has been important for the continuing refinement of the model. In the reference section of this article a list appears describing the research carried out on the motivational and instructional components of the model. These evaluations have included studies of the token economy (Phillips, 1968), the self-government system (Fixsen, Phillips, & Wolf, 1973), the elected-manager system (Phillips, Wolf, & Fixsen, 1973), the daily report card system (Bailey, Wolf, & Phillips, 1970), vocational training (Braukmann, Maloney, Fixsen, Phillips, & Wolf, 1974; Ayala, Minkin, Phillips, Fixsen, & Wolf, in press), speech correction (Bailey, Timbers, Phillips, & Wolf, 1970), social skill training (Maloney, Harper, Braukmann, Fixsen, Phillips, and Wolf, 1976; Werner, Minkin, Minkin, Fixsen, Phillips, & Wolf, 1975; and Minkin, Braukmann, Minkin, Timbers, Timbers, Fixsen, Phillips & Wolf, 1977), and general procedures (Wolf, Phillips, & Fixsen, 1972; Fixsen, Wolf, & Phillips, 1973; and Phillips, Phillips, Fixsen, & Wolf, 1974). These components have been demonstrated to be effective in teaching a variety of new skills. In addition, research has shown that youth-preferred teaching-parent interaction behaviors can be identified and taught to teaching-parent trainees.

Outcome Evaluation*

The evaluation of the overall Achievement Place program has been and continues to be concerned with the impact of the program on the lives of the youths. Our primary objective has been to develop a community-based group home program that would provide an alternative to institutionalization for youths who were in danger of being institutionalized, and that would help the youths in the treatment program to acquire skills which would enhance the likelihood of success in their community. Accordingly, our primary comparison of the Achievement Place youths should be with youths who have been treated in an institutional treatment program. However, there are unique problems inherent in evaluating a group home program by comparing it with the effects of an institutional treatment program. Random assignment is the ideal manner of assigning subjects to treatment programs that are compared. But, it is not usually feasible to assign youths randomly to a group home and to an institutional treatment program. Since these programs are vastly different in terms of their restrictiveness on the freedom of the individual, it is ethically questionable whether a youth, who normally would be considered eligible for treatment in his community in a group home, should be placed in an institution solely for purposes of evaluating the group home program. On the other hand, when the decision to randomly assign youths produces less restriction of the youth, then random assignment is a very defensible procedure. An example would be when a state agency which administers both institutional and community treatment programs takes youths who would normally be institutionalized and randomly assigns some to community placement (see Palmer, 1974).

In the case of the Achievement Place program, however, the local agencies consider it a service agency in a continuum of treatment services from a family counseling program in the community mental health center to actual institutionalization. Thus, a youth referred to Achievement Place is considered a youth *in danger* of institutionalization but one who has the right to at-

*The authors gratefully acknowledge the assistance of Jay Atwater in the collection and analysis of the follow-up data presented in this paper.

tempt to succeed with this less restrictive form of treatment. Thus, in our overall evaluation of the Achievement Place program we have had to rely on quasi-experimental methods (Campbell and Stanley, 1963) described below.

In addition, proper evaluation of the effects of a treatment program requires a substantial sample size. Unfortunately, a group home, unlike a large institution, only deals with a few youths each year. Thus, it will be necessary to continue to evaluate Achievement Place youths during the next few years and track the youths who are admitted to the replications of the Teaching-Family model before an acceptable sample size will exist.

We have gathered data on twenty-six youths who have been in the Achievement Place program and thirty-seven seemingly comparable youths who have not been in the Achievement Place program. The comparison youth were either treated in an institutional program or were considered by the selection committee to be in danger of institutionalization. The Achievement Place youths and the comparison youths each have two subgroups. The first set of subgroups consists of the first eighteen youths in the Achievement Place program and nineteen comparison youths who attended the state Boys School. This subgroup of comparison youths was determined by the probation officer who identified nineteen youths from the community who were potential candidates for Achievement Place.

The second set of subgroups originated by a process that we call *random selection*. With the Achievement Place program, typically, there were more candidates eligible for admission than there were openings available. When this occurs, random selection provides a fair way to determine who among the eligible candidates will enter the program. In addition, random selection reduces the likelihood of a biased selection based on a youth's "bad reputation," race, or other personal characteristics. To illustrate how random selection operates, if out of several referrals, three candidates meet the selection criteria, the selection of one of the youths would be determined randomly. The other two youths who were *randomly not selected* would be placed in the randomly determined comparison group. These youths would, of course, be considered for treatment by the other agencies that work with youths. If at a later time a youth in the randomly determined comparison group is reprocessed by the court and again becomes a candidate for the program, he could once again be included in the selection pool, but again the choice of the youth for admission would be made on a random basis. Thus far, data have been gathered for two years following selection for eight youths who were randomly selected to enter Achievement Place and for eighteen comparison youths who were randomly not selected to enter Achievement Place.

Achievement Place as an Alternative to Institutionalization

Some preliminary information about the role of Achievement Place as an alternative to institutionalization can be seen in Figure 7-1, which shows cumulative percent of youths institutionalized one year and two years after they were randomly either selected or not selected to enter Achievement Place. Of the eight youths who went to Achievement Place, one youth (12%) was institutionalized during the first year following selection. No additional youths were institutionalized during the second year. Of the eighteen youths randomly not selected, eight youths (44%) were institutionalized during the first year following selection. During the second year post-selection, the cumulative percent of youths institutionalized rose to 56 precent (2 additional youths).

Thus, these data tentatively suggest that the majority of youths considered for admission to Achievement Place are genuinely in danger of institutionalization and that Achievement Place is acting as an alternative to institutionalization for these youths.

The average age of the randomly selected youths admitted to Achievement Place was 14.7 years. The randomly determined comparison group youths were 15 years old, on the average, at the time of selection. The comparison youths who were institutionalized following selection were an average of 15.2 years old when they were admitted to an institution.

In addition to the comparability of age at the time of selection for both the randomly selected Achievement Place group and the randomly determined comparison group, the median police and court contacts during the year preceding selection provided another indication of comparability. The median contacts with the police and court prior to selection was 3.48 for the comparison group and 3.00 for the Achievement Place Youths.

Post-Treatment Institutionalization

A primary goal of Achievement Place has been to provide a community alternative for youths who were in danger of institutionalization. Consequently, an important question is, What proportion of the youths who enter the Achievement Place program are later institutionalized? Figure 7-2 shows the post-treatment institutionalization rate of the first eighteen youths who entered Achievement Place compared with the reinstitutionalization rate of the nineteen comparison youths who were placed in the state Boys School. (Post-treatment reinstitutionalization data for the

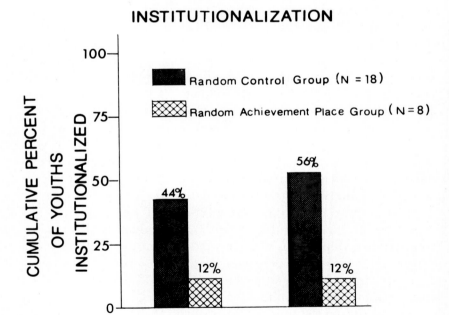

Figure 7-1. The cumulative percent of youths who were institutionalized one year and two years following the date they were selected or not selected into the Achievement Place program.

POST–TREATMENT
INSTITUTIONALIZATION

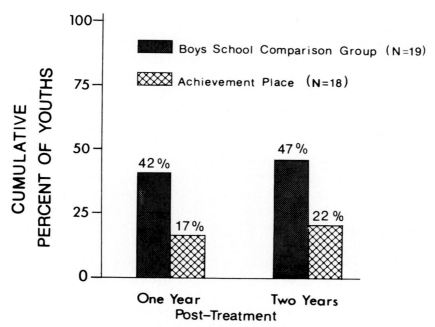

Figure 7-2. The cumulative percent of youths who were institutionalized one year and two years following release from treatment in an institution (Boys School group) or Achievement Place.

random group are unavailable due to the small number of those institutionalized who have completed the institutional program.) Approximately twice as many of the youths who went to the Boys School were institutionalized after their treatment as were youths who participated in the Achievement Place program. By the end of the first year post-treatment, 42 percent of the Boys School youths had been reinstitutionalized and 17 percent of the Achievement Place youths had been institutionalized. These figures include the in-program failures for both programs. During the second year the cumulative percent of youths institutionalized after their original treatment program increased to 47 percent for the Boys School group and to 22 percent for the Achievement Place group. Thus, approximately twice as many youths from the Boys School group were receiving further institutional treatment after having completed their original treatment program.

There are several possible explanations for these dramatic differences in the post-treatment institutionalization rates for youths in the two treatment programs. One real possibility is that since the youths were not assigned randomly to the two treatment programs, the two groups may have been distinctly different initially, e.g. the Boys School youths perhaps being more serious and thus more likely to engage in deviant behavior resulting in post-treatment institutionalization than the Achievement Place youths. This question can be partially answered by comparing the youths' rates of deviant behavior before they entered their respective programs.

The youths in the Achievement Place program and the Boys School group were not randomly determined. The Achievement Place youths were selected for their program by a selection committee on the basis of the recommendations of personnel from the juvenile court, social welfare, and public schools. Three years after the program had been operating, the probation officer was requested to review the youths who had been sent to the state Boys School over the preceding three years and to select those youths who, in the opinion of the probation officer would have been eligible for Achievement Place as an alternative to institutional treatment. The probation officer supplied the list and these youths became the nonrandom comparison group.

One striking difference between the Achievement Place youths and the Boys School youths that became immediately apparent was the difference in the average age at which the two groups of youths entered their respective programs. The Achievement Place youths were on the average 13.2 years old and the Boys School youths were on the average 14.5 years old when they entered their programs.

Information was gathered on the rates of police and court contacts and on school attendance for both groups for the years preceding their entry into the treatment programs. This information was recorded using procedures described in *An Evaluation*

Manual for Collecting Followup Information on Youths in Trouble (Kirigin, Fixsen, Phillips, & Wolf, 1974). Offenses were calculated for the time the youth was available in the community "at risk" (Palmer, 1974).

As can be seen in Table 7-I, the rates of police and court contacts and the percent of youths in school for the year preceding the commencement of their respective treatment programs were different. As Table 7-I shows there were more contacts and less school attendance on the part of the boys school group.

TABLE 7-I

POLICE AND COURT CONTACTS AND SCHOOL ATTENDANCE DURING
THE YEAR PRECEDING ADMISSION INTO ACHIEVEMENT
PLACE AND BOYS SCHOOL

	Mean Police and Court Contacts Per Year	*Percentage of Youths Attending School*
Achievement Place Youths		
N=18	2.89	72%
Boys School Youths		
N=19	3.89	44%

On the other hand, there were also large differences between the ages of the youths when they entered their programs. The Boys School youths were on the average one year and three months older than the Achievement Place youths were when they entered their programs. As was found with the randomly determined groups, youths who were institutionalized from the same county in which the group home was located usually were older than those placed in the group home. Since there is some possibility that rates of contacts and dropouts are related to age in this particular age range (Wolfgang, Figlio, and Sellin, 1972; Robin, 1964; Lerman, 1968; Robins, 1966), it was decided to compare the two groups of youths at equivalent ages. The youths were compared for rates of contacts and school attendance at the age at which the comparison youths were equivalent in age to the youths who went into Achievement Place.

The results of this *age equivalent analysis* are presented in Table 7-II. As can be seen in Table 7-II, the rate of contacts per

TABLE 7-II

MEAN POLICE AND COURT CONTACTS PER YEAR FOR THE ACHIEVE-
MENT PLACE YOUTHS AND FOR THE BOYS SCHOOL YOUTHS AT ONE,
TWO AND THREE YEARS PREVIOUS TO THE ONSET OF TREATMENT
FOR THE ACHIEVEMENT PLACE YOUTHS

	3 Years	*2 Years*	*1 Year*
Achievement Place Youths N=18	.22	.28	2.89
Boys School Youths N=19	0	16	.16

year for the Achievement Place youths was higher than the comparison youths for each of the three years preceding the point at
which the Achievement Place youths entered their program. In
the year just preceding the point at which the Achievement Place
youths entered their program, the Boys School youths had only
.16 contacts on the average while the Achievement Place youths
averaged 2.89 contacts. Thus, considering police and court contacts at equivalent ages, the evidence does not seem to support the
assumption that the Boys Schools youths were more frequent
offenders.

Table 7-III shows the percent of youths in school at equivalent
years prior to treatment. As can be seen, attendance in school for
the two groups of youths was very similar for years two and three.
In the year immediately preceding treatment of the Achievement
Place youths, 92 percent of the Boys School youths were attending
public school compared with 72 percent of the Achievement Place
youths. This examination of school attendance at equivalent ages
suggests that a greater percent of the Achievement Place youths
had school behavior problems at the same age.

TABLE 7-III

PERCENTAGE OF YOUTHS ATTENDING PUBLIC SCHOOL ONE, TWO,
AND THREE YEARS BEFORE THE ACHIEVEMENT PLACE YOUTHS
BEGAN THEIR TREATMENT PROGRAM

	3 Years	*2 Years*	*1 Year*
Achievement Place Youths	100%	90%	72%
Boys School Youths	100%	100%	92%

During Treatment Effects

The comparison youths in both the nonrandom and randomly determined comparison groups were older than the Achievement Place youths at the point in their lives when they entered their institutional treatment program. Thus, the comparison youths remained in the community for varying periods of time while the Achievement Place youths, who were also in the community, were being treated in the Achievement Place group home. This overlap allows an estimate of the in-treatment effects of the Achievement Place program by comparing the rate of police and court contacts and proportion of youths attending school for the Achievement Place youths while they were in the program with the equivalent age measures of the institutionalized youths who had not yet entered their institutional program and left the community.

The random groups and nonrandom groups were combined for the purpose of this analysis since the number of random Achievement Place youths is small. As the number of randomly selected youths entering Achievement Place increases during the next few years of the program, it will become more appropriate to analyze the randomly selected group separately from the nonrandom groups. Until this analysis of the in-treatment effect can be carried out with a credible number of randomly selected youths, the conclusions drawn from these data must be considered as tentative.

Figure 7-3 shows the during-treatment effects of Achievement Place on police and court contacts. Figure 7-4 shows the same effect for school attendance. As can be seen in each case, the Achievement Place youths improve markedly in both contacts and school attendance during treatment at Achievement Place.

Two-Year Follow-Up of the Achievement Place Youths

Another very important question relates to the frequency of continued police and court contacts and school attendance after participation in the Achievement Place program. At the present time the only comparison possible involves the nonrandom groups because an insufficient number of randomly selected youths have

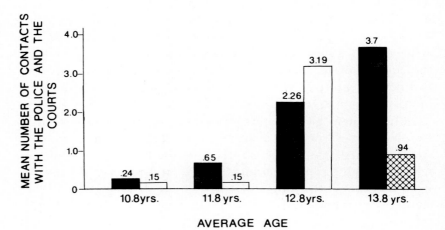
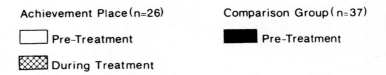

Figure 7-3. The mean number of contacts with the police and the courts when the youths in Achievement Place and the comparison group youths were at equivalent ages. The Achievement Place youths averaged 13.8 years of age when they entered treatment, thus, the three open bars represent data from 1, 2, and 3 years prior to treatment. The comparison group youths entered their treatment at an average age of 14.9 years, thus, the shaded bars represent data from 1, 2, 3, and 4 years prior to treatment.

completed their programs at this point. Also, this comparison must be made during the second year after treatment for the Achievement Place youths because the majority of the Boys School youths are institutionalized and thus are not in the community during the first Achievement Place post-treatment year. In addition, in each of the three years following their original institutionalization, the majority of the Boys School youths spent at least

SCHOOL ATTENDANCE
AT EQUIVALENT AGES

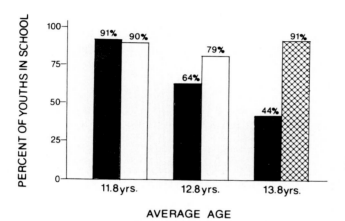

Figure 7-4. The percentage of youths in school each year when the youths in the Achievement Place for Boys and the youths in the comparison groups were at equivalent ages. The Achievement Place youths averaged 13.8 years of age when they entered treatment, thus, the two open bars represent data from 1 and 2 years prior to treatment. The comparison group entered treatment at an average age of 14.9 years, thus, the shaded bars represent data from 1, 2, and 3 years prior to treatment.

some time in an institution either originally or as reinstitutionalization and thus they have been away from their community. On the other hand, the overwhelming majority of the Achievement Place youths were in the community during the following treatment. Given the disproportionate number of Boys School youths who were reinstitutionalized and given the possibility that those same youths would have been the youths most likely to commit offenses had they been in the community, then the measure of post-treatment offenses may favor the Boys School group even though the offenses were prorated for actual time in the community. Consequently the comparison of post-treatment offense rate is difficult to interpret.

In order to make the comparison at equivalent ages for the two groups it was necessary to compare the Achievement Place youths during the second year after termination of their program with the Boys School youths during the first year after termination of their programs. At these points the youths averaged 15.8 years of age. As can be seen in Table 7-IV, at equivalent ages, the average frequency of police and court contacts was 1.5 per year for the Boys School and 1.7 per year for the Achievement Place youths.

TABLE 7-IV

POLICE AND COURT CONTACTS AND SCHOOL ATTENDANCE DURING THE AGE EQUIVALENT FOLLOW-UP YEAR

	Mean Police and Court Contacts Per Year	Percentage of Youths Attending School
Achievement Place Youths N=18	1.7	56%
Boys School Youths N=19	1.5	33%

The percent of youths attending school can also be seen in Table 7-IV. Of the youths who were in the community, 56 percent of the Achievement Place youths and 33 percent of the Boys School youths attended school in the community during the follow-up year. Again, since more of the Boys School graduates were institutionalized than the Achievement Place youths and since it is possible that those Boys School youths who were institutionalized would have been the least likely to have attended school, it is possible that this comparison is also confounded. That is, the percent of youths in school for the Boys School group is potentially inflated since the reinstitutionalization youths are eliminated from the calculation as they are not eligible to be in public school.

Cost of the Achievement Place Program

The cost of operating the Achievement Place program and the State Boys School program are shown in Table 7-V. As can be seen, the cost was about three times greater for operating the institutional program. In 1974, it cost fifteen dollars per day per youth in the Achievement Place program and forty-four dollars per day per youth in the institutional program.

TABLE 7-V

COMPARISON OF THE COST OF OPERATING ACHIEVEMENT PLACE, A COMMUNITY-BASED GROUP HOME AND BOYS SCHOOL, A STATE INSTITUTION

	Cost Per Youth Per Day
Achievement Place	$15
Boys School	$44

In addition to the differences in operating costs, there are also clear differences in the cost of construction of the two types of facilities. In 1971, the state of Kansas estimated that it would cost about twenty thousand dollars per bed to construct new institutions. In contrast, in that same year it cost only about six thousand dollars per bed to purchase and renovate Achievement Place homes for eight youths.

The figures on the building and operating costs show that there are many clear financial advantages to a community-based program. Because the program is community based there is no need to duplicate the facilities and resources that are already available to youths in their community, such as schools, recreational centers, medical facilities, etc. Also, the group home facility can be resold should the need for treatment diminish.

Evaluation of the Satisfaction of the Consumers of the Achievement Place Program

In order to assess the extent to which the Achievement Place program was accomplishing its goals according to its consumers, questionnaires were sent to members of the board of directors; the juvenile court; the department of social welfare; the principals, counselors, and teachers who had contacts with the youths at school; and the parents of the youths to provide them with the opportunity to give their opinions of the quality and effectiveness of the program in meeting their needs. These questionnaires were constructed using a seven-point rating scale (Osgood et al., 1957). Each individual was asked to rate the cooperativeness of the teaching-parents and their effectiveness in correcting the youths' problems. The board of directors was also asked to provide additional information about the teaching-parents' ability to operate within the police guidelines and the budget outlined for the program. The youths in the home were interviewed and asked to rate the teaching-parents in terms of their fairness, concern, effectiveness, and pleasantness. The youths also rated the program's effectiveness in helping them to get along better with their parents, teachers, employers, and friends. The youths' part of the evaluation was carried out without the teaching-parents being in the room, and the youths were assured that their individual responses would remain anonymous.

The two couples who have served as teaching-parents at Achievement Place for Boys have been evaluated by the consumer satisfaction measurement technique.

Figure 7-5 shows the mean levels of satisfaction indicated by the various consumers for the two sets of Achievement Place teaching-parents. As can be seen, the average for both couples was between six and seven on the seven-point scale on every dimension. The consumers clearly seem to be satisfied with the Achievement Place program.

While we have not been able to carry out a consumer evaluation of an institutional program, we have gathered data on six non-Achievement Place group homes in several communities in Kansas. Figure 7-5 also shows a comparison of the Achievement Place and the non-Achievement Place group homes. The Achievement Place couples averaged higher ratings on every dimension. According to the Mann Whitney U Test (Siegal, 1956) the differences in scores were significant for all dimensions of youth and teacher ratings and two of the board of director ratings.

It should be noted that there was no overlap in the mean

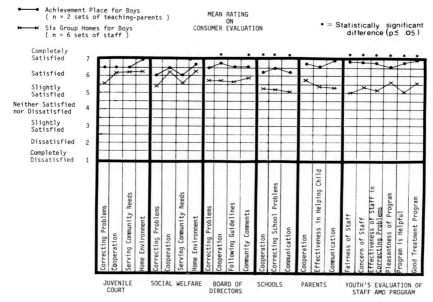

Figure 7-5. The mean consumer ratings for staff in the Achievement Place style group homes for boys located in Kansas. Five of the six non-Achievement Place homes provides family style residential care for youths between 12 and 15 years of age. The sixth home was staffed on a shift-work basis. The six homes had been in operation for an average of 3.5 years.

ratings for the Achievement Place couples and the comparison group homes and that in some categories there are large differences between the groups. However, due to the small sample size in each group, an overlap of one score was sufficient to render the difference statistically nonsignificant.

Replication of the Achievement Place Program

Central to the replication of the model has been the training of teaching-parent couples to operate replication programs. During the past three years, training and evaluation procedures for teaching-parents have been developed and are currently being implemented in several regional training sites throughout the country (Braukmann et al., 1976). The quality control of the treatment is ensured through routinized, systematic consumer and professional evaluations which lead to the couple's certification as teaching-parents. In the three-year period since the inception of the training program, the Teaching-Family treatment model has been implemented in over thirty-five group home programs.

CONCLUSIONS

The procedural and program evaluations that have been carried out over the past several years have provided important feedback integral to the development and refinement of the Achievement Place Teaching-Family Model. The procedural evaluations have assessed the effects of the program's components designed to train a variety of social, academic, prevocational, and self-care skills. The evaluation of the overall Achievement Place program has focused on the impact of the program on the youths who have participated. At present the data are quite preliminary due to methodological factors and a small sample size. For these reasons it is not yet possible to form definite conclusions about the effects of the Achievement Place treatment program or about its possible social policy implications for the role of group homes in the continuum of services for youths who become involved in the juvenile justice system. The tentative conclusions that the data suggest thus far are as follows:

> The Achievement Place group home model has acted as an alternative to institutionalization for the majority of the youths it served.
>
> The youths who took part in the Achievement Place program were much less likely to be institutionalized within two years after treatment than were similar youths who were originally treated in the institutional program.
>
> During treatment in Achievement Place there was a marked reduction in police and court contacts and an increase in school attendance.
>
> In the second year, after treatment, the Achievement Place youths had fewer police and court contacts than before treatment. However, equivalent aged youths who had been treated in an institution had a similar reduction.
>
> The Achievement Place youths were more likely to continue in school after treatment than the youths who were treated in the institute.

In addition, the preliminary data indicate that:

> The cost of treatment in Achievement Place was substantially less than the cost of treatment in the institution.
>
> The consumers (youths, parents, board of directors, school personnel, court personnel, social welfare personnel, and juvenile court personnel) were satisfied with the Achievement Place program.
>
> The Achievement Place research program produced a training program which resulted in approximately thirty-five replications of the original program.

The Achievement Place program was developed out of a need to provide the community with an effective, humane, replicable, and less costly alternative to institutional treatment. The preliminary data we have gathered have permitted an assessment of the achievement of our aims. As the data suggest, many of the aims have not been achieved with equal success. Of especial concern are the post-treatment rates of contact with the police and court for Achievement Place youths. This suggests that the model is still somewhat incomplete and that additional refinements are needed to maintain the level of effectiveness achieved during treatment. With additional refinements comes the recurring need to carry out both procedural and program evaluations to ensure that the quality of the services remains high and our aims to provide an effective alternative to institutionalization are being met.

REFERENCES

Editorial Comments

Liberman, R.P., Ferris, C., Salgado, P., & Salgado, J. Replication of the achievement place model in California. *Journal of Applied Behavior Analysis,* 1975, *8,* 287-299.

Text

Ayala, H.E., Minkin, N., Phillips, E.L., Fixsen, D.L., and Wolf, M.M. Achievement Place: The training and analysis of vocational behaviors. *Journal of Applied Behavior Analysis,* in press.

Bailey, J.S., Wolf, M.M., & Phillips, E.L. Home-based reinforcement and the modification of pre-delinquents' classroom behavior. *Journal of Applied Behavior Analysis,* 1970, *3,* 223-233.

Braukmann, C.J., Kirigin, K.A. ,and Wolf, M.M. *The Teaching-Parent Education Program.* Paper read at Association for the Advancement of Behavior Therapy, 1975.

Braukmann, C.J., Malone, D.M., Fixsen, D.L., Phillips, E.L., and Wolf, M.M. Analysis of a selection interview training package. *Criminal Justice and Behavior,* 1974, *1,* 30-42.

Campbell, D.T. and Stanley, J.C. Experimental and quasi-experimental designs for research and teaching. In N.L. Gage (Ed.) *Handbook of Research in Teaching.* Chicago, Illinois: Rand McNally, 1963, 171-246.

Empey, L.T. *Studies in delinquency: Alternatives to Incarceration.* Washington, D.C.: U.S. Deaprtment of Health, Education, and Welfare, Office of Juvenile Delinquent and Youth Development, 1967, (Publication No. 9001).

Fixsen, D.L., Phillips, E.L., and Wolf, M.M. Achievement Place: Experiments in self-government with pre-delinquents. *Journal of Applied Behavior Analysis,* 1973, *6,* 31-57.

Fixsen, D.L., Wolf, M.M., & Phillips, E.L. Achievement Place: A teaching-family model of community-based group homes for youths in trouble. In L.A. Hamerlynck, L.C. Handy, and E.J. Mash, (Eds.), *Critical Issues in Behavior Modification. Proceedings of the Fourth Banff International Conference on Behavioral Modification.* Champaign, Ill.: Research Press, 1973.

James, H. *Children In Trouble: The National Scandal.* New York: Pocket Books, 1971.

Keller, O.J. and Alper, B.S. *Halfway Houses: Community-centered Correction and Treatment.* Lexington, Mass.: Heath, 1970.

Kirigin, K.A., Fixsen, D.L., Phillips, E.L., and Wolf, M.M. *An Evaluation Manual for Collecting Follow-up Information on Youths in Trouble.* Lawrence, Kansas: Department of Human Development, unpublished, 1974.

Kirigin, K.A., Philips, E.L., Timbers, G.D., Fixsen, D.L., and Wolf, M.M. Achievement Place: The modification of academic behavior problems of youths in a group home setting. In B. Etzel, J.M. LeBlanc, and D.M. Baer (Eds.), *New Developments in Behavioral Research: Theory, Method, and Application.* Hillsdale, N.J.: Lawrence Erlbaum Associates, 1977.

Lerman, P. Individual values, peer values and subcultural delinquency. *American Sociological Review,* 1968, *33,* 219-235.

Maloney, D.M., Harper, T.M., Braukmann, C.J., Fixsen, D.L., Phillips, E.L., & Wolf, M.M. Teaching conversation-related skills to predelinquent girls. *Journal of Applied Behavior Analysis,* 1976, *9,* 371.

Minkin, N., Braukmann, C.J., Minkin, B.L., Timbers, G.D., Timbers, B.J., Fixsen, D.L., Phillips, E.L., and Wolf, M.M. The social validation and training of conversational skills. *Journal of Applied Behavior Analysis,* 1976, *9,* 127-139.

Osgood, C.E., Suci, G.J., Tannenbaum, Ph.H. *The Measurement of Meaning.* Urbana, Illinois: University of Illinois Press, 1957.

Palmer, T. The youth authority's community treatment program. *Federal Probation,* 1974, 3-14.

Phillips, E.L. Achievement Place: Token reinforcement procedures in a homestyle rehabilitation setting for "pre-delinquent" boys. *Journal of Applied Behavior Analysis,* 1968, *1,* 213-223.

Phillips, E.L., Phillips, E.A., Fixsen, D.L., and Wolf, M.M. *The Teaching-Family Handbook.* Lawrence, Kansas: University of Kansas Printing Service, 1974.

Phillips, E.L., Phillips, E.A., Wolf, M.M. and Fixsen, D.L. Achievement Place: Development of the elected manager system. *Journal of Applied Behavior Analysis,* 1973, *6,* 541-561.

Presidents' Commission on Law Enforcement and Administration of Justice. Task force report: *Juvenile Delinquency and Youth Crime.* Washington, D.C.: U.S. Government Printing Office, 1967.

Robin, G. Gang member delinquency: Its extent, sequence and typology. *Journal of Criminal Law, Criminology and Police Science,* 1964, *55,* 59-70.

Robins, L.N. *Deviant Children Grown Up.* Williams and Wilkins, 1966.

Sheridan, W.H. Juveniles who commit non-criminal acts—why treat in a correctional system. *Federal Probation,* 1967, *31,* 26-30.

Siegel, S. *Nonparametric Statistics.* Hightstown, N.J.: McGraw-Hill, 1956.

Werner, J.S., Minkin, N., Minkin, B.L., Fixsen, D.L., Phillips, E.L., and Wolf, M.M. Intervention Package: Analysis to prepare juvenile delinquents for encounters with police officers. *Criminal Justice and Behavior,* 1975, *2,* 55-83.

Wolf, M.M., Phillips, E.L., and Fixsen, D.L. *Achievement Place Project Phase II Final Report.* Lawrence, Kansas: University of Kansas Printing Service, 1974.

Wolfensberger, W. The principal of normalization and its implications to psychiatric service. *American Journal of Psychiatry,* 1970, *3,* 291-296.

Wolfgang, M.E., Figlio, R.M., & Sellin, T. *Delinquency in a Birth Cohort.* Chicago, Ill.: University of Chicago Press, 1972.

CHAPTER 8

THE EFFECTS OF BEHAVIOR MODIFI-CATION ON THE ATTITUDES OF DELINQUENTS*†

D. Stanley Eitzen

EDITORIAL COMMENTS

Some may argue that there is no need to document attitude change in behavior therapy but that behavior change is the major (only?) definitive criteria (see Burhart, Behles, & Stumphauzer, Chap. 11). Here, Eitzen suggests that a change in attitude **along with** a change in behavior will increase the probability of a lasting effect and that community agencies find attitude changes **are** important when they look at programs. To this the editor might add an observation on the increased use of "consumer evaluations" in behavioral programs (e.g. Chap. 7).

In this chapter Eitzen presents an independent evaluation of attitude changes in Achievement Place youth. Specifically, he investigated (1) achievement orientation, (2) internal-external locus of control, (3) Machiavellianism (manipulativeness), and (4) self-concept in Achievement Place youth as well as in a group of controls.

Results only seem to make a more compelling case for the Achievement Place model. Contrary to some naive views of behavior modification, these results found some positive changes in attitudes including the Achievement Place boys coming to view **themselves** as the ones in con-

*This project was supported by a grant from NIMH (Center for Studies of Crime and Delinquency) MH20030. My thanks to Mont Wolf, Dean Fixsen, Lonnie Phillips, and Willie Brown for their cooperation on this project.

†Reprinted with permission from *Behavior Research and Therapy,* 1975, *13,* 295-299. (Pergamon Press)

trol rather than being manipulated by others. Further, no evidence was found to support the idea that behavior modification made the youths more manipulative. Elsewhere, the author explores his findings on locus of control (Eitzen, 1974) and self-concept (Eitzen, 1976) in further detail.

ABSTRACT

THIS STUDY INVESTIGATES whether exposure to the rehabilitation techniques of behavior modification changes the attitudes of delinquents so that they more closely approximate the norms of the community. The attitudes of delinquent boys in a community-based home that uses behavior modification principles are contrasted over time with a control group of eighth-grade boys from the same community. The results suggest that the delinquent boys tend to improve dramatically in self-esteem and from externality to internality, actually scoring more favorably in each case than the control group at post-test. They improve also in achievement orientation but they remain below the control group. Finally, the delinquent boys are slightly less Machiavellian than the control group and this did not change across time.

Practitioners in the school of psychology known as *behavior modification* have shown that they can teach the skills deemed appropriate by the society to delinquents, retardates, and disadvantaged school children. The dependent variable for behavior modifiers has been limited, however, to overt behavior. As long as the behavior of a delinquent becomes more socially acceptable, for example, it matters little to them if there is a concomitant shift in attitudes. Whether there is a change in attitudes is an important question, however, for at least two reasons: (1) an attitude change corresponding with a change in behavior will increase the probability of a lasting effect; and (2) such a demonstration will make the case for behavior modification more compelling to community agencies contemplating the direction to take in their efforts to attack a particular social problem. The primary research question, then, for the study reported here is, Does exposure to the rehabilitation techniques of behavior modification change the attitudes of delinquents so that they more closely approximate the norms of the community?

METHODS

The Research Setting

The research setting is a community-based home (Achievement Place) for delinquent boys. It is part of the trend to find alternatives to the inhumane and debilitating conditions of traditional institutional treatment programs for children (Phillps *et al.*, 1973). The following is a description of the program by its orginators:

> Achievement Place is a community-based, family-style, behavior modification, group home treatment program for delinquent youths in Lawrence, Kansas. The goals of Achievement Place are to teach the youths appropriate social skills such as manners and introductions, academic skills such as study and homework behaviors, self-help skills such as meal preparation and personal hygiene, and pre-vocational skills that are thought to be necessary for them to be successful in the community. The youths who come to Achievement Place have been in trouble with the law and have been court adjudicated. They are typically 12-16 years old, in junior high school, and about 2-3 years below grade level on academic achievement tests.
>
> When a youth enters Achievement Place he is introduced to the point system that is used to help motivate the youths to learn new, appropriate behavior. Each youth uses a point card to record his behavior and the number of points he earns and loses. When a youth first enters the program his points are exchanged for privileges each day. After the youth learns the connection between earning points and earning privileges this daily-point-system is extended to a weekly-point-system where he exchanges points for privileges only once a week. Eventually, the point system is faded out to a merit system where no points are given or taken away and all privileges are free. The merit system is the last system a youth must progress through before returning to his natural home. However, almost all youths are on the weekly-point-system for most of their 9-12 month stay at Achievement Place. Because there are nearly unlimited opportunities to earn points most of the youths earn all of the privileges most of the time . . . .
>
> The main emphasis of the program is on *teaching* the youths the appropriate behavior they need to be successful participants in the community. We have found that a community-based group home that keeps the youths in daily contact with their community offers many opportunities to observe and modify deviant behaviors and to teach the youths alternative ways to deal with their parents, teachers, and friends. These behaviors are taught by the professional teaching-parents live at Achievement Place with their 'family' of six to eight

delinquent youths and provide them with 24 hour care and guidance. The teaching-parents also work with the youth's parents and teachers to help solve problems that occur at home and at school (Fixsen *et al.,* 1973).

The Achievement Place program has proven effective in changing behavior of delinquent boys. Research has shown that the boys improved in their classroom behavior (Bailey *et al.,* 1970), improved their grammar, punctuality, room cleanliness, reduced aggressive verbal behavior (Phillips, 1968; Phillips *et al.,* 1971), and modified their verbal interaction behavior (Timbers *et al.,* 1971).

The evaluation of the overall effectiveness of the Achievement Place program has begun and the preliminary data are supportive. The data include measures of police and court contacts, recidivism, and grades and school attendance. Information on these variables was obtained from 18 Achievement Place youths and 19 youths committed to Kansas Boys School (an institution for about 250 delinquent boys). All 37 youths were from the same community and had been released from treatment for at least 1 year at the time of data collection. The data show that:

(1) Two years after treatment 47 percent of both Boys School youth were placed in a state institution but only 22 percent of the Achievement Place youths were re-institutionalized.

(2) Fifty-six percent of Achievement Place youths were attending school, while 33 percent of Boys School youths were.

(3) There was no difference in the mean number of police and court contacts per year for the two groups.

The Instrument

A questionnaire was devised which included scales of achievement orientation, internal-external attitudes, Machiavellianism, and self-esteem. The questionnaire was administered to each boy at the beginning of his stay in Achievement Place, after 4 months, after 9 months, and at the completion of his stay. The findings reported in this paper come from 21 boys, six of whom were tested only in the during and/or post-test phases because the project was begun after their stay was underway at least 3 months. Two of the boys in the sample are recent arrivals to Achievement Place and therefore have only taken the initial administration of the questionnaire.

The Comparison Group

In order to assess whether the Achievement Place experience brings the attitudes of former delinquent boys in line with average boys, all eighth-grade boys from a Lawrence junior high school were given the same questionnaire. Eighth graders were selected because the average age of Achievement Place boys is 13 years. The junior high school chosen was in the school district from which most families of Achievement Place youngsters live.

THE FINDINGS

Achievement Orientation

Presumably, delinquent boys will be poorly motivated for achievement. This may result from their lack of success in school, their low social standing, the self-fulfilling prophecy resulting from the labels ascribed to them by significant others, or the lack of successful role models (especially parents). With regard to the latter point, research has shown that boys in homes where the father is absent tend to be (1) low in self-esteem and (2) poorly motivated for achievement (Bronfenbrenner, 1967). Experience in Achievement Place may alter this lack of motivation since the teaching-parents provide a stable environment and strong adult role models. Moreover, the teaching-parents teach social skills, school skills, and most importantly, provide a consistent system that rewards performance (achievement rather than ascription).

An eight-item achievement orientation scale devised by Fred Strodtbeck was used (1958). The results for achievement orientation and the other attitudinal scales are reported in Table 8-I. The data on achievement orientation show that the boys from Achievement Place enter relatively low on the scale (the difference between the means of the entering group and the control group is significant at the 0.05 level). The scores tend to increase in achievement orientation over time but as a group they remain below the mean of the control group.

TABLE 8-I

COMPARISON OF ACHIEVEMENT PLACE BOYS WITH A CONTROL GROUP
ON SELECTED ATTITUDE SCALES

Attitude dimension	Pre-test		4		9		Post-test		Control	
	$\overline{X}$	N	$\overline{X}$	N	$\overline{X}$	N	$\overline{X}$	N	$\overline{X}$	N
Achievement orientation*	4.47	(15)	4.63	(16)	4.93	(14)	4.80	(16)	5.33	(82)
Internal–external†	8.53	(15)	6.50	(16)	6.39	(14)	5.38‡	(16)	7.48	(82)
Machiavellianism§	92.93	(15)	92.25	(16)	92.43	(13)	92.50	(16)	94.24	(82)
Self-concept‖	37.47	(15)	27.00¶	(16)	25.36**	(14)	22.50††	(16)	30.90§§	(82)

*The higher the mean, the greater the achievement orientation (possible range of scores, 0–8).

†The higher the mean, the more external (possible range of scores, 0–21).

‡The difference between the mean score for the post-test and the pre-test is significant at the 0.01 level.

§The higher the mean, the more Machiavellianism (possible range of scores, 60–140).

‖The higher the mean, the lower the self-esteem (possible range of scores, 10–70).

¶The difference between the means for this category and the pre-test is significant at the 0.02 level.

**The difference between the means for this category and the pre-test is significant at the 0.01 level.

††The difference between the means for this category and the pre-test is significant at the 0.01 level.

§§The difference between the means for the control group and the pre-test is significant at the 0.01 level. So, too, are the means for the control group and the post-test.

Internal-External Attitudes

Previous research has shown that lower-class children and delinquents tend to be externals (i.e., they believe that things happen to them rather than their having any control over their own destinies) (Rotter, 1971). Rotter has suggested that rewarding a behavior strengthens an expectancy that the behavior will produce future rewards (1966). Thus, it would be expected that the external attitudes of delinquents should become more internal in a setting where behavior modification principles are consistently applied.

A children's version of Rotter's internal-external scale was used in this research (Nowicki and Strickland, 1973). This scale is for persons in grade 7 through 12 and is readable at the fifth grade level. The data in Table 8-1 for this scale are impressive in their support for the Achievement Place experience. Upon entering the program, the delinquent boys, as expected, tended to be externals, but by the time they left, the average score had dropped below the mean of the control group in the internal direction. The difference between the means of the entering group and the post-test group is significant at the 0.01 level. Examined another way, 72 percent of the boys became more internal during their stay in Achievement Place. A clear implication of this is that a person within a consistent behavior modification milieu, where his actions consistently receive appropriate credits or debits, tends to develop a feeling that he is the master of his fate.

Machiavellianism

A 20-item Machiavellian scale for children developed by Susan Nachamie was incorporated in the questionnaire (Christie, 1970). This scale was included because some critics have speculated that children in a behavior modification setting may become more manipulative and deceptive in their own social relationships since they have been the objects of manipulation by powerful others.

The data on Machiavellianism from Table 8-I show that the Achievement Place experience does not lead to greater Machiavellian attitudes among the boys. As a group they entered Achievement Place with a mean slightly less Machiavellian than the control group and they remain remarkably consistent across time.

Self-Concept

Albert K. Cohen has argued that the delinquent gang permits working-class boys to recoup self-esteem lost through defeat in middle-class institutions (1956). If this is the case, then delinquents in a behavior modification setting should gain in self-esteem because they (1) succeed in the token economy, (2) learn the skills that pay off in social relationships, (3) improve in skills useful for school, and (4) change from socially unacceptable to socially acceptable behavior.

To determine the degree of self-esteem a semantic differential scale devised by Swartz and Tangri (1965; 1967) was included in the questionnaire. With this method, the respondent was asked to rate himself on each of ten sets of bi-polar adjectives (e.g. I am: good . . . bad; useful . . . useless). The data on self-concept found in Table 8-I demonstrate overwhelmingly that the Achievement Place experience is conducive to a good self-concept. As expected, the mean score of the entering group was significantly more negative in self-esteem $(p < 0.01)$ than the control group mean. The greater the length of stay in Achievement Place, however, the more positive the self-concept. The post-test group mean was not only significantly different from the pre-test mean $(p < 0.01)$ but those completing the program also differed significantly from the control group, this time in the positive direction $(p < 0.01)$. When the data were analyzed across time for each boy, we find that 88 percent of the boys improved in self-concept. Examined another way, 80 percent of the boys entering Achievement Place were *above* the control group mean (i.e. had a more negative self-concept), while 75 percent of the boys at the post-test administration of the qeustionnaire were now *below* the control group mean $(p < 0.01)$. Clearly, the longer the stay at Achievement Place, the better the self-concept.

Summary

The findings reported here are impressive in their support of the Achievement Place experience. Accompanying the behavioral changes of these delinquent boys, are positive shifts in attitudes. The greatest shifts in attitudes were from poor to good self-esteem and from externality to internality. Not only were these changes more favorable over time, but they were dramatic—from much more negative than the control group at the beginning to much more favorable than the control group at the post-test.

No support was found for a behavior modification milieu making youngsters more Machiavellian. This "no-difference" finding is in fact a favorable one for this technique, since it negates the criticism often charged that the objects of behavior modification will become more manipulative in their social relationships as a consequence of their being manipulated.

In sum, the data reported here provide support for positive attitude change accompanying positive behavioral change in formerly delinquent adolescents. An important question is as yet unanswered, however. Are these positive attitudinal changes a function of the treatment model or the result of placing troubled boys in a stable environment with caring "parents." The next phase of the research will be a five-year study to answer this question. The sample will be enlarged to delinquent youngsters, both male and female, who reside in a large number of community-based, small treatment centers that use a variety of treatment philosophies.

REFERENCES

Editorial Comments

Eitzen, D.S. Impact of behavior modification techniques on locus of control of delinquent boys. *Psychological Reports,* 1974, *35,* 1317-1318.

Eitzen, D.S. The self-concept of delinquents in a behavior modification treatment program. *The Journal of Social Psychology,* 1976, *99,* 203-206.

Text

Bailey, J.S., Phillips, E.L., Phillips, E.A., Fixsen, D.L., and Wolf, M.M. (1970) Home-based reinforcement and the modification of pre-delinquents' classroom behavior. *J. Appl. Behav. Anal. 3,* 223-233.

Bronfenbrenner, U. (1967) The split level family. *Sat. Review,* October 7, 60-66.

Christie, R. (1970) Some correlates of Machiavellianism. In: *Studies in Machiavellianism* (Eds. Christie, R. and Geis, F.L.) 326-338, Academic Press, New York.

Cohen, A.K. (1956) Delinquent Boys. Free Press, Glencoe, Illinois.

Fixsen, D.L., Phillips, E.L., and Wolf, M.M. (1973) The teaching-family model: an example of mission-oriented research. Paper presented at the American Psychological Association, Montreal, Canada (September).

Nowicki, S., Jr. and Strickland, B.R. (1973) A locus of control scale for children. *J. Consult. Clin. Psychol. 40,* 148-154.

Phillips, E.L. (1968) Achievement place: token reinforcement procedures in a home-style rehabilitation setting for "pre-delinquent" boys. *J. Appl. Behav. Anal.* 213-223.

Phillips, E.L., Phillips, E.A., Fixsen, D.L., and Wolf, M.M. (1973) Behavior shaping works for delinquents. *Psychol. Today 7,* 75-59.

Rotter, J.B. (1966) Generalized expectations for internal versus external control of reinforcement. *Psychol. Monogr.: Gen and Applied* 80, whole No. 609.

Rotter, J.B. (1971) External control and internal control. *Psychol. Today* *5,* 37-42, 58-59.

Schwartz, M. and Tangri, S.S. (1965) A note of self-concept as an insulator against delinquency. *Amer. Sociol. Review 30,* 922-926.

Strodtbeck, F. (1958) Family orientation, values, and achievement. In: *Talent and Society* (Eds. McClelland et al.), *135-194.* D. Van Nostrand Co., New York.

Tangri, S.S. and Schwartz, M. (1967) Delinquency and the self-concept variable. *J. Crim. Law, Criminol, and Police Science 58,* 182-190.

Timbers, G.D., Phillips, E.L., Fixsen, D.L., and Wolf, M.M. (1971) Modification of the verbal interaction behavior of a pre-delinquent youth. Paper presented at the American Psychological Association, Washington, D.C. (September).

CHAPTER 9

LEARNING HOUSE: HELPING TROUBLED CHILDREN AND THEIR PARENTS CHANGE THEMSELVES

KATHERINE E. THORESEN, CARL E. THORESEN, STANLEY B. KLEIN, CURTIS S. WILBUR, JANE F. BECKER-HAVEN AND WILLIAM G. HAVEN*

EDITORIAL COMMENTS

In this original chapter the reader is introduced to Learning House of Palo Alto, California, a striking alternative group home model for elementary age problem children. While Learning House is undoubtedly a group effort (as seen by the multiple authorship and acknowledged input from others), Carl Thoresen's influence is seen in every phase of this impressive program in the emphasis on developing self-control (Thoresen

*Katherine E. Thoresen is Academic Skills Coordinator at Learning House; Carl E. Thoresen is Executive Director as well as Professor of Education and Psychology, Stanford University; Stanley B. Klein is Observation Systems - Assessment Coordinator; Curtis S. Wilbur is a former teaching parent and Program Coordinator; Jane F. Becker-Haven is formerly a teaching parent and Program Coordinator; and William G. Haven is a former teaching parent and current Program Coordinator. We are indebted to Brian T. Yates in helping to develop many of the procedures described in this chapter. We wish to acknowledge the teaching parents of Learning House, whose efforts made these ideas a reality: Tom and Karen Tobey, Robert and Kate Jeffery, Janis Wilbur, Jerry and Barbara Bradley, Paul and Teri Hanson, Jim and Linda Brown, Alan and Marilyn Silverman, Mike and Lynda Gilgun, Dennis Dow and Leslie Kramer Dow. Preparation of this chapter and support for some of the program developments described were made possible, in part, by the Boys Town Center for the Study of Youth Development at Stanford, the Spencer Foundation, and the Luke B. Hancock Foundation. The opinions expressed or the policies advocated do not necessarily reflect those of Boys Town, the Spencer Foundation, or the Luke B. Hancock Foundation.

& Mahoney, 1974; Mahoney & Thoresen, 1974).

Recognizing the problems of generalization, the staff of Learning House show us their progression of behavioral treatment from a point system to contracting, self-control training, academic skills training, self-rating, parent counseling, and continuing after-care for up to twelve months after children have left Learning House — all carefully planned to insure continued behavior improvement. The goal of the program is to help each child develop self-control and to insure that his or her home and school environment will continue to support this self-control.

As we might expect from this creative group, the chapter is packed with ideas and subprograms (for developing self-control, working with parents and schools) that might be replicated, extended, and utilized in other projects for children and adolescents with behavior problems.

In their conclusion, Thoresen et al. share a number of implications and future directions with us. In the following chapter Yates, Haven and Thoresen provide a thorough cost-effectiveness analysis of Learning House.

THE WORTH of any residential treatment program must be judged in large part on its ability to help clients acquire those skills necessary to control their own actions. Although behaviorally oriented programs have been effective in altering a great variety of behaviors in the short run, the evidence for the maintenance of these changes in the long run has been somewhat discouraging (cf. Bandura, 1977; Goldfried & Davison, 1976; Mahoney, 1974). Understandably, therapeutic gains cannot necessarily be expected to last and to generalize to other settings once the specific conditions influencing these gains have been removed. Teaching a child, for example, any number of social, educational, and self-care skills in a residential setting is of limited value unless these behaviors can be continued by the child after returning to his or her natural home and community setting. The current surge of theoretical and clinical interest in behavioral self-control processes has been prompted by the very practical problems of how to promote better maintenance and generalization of positive changes (cf. Kanfer, 1976; Karoly, 1977; Mahoney, 1976; Mahoney & Arnhoff, in press; Thoresen & Coates, 1976; Thoresen & Coates, in press; Thoresen & Mahoney, 1974).

At Learning House, a residential facility for elementary school age children, the maintenance and generalization of behavior change are major concerns. Continued contact with children and their families involved in the program over the past five years has provided the kind of information needed to assess and redesign treatment strategies. Each success and each failure have pointed out the strengths and weaknesses of the program. This chapter provides an introductory description of Learning House as it is today, emphasizing some of the things we have learned from past experience and some ideas for future directions. The steps of the Learning House program are presented as the child and his family would typically experience them, beginning with the point system and moving through contracting for target behaviors, individualized self-control training, academic skills training, self-rating, and continuing care phases of treatment.

THE BEGINNING OF CHANGE

The first step toward self-management is to learn new behaviors and to change problematic ones. Children are usually referred by local agencies, such as social services or juvenile probation, because of their inappropriate behavior in the community—arson, stealing, fighting, truancy and/or the family's inability to manage the child's behavior at home—violent tantrums, refusal to go to school, and other destructive or disruptive actions. Most referral families have experienced failure with other therapy attempts. The children typically come with an incorrigible, "out of control" label: out of control of their parents, their teachers, and their community.

How does one work with these children? Where does one begin? Viewing the genesis of many of these problems as poor interaction patterns in the family, Learning House proceeds as a family-style treatment program. There is a strong emphasis on training and counseling for the parents while their children are in residency. Heavy stress is placed on providing each child with a highly predictable, consistent, and positive environment. From the first day the child begins to learn that what happens is in large part a function of what he does ("if-then" relationships). Two sets of "teaching parents," specially trained married couples, live with the children on an alternate week basis; they serve as surrogate mother and father as well as treatment administrators for up to six elementary school age boys and girls (ages 6-13). No dichotomy exists between general residential care and specific treatment; learning the necessary personal, social, and academic skills for successful living in the family, school, and community is a twenty-four-hour-a-day process.*

THE POINT PHASE. When a child first arrives at Learning House, he is introduced to a highly structured environment. A comprehensive point system (token economy) helps define appropriate and inappropriate behaviors. The child quickly learns that behaviors have clearly stated, consistent consequences. The teaching parents act as participant observers of the child's day. They tally the frequency of positive and negative behaviors while verbally labeling the behavior for the child (see Fig. 9-1). Positive actions receive social support and praise ("Thanks for *helping* set the table, Bob. You did a fine job." or "Jim, I noticed that you got right to your homework. That's *good planning*.") Negative actions are identified; if they persist, teaching parents initiate a variety of logical consequences to help the child learn more appropriate behaviors ("That's *teasing*, Anne," or "You two are *arguing*. Let's try a different way. I'll role-play with you.") Brief social isolation helps break a chain of inappropriate behavior ("Mike, you're *off task*. Have a seat on Quiet Chair and think what you need to do to finish your job.") These interactions help the child develop the ability to observe and assess his own actions—basic skills for self-management. At the end of the day the teaching parents' observations provide a summary of each child's performance. The net points total is translated into the following day's privileges (see Fig. 9-2). Teaching parents' observations

---

*Most residential treatment programs and group homes operate on a "special treatment time" model, where a therapist, e.g. social worker, psychiatrist or psychologist, talks with the child on a one-to-one or small-group basis, often for less than one hour weekly.

NAME   DATE

PRIVILEGES					
BEDTIMES					
APPEARANCE/HYG					
COMPLIMENT					
COOPERATIVE					
HELPFUL					
HONEST					
ASSERTIVE					
ON-TASK					
P.A.I.					
P.P.I.					
POLITE					
GOOD ATTITUDE					
POS. SELF-TALK					
SELF-CONTROL					
GOOD PLANNING					
SHARING					
SPORTSMANSHIP					
THOUGHTFUL					
VOLUNTEER					
SCHOOL					
STUDY					
TUTOR					
WORK					

Figure 9-1a.   Positive behaviors.

	NAME				DATE		
APPEARANCE/HYG							
MANNERS							
CARELESS							
SLOPPY							
WASTEFUL							
FORGETFUL							
HELPLESS							
IMPROPER PERMISS							
INTERRUPTING							
LATE							
NONCOOPERATIVE							
NOT LISTENING							
OFF-TASK							
PESTERING							
ARGUE BACKTALK COMPLAIN							
BABYTALK WHINE							
INAPP. TALK							
LOUD							
OBNOXIOUS							
TEASE							
THEATRICAL							
ZINGER							
DANGEROUS							
DESTRUCTIVE							
HIT/THREATEN							
ROUGHHOUSE							
MANIPULATION/LIE							
MAJOR DISOBEDIENCE							
WARNINGS							
QUIET CHAIR							
TIME OUT							

Figure 9-1b.   Negative behaviors

Date	Name	Name	Name	Name	Name	Name
Mon.						
Tues.						
Wed.						
Thurs.						
Fri.						
Sat.						
Sun.						

POINTS/ PRIVILEGES EXCHANGE:

Points earned today	Points System	Contracting System
25,000 or more	—	Off- Grounds plus below
20,000 or more	—	Bikes plus below
15,000 or more	Basics, Snack, TV	Basics, Snack, TV
12-15,000	Basics, Snack	Basics, Snack
9-12,000	Basics	Basics
2- 9,000	1 work restriction, then Basics	1 work restriction, then Basics
2,000 or less	2 work restrictions, then Basics	2 work restrictions, then Basics
- 5,000 or less	Read, Write, Work or Sit (Earn Time Off)	Read, Write, Work or Sit (Earn Time Off)
-15,000 or less	Read, Write, Work or Sit, Subsystems	Read, Write, Work or Sit, Subsystems

ADDITIONAL PRIVILEGES:

Points System: Contract for special privileges available once per week. Criterion: cumulative point total.

Contracting System: Contract for special privilege, including extra allowance, money special, extra bedtime. Criterion: 4 of last 5 days at Learning House acceptable in terms of frequency of target behavior.

Figure 9-2. Weekly progress summary.

form a continuous record of each child's progress.*

Another measure of progress is provided by nonparticipant observers. They use an interactive observation system which gives insight into the behavior of the child and those interacting with

---

*The particular positive and negative categories on the point card have changed over the years. Initially the point system used at Achievement Place was used; the specific categories were changed to fit the types of problems experienced by elementary school age children as well as social and cultural factors characteristic of the San Francisco Bay Area.

him not only at Learning House but at school and during home visits as well. In this way multiple measures and methods are available on the behaviors of each child as well as on teaching parents, classroom teachers, tutors, natural parents, and siblings.

There are several advantages to using a structured point system in the beginning of treatment: it provides the child with a consistent and predictable environment plus direct encouragement for fairly rapid change. This system has proven to be an efficient way to bring inappropriate behaviors under some control so that training geared toward more permanent and positive long-term goals can be initiated.

CONTRACTING FOR CHANGE

Changes encouraged by a highly structured contingency procedure, although useful in the beginning stages of treatment, often have poor transfer to more noncontingent environments, such as the child's natural home and school. When a child's "thoughtfuls," "cooperatives," or "assertives" go unnoticed in the real world they often fade and old patterns return. Since points evaluate the day on an overall basis (total points earned and points lost), it is possible to have "successful" days while continuing to display problem behaviors. The goal is not to encourage children to earn large numbers of positive points by insincerely engaging in point-getting actions to stay ahead of the game. Rather, our primary concern is to help each child develop skills necessary to manage his own individualized problem behaviors.

Thus, when a child demonstrates the skills to work within defined limits by consistently earning more positive than negative points (typically after four to eight weeks), work is begun on behaviors problematic for that particular child. The child becomes more involved in decisions about his treatment program. Together the child and teaching parents identify a "target behavior." A contract is written specifying the change desired, how the change will be evaluated, and the consequences for meeting or failing to meet the goal. Progress toward the ultimate goal, returning home, is measured in successfully completed contracts. Contracting provides a bridge between the primarily external control of the child's behavior during the points phase and the internalization of that responsibility which the child develops during self-control training.

In Figure 9-3, Fred chose to work on reducing *arguing* with adults and kids. Baseline information (the frequency of arguing

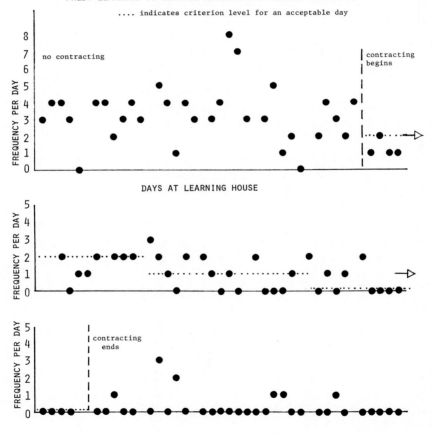

chip 2/77

Figure 9-3a.

CONTRACT

BETWEEN: (1) _____FRED_____ (ME)

                (2) ___Chip & Jane___ (THEM)

AGREEMENT: (1) __FRED__ AGREES _TO KEEP HIS_

ARGUING DOWN TO NOT MORE THAN 2 TIMES A DAY

WITH KIDS OR ADULTS FOR THE NEXT 4 OUT OF 5 DAYS.

REWARD, IF CONTRACT FULFILLED: _INVITE GEORGE TO_

DINNER.

GIVE UP, IF CONTRACT NOT FULFILLED: _DO AN EXTRA_

WORK RESTRICTION .

THIS CONTRACT BEGINS **MARCH 10TH** AND ENDS **MARCH 14TH.**

        SIGNED: _____FRED_____ (ME)

                ___Chip & Jane___ (THEM)

Figure 9-3b.

behavior *before* the agreement) was taken from teaching parent and nonparticipant observer records kept during his initial weeks at Learning House. In Figure 9-3 one of the contracts is presented; in this one he made an agreement with the teaching parents (Chip and Jane) covering a five-day period. Through successive brief contract periods, Fred demonstrated increasing self-control of his arguing. Once the goal of the contracting was achieved (most days with no arguing), Fred began contracting on another behavior that was a problem for him. The follow-up information on Fred's arguing suggested that he was able to maintain progress on arguing without additional contractual support.   Undoubtedly, by arguing less, Fred increased the positive interaction he had with peers and adults, a natural consequence of his self-controlling action.

SELF-CONTROL TRAINING

The major goal of the Learning House program is to teach families the skills necessary for solving problems effectively on their own.   To this end, training in self-management has become the heart of the residential treatment as well as the postresidential support program called Continuing Care (to be described later). A specific training program has been developed in the area of self-management of social skills (Wilbur, 1976) .

The training consists of a structured sequence of sessions (see Fig. 9-4) which teach children how to (1) increase *Commitment* to change, (2) develop *Awareness* of the cues and consequences associated with certain behaviors, (3) *Rearrange* thoughts, as well as social and physical surroundings to help bring about desired changes, and (4) *Evaluate* self-standards and utilize appropriate consequences to encourage progress.*

At first, self-control training concentrates on the acquisition of a desired social behavior.   Many times a child may not have learned the skills necessary to act appropriately.   He or she is put in a difficult position when asked to "control" one behavior or display another which has not yet been acquired.   For example, an uncooperative child may not know *how* to be cooperative or a physically abusive youngster may not know *how* to be assertive without using physical force.   Unfortunately, much of the work in using self-control methods with children—mostly self-reinforcement techniques—has failed to consider this point (Thoresen & Wilbur, 1976) .

Beginning training stresses teaching the desired response, such as cooperative responses.   The labeling of behavior begun during the point phase aids the child in identifying which of his behaviors constitutes a "cooperative" response.   The trainer demonstrates a

---

*A working model of self-control has been described by Thoresen and Coates (1976) and Thoresen and Ewart (1976).

Area	Skill
Commitment	1. Review reasons why self-control helpful
	2. Positive incentives to encourage the application of self-control skills
	3. Child perceiving himself as the "kind of person who can use self-control" through teaching another child the skills he has learned
	4. Review progress with peers and teaching parents during family meeting
	5. List positive consequences of demonstrating self-control
Awareness	1. Recognize target behaviors through role-playing and videotape feedback
	2. Count target behaviors in wrist counters
	3. Rate daily performance on target behaviors and compare with teaching parents' rating
Rearranging the Environment	
1. Cognitive	1. Self-instruction training
	2. Problem-solving training
2. Social	1. Teaching self-control skills to another child
	2. Discussing progress with peers and adults
3. Physical	1. Conspicuous display of charts indicating progress
	2. "Cue" card and signs to remind oneself of daily goals, use of self-instructions
Evaluation of Standards Consequences	1. Set daily goals for target behavior (contracts)
	2. Self-administer contingent consequences for completing contracts
	3. Uhe self-rating of daily performance to earn privileges

Figure 9-4.   Outline of self-control training.

wide range of cooperative behavior and evaluates each of his own performances aloud, e.g. "right on," "good going," "I could do better." Then the child rehearses (role-plays) similar behavior, using examples of actual events from home, school, or Learning House whenever possible. His performance is often videotaped, and the trainer and child immediately review and talk about the role-play and self-evaluation. Rehearsals continue until both child and trainer are satisfied.

To encourage the child to actually use his newly acquired

skills, a short "homework" assignment is completed each evening when the child's day is reviewed with the teaching parent. In Figure 9-5 (an assignment used midway in the sequence) Billy had a chance to report his use of a new skill and how it made him feel. He compared his count of the times he used the skill with the teaching parents' record. Finally, he anticipated a potential problem situation and considered alternative ways of solving it.

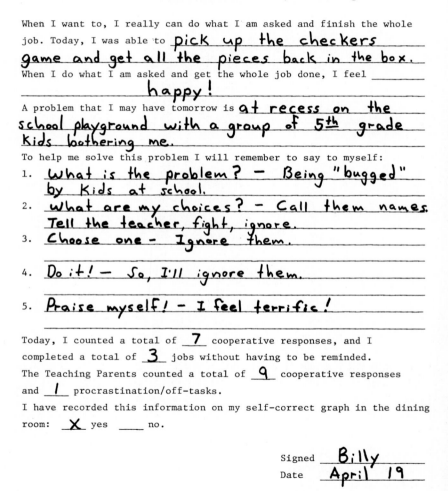

When I want to, I really can do what I am asked and finish the whole job. Today, I was able to **pick up the checkers game and get all the pieces back in the box.**
When I do what I am asked and get the whole job done, I feel **happy!**
A problem that I may have tomorrow is **at recess on the school playground with a group of 5th grade kids bothering me.**
To help me solve this problem I will remember to say to myself:
1. **What is the problem? — Being "bugged" by kids at school.**
2. **What are my choices? — Call them names. Tell the teacher, fight, ignore.**
3. **Choose one — Ignore them.**
4. **Do it! — So, I'll ignore them.**
5. **Praise myself! — I feel terrific!**

Today, I counted a total of **7** cooperative responses, and I completed a total of **3** jobs without having to be reminded.
The Teaching Parents counted a total of **9** cooperative responses and **1** procrastination/off-tasks.
I have recorded this information on my self-correct graph in the dining room: **X** yes _____ no.

Signed **Billy**
Date **April 19**

Figure 9-5. Learning House self-control training homework.

Performance of self-control skills is supported by the teaching parents, classroom teachers, and other staff members who pay special attention to behaviors that have been practiced during training sessions. Children may also earn points for desired privileges or special awards, such as a "self-control" T-shirt, special decals, or an outing.

Other important incentives contained in the training program include the following: (1) At regular intervals the child talks about his progress with the other Learning House children, school friends, and the staff. The process of openly and publicly discussing what he is trying to do and his successes and problems along the way appears to promote commitment to change. (2) During the maintenance stages of training the child may write contracts for desired rewards contingent upon a self-prescribed level of behavior. (3) Through role-play and modeling the child learns to evaluate himself and to make positive self-statements. The following are some examples of what Learning House children have said using the "I'm the kind of person who. . . ." format:

I'm the kind of person who can do a job and get the whole job done. Today I:

1. weeded the rose garden and raked and bagged weeds
2. got dressed and down to breakfast on time
3. read nineteen pages of *Charlotte's Web*.

I'm the kind of person who can get along well with my friends. Today I:

1. played well with Jerry and Ted at the swimming pool
2. told riddles with Frank after dinner
3. asked Mitch to play basketball at recess.

These commitment and self-evaluation features of training recognize that the success of the program ultimately rests with the child's ability to prompt and encourage himself to use the skills he has learned.*

---

*Much of the work in developing self-instructions and other cognitive restructuring methods at Learning House was done by Jane Becker-Haven.

IMPROVING SCHOOL PERFORMANCE

Learning House children often share a common problem—poor school performance. Both in academic achievement and appropriate classroom behaviors, these children lag behind most of their classmates. Besides home, school is the most important environment for young children and is often the locus of referral problems. The child's successful return to his home and school depends in a large part on reducing these deficits.

All children in the program attend public school. The Palo Alto Unified School District, particularly the highly competent staff at Addison Elementary School, provides excellent classroom instruction and remedial programs. The principal and teachers have been unusually cooperative with the Learning House staff and the staff, in turn, has taken care to strengthen this relationship by providing training in management techniques, extra help in the classroom and on the playground, and a general willingness to assist the school in any way necessary.

However, since most children come to Learning House approximately two years below grade level in reading and mathematics, even the best school program needs supplementary support. Over the years a tutoring program has been developed to reinforce the work accomplished at school and to increase the opportunity for academic success. Beginning as an informal volunteer effort to read to the children on a regular basis, the academic tutoring has continually evolved.

With the help of a grant from the National Science Foundation, an intensive tutoring project was conducted in the summer of 1975 which proved highly successful.* Tables 9-I and 9-II present some results from this initial study. The children receiving daily weekday tutoring for the twelve weeks made substantial and statistically significant improvements in their reading and arithmetic skills when compared to a matched group of peers from the same elementary school (matched and randomly selected) as well as for

*The project was developed by Leslie Chernan. For information, see Chernen, Leslie, *The Development of a Learning Laboratory at a Residential Treatment Center for Preadolescent Delinquents*. Report to National Science Foundation, Department of Psychology, San Jose State University, June 1976.

some previous Learning House residents who did not receive the tutoring.   These results, along with materials and equipment from the research project, provided impetus for the further development of tutoring.

At present, volunteers from the community and nearby colleges

TABLE 9-I

COMPARISON OF EXPERIMENTAL AND CONTROL GROUPS ON STANFORD DIAGNOSTIC TEST

Reading Comprehension
(Grade Equivalents)

LEARNING HOUSE EXPERIMENTAL GROUP

| | | Testings | | | | | Difference |
Grade Level	Subjects	1	2	3	Base	Final	Scores
6	Jane	6.2	4.3	9.0	5.25	9.0	4.75
6	Ken	5.0	4.6	5.8	4.80	5.8	1.00
5	Helen	3.2	3.1	5.1	3.15	5.1	1.95
3	Frank	2.0*	2.1	2.9	2.05	2.9	.85
5	Tom	3.2	2.3	3.9	3.25	3.9	.65
means 5.0		3.92	3.28	5.34	3.700	5.34	1.94

*Below 2.0

LEARNING HOUSE CONTROL GROUP (Former residents)

| | | Testings | | | | | Difference |
Grade Level	Subjects	1	2	3	Base	Final	Scores
3	Peter	3.1	3.0	3.2	3.05	3.2	.15
5	Ray	7.2	6.0	6.9	6.60	6.9	.30
6	Les	8.2	6.0	7.5	7.10	7.5	.40
6	Tom	3.1	3.1	4.5	3.10	4.5	1.40
means 5.0		5.4	4.525	5.525	4.963	5.525	.563

MATCHED CONTROL GROUP (Randomly selected)

| | | Testings | | | | | Difference |
Grade Level	Subjects	1	2	3	Base	Final	Scores
5	Pattie	6.0	5.7	4.6	5.85	4.6	—1.25
6	Mark	3.8	4.6	4.3	4.20	4.3	.10
6	Jim	4.2	4.8	6.9	4.50	6.9	2.40
5	Carl	6.0	5.5	5.8	5.75	5.8	.05
		5.0	5.15	5.40	5.0	5.48	.325

TABLE 9-II

COMPARISON OF EXPERIMENTAL AND CONTROL GROUPS ON
STANFORD DIAGNOSTIC TEST

Arithmetic Conceptualization
(Grade Equivalents)

EXPERIMENTAL GROUP

Grade Level	Subjects	Testings 1	2	3	Base	Final	Difference Scores
6	Jane	2.0	4.2	6.7	3.10	6.70	3.60
6	Ken	6.6	6.7	8.6	6.65	8.60	1.95
5	Helen	2.3	2.5	6.0	2.40	6.00	3.60
3	Frank	2.0*	2.3	4.5	2.15	4.50	2.35
5	Tom	3.3	2.5	6.9	2.90	6.90	4.00
means 5.0		3.24	3.64	6.54	3.44	6.54	3.10

*Below 2.0

LEARNING HOUSE CONTROL GROUP (Former Residents)

Grade Level	Subjects	Testings 1	2	3	Base	Final	Difference Scores
3	Peter	2.0*	1.9	2.7	1.95	2.70	.75
5	Ray	5.3	5.4	6.3	5.35	6.30	.95
6	Les	4.3	4.0	4.8	4.15	4.80	.65
6	Tom	4.5	4.3	5.1	4.40	5.10	.70
		4.025	3.90	4.73	3.96	4.73	.76

*Below 2.0

MATCHED CONTROL GROUP

Grade Level	Subjects	Testings 1	2	3	Base	Final	Difference Scores
5	Pattie	2.9	3.1	3.8	3.0	3.8	.80
6	Mark	3.8	4.5	5.4	4.15	5.4	1.25
6	Jim	6.7	6.0	6.4	6.35	6.4	.05
5	Carl	6.1	5.2	5.6	5.65	5.6	—.05
		4.89	4.70	5.30	4.79	5.3	.51

are trained in the use of materials, teaching techniques, and behavioral management skills by the Academic Skills Coordinator
and teaching parents†. Once trained, a volunteer spends thirty to

†The program to recruit and train tutors, as well as paraprofessional parent
consultants and staff assistants, was conceived and developed by Brian T. Yates.

forty-five minutes working with every child each week, an average of four hours of tutoring per tutor per week. Also, when a child has completed four successful sessions during one week, the tutor and the child plan an educational outing together. These outings range from a hunt for pollywogs to a tour of the Stanford Linear Accelerator; importantly, these special events have proven to be as rewarding for the tutor as for the child.

Continuous assessment of each child's reading and math skills combined with classroom teachers' recommendations provide the basis for planning individual instructional programs. Specific goals are set for each month, and every evening the tutoring session includes activities designed to reach these goals. Anne's teacher, for example, noted that she seemed particularly frustrated during math classes, tearing edges of her paper, frowning, and scribbling. Assessment showed that she understood the concepts involved but was very slow in computation. So the *general* goal for Anne was to increase her speed of computation beginning with the addition process. Her *specific* goal for the first month was to be able to immediately add any number facts with sums up to eighteen. Beginning where she could succeed (she could do sums up to seven automatically), the tutors started to spend a portion of each evening using dice games, number lotto, flashcards, and speed sheets to increase her proficiency. When she could complete a timed test correctly in less than three minutes at a given level, the difficulty was gradually increased until she could have the same success with her target goal. In a similar manner deficits in other basic skill areas are diagnosed and materials and activities designed to present work in the needed skill in small increments of difficulty. An individual assessment system, as contrasted to standardized testing, has made it possible to pinpoint more precisely instructional needs, allowing the child and tutor to see their progress and increase successful experiences.

Academic achievements mean little if the child lacks appropriate social behavior in the classroom. Working in close cooperation with the classroom teachers, the teaching parents develop techniques to deal with school problems and reward appropriate behaviors. These are individualized to both the particular child and the teacher's style of instruction. The most basic technique involves the daily School Note which each child carries to school and the teacher uses to evaluate the child's performance on a variety of behaviors pertinent to that child (See Fig. 9-6). For a change, a note brought home from school tells how *well* a child is doing! The better the day, the greater the praise and privileges

SCHOOL NOTE: NAME _____ DATE _____				
Please rate today's performance:	ALWAYS	MOST OF THE TIME	SOMETIMES	RARELY NEVER
1. ON TIME				
2. COOPERATES ON 1ST REQUEST				
3. ACCEPTABLE PEER INTERACTION				
4. IN-CLASS WORK COMPLETED				
5. HOMEWORK DONE				
6. FOLLOWED CLASS RULES				
7. STAYED ON TASK				
8.				
9.				
10.				

COMMENT/ASSIGNMENT:

_____
Teacher's signature   LH 3/77 wgh

Figure 9-6.

when the child returns to Learning House. The style and content of the School Note is flexible and easily revised to pinpoint problem behaviors as defined by the teacher and the child. Frequent visits by the teaching parents and the regular nonparticipant observation system increase understanding of the classroom interaction.

In the case of problems requiring immediate attention (classroom disruption, playground fights, etc.), the teaching parents can be in the classroom in minutes to assist the classroom teacher or school principal in disciplinary action. If the situation warrants, the child can return to Learning House for a short time (a type of brief contingent exclusion) to continue doing schoolwork.

Most important, however, is the development of the child's ability to control him/herself in the relative absence of special attention or preparations. Self-control training for the child is combined with training the school staff to identify and reward the child's efforts in this direction, e.g. correctly interpreting an abrupt move by the child to a desk at the rear of the class as an attempt to avoid a problem situation and stay on task or allowing a child to quietly "talk to himself" when first learning to use self-instruction. Slowly, through positive consequences for appropriate behavior, consistent discipline, regular tutoring, and increasing self-management, the natural positive consequences of participating in classroom activities make improvement in school performance more probable.

SELF-RATING: GETTING READY TO RETURN HOME

After learning to look more closely at his own behavior and to use his observations to set goals and evaluate progress, the child enters the final phase of residential treatment—self-rating. Point contingencies are no longer used. The child must make qualitative judgments about his own performance on a wide range of social and academic behaviors. Each evening the child and teaching parents review and assess the events of the day. They compare ratings and discuss standards of conduct, responsibilities, and rewards. Privileges for the next day are based on high ratings as well as the accuracy of ratings (See Fig. 9-7 and 9-8). The daily School Note is handled in a similar fashion: the child and the classroom teacher independently rate the child's performance and then compare notes at the end of the school day. As the child prepares to return home, matching ratings with the teaching parents and classroom teacher is reduced to once or twice a week; the child's self-evaluation of his day forms the primary method of determining his privileges. When he has left Learning House this daily self-evaluation fits easily and economically into the home routine.

DAILY SUMMARY

DATE _____

NAME _____

wgh/77

I'M THE KIND OF PERSON WHO: _____.

TODAY, I: _____

_____

Extremely Poor		Poor		So-So		Good		Extremely Good
: :	: :	: :	: :	: :
1	2	3	4	5	6	7	8	9	10

TODAY, MY PERFORMANCE IN MY CONTRACT BEHAVIOR(S) CAN BEST BE
DESCRIBED AS:

1. _____   _____   _____
2. _____   _____   _____
3. _____   _____   _____
4. _____   _____   _____
5. OVERALL, MY DAY WAS: _____   _____

POINTS GAINED _____   POINTS LOST _____   FINAL TOTAL _____

Figure 9-7.

PARENT COUNSELING

No matter how well a child has learned the principles of self-control, it is unrealistic to think that any youngster can return to his old environment and maintain appropriate behavior totally on his own. The child is not autonomous; parents, teachers, and relatives must be prepared to support the child's attempts at managing his own behavior.

While the child is at Learning House the parents attend weekly counseling sessions to develop child and self-management skills. These sessions are performance oriented, providing an opportunity for discussion, modeling, role-playing, and behavioral rehearsal of various child management, self-control, and decision-making strategies. The child's visits home, which gradually increase in

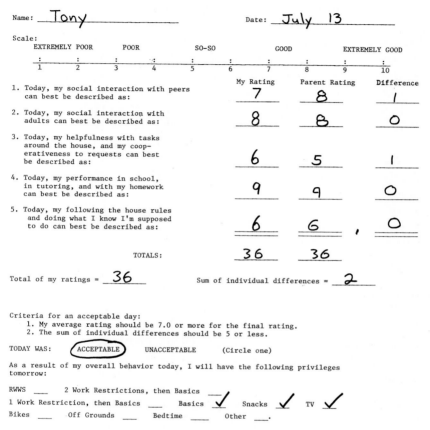

Name: __Tony_____   Date: __July   13_____

Scale:

EXTREMELY POOR	POOR	SO–SO	GOOD	EXTREMELY GOOD

```
 :      :      :      :      :      :      :      :      :
 1      2      3      4      5      6      7      8      9     10
```

	My Rating	Parent Rating	Difference
1. Today, my social interaction with peers can best be described as:	7	8	1
2. Today, my social interaction with adults can best be described as:	8	8	O
3. Today, my helpfulness with tasks around the house, and my cooperativeness to requests can best be described as:	6	5	1
4. Today, my performance in school, in tutoring, and with my homework can best be described as:	9	9	O
5. Today, my following the house rules and doing what I know I'm supposed to do can best be described as:	6	6	O
TOTALS:	36	36	

Total of my ratings = __36__   Sum of individual differences = __2__

Criteria for an acceptable day:
1. My average rating should be 7.0 or more for the final rating.
2. The sum of individual differences should be 5 or less.

TODAY WAS: (ACCEPTABLE)   UNACCEPTABLE   (Circle one)

As a result of my overall behavior today, I will have the following privileges tomorrow:

RWWS ____   2 Work Restrictions, then Basics ____ ✓
1 Work Restriction, then Basics ____   Basics ✓   Snacks ✓   TV ✓
Bikes ____   Off Grounds ____   Bedtime ____   Other ____.

Figure 9-8.   Learning House self-rating sheet.

length and number, maintain family ties and also allow parent and child to practice new skills. It is not unusual for the teaching parents to receive a weekend telephone call from a parent saying, "I tried this and this, now what do I do?" This is a time for both the staff and the family to learn what strategies are helpful and what changes need to be made in both the child's treatment and parent counseling. A parent consultant often visits the home on a periodic basis on weekends to give the family encouragement, suggestions, and on-the-spot demonstration of techniques.

When Learning House was first started, treatment was focused mainly on the child and his problems; over time more attention has been shifted to parent counseling and dealing with the total family environment. Again, these program changes have been based on follow-up data. Performance of former residents has been encouraging. So far, two out of three children (68%) who have completed the program (N = 22) have required no further intervention by any social service agencies. However, almost one half of the families have experienced some significant problems similar to the referral behaviors. The important point is that most families have learned how to cope with such problems successfully. Of the seven families who have had further contact with social service agencies after leaving, five of these families had *not* participated to any degree in the parent counseling program. Failure to participate was typically associated with serious marital problems, including problem drinking and physical abuse along with a strong investment in not assuming any responsibility for the child's behavior.*

The child's return home indicates that both he and his family have made progress in their ability to handle problems as they arise and to interact in a more positive, constructive manner. Such progress is evaluated in part on the basis of nonparticipant observations made of the parents and the child on weekends.

CONTINUING CARE

Even with parent counseling the child almost always changes more rapidly than the home and school settings. Despite the desire for treatment away from home to be as brief as possible, we have learned that returning a child to an environment which remains only slightly changed eventually strengthens deviant patterns once again. Self-control training is most effective when it is coupled with a systematic effort to alter this natural environment in ways that encourage change. This is the goal of the newest facet of the Learning House program: *Continuing Care.*†

*Thomas J. Coates and Craig K. Ewart have offered valuable assistance to the staff with problems concerning parents.

†The Continuing Care program has been made possible by a grant from the Luke B. Hancock Foundation.

Continuing Care provides support to the family during the first twelve months following the child's return home. The greatest emphasis has been during the first six months, since this is the time of greatest challenge (see Fig. 9-9). The return home is a welcomed yet frightening experience. Will the teachers and children remember me as a troublemaker? Has anything really changed? Members of the family are often uncertain how to react to the child's new behavior. They may continue to label him as a "troublemaker . . . unstable" and be overly sensitive to the slightest indication that he still has problems. Many a parent suddenly becomes aware of how convenient it has been not to have had the daily responsibility for his or her child for several months.

A full-time consultant, working about fifteen hours a week with the family and school, is sensitive to this situation and the emotions involved. Stress is placed upon developing realistic expectations for the child and teaching the family to deal with the problems that inevitably arise. For example, it is common for the child to push his parents to the limit to establish boundaries for his behavior at home. The consultant is there to offer help and encouragement to the parents at a time when natural rewards for their efforts are likely to be meager.

The specifics of Continuing Care are tailored to meet the special needs of each family as determined by (1) recommendations of the Learning House staff based on their contact with the family, (2) information relating to academic and in-school social behavior from the school attended while at Learning House, and (3) data collected by nonparticipant observers both while the child was at Learning House and at home and school. This information allows the consultant to develop a treatment plan that avoids reliance on a totally preplanned, inflexible model of care.

These sources of information along with the family's stated goals are also used to establish individualized criteria for success. This not only gives the consultant and the family a clear picture of what needs to be done before the family can "go it alone," but also enhances cooperation by having the family generate and work toward its *own* conception of a smoothly operating household.

A simple problem-solving model called the *Action Plan* is used

Residential Treatment at Learning House (Final Phase)	30-day Home Trial	Continuing Care
Child continues self-management skills training. Residential program continues.	Self-management by child and parent tested; return to Learning House on crisis basis. Child attends school at home. Graduation from Learning House upon successful completion.	*Emphasis on family performance including other siblings. Performance in school and community of all family members considered. Retraining as performance indicates is necessary.
Parent counseling continues, focus on child and self-management, and behavioral analysis skills.	Focus of counseling shifts to problem solving and skill performance. *Family consultant introduced.	*Family consultant assumes all counseling duties; sessions exclusively in child's home. Visits 2-3 times weekly, once weekly to school. Telephone contact to supplement visits. Community contacts established to assist child's return (e.g., Boy/Girl Scouts, athletic leagues).
Nonparticipant observation continues at Learning House and at school, providing independent assessment of child's performance.	*Nonparticipant observation continues, now in the child's home and school.	*Nonparticipant observation continues.
Time frame: residential program averages 9 months excluding 30-day trial.	Time frame: 30-45 days	Time frame: 6 months of support, followed by 6 months to gradually reduce services. Follow-up services to monitor family every 6th month thereafter.

*indicates additions to previous program

Figure 9-9. Integration of Continuing Care in the Learning House treatment program.

for training in family problem solving. It is composed of five parts: (1) Identifying what the problem is; (2) Deciding what one's choices are; (3) Choosing one; (4) Doing it; and (5) Praising oneself. Although introduced to child and parents earlier in treatment, the consultant supervises the use of this strategy during the vulnerable postresidency period; the consultant provides praise, feedback and, when necessary, instruction.

Contracting also forms an important part of developing good parent-child relationships during this time. Parents are expected to make contracts with the child on a weekly basis and to include *all* family members in the contracting process so that the child is not singled out as "the problem."

In the evenings parents and child fill out a daily self-rating form similar to the one used at Learning House. Together they plan the next day's privileges based on their discussion of the day and comparison of ratings. Having to sit down at a particular time every day and talk with each other about the ratings gives the child some attention for his efforts and reminds the parent that the child is actively trying to control himself during the day.

The Continuing Care Consultant needs to monitor the child's progress not only in his home but in other community settings as well. Of these, the school is often the most important. A School Note (Fig. 9-6) allows the consultant to get a good picture of the child's daily performance in the classroom.

Using a School Note serves two important functions. First, the card gives the teacher a concrete, self-generated report on the child's behavior. Teachers who remember the child from before residential treatment are often difficult to work with. Old labels and accompanying expectations of deviant behavior remain, despite the child's performance of new, socially acceptable behavior. Filling out the School Note every day prompts the teacher to observe and to evaluate the child on the very categories he or she has determined to be necessary for smooth classroom functioning. This feedback helps the teacher evaluate the child in light of current, not remembered, performance. Secondly, the note involves the parent directly with the school. The teacher has a means to inform the parent daily of his child's classroom performance. The parent, in turn, makes use of this information to work out contracts with the child to maintain appropriate behavior or modify areas that warrant improvement, thus reinforcing the teacher's efforts in filling out the note.

The Continuing Care program represents an ambitious attempt to enhance therapeutic gains made within residency by attacking the major obstacles to posttreatment generalization. The benefits are threefold. First, the child and family have greater likelihood of success in maintaining the skills needed to deal effectively with future problems. Second, future costs to the county social services are reduced to the extent that the family handles its own problems and does not create problems for the community. Finally, the shortened stay in residence reduces the financial costs of the county and the strain on family ties incurred by separation.

SOME FUTURE IMPLICATIONS

We have learned a great deal in trying to help disturbed children and their troubled parents bring about meaningful change. We have learned that the best of intentions often contradict everyday actions, that old expectations constantly disrupt new habits, and that social environments have a way of regularly discouraging small but positive changes. The traditional methods of psychological and neurological diagnosis, abnormal labeling, and various "nonspecific" treatments appear to us as hopelessly inadequate. We have learned firsthand of the "evils" of misdiagnosis and psychological labeling, how so often the child who is assessed as "prepsychotic . . . borderline brain damaged, suffering from an incipient character disorder" and labeled as "aggressive, hyperactive, dyslexic . . . . someone who obviously must be placed in a special classroom or excluded from public school" turns out to be suffering from a long learning history of bad experience. The child has a record of prolonged neglect, consistent inconsistency, and sometimes harsh punishment. Perhaps what we have come to understand more than anything is that children live up to their past learning and, to a lesser extent, to their labels—they do what they have experienced and what others "expect" them to do.

Fortunately we have experienced the great pleasure of seeing a child learn how to read, learn how to talk and listen more effectively, and, importantly, learn how to make a start at solving his own problems, making his own decisions, and managing his own actions. It is this powerful combination of skills in personal problem-solving, decision-making, and self-management which we believe is the mark of lasting success.

In cases where we have failed with a child—really with the child's family—it has been because we lacked leverage. We have lacked the power to lift the parents out of their routine ways of thinking, believing, and acting. We have failed when we have kept a child in residence too long, so much so that the child's positive changes have begun to decline and the parents have lost much of that crucial sense of responsibility and respect in themselves—the belief that they can succeed with their child. We have failed because we lacked specific enough information about this particular child and his or her own family.

To say we have succeeded or failed is of course a very relative thing. By conventional standards Learning House has been quite successful. Our recidivism rate in terms of a child requiring further institutional treatment of any kind has been encouraging (about 30%). But when we take a good hard look at success, we come away feeling that we have only just started. For us, several implications naturally follow from our experiences: (1) The major emphasis on treating the child as the client or patient should be reduced with primary attention given to the family as the focus of treatment. (2) Much more detailed *pretreatment* assessments of various types (external observations, self-report measures, structured interviews, participant observations) are needed of the child and the parents in the setting of their home, their school, and their neighborhood. (3) The length of residetnial treatment should be reduced, and the concept of continuing care—working with the neighborhood. (3) The length of residential treatment should be be expanded. (4) Use of the standardized token economy for all children should be de-emphasized, and a major curriculum for children and their parents in problem solving, decision making, and self-management should be developed and used as the primary treatment program. (5) Major efforts are needed to treat the family as a unit *before* the child is removed from the home and placed in residential treatment (intensive family intervention) .

We offer these implications as possibilities or as hypotheses worthy of controlled evaluation. They seem most reasonable to us, so much so that we are actively working to implement them. Yet they are not without major obstacles and problems. For example, orchestrating a dynamic combination of intensive "in-home" family treatment with the possibility of brief residential care, if needed, along with extended continuing care, tailored to a particular child and family, is no easy feat. Social and legal agencies, such as juvenile courts, probation, and social services agencies do not readily conceptualize services in this way. The child, for example, is often designated as in or out of the home. That is, he or she is either at home with the parents *or* in residential treatment. The notion of an individualized program combining family, residential, and continuing care is difficult to implement within existing agency categories—difficult but not impossible.

In coming years we hope to continue to learn about more effective ways of helping troubled children and their families. After five years we feel sufficiently challenged and yet encouraged to try out and carefully evaluate some new ways of working with children and parents along with their teachers and concerned agency personnel. We hope others will try to do so as well.

REFERENCES

Editorial Comments

Mahoney, M.J., & Thoresen, C.E.: *Self-control: Power to the Person.* Monterey, CA: Brooks-Cole, 1974.

Thoresen, C.E., & Mahoney, M.J. *Behavioral Self-control.* New York: Holt, 1974.

Text

Bandura, A. *Social Learning Theory.* Englewood Cliffs, NJ: Prentice-Hall, 1977.

Goldfried, M.R., & Davison, G.C. *Clinical Behavior Therapy.* New York: Holt, Rinehart and Winston, 1976.

Kanfer, F.H.   *The Many Faces of Self-Control, or Behavior Modification Changes Its Focus.*   Paper presented at the Eighth International Conference on Behavior Modification, University of Calgary, 1976.

Karoly, P.   Behavioral self-management in children: Concepts, methods, issues, and directions.   In M. Hersen, R.M. Eisler, and P. Miller (Eds.), *Progress in Behavior Modification,* Vol. 5, New York: Academic Press, 1977.

Mahoney, M.J.   *Cognition and Behavior Modification.*   Cambridge, MA: Ballinger, 1974.

Mahoney, M.J., & Arnoff, D.   Cognitive and self-control therapies.   In S. Garfield and A. Bergin, (Eds.).   *Handbook of Psychotherapy and Behavior Change,* New York: Wiley, in press.

Thoresen, C.E., & Coates, T.J.   Behavioral self-control: Some clinical concerns.   In M. Hersen, R. Eisler, and P. Miller (Eds.), *Progress in Behavior Modification,* Vol. 2, New York: Academic Press, 1976.

Thoresen, C.E., and Coates, T.J.   What does it mean to be a behavior therapist?   *The Counseling Psychologist,* Vol. 6, 1978.

Thoresen, C.E., & Mahoney, M.J.   *Behavioral Self-Control.*   New York: Holt, Rinehart & Winston, 1974.

Thoresen, C.E., & Wilbur, C.S.   Some encouraging thoughts about self-reinforcement.   *Journal of Applied Behavior Analysis,* 1976, *9,* 518-520.

Thoresen, C.E., & Ewart, C.K.   Behavioral self-management and career development.   *The Counseling Psychologist,* 1976, *6,* 29-43.

Wilbur, C.S.   *The Evaluation of a Program to Develop Self-Control of Social Skills Among Pre-delinquent Children.*   Unpublished doctoral dissertation, School of Education, Stanford University, 1977.

CHAPTER 10

COST-EFFECTIVENESS ANALYSES AT LEARN-ING HOUSE: HOW MUCH CHANGE FOR HOW MUCH MONEY?*

Brian T. Yates, William G. Haven, and Carl E. Thoresen

EDITORIAL COMMENTS

We hear a lot today about "cost-effectiveness," just as we do about "accountability." To most of us this may simply mean that we must demonstrate the effectiveness of a given program and perhaps show how many dollars it costs per person. These terms have been added to our vocabulary, in part, because of recent cuts in funding and related demands for proof that programs work and at what cost. It is not difficult to show that many programs for delinquents are cost-**in**effective. In general, behavioral programs have fared quite well since they are already data based and do document effects.

However Yates, Haven, and Thoresen take us several steps further in this important, original chapter. They provide a preliminary yet thorough model for cost-effectiveness analysis that should be a welcome tool for many struggling with these very problems. In addition, their model provides sensitive feedback for program evaluation, improvement, and "fine

*We wish to thank Learning House, Inc. of Palo Alto, California, the Stanford Boys Town Center for Youth Development, and the Stanford Center for Research and Development in Teaching for providing assistance in conducting this work. We also appreciate the cooperation of the Addison Elementary School staff in Palo Alto, California, as well as the American University in providing help to prepare the final writing of this chapter. Correspondence regarding this chapter should be directed to: Dr. Brian T. Yates, Department of Psychology, The American University, Nebraska and Massachusetts Avenues, N.W., Washington, D.C. 20016.

tuning" not seen before.

The model is used here to evaluate the cost-effectiveness of Learning House (Chap. 9) in enough detail to demonstrate a breakdown of cost per behavior treated as well as cost-effectiveness for each child ("micro"-cost-effectiveness). A "macro"-cost-effectiveness analysis was then utilized to look at important global outcome measures such as the cost of nonrecidivism. Not only does Learning House "work," but we see here a wealth of data on what these particular effects cost.

Since many chapters in this volume report what their programs cost, it might seem a fair question to ask how these costs and effects compare. Unfortunately, (as seen in this chapter) it is not simply a matter of comparing costs per youth or costs per day. Each program uses somewhat different measures of effectiveness, and many factors go into totaling their individual cost figures. Also, there is a problem in comparing locations with substantially different costs of living and in comparing a 1974 program with one in 1977. It is perhaps more meaningful to utilize this model in evaluating alternative programs in a given community.

MOUNTING DEMANDS for programs that successfully treat problem children, coupled with an almost paradoxical rash of budget cuts for such programs, have brought the term *cost-effectiveness* out of private industry and into the vernacular of behavior therapy. Contributing to the increasing frequency with which one hears "cost-effectiveness" mentioned is the growing realization that only looking at treatment cost or outcome is not enough. The decisions that funding agencies, treatment administrators, and therapists must make in the present fiscal situation involve consideration of cost *and* effectiveness. Faced with diminishing social resources and expanding social demands, we have a *dual* problem: maximizing effectiveness of treatment while minimizing its cost.

Despite general recognition of the importance of something called "cost-effectiveness" (Abelson, 1976; Balcerzak & Siddall, 1974; Bennis, 1966; Cain & Hollister, 1972; Cook, 1966; Elkin, 1969; O'Dell, 1974; O'Leary & Kent, 1973; Tavormina, 1974; Willems, 1974), there is little agreement on what "cost-effectiveness" means. Some psychologists confuse cost-effectiveness analysis, in which effectiveness is measured in typically nonmonetary units, with cost-benefit analysis, in which costs and benefits are measured in the same, often monetary, units (cf. Levin, 1975; Thomas, 1971). Others confuse the analysis of cost-effectiveness, which is usually done on the basis of previously collected data, with the analysis of cost-utility (Krapfl, 1974) which is conducted a priori with probabilistic estimates of cost and utility (cf. Levin, 1975; Thomas, 1971).

Lack of agreement is also found in what cost-effectiveness models should be used for psychological treatment programs (Fox & Kuldau, 1968; Krumboltz, 1974; Carter & Newman, 1974; Yates, 1977a). Current models have received little, if any testing in a treatment setting; those actually implemented are typically more concerned with measuring effectiveness than with assessing costs (Pennypacker, Koenig & Seaver, 1974; Sexton, Merbitz & Penny-packer, 1975). Unfortunately, models used to date have largely ignored the procedures and applications of cost-effectiveness analysis that have been developed and thoroughly tested over decades of routine use by private industry (cf. Ackoff & Rivett, 1963; Ackoff & Sasieni, 1968; Goldman, 1967; Martin & Denison, 1971; Yates, 1976c).

The lack of constructive discussion of how assessing the cost-effectiveness of a treatment program could facilitate the systematic improvement of the program has been a major shortcoming. Presumably a major benefit of a comprehensive analysis of costs and effects should reflect directly on how treatment can be improved.

In this chapter we propose a model of cost-effectiveness analysis and try to show how we tested it in the context of a residential treatment program for problem children. The model is neither original nor perfect; it is a synthesis of other models of cost-effectiveness analysis (especially Levin, 1975) as well as a product of our own experience. We believe that the model is simply a good first approximation to one that could be adopted for widespread use in psychological treatment programs.

A MODEL OF COST-EFFECTIVENESS ANALYSIS

All human endeavors have two things in common: they consume resources and they produce outcomes. At the very least, human activities consume time and yield an outcome of no change. The purpose of cost-effectiveness analysis, in the most general sense, is minimizing the use of resources while maximizing the outcomes of activities. To do this, three basic steps are required: (a) measuring amount of resources consumed, (b) measuring outcomes produced, and (c) integrating information on outcomes produced versus resources consumed to reflect the ratio of "output" to "input."

Social service systems, such as behavioral programs for delinquent children, consume a mixture of resources such as facilities, equipment, materials, people's time, and the services of other programs. The amount and value of resources consumed by the social program are quantified as *cost* and can usually be expressed in common units of dollars and cents. Social service programs also produce outcomes or "results" which can be quantified as *effectiveness*. Although effectiveness cannot be readily expressed in monetary units, other common units usually can be found (Pennypacker, Koenig, & Seaver, 1974). The ways in which the cost and effectiveness of social service programs can be quantified, contrasted, and improved are the primary focus of the present model and are discussed in the following sections.

Levels of Specificity

Data on cost and effectiveness can be collected at different levels of specificity, depending on the purpose of the cost-effectiveness analysis (cf. Katz & Kahn, 1966; Neufeldt, 1974). If the purpose of analysis is to improve a treatment program, data must be collected at a very specific and detailed *micro* level. In order to identify those components of a social service system that are (or are not) performing at desirable ratios of cost to effectiveness, cost and effectiveness should be measured for each component. For example, in our micro-level analysis at Learning House, we measured cost and effectiveness separately for each of twenty behaviors for each child who was in the program.

If the purpose of the analysis is to compare the cost-effectiveness of different treatment programs, then cost and effectiveness data should be collected at a very global, *macro* level. Comparisons between programs must often be conducted by using the "lowest common denominator" of available cost and outcome measures. This is due to the diversity of resources, goals, and empirical sophistication found in different programs. For example in our macro-level analysis of the residential program, cost was measured as the amount of money allocated by a funding agency for each child at Learning House, and effectiveness was measured in terms of recidivism, i.e. after leaving the Learning House program, was the child referred again for treatment?

Perspectives on Cost and Effectiveness

Cost and effectiveness can be measured in different ways. Whether the analysis is being conducted to improve a particular program or to compare different programs, a variety of interest groups may become involved (Hiebert, 1974). Interest groups may have different views on how cost and effectiveness should be measured, and they may argue that their perspective should be adopted. Each of the following four interest groups, for example, could have different opinions on how to assess cost and effectiveness: (a) therapists and program administrators, (b) funding agencies (local, state, or national level), (c) clients, their relatives and associates, and (d) advocacy organizations representing clients or citizens. "Political" problems can be reduced or at least postponed by measuring cost and effectiveness from the perspectives of each interest group (cf. Williams & Evans, 1972). Decisions can be made later about the way in which different perspectives should be weighted in the final analysis.

Perspectives on Cost

Therapists and program administrators are usually concerned with the amount of funds consumed in operation of the program. From this *operations* perspective, cost is measured as the number of dollars entered on the bottom line of the accounting record. This operations cost includes all monetary outlays and depreciation of facilities and equipment. Funding agencies often adopt the operations perspective on costs. Clients, however, are not as concerned with the amount of funds consumed by the program as with the amount of money that they must pay to the program (Born & Davis, 1974). The "private" or *client* perspective on cost may also include foregone earnings, the amount of time required by program activities, and the subjective cost or "hassle" of undergoing treatment. Consumer advocacy organizations often adopt the client perspective on costs; taxpayer organizations typically adopt the operations perspective on costs (cf. Trotter, 1975).

Another perspective that may be adopted in the measurement of costs is the *opportunity* perspective (Bowman, 1966; Conley, Conwell, & Arrill, 1967). The opportunity value of resources consumed by a program is directly related to the benefit that would accrue to society in general if resources consumed by the program were used elsewhere. Thus, the opportunity value cost of a psychological service for delinquent children includes not only the operations cost but also the estimated salary that would have been received from another program by volunteer personnel who donate their services to the program, and the open-market value of donated facilities, equipment, and materials. Also included in the opportunity cost would be tax exemptions and the interest paid on outstanding bonds such as those paying for construction of facilities (Thomas, 1971).

Perspectives on Effectiveness

Therapists and administrators are concerned about their efforts and results; do the outcomes match their expectations of change? Effectiveness measures favored by therapists and administrators involve changes in clients' behaviors relative to treatment goals. The *goal* perspective on effectiveness may also be adopted by clients; some have argued that therapists and clients should always work on a contractual basis with goals clearly stated in terms of specific changes in client behavior (Krumboltz & Thoresen, 1976). The majority of clients, however, seem to want a "positive change" to occur. This *change* perspective is more vague when compared to the previously described *goal* perspective, e.g. "act better" vs. "reduce the frequency of tantrums to less than one per week."

Some agencies and organizations will ask that effectiveness be assessed in terms of how "normal" the client becomes during and after treatment. This *normative* perspective involves goals but it largely avoids the delicate issue of establishing specific goals for each client. Instead, the issue becomes one of defining goals in terms of what constitutes a significant deviation from "normality." We discuss the issue of normality from an empirical view later in this chapter. The many problems of using typical behavior—the norm—as value criteria are beyond the scope of this chapter (see Mischel, 1976; Yates, 1977a).

Variables for Measuring Cost and Effectiveness

It is useful to distinguish between the different types of variables that can be employed in the measurement of cost and effectiveness.

Cost Variables

The variables selected to measure cost of a social service system can be defined in terms of the major "ingredients" of the system (Fanshel & Shinn, 1972; Levin, 1975; Wolins, 1962). Typically, these are (a) personnel, (b) facilities, and (c) equipment and materials.

The personnel cost variable may include the major variables of time and skills given to the service system by therapists, administrators, paraprofessionals, and volunteers. Personnel cost would also include "support" services such as secretaries, accountants, janitors, doctors, and lawyers.

The facilities cost variable is the rent paid for use of space or the mortgage payments and depreciation of buildings used by the service system. Rental or mortgage payments for land, loan payments for or the depreciation of vehicles used by the program, and the depreciation of furniture and fixtures can be included.

The equipment and materials cost variable includes all the other resources consumed by the social service system, e.g. office supplies and equipment, food, utilities, telephone service, insurance, advertising, sundries, and recreation expenses. Of course, different values can be assigned to each cost variable depending on the amounts of each resource consumed. Deciding on the amounts is where the different perspectives cited earlier make a difference. For example, an operations perspective would use different estimates than a combined operations-client perspective or one that also included the opportunities factor.

Effectiveness Variables

The variables that measure cost can be defined in terms of the types of resources consumed by the service system. Unfortunately there are usually no convenient analogues for the definition of effectiveness variables.

If the psychological problem treated by the program is complex, as is often the case with delinquency, the outcome of a program may best be measured in terms of a composite effectiveness index comprised of a number of behaviors (Patterson, Reid, Jones, & Conger, 1975). Effectiveness variables may be defined empirically as those classes of behavior that differentiate problem children from normal children (Johnson & Bolstad, 1973). Alternatively, the effectiveness variables might be defined as those behaviors that have been empirically shown to best predict long-term outcome (recidivism). Effectiveness variables can also be defined as those behaviors of concern to one or more of the interest groups. For any of these purposes, the composite index of effectiveness can be defined in a precise manner as a combination of effectiveness variables, such as behavior frequencies, that are weighted mathematically according to their relative importance (Walker, 1972). These "importance weightings" can be derived from regression analyses of predictor variables or from questionnaires completed by interest groups.

Steps in Using the Model

Levels of specificity, perspectives on measurement, and variables of cost and effectiveness are important considerations in cost-effectiveness analysis. However, these factors do not provide a complete model of how to conduct cost-effectiveness analysis. The final component of the model is a series of steps for the measurement and improvement of cost-effectiveness. These steps are described and illustrated using an example from a residential treatment program.

AN EXAMPLE AT THE MICRO LEVEL: LEARNING HOUSE

Learning House is a family-style residential treatment program for elementary school age problem children located in Palo Alto, California (Tobey & Thoresen, 1976; Russell & Thoresen, 1976; Thoresen, Haven, Wilbur, Klein, & Thoresen, 1978). The context supplied by Learning House provided a test of the feasibility of our model, as well as an opportunity to illustrate its implementation.   In doing so, we acknowledge the temporal nature of the data in that the treatment program has since been altered.   Nevertheless, the analysis is one of the first completed and serves well as a working example.

How Effective is Learning House?

The basic objective of Learning House, agreed upon by all concerned interest groups, is to prevent future occurrences of the problem behaviors that instigated treatment. Unfortunately, the reasons for referral (as recorded in client files) were not readily measurable ("suffers from preschizophrenic tendencies") or occurred seldom (arson) and sometimes were difficult to measure reliably (peer abuse, theft) .

A normative perspective on effectiveness was selected as one way to measure treatment effectiveness on a short-term basis. Given the social-learning orientation of the Learning House staff, it seemed appropriate to measure effectiveness using personal and social behaviors of each child rather than global ratings by therapists or score changes on various personality inventories. Using the normative perspective and behavioral variables, effectiveness was defined (at the micro level) in terms of how closely the behaviors of Learning House children fit the observed frequencies of "normal" children of the same age.

Learning House staff members considered more than eighty different behaviors that fell into one of two classes: (a) *positive* behaviors (those that seemed desirable) and (b) *negative* behaviors (those that seemed undesirable) . After considerable discussion over several meetings and independent rankings of the most important positive and negative behaviors, the staff agreed upon ten positive and ten negative behaviors. Labels for these behaviors, that is, for effectiveness variables, are listed in Table 10-I Operational definitions for each variable were also developed (Yates, 1975).

TABLE 10-I

EFFECTIVENESS VARIABLES OF A RESIDENTIAL TREATMENT PROGRAM FOR BEHAVIORALLY DISTURBED PREADOLESCENTS

Number	Negative Variable	Positive Variable
1	Lying/Cheating/Stealing	Honesty
2	Noncooperative Verbal Response to Adult or Peer Request	Cooperative Verbal Response to Adult or Peer Request
3	Noncooperative Nonverbal Response to Adult or Peer Request	Cooperative Nonverbal Response to Adult or Peer Request
4	Late/Off-Task	On-Time/On-Task
5	Pestering Following Denial	Taking No for an Answer
6	Complaining/Crying/ Bitching to Adults	Complimenting/Thanking/ Smiling to Adults
7	Negative Verbal Interaction with Adults or Peers	Positive Verbal Interaction with Adults or Peers
8	Negative Nonverbal Interaction with Adults or Peers	Positive Nonverbal Interaction with Adults or Peers
9	Playing Alone	Playing with Adults or Peers
10	Improper Manners	Proper Manners

Note. Operational definitions for each effectiveness variable are provided in Yates (1975).

Importance Weightings

During staff discussions, it became apparent that not all behaviors were considered to be equally important. It was decided that the relative importance of each behavior should be incorporated into a composite index of effectiveness that would be formed from the effectiveness variables. Each staff member was asked to independently assign ratings of relative importance using a ten-point scale for each of the twenty behaviors. Agreement was reasonably high; the average standard deviation of ratings was 1.32 (range 0.47 to 2.58). The importance ratings were transformed by Equation 1 to provide an importance weighting, W, for each variable, b, that could be used in calculation of the composite effectiveness index. A weighting W_b that was less than 1.00 indicated that behavior b was considered somewhat less important than most other behaviors, and a weighting greater than 1.00 indicated that the behavior was more important than most.

$$W_{(b)} = [\sum_{i=1}^{m} r_{(i,b)}] \div [\frac{1}{n} \sum_{b=1}^{n} \sum_{i=1}^{m} r_{(i,b)}] \tag{1},$$

where m is the total number of staff members who supplied ratings,
      n is the total number of effectiveness variables, and
      $r_{(i,b)}$ is the rating of importance given by staff member i for effectiveness variable b.

The importance weightings ranged from .41 to 1.30. The similarity of the average importance weighting for positive behaviors ($\overline{W} = .99$) and for negative behaviors ($\overline{W} = 1.01$) indicated that the importance of normalizing each type of behavior was considered equivalent by the staff.

Obtaining Values for Effectiveness Variables

An observation procedure was designed to collect data on the frequencies of the twenty positive and negative behaviors. Each child at Learning House, as well as a randomly selected sample of "normal" children, was observed separately in two-hour sessions. The occurrence of each behavior was recorded in thirty-second time blocks. Only one child was observed per session.

This long observation period, and the repeated number of sessions conducted for each child, was used to provide a more representative sample of the twenty behaviors since some occurred much less frequently than others. Also, the two-hour observation sessions helped reduce the reactivity of observation (cf. Haggard, Hiken, & Isaacs, 1965; Martin, Gelfand, & Hartmann, 1971; Sternberg, Chapman, & Shakow, 1958). To further reduce observation reactivity, the Learning House children were told that observations would not affect the contingencies used at Learning House for "good" and "bad" behavior. Also, having trained observers around using clipboards and stop watches was routine at Learning House.

In order to minimize systematic observer bias (Rosenthal, 1963, 1966), the observers had no previous acquaintance with the children or with Learning House (Yates, 1976b). To further minimize bias, the observers were told nothing about the children in terms of their problems or treatment (cf. O'Leary, Kent, & Kanowitz, 1975; Skindrud, 1973).

Two randomly selected observers each simultaneously and independently collected data for one randomly assigned child. Data for each session were collected by two observers rather than one to improve reliability. In this way, each observer knew that the data would be compared to the records of another observer (Romanczyk, Kent, Diament, & O'Leary, 1973). Observers were repeatedly cautioned to refrain from discussing their data with any other observers; reliability coefficients also were not communicated to the observers at any time (cf. O'Leary & Kent, 1973).

The mean reliability per session was .83 with a range of .75 to .99, using the Pearson product moment correlation coefficient. The value of an effectiveness variable for a particular session was the mean frequency recorded for that behavior by the two observers. A limitation of using an overall measure of reliability, however, is the lack of information provided about the nature of interval by interval agreement. A more complex, yet more informative index of reliability can be calculated in terms of generalizability (Cronbach, Gleser, Nanda, & Rajaratnam, 1972), which approach we are currently pursuing (Coates & Thoresen, 1976).

Observational data on values of effectiveness variables were collected regularly for Learning House children in their natural home setting, in school, and at Learning House. Observational data included in the present analysis were collected during five consecutive eight-week periods; the total time covered was sixty-four weeks. Each of the five periods corresponded to the last eight weeks of an academic quarter (winter 1975, spring 1975, autumn 1975, winter 1976, and spring 1976). Data were not recorded during summer 1975 because observers were not available. The average number of two-hour observation sessions for each child was 4.8 per quarter; the range was from 2 to 9. There were between five and ten observers working per quarter. To further reduce the possibility of systematic bias in observation data, no observer spent more than one quarter collecting data.

Data on the behavior of randomly selected "normal" children, i.e. children who attended public schools and who were not in any form of therapy, were collected by the same observers in those schools attended by the Learning House children. Identical procedures were used in the observation of normal and Learning House children. Unfortunately, observation data on the behavior of normal children were not collected during the final quarter because of a change in school policy.

Quantifying Approximation to Normality

Standardized scores were used to quantify the normative perspective on effectiveness. This measure of effectiveness, E, was calculated each quarter, q, for each effectiveness variable, b, of each child, c. The scores were computed by first finding the difference between the mean frequency of behavior of a Learning House child and the mean frequency of normal children for the same behavior, as shown in Equation 2. This difference was then divided by the standard deviation of the frequencies at which normal children engaged in the behavior. Due to the possibility that apparent changes in effectiveness could be caused by fluctuations in the mean normal frequency or in the standard deviation of normal frequencies, each standardized score used normative data from all quarters.

$$E_{(b,\, c,\, q)} = \frac{k_{(b)}\left[\overline{f}_{(b,\, c,\, q)} - \overline{f}_{(norm,\, b)}\right]}{s_{(norm,\, b)}} \tag{2},$$

where $\overline{f}_{(b,\, c,\, q)}$ is the mean frequency of behavior b for Learning House child c during quarter q,

$\overline{f}_{(norm,\, b)}$ is the mean frequency of behavior b for normal children, averaged over all quarters,

$s_{(norm,\, b)}$ is the standard deviation of the frequencies at which normal children emitted behavior b during all quarters,

$k_{(b)}$ is +1 of behavior b is a positive behavior and is −1 if behavior b is a negative behavior.

The variable $k_{(b)}$ was introduced into Equation 2 so that the effectiveness score $E_{(b, c, q)}$ would be positive if the Learning House child was showing the positive or negative behavior at a frequency that was on the "good side" of normality. That is, Equation 2 is designed so that a positively signed E score indicated that the child emitted a positive behavior more frequently than did normal children, or that the child emitted a negative behavior less frequently than did normal children. Equation 2 is also designed such that a negatively signed E score indicated that the child engaged in a positive behavior less frequently than did normal children, or that the child acted more negatively than normal children. The absolute value of the E scores indicated the number of standard deviations between the mean normative frequency for a behavior and the mean frequency at which Learning House child c emitted the same behavior during quarter q. Thus, the smaller the absolute value of E, the more closely the Learning House child approximated normative behavior.

Mean Effectiveness Values

To provide a general index of how effectively Learning House treated a particular child, the child's effectiveness score for each variable was multiplied by the importance weighting for that variable (see Equation 1), and the weighted scores were averaged. These weighted averages of standard deviation from normality were calculated separately for the positive and negative behaviors of each child and are displayed in Figure 10-1 for each quarter. The lower case letters in Figure 10-1 represent different children. The circles represent mean effectiveness scores for the positive behaviors of a particular child, and the squares represent mean effectiveness scores for the negative behaviors of a particular child. A score of 0.0 indicates that the child was "perfectly normal" in his behavior. The farther a score is from zero in either direction, the more different the child was from normal behavior levels.

Discussion of Micro Effectiveness

Figure 10-1 shows that two different groups or "waves" of children were treated at Learning House during the five-quarter period over which the micro cost-effectiveness analysis was con-

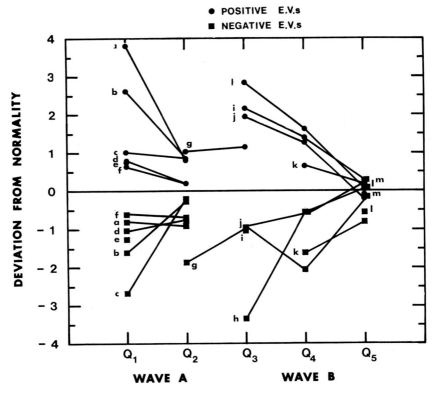

Figure 10-1. Micro-level Learning House effectiveness for positive and negative effectiveness variables (EVs) over two successive groups of children.

ducted. The first group (Group Wave A in Fig. 10-1) contained five children (a, b, c, d, f). The second group consisted of h, i, j, k. Four children (e, g, l, m) who were not members of either group for more than one quarter are also shown. The children in the first group had been at Learning House for one quarter before the first quarter (Q_1) of data collection. Thus, for the first wave of children, Figure 10-1 shows effectiveness scores for only the last two quarters of treatment.

The general convergence toward zero of the mean effectiveness scores for both positive and negative behaviors of children in both groups suggests that the Learning House program was effective in helping children to be more normal. At the beginning of treatment, children were "hyperactive" in that the frequencies of negative behaviors were, on the average, from .6 to more than 3 standard deviations higher than normal levels; positive behaviors averaged from .5 to almost 4 standard deviations higher than normal levels. However, during the last quarter of treatment, all children in both groups demonstrated positive and negative behaviors at frequencies that were less than 1 standard deviation from normal levels.

The data presented in Figure 10-1 also suggest that treating children in "waves", rather than admitting and releasing them individually, may facilitate normalization of behavior. Note that children who were admitted to Learning House in the middle of a wave (child k) or at the end of a wave (children g, l, and m) showed positive and negative behaviors at levels quite similar to those observed for other children who had been admitted during previous quarters. This similarity may have been in part due to the modeling of more normal levels of behavior by children who had been admitted previously (cf. Bandura, 1977). Evidence of the influence of peer models is also provided by one child (g) who was admitted during the last quarter of Group A, and who resided at Learning House during the first quarter of Group B.

The convergence of effectiveness scores toward zero in two consecutive groups of children provides a replication of treatment effectiveness. The conclusion that Learning House "normalized" children receives support from additional analyses. The convergence of scores toward zero cannot be explained in terms of a systematic change in the number of observations conducted during consecutive quarters for each group, because the change in scores was not correlated highly with corresponding changes in numbers of observations (for positive behaviors, $r_s = .25$, n. s.; for negative behaviors, $r_s = .09$). Convergence of effectiveness scores toward normality is not an artifact of a systematic increase in the number of observations of Learning House children compared with normal children; there was not a significant change in the relative number of observations conducted at the school, χ^2

$(3) = 2.6, p > .25$. Finally, it is unlikely that the change to normal frequencies is a "regression to the mean" phenomenon. A comparison group of problem children who did not receive treatment was unavailable. However, inspection of the weekly frequencies of behavior for each child suggests that changes were gradual and somewhat variable over time. Also, the "hyperactive" behavior patterns of these children were of long standing—so much so that they had been referred for residential treatment often after failing in foster home placements. The regression to the mean problem is a measurement artifact of selecting subjects with extreme scores from a sample *at one point in time* and, upon retesting, finding that the mean scores have moved closer to the average score (Hayes, 1963, pp. 500-501). By contrast, the Learning House data were collected daily over many weeks, precluding any single test-retest regression effect.

In sum, the Learning House program seems to have been effective in "normalizing" the behavior of children after approximately nine months of treatment. An overall view of its effectiveness is supplied by Table 10-II and Figure 10-2, which display the grand means of the effectiveness scores for positive and negative behaviors of children who were members of either group for more than one quarter. The broken horizontal lines in Figure 10-2 represent the outer bound of normality as we defined it—a conservative one standard deviation from normal behavior frequencies.

Of course, the exact mechanism by which Learning House

TABLE 10-II

OVERALL NEGATIVE AND POSITIVE MEAN EFFECTIVENESS SCORES
FOR GROUPS A AND B

Group	Quarter	Negative Effectiveness Variables	Positive Effectiveness Variables
A	1	1.34	1.60
	2	.56	.58
B	3	1.78	2.32
	4	1.18	1.23
	5	.17	.06

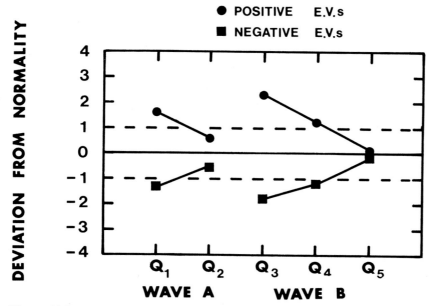

Figure 10-2. Mean effectiveness scores for positive and negative effectiveness variables (EVs) of children in the first and second group. (Dash lines indicate one standard deviation from normative frequencies of positive and negative effectiveness variables.)

accomplished its objective cannot be specified by the present analyses. It is conceivable that the structured home environment provided by Learning House and/or the modeling provided by "mainstreaming" the children into regular public school classes were responsible for some or all of the normalized behavior. Nevertheless, the effectiveness of Learning House has been measured and seems considerable. For the purpose of the cost-effectiveness analysis, the next step in implementation is the measurement of Learning House costs.

How Much Does It Cost?

From the operations and opportunity perspectives, the cost of Learning House was measured separately for each of the same quarters during which effectiveness data were collected. The variables used in measurement of cost from both perspectives were (a) personnel, (b) facilities, and (c) equipment and materials. These major resource ingredients were broken down into minor cost variables, as explained in the following paragraphs.

Personnel Cost

From the operations perspective, the cost of Learning House personnel was simply the sum of salaries received by paid staff members and fees collected by extraprogram professionals for services rendered to the program. The minor personnel cost variables corresponded to salary classifications that were based primarily on education level. An exemplary list of the minor personnel cost variables and their operations values for one quarter is provided in the left column of Table 10-III.

Measurement of personnel costs was more involved when the opportunity perspective was adopted, because a considerable proportion of Learning House personnel were volunteers or worked overtime without extra pay. In return for their time, these personnel received paraprofessional training or the opportunity to conduct research at Learning House. It was decided that the opportunity value of all personnel time might be best measured in terms of the number of hours engaged in activities related to Learning House.

In order to collect data on the amount of time that different personnel devoted to Learning House, all personnel connected in any way with the program kept daily records of the amount of time that they devoted to treatment-related activities. The number of hours worked by each staff member was multiplied by the hourly wage rate which that staff member would have received elsewhere for similar services. The wage rates used in these calculations were those of the local county mental health clinic and varied according to level of education attained by the staff member.

An exemplary listing of the opportunity value of time involved in Learning House activities by different personnel during one quarter is provided in the right column of Table 10-III. The profound difference in the summary values of operations versus opportunity value cost illustrates the importance of considering the perspective adopted in cost measurement.

TABLE 10-III

EXEMPLARY VALUES OF THE OPERATIONS AND OPPORTUNITY COST FOR THE PERSONNEL VARIABLES

Educational Level	Operations Cost	Opportunity Cost
MD, DJS	$ 1,461	$ 1,461
PhD	$ 849	$ 798
MA	$ 2,706	$ 6,452
BA	$ 2,972	$13,675
Paraprofessional		$ 2,943
Undergraduate		$ 1,189
Other		$ 594
Total Cost for Personnel	$ 7,988	$27,112

Note. These operations and social cost values were compiled over the second quarter only. No staff benefits are listed because no such benefits were paid by Learning House during this quarter.

Facilities Cost

The operations cost of facilities was calculated by summing various entries in the Learning House accounting records. The minor cost variables subsumed under the facilities variable are listed in Table 10-IV, along with their operations value for one quarter. Vehicles were depreciated at an annual rate of 15 percent and furniture and fixtures were depreciated at an annual rate of 20 percent, in accord with the practice of local accountants.

Table 10-IV also lists the values of the minor facilities variables as tabulated from the opportunity perspective. These values included the estimated cost of facilities, e.g. offices at a nearby university, used on a part-time basis by personnel for activities related to treatment. The cost of using such facilities was estimated by multiplying local rental rates for comparable office space by the proportion of time that the facilities were used for Learning House activities.

TABLE 10-IV

EXEMPLARY VALUES OF THE OPERATIONS AND OPPORTUNITY COST
FOR THE FACILITIES, EQUIPMENT AND MATERIALS VARIABLES

Cost Variables	Operations Cost	Opportunity Cost
Facilities:		
Mortgage and Depreciation	$ 1,160	$ 1,584
Furniture Depreciation	$ 12	$ 12
Vehicle Depreciation	$ 7	$ 7
Repairs	$ 49	$ 121
Total Cost for Facilities:	$ 1,228	$ 1,724
Equipment and Materials:		
Gasoline and Oil	$ 173	$ 173
Food	$ 746	$ 748
Recreation	$ 271	$ 276
Advertising	—	$ 21
Utilities	$ 154	$ 154
Telephones	$ 157	$ 210
Clothes	$ 89	$ 95
Insurance	$ 170	$ 170
Sundries	$ 835	$ 867
Total Cost for Equipment and Materials	$ 2,595	$ 2,714

Note. These operations and opportunity cost values were compiled over
the second quarter.

Equipment and Materials Cost

The operations cost of equipment and materials used by
Learning House was taken directly from accounting records and
is itemized in terms of minor variables of equipment and materials in Table 10-IV. The opportunity cost of equipment and
materials included the estimated value of donated or freely loaned
equipment and materials in addition to operations cost and is
listed in Table 10-IV for each minor variable.

Operations Versus Opportunity Cost Values

Comparison of the operations and opportunity values of the
personnel and facilities cost variables in Tables 10-III and 10-IV
indicates that the opportunity cost of Learning House personnel

was much higher, at least during this quarter, than was the operations cost. Closer examination reveals that the difference between the operations and opportunity personnel cost values was largest for those personnel who had not exceeded the master's level of education. Localization of the cost difference at these personnel levels suggests, as was indeed the case, that many undergraduate students, paraprofessionals, and graduate students were receiving nonmonetary benefits from their participation in Learning House. These nonmonetary benefits seemed to be research opportunities, education, and training. Because working at Learning House was by no means compulsory, the educational, training, and research benefits received by personnel with lower levels of education may balance out the difference between the operations and opportunity cost of those personnel. To avoid complicating the cost-effectiveness analysis by attempting to consider the research opportunities, education, and training benefits as other outcomes of the program, only the operations cost values were considered in the final measurement of cost and cost-effectiveness.

Estimating Cost Per Child and Per Effectiveness Variable

The operations cost of Learning House had to be transformed from the units in which it was available into units that were compatible with the effectiveness variables. The first step in this transformation was to calculate the total operations cost of Learning House for each of the quarters during which effectiveness data were collected. Because there was a high rate of inflation during the five-quarter period over which cost and effectiveness were measured, all cost data were adjusted for inflation in terms of the quarterly consumer price index for middle-class families that lived in the same locale as Learning House (Bureau of Labor Statistics, 1976). Adjustment for inflation was conducted so that the cost of resources was in units of spring 1976 dollars in order to provide a more up-to-date picture of cost. The adjusted quarterly cost data are listed in Table 10-V for each major cost variable.

Table 10-V shows that personnel accounted for an average of 64 percent of the total operations cost of Learning House over the

TABLE 10-V

QUARTERLY OPERATIONS COST VALUES FOR LEARNING HOUSE

	Quarter					Overall Mean
	Group A		Group B			
Cost Variable	Q_1	Q_2	Q_3	Q_4	Q_5	
Personnel	$ 6,632	$ 7,988	$ 6,909	$ 6,809	$ 5,828	$ 6,833
Facilities	$ 1,245	$ 1,228	$ 1,140	$ 2,788	$ 914	$ 1,463
Equipment and Materials	$ 2,137	$ 2,595	$ 2,467	$ 2,470	$ 2,054	$ 2,344
Total	$10,014	$11,811	$10,516	$12,067	$ 8,796	$10,640
Personnel Costs as a Percentage of Total Costs	66%	68%	66%	56%	66%	64%

Note. Cost data have been adjusted for inflation in terms of spring 1976 dollars.

five quarters, with facilities being an average of 13 percent of the total cost. The increase in facilities cost during Quarter 4 reflects the purchase of a small used car. Equipment and materials accounted for 23 percent of Learning House costs on the average.

The second step was to calculate the cost per quarter of treating each effectiveness variable for each child. It might be thought that the cost per child per effectiveness variable could be estimated by simply dividing the total cost per quarter by the number of effectiveness variables and by the number of children who resided at Learning House during that quarter. Implicit in this calculation scheme is the assumption that an equal proportion of personnel time was devoted to treatment of each child. Although this assumption seemed tenable for personnel who spent most of their time in administrative or evaluation activities, it did not seem plausible for treatment personnel, i.e. teaching parents, who interacted directly with the children.

The amount of time devoted to treatment of different children by therapists could have been assessed by a nonparticipant observation system similar to that used to collect data on behaviors of the children. Unfortunately, there was not a sufficient number of observers to collect such data. Instead, the relative amount of time devoted to the different children by therapeutic personnel was measured by monthly self-reports to the question, "I spent _____ time with _____ (one of the children) than with the other children during this quarter." Therapists' reports to this question were provided independently for each child on a ten-point rating scale that had the anchor points "much less" (1) and "much more" (10). Analyses of ratings provided during the first quarter indicated that there was fair agreement among therapists as to the relative amount of time devoted to the different children ($\bar{s} = 1.9$ on the 10-point scale, range of s: 1.1 to 2.6). Equation 3 was used to transform the ratings into a composite weighting index, $W_{(c, q)}$, that expressed the proportion of therapist time devoted to treatment of a particular child, c, during a given quarter, q.

$$W_{(c, q)} = [\sum_{t = 1}^{m} r_{(t, c, q)}] \div [\sum_{c = 1}^{p} \sum_{t = 1}^{m} r_{(t, c, q)}] \tag{3},$$

where $r_{(t, c, q)}$ is the rating supplied by therapist t for child c during quarter q
m is the total number of therapists, and
p is the total number of children in treatment during quarter q.

To compute the cost of therapist time for a child during a given quarter, the cost of therapist time for that quarter was multiplied by the weighting $W_{(c, q)}$. The total cost of treatment for a child during a particular quarter was calculated by first dividing the cost of nontherapist personnel and the cost of facilities, equipment, and materials by the number of children who lived at Learning House during that quarter, and then adding this average cost to the estimated cost of therapist time for that child. The total cost of treatment for a child was then divided by the number of effectiveness variables to arrive at the estimated cost of treating an effectiveness variable for a particular child during a given quarter.

The mean cost per child per effectiveness variable is displayed in Figure 10-3 separately for each quarter. Figure 10-3 shows that even after adjustment for inflation, the average cost of treating a behavior of a child at Learning House rose during the first four quarters of the analysis period. The primary reason for this increase was a decrease in the number of children treated at Learning House during the third and fourth quarters. Whereas six children resided at Learning House during the first, second, and fifth quarters of the analysis period, only four children were in the program during the third and fourth quarters. Learning House could not readily reduce operations cost when the number of children decreased because many of the personnel, facilities, and equipment and materials costs were fixed as opposed to variable costs; that is, salaries and mortgage payments were the same regardless of how many children were in the program. Thus, the cost per child per effectiveness variable increased when the number of children decreased. Compounding the problem of having many fixed costs was a gradual increase in the total cost of program operation that, on the basis of data in Table 10-V, was due to transient increases in the value of each major cost variable.

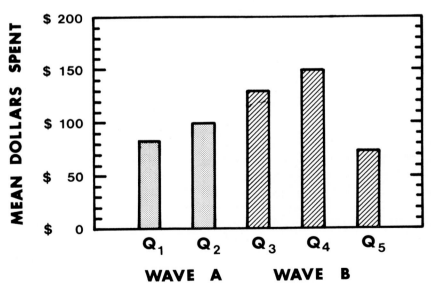

Figure 10-3. Mean operations cost of treating one effectiveness variable for one child at Learning House (data are adjusted for inflation in spring, 1976 dollar units).

How Cost-Effective Is It?

Operationalizing and Quantifying Cost-Effectiveness

The cost-effectiveness indices generated in the microlevel analysis of Learning House were designed to indicate how much change in behavior was achieved per dollar spent during each quarter. Cost-Effectiveness Indices (CEIs) were formed for each child by dividing the difference between the means of the effectiveness variables (Equation 2) for each child for two consecutive time periods by the cost of treating an effectiveness variable for that child during the latter quarter, as shown in Equation 4.

$$CEI_{(b,c,q+1)} = [\frac{|\overline{E}_{(b,c,q)}| - |\overline{E}_{(b,c,q+1)}|}{\$_{(b,c,q+1)}}] \qquad (4),$$

where q is a particular quarter during a child's treatment,

$|\overline{E}_{(b,c,q)}|$ is the absolute value of the mean of effectiveness variable b for child c during quarter q (see Equation 2), and

$\$_{(b,c,q+1)}$ is the cost of treating one effectiveness variable for child c for the following $(q+1)$ quarter.

In order to interpret correctly the values of cost-effectiveness generated by Equation 4, it is important to note that a positively signed cost-effectiveness index means that a decrease in extreme behavior occurred between quarters q and $q+1$. A negatively signed index means that extreme behavior increased. Thus, if a CEI is positive in sign and large in magnitude, more change per dollar was achieved by that child in that behavior class than by a child with a small, positive CEI. If a CEI is negative in sign, then the child's behavior deteriorated, despite the resources spent in treatment. The magnitude of a negative CEI indicates the size of the setback in that effectiveness variable. When comparing these cost-effectiveness indices, it should be remembered that a difference between indices could be caused by different rates of progress *or* by different costs of treatment. For example, a doubling of cost-effectiveness could be caused by doubling the progress made (effectiveness), reducing the cost by one-half, or some combination of change in both cost and effectiveness. For purposes of both program evaluation and individual treatment decisions, highly specific indices of both costs and effectiveness are important.

Mean Cost-Effectiveness Per Child Per Effectiveness Variable

Figure 10-4 displays mean cost-effectiveness indices separately for the positive and negative variables of each child in the first group. These indices were formed by multiplying the CEIs by 100 to facilitate graphic display. Figure 10-5 displays the indices for each child in the second group. There are two sets of indices for most children in the second group because behavior change was measured over three quarters instead of two.

Comparison of the cost-effectiveness indices in Figure 10-4 suggests that the program was most cost-effective in dealing with the most deviant behaviors. Positive behaviors of children *a* and *b*, and negative behaviors of child *c* started out as the most extreme of Quarter 1 (see Fig. 10-1), and they achieved the greatest

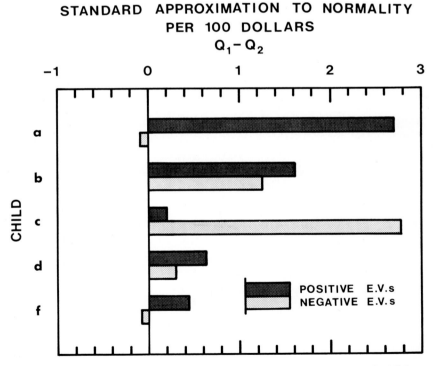

Figure 10-4. Micro cost-effectiveness of treating the first group of children (mean standard approximation to normality per 100 dollars spent).

STANDARD APPROXIMATION TO NORMALITY PER 100 DOLLARS

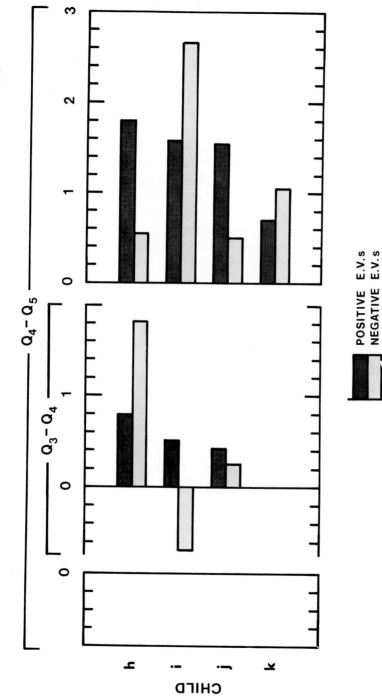

POSITIVE E.V.s
NEGATIVE E.V.s

Figure 10-5. Micro cost-effectivenes of treating the second group of children (mean standard approximation to normality per 100 dollars spent).

change. Two indices indicate undesirable change occurred: the negative behaviors of children *a* and *f* increased slightly. This change may be attributed to a modeling effect. Children *a* and *f* were roommates and girls; children *b, c,* and *d* were boys.

Compared to the cost-effectiveness indices found for the first group, those in the second group were less variable. Children *h, i,* and *j* entered the program during Quarter 3, exhibiting extreme behaviors (see Fig. 10-1). Their progress was good, but treatment costs per child were higher during this period (see Fig. 10-3). Hence their cost-effectiveness indices are generally lower for Q_3-Q_4 than for Q_4-Q_5. An exception are the negative behaviors of child *i,* which increased dramatically during Q_4. For this child, the "honeymoon period" of trying to be on one's best behavior in a new environment may have been longer lasting than for most children. By Q_5, there was a change for the better, resulting in a high cost-effectiveness value for child *i* for Q_4-Q_5.

Improving Micro-Level Cost-Effectiveness

There are a variety of ways in which factors related to improvement in cost-effectiveness might be discovered. One might conduct a multiple regression analysis with those input variables that could affect the output of cost-effectiveness (cf. Thomas, 1971; Yates & Jeffery, 1976). In a small program like Learning House, the number of children for whom data on input variables can be collected may be insufficient to do multiple regression analyses. The lack of independence between cost-effectiveness indices for successive quarters and for different effectiveness variables, e.g. reduction of arguing and increase of playing together may not be independent, further violates the assumptions necessary for multiple regression analyses (cf. Elashoff and Thoresen, in press).

An alternative method would be to plot a time-series display of children's behavior and look for influences from possible significant events, such as change in number of children in residence, change in staff, or change in treatment procedures. Another method would involve regular feedback to treatment staff of cost, effectiveness, and cost-effectiveness data.

When Should Cost-Effectiveness Analyses Be Stopped?

If a program is found to be achieving its short-term goals to an acceptable degree, additional efforts to improve cost-effectiveness may not succeed. The costs of conducting assessments of cost-effectiveness can be minimized by the use of specially designed computer programs (Yates & Haven, 1976). However, the cost of collecting the observational and rating data must be considered.

Using cost-effectiveness analyses on a selected time basis, such as one quarter per year, might save enough personnel time and money to produce a further improvement in program effectiveness. Alternatively, resources might be directed toward conducting cost-effectiveness analyses at a more global or macro level. Macro-level analysis could assess how well Learning House was achieving its long-range goal of nonrecidivism, and at what cost. Such an analysis and the issues surrounding interprogram comparisons of cost-effectiveness are described briefly in the following section.

AN EXEMPLARY MACRO-LEVEL COST-EFFECTIVENESS ANALYSIS

How Effective Is It?

Nonrecidivism was used as the effectiveness measure in the macro-level analysis of Learning House because it best represented the goal commonly advocated by all concerned interest groups, i.e. preventing future occurrences of the referral behavior. Another reason for measuring effectiveness in terms of nonrecidivism was that other treatment programs were most likely to have collected data on as basic a measure as nonrecidivism. Nonrecidivism was operationally defined as not being contacted by county officials for anything other than a regular report. A follow-up found that nine or 69 percent of the thirteen children who had completed the Learning House program by the spring of 1975 and who had been released to their parents or to foster care did not recede during their first year after release. A longer follow-up period is more desirable; two-year data are now being collected.

How Much Does It Cost?

The operations perspective was used to measure costs at the macro level because it seemed to be the perspective that would produce the most reliable and valid cost data. The operations perspective also was adopted because it was the perspective that funding agencies interested in interprogram comparisons were most likely to prefer.

The basic cost of treatment at Learning House was defined as the amount of money that was allocated to Learning House per child per month by the county funding agency. This operations cost was $978 per child per month. To compute the cost of treating children who were released during the follow-up period, the cost per child per day was calculated ($978 per child per month ÷ 30 = $32.60 per child per day). To compute the cost of treating each child, the daily cost was multiplied by the number of days that the child stayed at Learning House. The average cost of treating a child at Learning House was found to be $12,847.[1]

How Cost-Effective Is It?

One could calculate cost-effectiveness in terms of treating children who did not recede after treatment. This index of cost-effectiveness would be computed by dividing the total cost of treating all nonreceded children by the number of nonreceded children. For Learning House, this figure was $13,731 per nonreceded child.

However, this information is not as useful, especially for interprogram comparisons, as is the average amount of money that was expended for all children (not just the successful ones). The latter type of information was obtained by computing the total cost of treating *all* children who were in the follow-up population and then dividing that cost by the number of children in the population who did not recede. This figure was $167,012 ÷ 9 nonreceded children or $18,557 per nonreceded child on the aver-

----

[1]Although the figures vary widely, the average cost per child of public residential care (primarily custodial) for youth in California is approximately $15,000 per year. This figure does not include indirect costs such as construction bonds, building depreciation, and some administrative costs. Unfortunately, effectiveness data on these costs were unavailable.

age. The difference between this figure and the one cited above illustrates the importance of defining cost-effectiveness very operationally, especially before conducting interprogram comparisons of cost-effectiveness.

How Can Macro Cost-Effectiveness Be Improved?

One way to answer this question is to conduct micro cost-effectiveness analysis to pinpoint treatment components that are more and less effective. Another improvement strategy is to find another program that deals with similar clientele but which is superior in the cost-effectiveness of one or more of its treatment components. After such interprogram comparisons of cost-effectiveness, each program might adopt some of the procedures that seemed to make the component(s) of other programs more cost-effective. If data from a sufficient number of programs were available, a production function might be established which, after a multiple regression analysis of various input variables, could specify which resources should be increased in amount and which should be decreased so as to optimize cost-effectiveness of treatment (cf. Levin, 1970, 1971). In this way, interprogram cost-effectiveness analysis could improve all programs involved, instead of providing ill-founded justification for the "axing" of less cost-effective programs (Wortman, 1975).

We attempted to collect macro-level cost and effectiveness data from other residential treatment programs in the area. Unfortunately, data on the macro effectiveness of the other treatments were not available—even for as basic a measure as nonrecidivism. Most of the treatment facilities contacted were not conducting any follow-up. The few treatments that were collecting nonrecidivism data did not wish to disclose it. No follow-up data were available through local county agencies that funded the treatments, although they did plan to begin collecting follow-up data on treatments "in a few years."

CLOSING COMMENT

We hope that the model of cost-effectiveness analysis presented here will be of use to others. It has been implemented recently in a different treatment setting—an obesity treatment clinic—and has generated useful information on cost-effectiveness (Yates, 1976a; Yates, 1977b). We realize the many limitations of any model but offer ours as a preliminary and *working* version. We welcome its use by others and will be revising it with more experience. For many reasons, behaviorally oriented programs are well suited to applying this model, due to their emphasis on systematic data collection over time. A profound need exists to evaluate and improve the cost-effectiveness of treatment programs for delinquent youth and troubled persons in general. The demand for fiscal and efficacious accountability is growing. We hope others will venture forth in trying to conduct cost-effectiveness analyses of social service programs. We can benefit by learning more about how to increase positive treatment effects and decrease treatment costs.

REFERENCES

Text

Abelson, P.H. Cost-effective health care. *Science,* 1976, *192,* 1.

Ackoff, R.L., & Rivett, P. *A manager's guide to operations research.* New York: Wiley, 1963.

Ackoff, R.L., & Sasieni, N.W. *Fundamentals of operations research.* New York: Wiley, 1968.

Balcerzak, W.S., & Siddall, J.W. A brief discussion of a model for improving the cost effectiveness of a token economy in a rehabilitative setting. *Journal of Applied Behavior Analysis,* 1974, *7,* 501-504.

Bandura, A. *Social learning theory.* Englewood Cliffs, N.J.: Prentice-Hall, 1977.

Bennis, W. (Ed.), *The planning of change: Readings in the applied behavioral sciences.* New York: Holt, Rinehart & Winston, 1966.

Born, D.G., & Davis, M.L. Amount and distribution of study in a personalized instruction course and in a lecture course. *Journal of Applied Behavior Analysis,* 1974, *7,* 365-375.

Bowman, M.J. The costing of human resource development. In E.A. Robinson & J.E. Vaizey (Eds.), *The economics of education.* New York: St. Martin's Press, 1966.

Bureau of Labor Statistics. *Consumer price index for urban wage earners and clerical workers: San Francisco-Oakland, California, 1946-1976.* Washington, D.C.: U.S. Department of Labor, 1976.

Cain, G.G., & Hollister, R.G. The methodology of evaluating social programs. In P.H. Rossi & W. Williams (Eds.), *Evaluating social programs: Theory, practice, and politics.* New York: Seminar Press, 1972.

Carter, D.E., & Newman, F.L. *A client oriented system of mental health service delivery and program management: A workbook and guide.* Philadelphia: Eastern Pennsylvania Psychiatric Institute, 1974.

Coates, T.J., & Thoresen, C.E. *Using generalizability theory in behavioral observations.* Unpublished manuscript, Stanford University, 1976.

Conley, R.W., Conwell, M., & Arrill, M.B. An approach to measuring the cost of mental illness. *American Journal of Psychiatry,* 1967, *124,* 63-70.

Cook, S.L. Introduction: Organization and control. In J.R. Lawrence (Ed.), *Operations research and the social sciences.* New York: Tavistock, 1966.

Cronbach, L.J., Gleser, G.C., Nanda, H. and Rajaratnam, N. *The dependability of behavioral measures.* New York: Wiley, 1972.

Elashoff, J.D., & Thoresen, C.E. Selecting statistical method analysis of intensive research data. In Kratochwill (Ed.), *Strategies to evaluate change in single subject research.* New York: Academic Press, in press.

Elkin, R. *Relating programs to costs in children's residential institutions.* Washington, D.C.: The American University, 1969.

Fanshel, D., & Shinn, E.B. *Dollars and sense in the foster care of children: A look at cost factors.* New York: Child Welfare League of America, 1972.

Fox, P.D., & Kuldau, J.M. Expanding the framework for mental health program evaluation. *Archives of General Psychiatry,* 1968, *19,* 538-544.

Goldman, T.A. (Ed.), *Cost-effectiveness analysis: New approaches in decision-making.* New York: Praeger, 1967.

Haggard, E.A., Hiken, J.R., & Isaac, K.S. Some effects of recording and filming in the psychotherapeutic process. *Psychiatry,* 1965, *28,* 169-191.

Hays, W.L. *Statistics,* New York: Holt, Rinehart & Winston, 1963.

Hiebert, S. Who benefits from the program? Criteria selection. In P.O. Davidson, F.W. Clark, & L.A. Hamerlynck (Eds.), *Evaluation of behavioral programs.* Champaign, Ill.: Research Press, 1974.

Johnson, S.M., & Bolstad, O.D. Methodological issues in naturalistic observations: Some problems and solutions for field research. In L.A. Hamerlynck, L.C. Handy, & E.J. Mash (Eds.), *Behavior change: Methodology, concepts, and practice.* Champaign, Ill.: Research Press, 1973.

Katz, D., & Kahn, R.L. *The social psychology of organizations.* New York: Wiley, 1966.

Krapfl, J.E. Accountability through cost-benefit analysis. In D. Harshberger & R.F. Maley (Eds.), *Behavior analysis and systems analysis: An integrative approach to mental health programs.* Kalamazoo, Michigan: Behaviordelia, 1974.

Krumboltz, J.D.   An accountability model for counselors.   *Personnel and Guidance Journal,* 1974, *52,* 639-646.

Krumboltz, J.D., & Thoresen, C.E.   *Counseling methods.*   New York: Holt, Rinehart & Winston, 1976.

Levin, H.M.   A cost-effectiveness analysis of teacher selection.   *Journal of Human Resources,* 1970, *5,* 24-33.

Levin, H.M.   The effect of different levels of expenditure on educational output.   In R.L. Johns (Ed.), *Economic factors affecting the financing of education in the decade ahead.*   Gainesville, Fla.:   National Education Finance Project, 1971.

Levin, H.M.   Cost-effectiveness analysis in evaluation research.   In M. Guttentag & E.H. Struening (Eds.), *Handbook of evaluation research* (Vol. 2).   Beverly Hills, Calif.:   Sage, 1975.

Martin, M.F., Gelfand, D.M., & Hartmann, D.P.   Effects of adult and peer observers on boys' and girls' responses to an aggressive model.   *Child Development,* 1971, *42,* 1271-1275.

Martin, M.J., & Denison, R.A.   *Case exercises in operations research.*   New York: Wiley, 1971.

Mischel, W.   *Introduction to personality* (2nd ed.).   New York: Holt, Rinehart & Winston, 1976.

Neufeldt, A.H.   Considerations in the implementation of program evaluation.   In P.O. Davidson, F.W. Clark, & L.A. Hamerlynck (Eds.), *Evaluation of behavioral programs.*   Champaign, Ill.:   Research Press, 1974.

O'Dell, S.   Training parents in behavior modification: A review.   *Psychological Bulletin,* 1974, *81,* 418-433.

O'Leary, K.D., & Kent, R.   Behavior modification for social action: Research tactics and problems.   In L.A. Hamerlynck, L.C. Handy, & E.J. Mash (Eds.), *Behavior change: Methodology, concepts, and practice.*   Champaign, Ill.:   Research Press, 1973.

O'Leary, K.D., Kent, R.N., & Kanowitz, J.   Shaping data collection congruent with experimental hypotheses.   *Journal of Applied Behavior Analysis,* 1975, *8,* 43-51.

Patterson, G.R., Reid, J.B., Jones, R.R., & Conger, R.E.   *A social learning approach to family interaction.*   Eugene, Oregon: Castalia, 1975.

Pennypacker, H.S., Koenig, C.H., & Seaver, W.H.   Cost efficiency and effectiveness in the early detection and improvement of learning abilities.   In P.O. Davidson, F.W. Clark, & L.A. Hamerlynck (Eds.), *Evaluation of behavioral programs.*   Champaign, Ill.:   Research Press, 1974.

Romanczyk, R.G., Kent, R.N., Diament, C., & O'Leary, K.D.   Measuring the reliability of observational data: A reactive process.   *Journal of Applied Behavior Analysis,* 1973, *6,* 175-184.

Rosenthal, R.   On the social psychology of the psychological experiment: The experimenter's hypotheses as an unintended determinant of the experimental results.   *American Scientist,* 1963, *51,* 268-283.

Rosenthal, R. *Experimenter effects in behavioral research.* New York: Appleton-Century-Crofts, 1966.

Russell, M.L., & Thoresen, C.E. Teaching decision-making skills to children. In J.D. Krumboltz, and C.E. Thoresen, (Eds.), *Counseling Methods.* New York: Holt, Rinehart & Winston, 1976.

Sexton, J.W., Merbitz, C., & Pennypacker, H.S. Accountability: Cost efficiency and effectiveness measures in behavioral college teaching. In J.M. Johnston (Ed.), *Behavior research and technology in higher education.* Springfield, Ill.: Charles C Thomas, 1975.

Skindrud, K. A preliminary evaluation of observer bias in multivariate studies of social interaction. In L.A. Hamerlynck, L.C. Handy, & E.J. Mash (Eds.), Behavior change: *Methodology, concepts, and practice.* Champaign, Ill.: Research Press, 1973.

Sternberg, R.S., Chapman, J., & Shakow, D. Psychotherapy research and the probem of intrusions on privacy. *Psychiatry,* 1958, *21,* 195-203.

Tavormina, J.B. Basic models of parent counseling: A critical review. *Psychological Bulletin,* 1974, *81,* 827-835.

Thomas, J.A. *The productive school: A systems analysis approach to educational administration.* New York: Wiley, 1971.

Thoresen, K.E., Thoresen, C.E., Klein, S.B., Wilbur, C.SC., Becker-Haven, J.F., and Haven, W.G. Learning House: helping troubled children and their parents change themselves. In J.S. Stumphauzer (Ed.), *Progress in behavior therapy with delinquents* (2nd ed.). Springfield, Ill.: Charles C Thomas, 1978.

Tobey, T.S., & Thoresen, C.E. Helping Bill reduce aggressive behaviors. In J.D. Krumboltz and C.E. Thoresen (Eds.), *Counseling methods.* New York: Holt, Rinehart & Winston, 1976.

Trotter, S. Nader group releases first consumer guide to psychotherapists. *APA Monitor,* 1975, *6,* 11ff.

Walker, R.A. The ninth panacea: Program evaluation. *Evaluation,* 1972, *1,* 45-53.

Willems, E.P. Behavioral technology and behavioral ecology. *Journal of Applied Behavior Analysis,* 1974, 7, 151-165.

Williams, W., & Evans, J.W. The politics of evaluation: The case of Head Start. In P.H. Rossi & W. Williams (Eds.), *Evaluating social programs: Theory, practice, and politics.* New York: Seminar Press, 1972.

Wolins, M. *A manual for cost analysis in institutions for children.* New York: Child Welfare League of America, 1962.

Wortman, P.M. Evaluation research: A psychological perspective. *American Psychologist,* 1975, *30,* 562-573.

Yates, B.T. *The first quarter at Learning House: Observation manual* (5th ed.). Palo Alto, California: Learning House, 1975.

Yates, B.T. *Intra- and inter-program cost-effectiveness analysis of obesity treatments.* Paper presented at the Western Psychological Association,

Los Angeles, April, 1976 (a).

Yates, B.T. *Students as paraprofessionals: Systematic instruction in residential treatment of behaviorally disturbed children.* Manuscript submitted for publication, 1976 (b).

Yates, B.T. *The use of operations research to improve psychological treatments: Prescriptions from an historical perspective.* Paper presented at the meeting of the Western Psychological Association, Los Angeles, April 1976 (c).

Yates, B.T. *Cost-effectiveness analysis of psychological service systems.* Requested revision of manuscript, resubmitted for publication, 1977 (a).

Yates, B.T. *Improving the cost-effectiveness of behavioral programs for obesity reduction.* Manuscript submitted for publication, 1977 (b).

Yates, B.T., & Haven, W.G. A 1115-statement computer program (in ALGOLW) for regular multilevel assessment of cost-effectiveness. Unpublished program, Stanford University, 1976.

Yates, B.T., & Jeffery, R.W. *Toward an empirical answer to a clinical question: Changing which eating behavior contributes most to the reduction of obesity?* Paper presented at the Western Psychological Association, Los Angeles, April 1976.

CHAPTER 11

TRAINING JUVENILE PROBATION OFFICERS IN BEHAVIOR MODIFI-CATION: KNOWLEDGE, ATTITUDE CHANGE, OR BEHAVIORAL COMPETENCE?*†

Barry R. Burkhart, Michael W. Behles, and Jerome S. Stumphauzer

EDITORIAL COMMENTS

In understanding, modifying, and preventing delinquent behavior we must look beyond the delinquents themselves to their social environment: their neighborhoods (Chap. 19 & 20), their schools (Chap. 13), their families (Chap. 14) and also, since we must deal with juvenile **crime**, to law enforcement and probation — all vital parts of the "delinquency equation."

In these next two chapters, the focus is the training of juvenile probation officers in behavior modification. The implicit goal of probation for juveniles is to curtail and prevent further problems. The methods utilized to attain these goals are appalling if analyzed in light of our current understanding of principles of behavior change (Stumphauzer, 1977). Probation is often a series of loose contingency contracts such as "stay out of trouble or you're headed for juvenile hall. . . " and "obey your parents

*The authors thank Art Weingartner, of the Rio Hondo Community Mental Health Center, for arranging the initial consultation; Dave Zoellner, Director of the Bellflower Probation Department, for his generous cooperation; Robert L. Pola-kow of the probation department's Behavioral Research and Training Program, who served as a guest lecturer; and Victor Haluska who served as a research assistant on the project.

†Reprinted with permission from *Behavior Therapy*, 1976, 7, 47-53. (Association for Advancement of Behavior Therapy)

or else. . ." Behaviors are not specified, usually not measured. Positive controls (modeling, shaping, reinforcement) are not utilized. Punishment is the major — often only — principle used (Stumphauzer, 1974).

Burkhart, Behles, and Stumphauzer (Chap. 11) conducted a behavior modification training program with juvenile probation officers. They focused on a behavioral understanding of the officers' day to day work, on behavior modification principles, on behavioral analyses of probation cases, and finally on behavioral contracting in probation. Results were indeed promising. With this brief training, officers showed that they could both do a behavioral analysis and construct behavioral probation plans.

In a follow-up done six months later (Chap. 12) Stumphauzer, Candelora, and Venema found that the trained officers were still utilizing their training (both in their work and in their personal lives), but only to a limited degree. It seems that we not only have to look at the controlling social variables of the youth's environment, but also at those variables controlling the behavior of the change agents. If there is no modeling and reinforcement from supervisors, and if behavioral contracting is "more work" than the old "system," then we should not expect it to be used.

Probation and law enforcement are obviously potentially very fruitful areas in which to use behavior analysis and modification. But serious questions and issues arise. Should we blindly hand over this new technology to an often damaging juvenile justice system without considering how it will be used? Will these new "means" be used simply to better achieve the old "ends" of control and conformity (Davidson & Seidman, 1974)? Ethical and legal issues will necessarily be thrust upon us and may well temper our eagerness to find new, useful applications for our principles (Stumphauzer, 1977).

ABSTRACT

IN A SOLOMON CONTROL GROUP DESIGN, nine juvenile probation officers received six weeks of training in behavior modification, while nine others did not. The trained group did not differ significantly from the control group on paper and pencil measures of knowledge and attitudes. However, the trained group did demonstrate significantly that they could, in fact, do a behavior analysis and construct a behavioral probation plan. Behavioral competence measures are discussed as the most definitive criteria for evaluation of behavior therapy training programs.

The clarion call for psychologists in the last decade has been to "give psychology away." In this regard, psychologists and other mental health professionals increasingly are finding themselves being called on to train other professionals and paraprofessionals in the technology of behavior change.

Behavior therapy, or behavior modification, with its intrinsic operational validity, ready translation from theory to action, and freedom from nonoperationally defined constructs, lends itself to many applications within the mental health field, as well as other professional areas concerned with behavior change. One profound social problem, which has recently become the focus of attention of behavior therapists, has been juvenile delinquency. Although predelinquent and delinquent behaviors constitute a major social problem, traditional mental health approaches have been consistently ineffective, while many behavior therapy approaches show considerable promise (Stumphauzer, 1973, 1974, in press; Davidson & Seidman, in press). Tharp and Wetzel (1969), in outlining the direction for the future of helping professions with specific reference to delinquent behavior, delineate three factors of cardinal importance: "use of the natural environment, reliance on the nontraditional worker, and behavior modification" (p. vii). Being in essential agreement with Tharp and Wetzel, we have endeavored to conduct the present study to reflect all three factors.

Hand in hand with the responsibility of training other workers in behavioral technology goes the responsibility of evaluating the effect of training programs. Of interest is the paucity of evaluative research on the efficacy of behavior modification programs as reported in the literature. In the only article detailing the results of a training program for juvenile probation officers, Deibert and Golden (1973) have indicated that most research activity has focused on the changes effected in the client, the recipient of the behavior therapy, rather than on the behavior changes occurring in the newly trained behavior therapist himself. It is apparent that there are many problems developing, with behavioral technology being misrepresented, misapplied, and misused by recently or poorly trained change agents. The recent decision of the Federal Bureau of Prisons and the Law Enforcement Assistance Administration to withdraw support to behavior modification programs is a painful case in point. It is as important for behavior therapy

trainers and consultants to document and specify changes in the
behavior of trainees, as a *function* of a behavioral training program, as it is to document the later therapeutic successfulness of
the trainees with their clients.

Very few studies have been reported on the direct effects on
trainees of a behavioral training program. For a discipline which
places a premium on operational purity, such a state is deplorable.
Deibert and Golden's (1973) study is the only report on the outcome of a behavioral training program for probation officers.
Outcome of training was evaluated by changes in knowledge, perceived competence, attitudes, and preference for behavioral explanations. Their study, however, though a needed pioneering
effort, had several major omissions. Although a study of behavior
modification, no behavioral measure was utilized. The low order
correlation between attitudes and behavior cannot be ignored in
a behavioral training project. Additionally, the authors relied on
an unsophisticated pre-postexperimental design without a control
group. Campbell and Stanley (1963) have documented the in-
adequacies of such a design for evaluative research. The current
study complements the initial work of Deibert and Golden (1973)
with design refinements and more adequate behavioral measures.

METHOD

Trainees

The 18 trainees[1] (nine experimental and nine control) were
randomly selected from a pool of 38 probation officers from the
Los Angeles County Probation Department (Bellflower), who had
requested to participate in the program after hearing the introductory lecture on the application of behavioral technology to probation. In accordance with the experimental design, a randomly
selected half of the experimental group *(N = 4)* and half of the
control group *(N = 4)* were given the paper and pencil premeasures. The experimental group then participated in the 6-week
workshop, while the control group received no training. Two
weeks after the end of the training program, all the officers com-

---

[1]Originally, 20 officers were selected, but two were promoted and left the program
prior to completion.

pleted the paper and pencil measures as well as the behavioral measure.

All trainees were juvenile probation officers who had had at least 5 years of previous experience in probation work $(\overline{\chi} = 7.4)$. All had at least a bachelor's degree and over half had some graduate credits. None of the officers had ever had formal training in behavioral technology, but all had attended the introductory lecture.

Training Program

The training program was the outcome of ongoing psychological consultation between the Rio Hondo (Los Angeles County) Community Mental Health Center and the Bellflower Probation Department. As a consultant, the first author presented a lecture on application of behavioral technology to the probation officers. The training program described here was the result of requests from those probation officers in attendance for more detailed and advanced training in behavior therapy.

The workshop consisted of six, 2-hr sessions conducted by the first two authors and two guest lecturers. The primary training manual, *Behavior Modification Principles* (Stumphauzer, 1977), consists of programmed instructions of 22 basic principles of behavior therapy along with modeled examples of each with both children and adults. Relevant research articles, and selections from texts in behavior therapy were used as well. The course was divided into four major sections: general principles of behavior therapy, behavioral assessment, techniques of intervention, and generalization to the natural environment. The class sessions were divided into two parts; the first hour was used for didactic presentations and the second for experiential activities, discussion of cases, modeled interviewing, and group problem solving. As part of their homework, all participants completed the programmed text, did a behavioral analysis, and developed a behavioral intervention plan for one of their clients.

MEASURES AND EXPERIMENTAL DESIGN

Three types of measures were utilized. The first, a paper and pencil 30-item, multiple choice test adapted from Becker (1971)

assesses general, fundamental knowledge of behavioral principles.[2]
The second, a 7-point semantic differential scale, measures attitudes toward behavior modification involving eight concepts
(sincerity, effectiveness, naturalness, superficiality, warmth, cruelty,
speed of treatment, and lasting effects) .[3]

The second facet of the evaluation procedure was a behavioral
measure of the effectiveness of the training. One precedent which
this study hopes to establish is the utilization of behavioral criteria
in the evaluation of behaviorally oriented training programs.
The need was to assess the ability of the probation officer, when
faced with a client, to do a behaviorally oriented interview, write
up a behavioral analysis of the client, and outline a therapeutic
intervention based on sound behavioral principles. Our procedure was to have the officer interview a client (a confederate who
had been trained to role-play a probationer) with a standard probation information fact sheet, complete a behavior analysis, and
write a treatment plan based on their interview and their analysis
of the problem behaviors and the environment of the confederate.

The confederate was a young adult male who was, in fact, currently on federal probation. To complete service requirements
for his probation, he was working at the Los Angeles County-
USC Medical Center under the direction of the third author.
The background information with which his role was prepared
was, in all essential respects, a synthesis of his real life history.
When the probation officers were queried about the "realness" of
the evaluation procedure, their unanimous feedback was that the
confederate was "just like a real client." The confederate was, of
course, blind to the control/experimental assignment of the officers. The behavior analysis and intervention plans of the officers
were recorded on a standard form which had four sections. The
first was titled problem behaviors; the second, causes and consequences of behavior problems; the third labeled potential agents
of control; and the fourth directed the probation officer to specify
a plan of treatment.

The probation officers were given the standard probation work-

---

[2]Copies of these measures may be obtained from the first author.
[3]Copies of these measures may be obtained from the first author.

sheet, usually received from an investigating officer the day before they were to see the "client." On the evaluation day, the officers were given the behavioral research form and its use explained. The 30-min period allotted for each interview was chosen because it represented the modal time usually given to a first interview by the officers.

The behavioral research form was scored according to a 35-item checklist specially derived to measure the most salient facets of a behavioral analysis and behavioral probation intervention.[4] For example, in the first section, Problem Behaviors, credits were given if the probation officer listed actual behaviors (e.g. "theft of car radio") as opposed to generalities ("bad attitude" or "immature"). In the second section, Causes of Problem Behaviors, credits were given if modeling or reinforcement for problem behaviors was specified, or if lack of reinforcement for pro-social behavior was noted. Credits were gained in the third section, Potential Controls On Behaviors, for utilizing pro-social models, listing reinforcers derived from the interview, or with specific plans to reinforce incompatible behavior. The last section, Intervention Plan, was scored for clear contingency units (e.g., wanted behavior specified followed by positive consequent contingency), and use of self-control. Bonus points were given if a step-by-step behavioral contract was specified as done in training sessions.

Following the recommendation of Campbell and Stanley (1963) for evaluative research, a Solomon four group design was used for the paper and pencil measures. For the behavioral measure, a post-test only control group design was used.

RESULTS

Data were gathered on three dimensions to assess the effects of the training program: (1) differences between groups in knowledge of behavioral principles, (2) changes in attitudes toward behavior therapy, and (3) demonstration of behavioral competence.

A Solomon four group design was used for the two paper and pencil measures. With regard to knowledge of behavior modification, the pretest results indicate a fairly high level of knowledge

---

[4]Copies of these measures may be obtained from the first author.

before training for all officers $(\overline{x} = 17.88$ correct out of 30) with no statistically significant difference between groups *(t = .15)*. The post-test scores were analyzed following the recommendations of Campbell and Stanley (1963) using the treatment variable as one factor and the pretest variable as the second factor in a 2 × 2 analysis of variance. There was no statistically significant main effect or a significant interaction. The semantic differential measure was analyzed similarly. Again the pretest scores do not show significant differences between groups at the start of the program *(t = 1.21)*, indicating that the groups were not skewed or non-randomly assigned. The 2 × 2 analysis of variance of the post-test scores failed to demonstrate significant difference between groups.

The critical measure of the training program was the behavioral competency measure. The measure consisted of the scores derived from the behavioral analysis and intervention plan which the officers had completed in conjunction with interviewing the confederate client. Each of these forms was scored by two of the authors to determine the reliability of the scale. The reliability coefficient indicated that the measure was indeed reliable *(r = .98)*. The means for the experimental and control groups were 45.44 and 16.88, respectively.[5] A *t*-test performed on the scores of the experimental and control groups was significant (p < .001).

DISCUSSION

The lack of significant differences between the experimental and control groups on the paper and pencil measures of knowledge and attitudes toward behavior modification appeared to be a function of the selection procedure and limits of the measures used. All of the officers who completed the program were selected from a large pool of officers who had volunteered to participate after attending the 2-hour lecture on behavioral principles and probation. As such, all participants had fairly positive attitudes towards behavior therapy, as well as a basic grounding in the principles of behavior therapy. The virtually identical pretest

---

[5]Only 16 officers were able to complete the behavioral measure; one from each group was unavailable at the time of the post-measure.

scores attest to the equivalence of the experimental and control groups with regard to the dependent variable. Secondly, both measures seem to possess a ceiling effect, the net result being that little pre-post differences could be demonstrated.

However, the cardinal significance of this study is the demonstration of marked, significant behavioral competence by the probation officers who were trained in comparison to the control group officers. From these data, it would appear that a basic foundation in principles of learning and a positive attitude simply are not enough in evaluating training programs. What is needed, additionally, is training in the specific behaviors and demonstration of the resultant *application* of the knowledge.

Several probation officers in the training program suggested informally that the most valuable part of the training program was the experiential and modeled practical experiences. The closer these exercises were to their on-line job behavior, the more valuable the training. A substantial part of training time should be devoted to stimulated or actual behavioral experiences; first modeled, then under direct supervision with extensive feedback. A circumstantial measure of this effect was noted in that the two lowest scores in the training group were obtained by members who missed two sessions dealing almost exclusively with practical applications.

The next step in such a training program is to document further the behavioral competence of the trainee in their day-to-day job activities and concomitant change in client behavior. Hand in hand with the responsibility of training other workers in behavioral technology goes the responsibility of evaluating the effect of such training. It borders on malfeasance (certainly misfeasance) to conduct training programs without the guidance and feedback supplied by an extensive evaluation procedure which is intrinsic to the training program. Certainly, in the training of behavior therapists, it is necessary to model the importance of looking at the data, and to adjust programs in line with the evaluation and feedback to determine the effectiveness and then to decide on the future directions of training.

The definitive criterion must always be behavioral competency. Can probation officers, when trained in this manner, conduct a behaviorally oriented interview with a live client, complete a thorough behavioral analysis, and outline an effective therapeutic intervention based on sound behavioral principles? The answer here was yes. Given a brief 6-week workshop, juvenile probation officers were able to demonstrate marked behavioral competency over similar untrained peers. In addition, our results undermine the common practice, in general, in behavior therapy training programs, of using knowledge or attitude differences as a demonstration of overall training effectiveness.

REFERENCES

Editorial Comments

Davidson, W.S., & Seidman, E. Studies of behavior modification and juvenile delinquency: a review, methodological critique, and social perspective. *Psychological Bulletin,* 1974, *81,* 998-1011.

Stumphauzer, J.S. *Six techniques of modifying delinquent behavior.* Teaneck, NJ: Behavioral Sciences Tape Library, 1974.

Stumphauzer, J.S. *Behavior modification principles.* Kalamazoo, MI: Behaviordelia, 1977.

Text

Becker, W.C. *Parents are teachers.* Champaign, IL: Research Press, 1971.

Campbell, T., & Stanley, J.C. *Experimental and quasi-experimental designs for research.* Chicago: Rand McNally, 1963.

Davidson, W.S., & Seidman, E. Studies of behavior modification and juvenile delinquency: A review, methodological critique, and social perspective. *Psychological Bulletin,* in press.

Deibert, A.N.., & Golden, F. Behavior modification workshop with juvenile officers: Brief report. *Behavior Therapy,* 1973, *4,* 586-588.

Stumphauzer, J.S. (Ed.) *Behavior therapy with delinquents.* Springfield, IL: Thomas, 1973.

Stumphauzer, J.S.: *Six techniques of modifying delinquent behavior.* Leona, NJ: Behavioral Sciences Tape Library, 1974.

Stumphauzer, J.S. *Behavior modification principles: An introduction and training manual.* Kalamazoo, MI: Behaviordelia, 1977.

Stumphauzer, J.S. Modifying delinquent behavior: Beginning and current practices. *Adolescence,* in press.

Tharp, R.G., & Wetzel, R.J. *Behavior modification in the natural environment.* New York: Academic Press, 1969.

CHAPTER 12

A FOLLOW-UP OF PROBATION OFFICERS TRAINED IN BEHAVIOR MODIFICATION*

JEROME S. STUMPHAUZER, KENT CANDELORA, AND HENRY B. VENEMA

COLLECTION OF FOLLOW-UP DATA has become common practice in behavior therapy; however, little has been done to assess the long-range effects of behavioral training programs. A related issue has also been raised concerning the effectiveness and ethics of widely practiced behavior modification training "workshops" (Stein, 1975). Extent of application, generalization, and durability of training effects are issues which need to be attended to if potential gains from these programs are to be realized. Thus far, for example, there has been no report in the literature of a follow-up of probation officers trained in behavior modification. Burkhart, Behles, and Stumphauzer (1976) demonstrated that juvenile probation officers who received 6 weeks of training could complete a behavioral analysis and construct a behaviorally oriented probation plan. The purpose of the present report is to answer the following questions regarding the long-range effects of that particular training course: (1) To what extent was behavior modification being utilized in day to day casework? (2) What changes in the training or in the probation department would have to be made in order to fully utilize behavior modification principles?

Six months after the training was completed, we conducted individual follow-up interviews with the nine officers who had com-

---

*Reprinted with permission from *Behavior Therapy*, 1976, 7, 713-715. (Association for Advancement of Behavior Therapy)

233

pleted training.   Fortunately, all nine officers had remained with
the Bellflower division of the Los Angeles County Probation Department.   However, one had become a supervisor, one a probation investigator, and two had been reassigned to the adult division.   Of the five who continued as juvenile probation officers, two
were participants in a special after-care program with a reduced
case load.   Interviews followed an outline constructed by the
authors to cover the two questions listed above.   Specific examples
of application were requested and responses recorded verbatim.
Information on size and type of current case load was also gathered.

Case loads among the eight trainees who worked directly with
probationers (the ninth was a supervisor) varied from 20 to 150
with a mean of 74.   Seven of the nine trainees reported that they
were utilizing some aspect of the training in their day to day work.
The two who reported not currently using the training had been
reassigned and saw less chance for application, although one of
them did report that he had used the training with his daughter.
In general, a shift from the usual focus by probation officers on
"bad" behavior to assets was noteworthy (e.g., "I now look for
positive behaviors").   Use of positive reinforcement was often
mentioned by the officers ("I now tell them what I like") as was
the concept of behavioral contracting (e.g., "getting off probation
in exchange for regular school attendance").   The behavioral approach was seen as especially useful in getting parents and schools
involved in "taking responsibility" for improving behavior.   The
officer who became a probation supervisor reported using the
training in her supervision of other officers, especially in her use
of modeling and praise.   All but one of the trainees stated that
they had applied various components of the training with either
their families (e.g., "reinforcing children for completing homework" and "punishment of mother-in-law!") or themselves (e.g.,
"weight control") since the program ended.

Regarding changes in the training or department which would
facilitate the application of behavioral methods, the officers were
unanimous in stressing the need for reduced case loads, i.e., from
as many as 150 to an optimum of 30.   They also recommended
familiarizing the entire department and especially supervisory staff

with the methods and adapting existing forms and procedures to accommodate the behavioral approach. Additional suggestions were to have continued, on-going consultation from the trainers with a focus on actual rather than hypothetical cases.

The results of this 6-month follow-up were encouraging in that the majority of those trained were applying some form of behavior modification in their work with probationers. All of the trainees expressed the belief, however, that greater use of the methodology would have occurred if support and assistance were provided from within the department. Similar findings regarding the importance of reinforcement from within the system were reported by Ryan (1976) who collected follow-up data on teachers 12 months after they had received behavioral training. If we are to continue the wide scale practice of conducting behavioral training programs, and it seems certain that we will, then we should keep in mind some of the very principles that we are teaching. We must examine closely and manipulate those variables which control generalization and extinction of training.

REFERENCES

Text

Burkhart, B.R., Behles, M.W., & Stumphauzer, J.S. Training juvenile probation officers in behavior modification: Knowledge, attitude change, or behavioral competence? *Behavior Therapy*, 1976, *7*, 47-53.

Ryan, B.A. Teacher attitudes toward behaivor modification one year after an in-service training program. *Behavior Therapy*, 1976, *7*, 264-265.

Stein, T.J. Some ethical considerations of short-term workshops in the principles and methods of behavior modification. *Journal of Applied Behavior Analysis*, 1975, *8*, 113-115.

CHAPTER 13

PREP: EDUCATIONAL PROGRAMMING TO PREVENT JUVENILE PROBLEMS*

JAMES FILIPCZAK, ROBERT M. FRIEDMAN, AND SANDRA C. REESE

EDITORIAL COMMENTS

Virtually every delinquent has attended school. Could the school system have been more effective in preventing the delinquency? This has long been the general belief, but little hard evidence has been forthcoming. In this original chapter, Filipczak, Friedman, and Reese present PREP (Preparation through Responsive Educational Programs), a large-scale program to prevent juvenile problems. The project has an impressive historical lineage — beginning with the early demonstration projects at the National Training School (see Chap. 1) and more recently the three year Programming Interpersonal Curricula for Adolescents (PICA) program (Cohen et al., 1971) in which adolescents were referred to a centralized token-economy school curriculum at the Institute for Behavioral Research, Silver Spring, Maryland. PREP began in 1971 and continues directly **in public schools** with four basic elements: (1) individualized programming for math and English for those students who are both referred and volunteer to participate, (2) group interpersonal skills classes, (3) a behavioral educational and counseling program for parents, and (4)

*The research on which this description is based was conducted at the Institute for Behavioral Research through PHS Research Grants No. MH14443 and No. MH21950 from the Center for Studies of ·Crime and Delinquency, National Institute of Mental Health, and with support of local cooperating school districts and personnel. Thanks must be accorded these districts and personnel (anonymously) and all PREP staff who have worked to stimulate and carry out the research. Special appreciation is also extended to Mr. Harold L. Cohen for his early guidance and direction in the PREP project.

teacher/staff training.   The program is being evaluated in three diverse schools — suburban, rural, and urban.

The investigators differentiate between short– and long–range goals. Substantial data on some 600 students over a period of five years are available.   Significant but short-range goals were reached with regard to academic tests, grades in PREP classes, discipline, and school attendance. In addition, improvement also generalized to other classes in which these PREP students participated.

One year follow-up indicated that program effects were maintained. Longer range and more varied assessments are an integral part of the PREP program.   While it seems safe to assume that replacing failure with successful school and social experience will increase the chances that youth will stay out of trouble later, the definitive data are not yet in. Because PREP results have generalized to other classes as well as been maintained over time, there is reason for encouragement in their long-range goal of preventing juvenile problems.   This link between school efforts and juvenile problems should remain a focal point for our continued interest.

D URING MOST DISCUSSIONS on juvenile problems and delinquency, the schools, as a principal source of youth training, are indicted for not doing their job. The United States Office of Education (1967), for example, while asserting that schools are perhaps the "major socializing institution affecting the lives of today's youth," admits to deficiencies in schools that "probably contribute to (their) delinquent behavior . . . . "

The belief that schools can contribute to or prevent juvenile delinquency has considerable support.   For example, Wenk (1974) indicates that changes in educational policy must be made to insure students are prepared for constructive personal and social behavior, as such training is "the key for decision impact on the problem of juvenile delinquency and youth crime that could not be produced or maintained by the criminal justice system alone." The American educational system has been strongly criticized by the National Advisory Commission on Criminal Justice Standards and Goals (1973) for failing to recognize its role in either the production or prevention of crime.   Schafer and Polk (1967) maintain that "available evidence strongly suggests that delinquent commitments result in part from adverse or negative experiences of some youth." They further note that "there are fundamental defects within the educational system, especially as it touches the lower income youth, that actively contribute to these negative experiences, thereby increasing rather than decreasing the chances that some youth will choose the illegitimate alternative." Educational failure, Schafer and Polk contend, is one of the school experiences that most prominently contributes to delinquency. A recent survey queried 154 juvenile court and aftercare staff in the state of Maryland on their impressions of the most urgent problems and needs in "the entire field of juvenile delinquency." The single item ranked highest by this sample of juvenile service personnel was "the need to restructure the public schools" (Howard Association, 1972).

A number of large-scale research studies have demonstrated empirically the relationship between school achievement and delinquent behavior (see Elliott and Voss, 1974; Frease, 1972, 1973; Gold, 1970; Hirschi, 1969; Wolfgang, Figlio, and Sellin, 1972, for example). These different researchers have provided various interpretations of their results and have given many theoretical explanations of the relationships between school achievement and delinquency. Yet, the major conclusion of them all parallels that voiced by Burns and Stern (1967): "The inability to cope successfully with school sets up wider problems of troublesome behavior for the student and the community."

A number of attempts have been made over the past decade to respond to the insistent demand to "restructure the public schools," attempting to help troubled or troubling youth learn the skills they required for successful interaction with society. Certain of these have avoided the principal issue by creating successful alternative programs outside the normal public school domain (see, for example, Graubard, 1972). In other cases, activities have been built that provide a supplement to the public school programs, helping insure that the students receive the training they need outside the school day and normal program structure (see, for example, descriptions of the Hunt School Program, Burchard & Harig, 1976).

This discussion focuses on a project that attempted to more

directly influence public school programs and make them more responsive to the need of such students. The project, entitled Preparation through Responsive Educational Programs (PREP), was conceived in an unlikely location (a federal juvenile correctional institution), born in an alternative school setting (a laboratory program outside the public schools), and has now been applied in settings relevant to large numbers of youth (urban, suburban, and rural junior high schools in the metropolitan area of a large East Coast city).

DEVELOPMENT OF THE PREP PROGRAM

PREP grew out of issues confronted in programs called CASE (Cohen, Filipczak, & Bis, 1967) and CASE II (Cohen & Filipczak, 1971). These programs concentrated on the academic and social skill training of juveniles committed to a juvenile correctional facility. The programs intended to assist these students in developing skills that would permit them to take advantage of educational and vocational opportunities after release and to foster behaviors and attitudes more appropriate to the requirements imposed by society in general.

The CASE II project was managed as a large-scale point economy, housed in a separate cottage on institutional grounds. Students' academic skills were assessed, and they were placed in individualized instructional programs under the direction of trained institutional staff. Unlike students in many juvenile institutions of that time, CASE students maintained a full academic load of study, whatever their perceived academic "capabilities." They earned "points" for successful completion of their self-instructional and small-group work completed at high criterion standards. These points were spent for private rooms, special meals, access to more advanced courses of study, leisure activities at night and on the weekends, and other consequences that the students and staff found appropriate in such a setting.

When a student had shown high success and major progress in the academic phase of the program, he was able to select from a range of part-time jobs in the cottage or to purchase other vocational training from qualified instructors in the program. Social skills were trained, as well, by program counselors in both residential and recreational activities. Students literally earned their release from the institution, contingent on successful demonstration of attainment of academic and social goals established during the term of commitment.

Students enrolled in these programs were found to make impressive and large-scale academic and social change during their term of commitment. A number of students were enrolled in local public schools during their term of confinement through a school-release program. After release, students for whom the strongest community-based contacts and relationships had been established were found to have the longest-term success. Yet, almost to a (young) man, these students reported to the staff that such a program should have been offered to them before they found themselves in serious trouble. They indicated that their successful experiences in the CASE school program were unlike anything they had previously experienced in their public schools. They recognized that the school was not the only "bad rap" in their lives, but that a school situation such as they found in CASE II could have made their adjustment to the rest of their problems easier to manage. As the CASE projects terminated, staff made plans to build such a reinforcing and behaviorally based program in the non-juvenile justice segment of the society, hopefully, to function as a part of the traditional public school system.

This new program, much like its predecessor at the National Training School, was to be based on several important premises. First, juvenile problem behavior was not viewed as a symptom of an underlying psychopathology. Rather, it was seen as reflective of an inadequate, ineffective, or inappropriate repertoire of social and academic skills. Second, this problem-promoting behavioral repertoire was not considered to be due to an "inability" of the youths to learn, but rather to the presence of learning conditions that promoted failure rather than success, that exposed students to models of problem behavior, and that shaped and reinforced nonproductivity and troublesome behavior. Third, it was assumed that the academic, social, and family behaviors of youngsters were interrelated and had reciprocal effects upon each other. Based on these assumptions, the staff decided to develop a program that would, on the one hand, emphasize instructional procedures (to promote successful learning) and reinforcement procedures (to strengthen this learning) ; and would, on the other hand, focus on the academic, social, and family spheres of the students' lives.

Former CASE staff began planning such a program by dealing directly with administrators from three metropolitan school jurisdictions. A number of students were viewed by school staff as requiring services more comprehensive and intensive than the schools could provide. They were willing to permit these students to be enrolled in an "alternative school" managed by these former CASE staff. Objectives were developed for this alternative program (eventually called PREP) that encompassed training in social and academic skills in addition to elements of parent training. All objectives were formulated with the aid of parents, project staff, and school officials or teachers.

Both training programs and procedures that facilitated student and parent learning were developed by project staff and tested with twelve students during each of three different school years. The outcome of these three program years was used to revise and expand the training programs and analysis procedures to insure that the most appropriate set of training was provided. (See Cohen, Filipczak, Boren, and Slavin, 1971, for a description of this program.)

During the last of these three years, PREP staff began negotiations with the personnel of one local school jurisdiction for the installation of the project in a public junior high school. PREP recognized that cost-effective programs of change for such students were possible only if they were institutionalized and afforded the public support available to other public educational efforts. A program of training was developed that would insure that teachers and other staff would eventually carry out the PREP procedures under the limited direction of PREP staff. Community liaisons were established and lines of communication were established to pertinent school system personnel.

A set of objectives was defined which established evaluation, demonstration, and research procedures that have continued with minor change over five school years. These procedures comprise a program incorporating three distinct, but interrelated, training efforts for its students: academic skills training, social skills training, and family training and liaison   (see Filipczak, Storm, and Breiling, 1973) .

PREP'S WORKING MODEL

This training program hopes to achieve a number of short- and long-range goals.   All of these goals attempt to expand student skills (permitting them to function more appropriately and harmoniously with their environment) and to enhance public school programs (so that special programs of this kind would be needed less in the future) .

Conceptually, the goals for enhancement of student skills relate to a variety of potentially important social outcomes.   PREP directs its efforts so that students will realize benefits as noted in Figure 13-1.

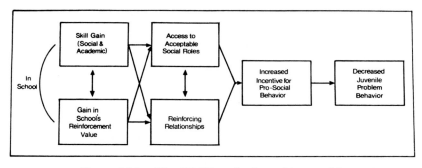

Figure 13-1.   The PREP project's working model.

This model has guided all of PREP's developmental work with training procedures and outcome measures.   It is based on both a theoretical analysis of the effects school programs can have on student performance and on the need for cost-effectiveness in juvenile problem prevention.   The model contains elements of social control and social learning theories, combining features of proven sociological and behavioral perspectives.

As noted, PREP has tried to achieve two different types of short-term objectives for problem-prone adolescents: first, the improvement of their academic and social skills; and second, the development of a school environment that would provide positive incentives for school attendance and participation. Student skill gains and improvement in the reinforcing value of the school are considered by PREP to be reciprocally related. To the extent that students acquired new skills, the reinforcement of school should also increase. To the extent that the school provides positive incentives for attendance and participation, students should find increased opportunity to improve their skills.

PREP also presumes that when students achieve these short-term objectives, they are more likely to adopt socially acceptable roles and become involved in mutually reinforcing relationships with prosocial others. Access to roles such as "employee," "leader," "friend," or "good student" should occur more often for the individual who has a repertoire of effective social and academic skills. Again, these outcomes may be reciprocally related. Students who have success experiences in the more short-term academic area should have greater access to prosocial roles. Assessment of the degree to which these outcomes are obtained is more difficult than in the purely academic areas.

PREP further postulates that academic and social skill improvement, access to and use of acceptable social roles, and the reinforcement by prosocial persons and institutions for these changes can lead directly to increases in the incentives for prosocial behavior. These potentially increased incentives for prosocial behavior (such as social role access and reinforcement for it) are important both within and outside the limited school environment. Here, such objectives require the potential for generalization of skills from the school training setting to other settings (such as the family milieu and the community at large). Assessment of such generalization is again a difficult matter, but one that seems necessary to determine the overall effect of such a training procedure.

Finally, PREP presumes that each of these foregoing changes will permit the student to either avoid or reduce the likelihood of having large-scale juvenile problem behavior. Such problem behavior could be associated with either the school or community life of the student or both. Therefore, the assessment of either its avoidance or reduction must occur in both settings. Hence, PREP postulates that its program may be found to have effects on such juvenile problems through assessment of the extent to which each cell of this model indicates student performance changes.

Assessment of the in-school cells takes place routinely during each PREP school year. Assessment of the latter cells occurs during planned follow-up procedures.

PREP PROGRAM OPERATIONS

PREP's training program encompasses one school year for each student who is selected and voluntarily participates. Students are recommended for PREP by school staff on the basis of strong evidence of academic and/or social problems: failing grades, high number of disciplinary referrals, chronic absenteeism, frequent tardiness or suspension, poor performance on standardized tests or teacher observations of poor classroom performance, contacts with the police or other juvenile problem agencies, and so forth. Thereafter, staff members assess each student's skills and problems in reference to specific entrance criteria, solicit informed consent of parent and child to participate, develop experimental and control groups as required for research purposes, and enroll students in the program for that school year. In this way, PREP finds itself dealing with the students who present the school with the most severe academic and/or social problems each year.

Over the last five years, PREP has been conducted in three different schools in three different school jurisdictions (suburban, rural, and urban). Between 60 and 120 students have participated each year, and more than 600 students have enrolled in PREP over this five-year term. The decision to work in such diverse settings with such a large number of students has been prompted by PREP's concern with developing a program that has been well tested with a variety of student populations.

The program developed for PREP and applied in these settings includes four distinct but interrelated components:

- academic training in reading, English language, and mathematics that permits rapid and thorough skill development;
- social or interpersonal skill training that facilitates im-

mediate and generalizable behavioral skill development for both in- and out-of-school problems;

- family liaison and skills training that promotes increased involvement of the parents in school activities and reasonable programs of family management in the home; and
- teacher and other staff training that helps them conduct all phases of the program.

PREP's evaluation procedures begin at the time students are enrolled. Data from the criterion-referenced selection procedure form a major part of the baseline information on each student. PREP uses such information to assess the change in student performance from before entrance over the program year on measures such as grades, office referrals (for reasons of discipline), suspensions, and attendance. PREP also administers standardized achievement and/or diagnostic tests, the results of which are compared on a pre- and postprogram basis to assess academic skill change. A number of personality, attitudinal, and behavioral measures are also taken for such program evaluations. Comparisons are made on these outcome measures between experimental and control groups or across multiple experimental groups, permitting valid determination of the program's effects.

PREP's training program of academic social, and family skills is comprised of a number of separate but interrelated elements. In certain years, students assigned to PREP take either all of the training elements or none of the elements, yielding pure experimental and control groups. In other years, some students take none, one, or more of the elements, yielding analyses of different component effects. These different training elements are illustrated in Figure 13-2.

The majority of student activity each day is spent in a "skills center" where all academic training is scheduled for a class size of between sixteen and twenty-four students. The students receive training in English and mathematics (in certain years, reading, as well) during these skill center periods, which may be scheduled in a block or during select class periods through the day. Most academic learning is managed in a self-instructional medium, with a number of specific topics or objectives organized for small-

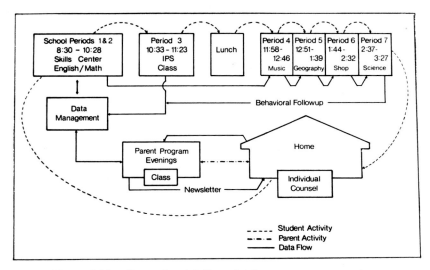

Figure 13-2.   Example of daily activities in the PREP project.

group instruction.   Public school teachers conduct all such programs after receiving training from PREP project staff.   Following
diagnosis and prescriptive placement, students work at their own
pace on these instructional programs.   Learning programs are
geared for all major topics and skill levels across a continuum of
approximately 2nd through 11th grade objectives.   The students'
learning progress is assessed continually, through curriculum-em-
bedded tests and with parallel periodic tests.   Data are maintained
in the program concerning the students' rate of work, their on-
task activities, and their social behavior (according to a number
of criteria).   These data form the basis for student ratings by the
teachers and eventually determine grades and other means of recognition.   Teachers are also trained to create a highly reinforcing atmosphere in the classroom by praising students for their
immediate achievements.   Yet, they provide a structured atmosphere and practice assertive teaching procedures to insure that all
classroom rules are clearly defined and instruction can be conducted without major disruption.

A limited number of social skills are also trained in these academic classes, principally concerning objectives for self-management of study behavior and individual interaction with other students in a self-study setting.

During a different class period, students participate in a more elaborate social skills training element, often entitled IPS (interpersonal skills) class. The number of students in such classes has ranged between eighteen and thirty-two in different years. Here, a large set of social behavior objectives is related to current student skills, and the teacher assists the students in learning those skills needed for survival in the school, home, and community environments. A curriculum of study is available that provides instruction in such basic areas of concern as verbal behavior with teachers, administrators, parents, peers, and persons of authority. Students can also be scheduled for work in verbal and real-life problem solving over issues that relate to in-school and community events. Other basic topics can include nonverbal behavior training (such as facial expressions and gestures); small-group interaction, leadership, and fellowship; personal behavior recording and management; following instructions (in oral, written, and visual forms); and test-taking behavior requirements. In addition, more cognitively oriented instructional sequences may be scheduled for group learning. Among the more prominent of these are family processes and interactions, career preparation and practical skills training, teenagers' rights and responsibilities under the law, drug information, and sex education and hygiene.

Obviously, the majority of these skills cannot be trained on a one-to-one basis, and both small- and large-group instructional processes predominant in this IPS class. Students occasionally work on individually prescribed units, but most frequently work on a group basis is handled by a single teacher with the assistance of student aides (from outside the class and inside—using better-skilled class members). Student behavior is rated and recorded for both content and behavior acquisition. Like the academic classes, students also earn praise from their teacher and the aides when they perform well, earn grades and school credits for skill building, and receive other reinforcers for specified achievement. The entire class is run on a behavioral system, with appropriate behavior rewarded and inappropriate behavior ignored or systematically eliminated.

Students are also involved in regular school classes. These are usually limited to four or five other classes per day—including science, physical education, music or art, social studies, or others as routinely scheduled by the school administration. PREP students participate in these classes to help insure that they are not significantly labeled by participation in PREP and to provide them with other critical skills not a part of PREP training. Yet these other classes also provide PREP with a means of assessing the degree to which the skills learned in PREP carry over to other settings—an important measure of PREP's success. In some cases, students have carried to each of these classes a daily form on which their other class teachers rated their academic and social skills. These forms were returned to PREP by the students, and the data from them formed the basis for routine feedback to the parents. Teachers from these other classes found such daily evaluation to be an important means of providing the student with the additional feedback and control that was often needed.

Family liaison and training has taken many forms over the various years of the program. One of the more important features of this program is the "other class" rating described above. However, more substantial elements have been devised and used as well. Actual programs of parent training have formed a part of PREP's program in the schools. They have been conducted by both PREP and school staff, focusing on the development of parent skills in supporting and maintaining student behavior in the home as it pertains to school- and community-related activities. This training has been given within the school, during evening hours, along with other community-related training programs. In addition, staff have helped the parents develop and conduct programs of individualized behavior management with their children, often working in concert with the IPS class where the students learned comparable skills, all with the consent of both students and parents. Staff worked with the parents and students in their homes as well, assisting them in the specific conduct of programs of mutual interest and need.

Feedback among the PREP staff, students, and their parents

has proceeded in a number of ways. Among these has been a project newsletter that detailed important progress of the students and ongoing activities of the program. In addition, systematic telephone and personal contacts have been used to stimulate or maintain performance such as homework completion, attendance, and interaction with teachers or other students.

Within each of these different program elements, there has been some type of specified and managed reinforcement system for students, parents, and teaching staff. For students, this has included the praise, ratings, and grades given by teachers. In addition, students have earned (in different combinations, over different program years) tangible rewards (such as leisure-time coke breaks) or activity rewards (such as movies, field trips, or game time). In each instance, the use of these different reinforcers was dictated either by the severity of the students' problems or by the social milieu of the school and its parent constituents. Parents receive their reinforcement from the improved performance of their children and contact with staff. Teachers are reinforced similarly, but may also earn college credit for successful performance in the training program.

Data from each of these program elements have been channeled through a data control and evaluation center that has been an ongoing part of PREP's efforts since its inception. Here, the moment-to-moment performance of students in PREP program elements and the project pre- and postassessment have been managed. All outcome information from the project that concerns both student performance and program effectiveness is routinely analyzed by PREP and reported in the appropriate medium.

Obviously, information on the performance of students over the course of the program is important in determining the extent to which the program demonstrates success. However, other issues, of longer range concern, are of even greater importance in the prevention of juvenile problems today. It becomes important to know for how long and to what extent these new skills have generalized to other settings and have been maintained over time.

To answer these concerns, PREP conducts a number of rigorous follow-up evaluations of its students' performance after leaving the project. These are of two different types: one-year postassessment of generalization and maintenance in the schools; and long-term retrospective follow-up on in-school, at-home, and in-community performance. The one-year assessment has been limited to an evaluation of student grades in school for that year and a self-report by the students' parents on successful and unsuccessful experiences at school and in the community. The long-term follow-up is currently in process and includes both student and parent self-reports on the students' home and community adjustment; the students' perceived self-esteem, aspirations, and expectations; ratings of aversive consequences for misbehavior, and socialization; information from the schools on grades, attendance, test scores, disciplinary problems, etc.; and evidentiary information on juvenile problems from the police and courts.

PREP'S RESULTS

PREP's conceptual model incorporates a number of specific short- and long-range goals for its students. The programmatic efforts made within PREP are directed toward the attainment of the goals embedded in each part of the model, from immediate academic through longer-range juvenile problem behavior. Using all of the data that PREP will eventually gather, it may be possible to determine the degree to which each of these parts of the model relates to the whole. Currently, substantial data are available on the short-range, school-based parts of the model. Minimal data are available for the longer-range portions.

One important short-range goal for PREP is to implement a program that facilitates student gains in academic and social competence. Certain of these gains can be measured through changes in standardized test scores and grades the students earn in their school classes over the program year. Another measure of program effectiveness is the extent to which skill changes found in PREP classes carry over to other class settings in the school. Measures of program effectiveness in increasing the reinforcement value of the school to the student can be reflected by changes in the students' attendance. All of these measures pertain to short-range outcomes of high importance to PREP.

Table 13-I summarizes, by year and group, nearly 120 measures

TABLE 13-I

PRESENCE OF SIGNIFICANCE IN FAVOR OF PERTINENT EXPERIMENTAL GROUP ON GROUPED MEASURES, BY YEAR IN EACH SCHOOL SETTING

GROUPS OF MEASURES	YEAR 1 SUBURBAN 2 Groups (N=60)	YEAR 2 SUBURBAN 5 Groups (N=80)	YEAR 3 RURAL 2 Groups (N=78)	YEAR 4 RURAL 3 Groups (N=107)	YEAR 4 URBAN 2 Groups (N=83)	YEAR 5 RURAL 2×2 Factorial (N=96)	YEAR 5 URBAN 2 Groups (N=112)
ACADEMIC TESTS							
Number Significant	5**	1** 2*	1** 1*	8**	NA	4** 1*	2**
Number of Measures	6	6	2	10	NA	12	12
PREP CLASS GRADES							
Number Significant	1**	1**	1**	2**	1**	2**	4**
Number of Measures	1	1	1	2	1	4	6
OTHER CLASS GRADES							
Number Significant	2**	1*	2**	1**	0	1*	3**
Number of Measures	2	2	2	1	1	1	6
DISCIPLINE & SOCIAL							
Number Significant	2**	1*	0	0	NA	7** 4*	2** 1*
Number of Measures	4	4	2	2	NA	16	5
SCHOOL ATTENDANCE							
Number Significant	0	0	0	1**	1**	1**	1**
Number of Measures	1	1	1	1	1	1	1

**Indicates significance $p < .05$ or less.

*Indicates significance between $p < .10 - p < .06$.

on which data were gathered in PREP over the last five years.
The number and types of measures cited here for each year vary
according to the project's need and ability to conduct them at that
time.   Academic tests refer principally to standardized achievement tests (using skill area subtests such as English language, reading, and mathematics) or diagnostic tests (in similar skills).
Measures of PREP class grades are the average grades students receive in classes with which PREP deals (principally English,
reading, and mathematics).   The measures of other class grades
are drawn from classes in which PREP does not do its training
work (such as science, history, home economics, or physical education).   Disciplinary and social measures vary widely from year to
year, but include disciplinary referrals, suspensions, teacher behavior ratings, etc.   The attendance measure refers to the average
number of days students attended school that year.   The outcomes
cited in this table are the number of measures on which significance was obtained in favor of the pertinent experimental group.
The minimally accepted level of significance used for this summary is $p = < .10$.   Outcomes not meeting this standard may be
seen as the difference between the "number of measures" and the
"number significant."   In no instance were significant differences
on social measures or grades obtained in favor of the control
group.

The magnitude of the outcomes obtained for academic test
measures has varied from year to year.   During the first four years,
the differences on most measures were found to be significant.
The relatively low proportion (one-half) of significant differences
in Year Two (suburban) was related to an intense controversy
created by outsiders about the program that affected the students'
performance throughout the year.   Valid testing conditions were
not possible during Year Four (urban), and results are therefore
not available (NA).   During the fifth program year (rural and
urban), emphasis was directed away from academic training effort
relevant to such test measures, with a corresponding reduction in
outcome effect.

PREP students were found to consistently earn higher grades
in PREP subjects than control students earned in such classes
(English, reading, and mathematics).   Although this effect is prob-

ably due to PREP students demonstrating better skills, it is also possible that teachers who worked with PREP (through expectancy or their own desire to see the students' grades improve) may have artificially inflated these grades. However, data from progress measures within the program demonstrate skill improvement comparable to or better than the outcomes obtained on the academic tests. Despite this question, it is fair to note that such improvement in grades for these PREP students serves to decrease the negative labels that can be ascribed to them and potentially enhances their ability to gain more socially acceptable roles in school and elsewhere.

Another important measure of PREP student success is the degree to which skills learned in PREP classes help enhance grades in other (non-PREP) classes. During six of seven setting/years, PREP students showed significantly higher grade gains in non-PREP classes than the controls. Here, grade change results are unlikely to be the product of teacher expectancy or other bias and more clearly indicate the extent to which PREP students demonstrate successful academic and social skill performances in school. Again, improvement in grades can produce either a reduction in negative labeling or an increase in positive labeling throughout the school during that year and in the future.

The disciplinary measures provide an important and major outcome assessment of the students' overall social skill development within the school setting. The degree to which such students are not referred to the administration for reasons of discipline, suspended from school for major or chronic misbehavioral incidents, or receive negative social behavior ratings (or report cards or other routine process in school) indicates to the school and community at large improvement in social competence. Information provided in the table shows that PREP has had less consistent impact on these behaviors than on either tests or grades. During the first two years (suburban school) major differences were obtained in favor of the experimental group (particularly on disciplinary referrals). However, problems were again encountered during Year Two because of the controversy surrounding the program's operations. During both the third and fourth years, no significant differences were obtained, due either to the unavailability of data within the school or to the lack of quality control for such records. When these problems were resolved during the fifth project year (both urban and rural), a greater number of data measures were available and significant differences between experimental and control groups were obtained.

Attendance data shows marked differences across the three school sites. During the first two years (suburban school), attendance for both the experimental and control groups ranged near 90 percent. Little change could be expected with such high-level attendance. Although the experimental group(s) attendance was markedly better than that of the control group(s), no significant differences were found during these two years. During Year Three (rural), overall attendance was lower, but PREP did not mount an effective effort for deterring absenteeism. No differences were obtained on this measure during Year Three. Starting in Year Four, PREP began conducting rigorous attendance-improvement programs in each of the participating schools. As noted in the table, significant differences were found in attendance in both settings over the fourth and fifth program years in favor of the experimental group(s). However, a note of caution is in order. PREP had originally postulated improvement in attendance to be one of the signs of the increased reinforcing value of school for these students. Such a conclusion is not necessarily supported by these data, as the "special" attendance program effects confound the effects obtained through PREP's general efforts. The differences in attendance have always been in favor of the experimental group. However, the effect of the program alone has resulted in significant differences in only one setting (the urban setting, Years Four and Five).

Generalization of student skills from the training program to other settings is a major test of the program's utility. One measure of generalization of skill gains is the degree of relationship between success in the PREP classes and these grades in other classes. The first step taken in assessing this relationship was to calculate residual gain scores on grades for each type of class. A Pearson product-moment correlation computed between the residual gain scores would indicate the extent to which these skills had generalized. Significant relationships were found beween success in

PREP and non-PREP classes in four out of six instances where it could be tested (Year One, suburban; Year Three, rural; Year Five, rural; and Year Five, urban). Research design incompatibility precluded assessment for the Year Four rural program. Another measure of the generalization of program effectiveness is the relationship between program success (grades in PREP classes) and the number of days attended. The PREP model postulated a reciprocal relationship between skill gain and gain in the school's reinforcement value. Therefore, a significant correlation between residual gain scores on PREP grades and school attendance would tend to demonstrate generalization of program effectiveness. In program Year Five (at the urban school, for example), significant correlations were obtained between these measures. The magnitude of the relationship was related to the magnitude of change within the PREP classes, demonstrating that such generalization may have occurred.

PREP's longer-term goals are to (a) increase access to acceptable social roles, (b) increase reinforcing relationships, (c) increase incentive for prosocial behavior, and (d) decrease juvenile problem behavior. The project's ability to help students achieve these goals will be assessed through a number of long- and short-term follow-up procedures for each prior program year.

A one-year follow-up of student performance has been made for certain program years. Results from a follow-up on Year One students indicate that program effects were maintained on a number of measures. For example, the significant improvement in grades for English language and mathematics (PREP classes) and social studies and science (non-PREP classes) found during the program year were maintained for the year following the program, indicating generalization and maintenance of effects.

A long-term follow-up utilizing self-reports and evidentiary measures is currently in progress. Each program year's students are the subject of a follow-up four years after participation in PREP. Results of this long-term follow-up are needed to assess the degree to which PREP has attained its major objectives with its former students and to assess the validity of the working model PREP proposed for juvenile problem prevention.

In summary, five years of program operation in three different school settings have indicated the effectiveness of PREP in achieving the two short-term goals: the improvement of academic and social skills and the development of the school as a more reinforcing environment for the students. Here, a total of 68 differences significantly favoring the experimental group were found in a total of 119 measures. The skill gains and the gains in the school's reinforcing value were found to be related, creating a cycle in which gains in each area contributed to gains in the other.

As a result of achieving these short-term goals, PREP presumes that these former students should be more likely to achieve the longer-term goals as well. However, long-term assessments are required to provide evidence that PREP serves to deter or reduce large-scale or long-range juvenile problems. If the long-range findings indicate that PREP decreases or deters juvenile problems, the original theoretical assumption about the link between school efforts and juvenile problems could be supported. If such findings are absent, this link becomes more suspect; the potential utility of PREP in reducing juvenile problems is decreased, and PREP would face a major dilemma.

Should such a program for behavior problem students be continued because of demonstrated high-level, short-term success or be abandoned due to lack of success in the ultimate test for delinquency prevention programs? This question may be impossible to answer even when all follow-up results on PREP are available. Yet, like most questions in the behavioral sciences, it could serve the best possible ends: to prompt further research that ultimately provides substantive reduction in juvenile delinquency.

REFERENCES

Editorial Comments

Cohen, H.L., Filipczak, J., Slavin, J., & Boren, J. *Programming interpersonal curricula for adolescents (PICA), project year three: A laboratory model.* Silver Spring, Maryland: Educational Facility Press—Institute for Behavioral Research, 1971.

Text

Burchard, J.D., & Harig, P.T.   Behavior modification and juvenile delinquency.   In H. Leitenberg (Ed.), *Handbook of behavior modification and behavior therapy*.   Englewood Cliffs, N.J.:   Prentice-Hall, 1976.

Burns, V.M., & Stern, L.W.   The prevention of juvenile delinquency.   In The President's Commission on Law Enforcement and Administration of Justice, *Task force report: Juvenile delinquency and youth crime.* Washington, D.C.:   U.S. Government Printing Office, 1967.

Cohen, H.L., & Filipczak, J.   *A new learning environment*.   San Francisco, Calif.:   Jossey-Bass, 1971.

Cohen, H.L., Filipczak, J., & Bis, J.S.   *CASE I: An initial study of contingencies applicable to special education*.   Silver Spring, Maryland: Educational Facility Press—Institute for Behavioral Research, 1967.

Cohen, H.L., Filipczak, J., Slavin, J., & Boren, J.   *Programming interpersonal curricula for adolescents (PICA), project year three: A laboratory model*. Silver Spring, Maryland: Educational Facility Press—Institute for Behavioral Research, 1971.

Elliott, D.S., & Voss, H.L.   *Delinquency and dropout*.   Lexington, Mass.: D.C. Heath & Co., 1974.

Filipczak, J., Storm, R., & Breiling, J.   Programming for disruptive and low-achieving students: An experimental in-school alternative.   *Journal of the International Association of Pupil Personnel Workers*, 1973, *17*, 38-42.

Frease, D.E.   The schools, self-concept, and juvenile delinquency.   *Journal of Criminology, Delinquency, and Deviant Social Behavior*, 1972, *12*, 133-146.

Frease, D.E.   Delinquency, social class, and the schools.   *Sociology and Social Research*, 1973, *4*, 443-459.

Gold, M.   *Delinquent behavior in an American city*.   Belmont, Calif.: Brooks-Cole, 1970.

Graubard, A.   The free school movement, *Harvard Educational Review*, 1972, *42*, 351-373.

Hirschi, T.   *Causes of delinquency*.   Berkeley: University of California Press, 1969.

Howard Association.   *Comprehensive long range master plan.   Department of Juvenile Services, State of Maryland* (a survey and consultation report). Chicago: John Howard Association, 1972.

National Advisory Commission on Criminal Justice Standards and Goals. *Community crime prevention*.   Washington, D.C.:   Department of Justice, 1973.

Office of Education, U.S. Department of Health, Education, and Welfare. Delinquency and the schools.   In The President's Commission on Law Enforcement and Administration of Justice, *Task force report: Juvenile delinquency and youth crime*.   Washington, D.C.:   U.S. Government

Printing Office, 1967.

Schafer, W.E., & Polk, K. Delinquency and the schools. In The President's Commission on Law Enforcement and Administration of Justice, *Task force report: Juvenile delinquency and youth crime.* Washington, D.C.: U.S. Government Printing Office, 1967.

Wenk, E.A. Schools and delinquency prevention. *Crime and Delinquency Literature*, 1974, *6*, 236-258.

Wolfgang, M.E., Figlio, R.M., & Sellin, T. *Delinquency in a birth cohort.* Chicago: University of Chicago Press, 1972.

CHAPTER 14

ELIMINATION OF STEALING BY SELF-REINFORCEMENT OF ALTERNATIVE BEHAVIOR AND FAMILY CONTRACTING*

JEROME S. STUMPHAUZER

EDITORIAL COMMENTS

Stealing is a major delinquent behavior. In fact, the FBI's "Uniform Crime Report" for 1974 suggests that 55 percent of serious theft is committed by youths under eighteen—and this amounted to nearly three million arrests of young thieves that year alone! However, curiously little work has been aimed directly at modifying theft behavior in adolescents. Why is this so? One reason may be that, per individual, theft is quite a low frequency behavior. Also, by its very nature it is exceedingly difficult to observe or measure — if successful!

In this chapter the case study of a twelve-year-old girl is presented in which frequent theft of several year's duration is treated. A combination of family contracting and self-reinforcement resulted in rapid cessation of theft, and no return to stealing was found at eighteen-month follow-up. Some hints at the development of rather remarkable cognitive self-control were found. The combined treatment (also including behavioral bibliotherapy with parents and assertion training for the girl) makes it impossible to determine which aspect (or combination) caused the change, and more highly controlled study is warranted. Such study might well be carried out by a probation department (see Chaps. 5 and 6), where a vast number of adolescent thieves are already being "treated."

---

*Reprinted with permission from *Journal of Behavior Therapy and Experimental Psychiatry,* 1976, 7, 265-268. (Pergamon Press)

As part of a large project assessing behavioral interventions with families, Reid and Patterson (1973) present a preliminary evaluation of their work with seven families in which stealing by one of the boys was a problem. As in the present chapter, they describe a variety of behavioral family interventions coupled with behavioral bibliotherapy for parents (Patterson's **Families,** 1971) which resulted in cessation of stealing, although only short-term follow-ups were reported. Reid (personal communication, Sept. 4, 1976) reports replication of these results with nine to twelve month follow-ups.

The parallel findings of this case (with a girl) and those of Reid and Patterson (with boys) suggest that stealing can be treated successfully within a behavioral/family paradigm. Cognitive self-control strategies for treating theft remain relatively unexplored (see also Chaps. 2 and 3).

ABSTRACT

STEALING BEHAVIOR of 5 years duration in a 12-year-old girl was overcome by a combination of self-reinforcement of alternative behavior and family contracting. The stealing stopped within 6 weeks. Family functioning also improved and continued to do so during 5 months of treatment. Follow-ups at 6, 12, and 18 months showed no return to stealing.

Stealing behavior presents a most perplexing problem; its successful treatment has only rarely been reported (Stumphauzer, 1973). Theft is self-reinforcing in that the desired object is immediately acquired. As with other criminal behavior, aversive controls are usually ineffective: any punishment from authority or through legal proceedings is variable, intermittent, and delayed.

While many other delinquent behaviors have been successfully modified through the application of behavior therapy principles (Davidson and Seidman, 1974; Stumphauzer, 1974a, 1976) only one case (Wetzel, 1966) is available in the literature which focuses on the treatment of stealing in a child—which seems incredible since theft is such a major component of delinquent behavior. Wetzel helped stop the stealing of a 10-year-old boy over a $3\frac{1}{2}$ month period utilizing contingency contracting. Treatment was conducted in an institution where the staff were trained, and where direct observation and recording were relatively easy to control. Follow-up was limited to only one month. In the present study, the case was followed up $1\frac{1}{2}$ years after treatment.

CASE HISTORY

The patient was a 12-year-old, black girl who was referred for treatment by school officials who were concerned that they could not keep her in school because of repeated incidences of theft. She lived with her parents and two younger siblings and was attending regular sixth grade classes in a Catholic school. According to reports from school and parents, the girl had suffered from "uncontrollable stealing" almost daily for 5 years (taking small amounts of money and small objects at home, at school, and most recently in stores). The stolen money was often spent on sweets and ice cream. Her teacher and principal were very concerned because, besides the stealing, she was a very good student with above average grades. They suggested that she "had a sickness" and together with the patient had prayed for her recovery. The parents and school officials had managed to keep the girl outside the attention of the law but both feared eventual arrest and embarrassment. As a result she was "watched" closely and was quite isolated—her time being spent either in school, at home with her family, or at bi-weekly church services. She was not allowed to leave home alone as parents feared her stealing would be revealed publicly.

A behavioral analysis of the family (Kanfer and Saslow, 1969) revealed that stealing was the only major problem, occurring at a base rate of four to five times a week, especially at school. Reinforcers that were listed by the patient were attention, praise, sweets, and special activities. These were also recognized by the parents as important to the girl. Stealing behavior appeared to be reinforced in many ways. First, she would have the object she wanted immediately. Second, she gained a great deal of attention from the teachers at school, the principal, and her parents. It is noteworthy that the mother smiled as she told about the stealing and, thus, subtly reinforced it again. The parents' chief method of discipline was a combination of loosely contingent punishment and restriction for bad behavior, and religious activities (praying for help). The patient's father did a great deal of reading and lately had been reading medical books to support his belief that the patient's craving for sweets was due to diabetes. The mother had been trained as a practical nurse, but had dropped out as she felt she had to keep an eye on her daughter.   There was a 7-year-old sister and a 4-year-old brother who seemed to pose no particular problem.   The patient's assets were many: she was bright, above average, very interested in school, liked to please others, and was creative in doing and making things.   In sum, it seemed that the stealing was maintained by a great deal of attention and reinforcement.   Her environment (home and school) , however, did not reinforce her for any prosocial, incompatible behavior.

TREATMENT

The treatment strategy, based on conclusions drawn from the behavioral analysis, was a combination of self-control techniques (Meichenbaum and Goodman, 1971; Kanfer and Karoly, 1972) and family contingency contracting (Stuart, 1971; Stumphauzer, 1974a) .   The patient was seen on an outpatient basis for a total of 15 treatment sessions over a period of five months, initially once a week and later once every 4 weeks.   Each session was a combination of individual therapy and family meetings.

The first three weekly sessions were devoted to the initial behavioral analysis.   Stealing was measured by the patient's mother on Daily Behavior Graphs (Stumphauzer, 1971) and by her teacher on Daily Behavior Cards (Stumphauzer, 1974b) .   The base rate of 4 to 5 thefts a week was consistent with the school records and with parental recollections over the previous several months and years.   Referral to a pediatric clinic resulted in negative findings that helped convince the parents that the problem was not of a "physical" nature.

Self-control techniques were based on an analysis of the exact circumstances under which theft occurred and what the patient said to herself (Mechenbaum and Goodman, 1971).   She expressed interest in stopping but said, "I can't control myself."   We role-played seeing the usual kind of things she would steal (e.g. money in a classmate's purse on the playground) and then alternate interesting things and activities she could shift her attention to which were to be followed by self-reinforcement (e.g. "I'm proud of myself") .   Included in this development of self-control was Kanfer and Karoly's (1972) triad: self-monitoring, self-evaluation, and self-reinforcement. Beginning with the fourth session the patient was encouraged also to measure her own stealing on Daily Behavior Graphs in addition to the measures from parents and teacher, which agreed. Initially she measured, in the *therapist's* words, "the number of times I steal" in school, at home, and in the store. On refraining from stealing she was to use self-reinforcing language. At the sixth session the patient suggested measurement using *her own* words, which strikingly reflects Kanfer and Karoly's (1972) second aspect of self-control (self-evaluation or a qualitative analysis of one's own behavior) : at first daily measures of "I did very well, I did not steal . . .," the following week "I have done so well in the past that I did not think to steal . . .," and for the last two months of treatment she composed these self-evaluative daily measures: (1) "I'm trustworthy. I keep my hands to myself, they are not gummy, and my mind is on learning at school." (2) "I watch to make sure everything is in its place at home. My hands aren't sticky." (3) "At the store I look for what I'm supposed to and not things that will get my interest."

Simple family contracts (Stuart, 1971; Stumphauzer, 1974b) comprised joint agreements to shift parental and school attention away from stealing toward nonstealing. Praise and twenty cents allowance were given for each day of no stealing, but not after stealing incidents. Special activities and her favorite meal on Sundays were used as bonuses for entire weeks of not stealing.

During the initial 5 weeks of treatment, the combination of the self-control and family contracting resulted in a drop of stealing from the four to five times a week base rate to two minor incidents (food from the refrigerator, an apple from a neighbor's tree). Beginning on the sixth week of the treatment combination, stealing stopped altogether, and continued at zero rate up to discharge 3 months later. Follow-ups at 6, 12, and 18 months revealed no further stealing and much improved family functioning.

Two other aspects of work with the family should be noted. First, along with family contracting, behavioral bibliotherapy was introduced. The patient's father, as previously noted, was an avid reader and had been searching in medical books for explanations of his daughter's behavior. Recognizing this, I gave him a series of behavioral books for parents, which he read with great interest and which helped him in shifting his and his wife's attention from stealing to alternate behaviors. They also set up behavioral programs for their other two children.

Second, the social isolation of the patient became an issue, leading me to stress the shaping of gradual independent and assertive behaviors. In family sessions we explored ways in which the patient could gradually go out on her own, go to the store, and take part in school activities. One plan implemented was for her to take a weekly walk to the store to buy some small item for her mother, and to bring home the change from a dollar and a receipt. It is noteworthy that she did not have complete self-control at first and insisted on taking her sister with her, perhaps indicating the transitory phase between external and self-control outlined by Bishop (1973). Many such trips were made, and the family found other ways to encourage and praise out-of-home activities.

During the first year of follow-up the patient became active in a school speech club and developed new friendships. Other changes took place in the family. The patient's mother returned to nursing school saying she no longer had to worry about watching her daughter. At $1\frac{1}{2}$ years' follow-up, the patient does not steal, and has many alternate sources of gratification and reinforcement. She is no longer isolated and is an active 14-year-old. Her parents have continued applying behavioral principles successfully to training their other children and have become able to pursue interests they had thought beyond their reach.

While the present results are encouraging for the treatment of juvenile theft and add a potentially important strategy for this general problem, the generality of these results is limited within the case study approach. The extent of juvenile theft does warrant further controlled study if behavior therapy is to contribute meaningfully to delinquency control and prevention.

REFERENCES

Editorial Comments

Patterson, G.R. *Families: applications of social learning to family life.* Champaign, IL: Research Press, 1971, 1975.

Reid, J.B., & Patterson, G.R. The modification of aggression and stealing behavior of boys in the home setting. In E. Ribes & A. Bandura (Eds.) *Analysis of delinquency and aggression.* Hillsdale, NJ: Lawrence Erlbaum, 1973, 123-145.

Text

Bishop, B.R. (1973) Self-control is learned in *Behavior Therapy with Delinquents* (Edited by Stumphauzer, J.S.), pp. 54-65, Thomas, Springfield, Ill.

Davidson, W.S. and Seidman, E. (1974). Studies of behavior modification and juvenile delinquency: a review, methodological critique, and social perspective, *Psychol. Bull. 81,* 998-1011.

Kanfer, F.H. and Karoly, P. (1972) Self-control: a behavioristic excursion into the lion's den, *Behav. Ther. 3,* 398-416.

Kanfer, F.H. and Saslow, G. (1969) Behavioral diagnosis. In *Behavioral Therapy: Appraisal and Status* (Edited by Franks, C.M.), pp. 417-444, McGraw-Hill, New York.

Meichenbaum, D. and Goodman, J. (1971) Training impulsive children to talk to themselves: a means of developing self-control, *J. Abnorm. Psychol. 77,* 115-126.

Stuart, R.B. (1971) Behavioral contracting within the families of delinquents, *J. Behav. Ther. & Exp. Psychiat. 2,* 1-11.

Stumphauzer, J.S. (1971) *Daily Behavior Graph Manual,* Behaviormetrics, Venice, California.

Stumphauzer, J.S. (1973) *Behavior Therapy with Delinquents,* Thomas, Springfield, Ill.

Stumphauzer, J.S. (1974a) *Six Techniques of Modifying Delinquent Behavior,* Behavioral Sciences Tape Library, Leonia, New Jersey.

Stumphauzer, J.S. (1974b) *Daily Behavior Card Manual,* Behaviormetrics, Venice, California.

Stumphauzer, J.S. (1976) Modifying delinquent behavior: beginnings and current practices, *Adolescence, 1,* 13-28.

Wetzel, R. (1966) Use of behavioral techniques in a case of compulsive stealing, *J. Consult. Clin. Psychol. 30,* 367-374.

CHAPTER 15

COMMUNITY PSYCHOLOGY AND BEHAVIOR MODIFICATION: A COMMUNITY-BASED PROGRAM FOR THE PREVENTION OF DELINQUENCY*†

WILLIAM S. DAVIDSON II AND MICHAEL J. ROBINSON

EDITORIAL COMMENTS

A behavioral community program would be especially remarkable if it could demonstrate effectiveness with "hard core" delinquents. It would deserve even further attention if the program could do this for less money than the usual "treatment" program. The Kentfields Rehabilitation Program, presented in this chapter by Davidson and Robinson, can boast these very results.

Juvenile justice programs for "hard core" (relatively serious and repetitive) offenders are the most costly of programs because they usually require institutionalization and high staff/youth ratios. In spite of the great expense throughout the world for such programs, there is little reason to

*This project was supported by the County of Kent, Michigan. Funds were administered by the Kent County Juvenile Court, Grand Rapids, Michigan. This manuscript was submitted to the University of Illinois at Urbana-Champaign in partial fulfillment of the requirements for the Master of Arts degree. The authors wish to express appreciation for assistance and encouragement to Roger Lewis, Judge John Steketee, Judge Richard Loughrin; to Robert D. O'Connor, of the University of Colorado, for invaluable consultation of the operation of the program; to Julian Rappaport and Edward Seidman, of the University of Illinois, for critical reading of the manuscript; to Lynne A. Davidson for preparation of included figures and support throughout.

†Reprinted with permission from *Journal of Corrective Psychiatry and Behavior Therapy,* 1975, 21, 1-12.

believe that they work in terms of teaching more adaptive behavior or in terms of preventing further offenses.

The ambitious and exemplary Kentfields Program in Kent County, Michigan provides a really **comprehensive** community-based program which includes keeping youths in their own homes, public works participation each morning for wages, an afternoon school program based on programmed instruction as well as performance contracts, behavioral group sessions twice a week, and an overall level and point system. The only obvious extension which they do not report is behavioral contracting with the families as well.

This is a model program not only because of its comprehensiveness and results, but also in the way in which the project staff were able to convince community leaders and the court to refer virtually every youth to this program who otherwise would be institutionalized (125 out of 131). Local government skeptics were so impressed with results—and, no doubt, the money saved—that the program continues with **local** financial support. An outstanding, cost-effective program like this certainly warrants replication in other municipalities.

Abstract

THE APPROACHES of community psychology and behavior modification are combined in establishing a nonresidential, community-based program for hard-core male delinquents. A single group time series design and contingency system analysis are presented. Results indicate a significant increase in prosocial performances, a significant reduction in delinquent behavior, and a significant reduction in costs. It is concluded that the combined strategy makes both empirical and conceptual sense and that a sound basis for further control group and factorial design replication has been established.

Contemporary developments in strategy for the prevention and treatment of juvenile delinquency have found two parallel but relatively independent avenues of promise: community-based rather than institutional interventions, and behavior modification. While such avenues each seem prospectively worthwhile, with the possible exception of Sarason and Ganzer (1969) and Tharp and Wetzel (1969), proponents of these two approaches have tended to ignore one another. Whether for reasons of polemic or for more scientifically defensible reasons, researchers in the behavior modification camp have tended to ignore the community psychology movement, while community psychologists have frequently failed to make use of the conceptual and technological advances in behavior modification. Interestingly, each of these two independent movements has had its beginnings in a climate of dissatisfaction with the medical model of psychological treatment. The problems with a medical model are well known and need no discussion here. However, what is frequently overlooked is the fact that many who, on the one hand reject the medical model, on the other hand fail to develop a viable alternative to it.

Rappaport and Chinsky (1973) have distinguished between two components in any model for delivery of services: the conceptual component and the style of delivery component. Behavior-modification-oriented psychologists frequently reject the medical conception of psychological treatment while retaining the medical style of service delivery. For example, many behavior modifiers conceptualize psychological disturbance in nonmedical terms, but continue to see clients in their private offices, clinics, and hospitals within a doctor-patient relationship. At the same time, while focusing on environmental contingencies in conceptualizing the problem of delinquency, they fail to deal directly with the legal system. Conversely, community psychologists are frequently critical of this doctor-patient, in-the-office style of delivery, but continue to use traditional medical model conceptions of psychopathology. While ostensibly rejecting the medical model in favor of an environmental contingency conception, few community psychologists have taken advantage of the most fully developed psychological conception of the environment: behavior modification. This paper demonstrates a viable bringing together of the community psychology and behavior modification approaches within one problem area: the prevention and treatment of juvenile delinquency.

To date, most rehabilitation efforts for hard-core male delinquent populations, though well intended, have called for large expenditures of money, with less than optimal results (James 1969). While the principles and techniques of behavior modification have in general, demonstrated effectiveness in treatment of a wide variety of disorders (Ullmann & Krasner, 1965; Franks, 1969; Ullrich, Stachnik, & Mabry, 1970), specific attempts to apply a behavioral approach to delinquency have been limited. Yates (1970) reports that a symposium held in 1965 to discuss the application of behavior therapy to delinquency was restricted exclusively to theoretical issues. Since that time, research has been limited in scope, except for educational interventions generally considered critical to successful rehabilitation (Cohen, 1968; Bedner, Zelhart, Greathouse, & Weinberg, 1970; Meichenbaum, Bowers, & Ross, 1968). Other interventions reported to date include demonstration of token economy effectiveness (Burchard, 1967), examination of natural reinforcement systems (Buehler, Patterson, & Furness, 1966), and enhancement of parole success (Petrock, 1969), all within institutional settings. A number of programs have achieved excellent success with delinquent youth in community-based settings (Goldenberg, 1971; Klein, 1967). However, they have not conceived their interventions in a behavioral framework.

Nevertheless, a conceptual model for behavioral interventions in the natural environment has been suggested by Tharp and Wetzel (1969). Research utilizing behavioral techniques in community settings includes shaping interview attendance and content in a street corner project (Schwitzgebel, 1969), increasing self-care and academic performance in a family-style residential program for predelinquents (Phillips, Phillips, Fixsen, & Wolf, 1971), and training parents to reduce deviant behavior in their children (Patterson, Ray, & Shaw, 1969).

The program to be discussed here had as its focus four problem areas: (1) to provide a community-based, nonresidential program as an alternative to institutionalization for hard core male offenders; (2) to increase prosocial behavior in the target population; (3) to reduce delinquent behavior in the target population; (4) to reduce the monetary expenditure required for treatment of chronic juvenile offenders. Before turning to an explicit description of the methods utilized, it is important to describe the social setting in which the program was initiated.

SOCIAL CONDITIONS

The Kent County Juvenile Court, in Grand Rapids, Michigan, began administering the Kentfields Rehabilitation Program in 1969. Prior to that time the Court had been institutionalizing large numbers of chronic male offenders. Such a strategy was costing large amounts of money and bringing less than desirable results.

There were many sources of resistance to a nonresidential community-based program for hard-core delinquents. Many of the objections centered around keeping "those kinds of kids" in the community. It is to be remembered that this project was initiated at the high point in the nationwide campaign for "law and order." Primary resistances were centered around the police departments, school administrations, and local governmental officials. The police objected to the Court "mollycoddling" offenders and not forcing them to take full responsibility for their actions. The school had been generally quite satisfied when the *subjects* (Ss) with which Kentfields dealt were removed from the community. Now they were being asked to reenroll and deal with these young men after they had completed Kentfields. The local governmental officials were highly resistant to any further expenditures of tax dollars for new programs which had no guaranteed outcome.

In overcoming such resistances, a number of strategies were implemented. First, a great deal of effort was put into providing the two juvenile court judges with information about the program's potential. Here there was substantial behavior modification literature upon which to draw. Once convinced, the judges were active in both local and state political arenas and utilized their personal influence in convincing community leaders of the need for the Kentfields endeavor. Second, the Director of Court Services, the administrative parallel of the judges, was personally committed to a community-based behavorial approach and to convincing the governmental bodies of its efficiency and effectiveness. He was instrumental in providing local officials with the information and rationale for supporting a community-based behavioral approach. Third, constant efforts were made to provide concerned individuals with monthly, quarterly, and annual reports about the program's progress. In this instance, the local media, TV and newspapers were helpful in dissemination of progress data. Their interest was both in the experimental nature of the project and coverage of what had become, at least during the early months, a politically hot issue. Fourth, every effort was made throughout the project to cooperate with other community agencies. This is not to say that at many times our goals were not diametrically opposed to those of other social and educational agencies. However, through consistent contact, both social and professional, cooperative efforts were maintained. The fifth strategy involved one of the program components. The work projects, to be described in detail later, had excellent public relations value. Part of the rationale for initiating the community-based approach was that local municipalities and the county would receive partial payback for their investments. Such information was included in program reports and communications.

METHOD

Subjects

From September 1, 1969 through August 31, 1971, 131 males were considered for long-term institutional placement by the Kent County Juvenile Court due to chronic delinquency. Of the 131, 125 were referred to the Kentfields Program as an alternative. The remaining six were sent directly to institutions because of serious crimes against persons. All 125 Ss were accepted. Thus, no special criteria for admission were in effect.

An average S was sixteen years of age (range 14 to 17 years), and tended to live in the inner-city area of Grand Rapids, Michigan (80%). Approximately 60 percent of the target population were nonwhites. The Ss had been on probation to the Kent County Juvenile Court a mean of 2.6 years (range 2 months to 7 years).

Program Description

The Kentfields Program consisted of a contingency point system, utilized in the areas of work performance, academic performance, and appropriate verbalizations in group sessions. The Ss lived in their own homes and were picked up by bus five mornings per week. Each morning, for three hours, the group engaged in various public works projects in the community. These included: tree trimming for local park departments, litter removal for the county highway department, spreading wood chips around playground equipment for the board of education, painting camp buildings for the YMCA, and building renovation for the local

Community Action Programs. Specific individual and group tasks were established each hour, with specific point payoff for successful performance. The work projects were run by a nonprofessional who was taking undergraduate courses part time. Lunch was provided by the program. Again, contingencies for various self-care performances were in effect during the lunch period.

The afternoon classroom consisted of individualized (by grade performance level) programmed instruction and performance contracts, which involved contingencies for accurate performance, for three hours per day. At the beginning of the educational session each student was given an outline of the specific tasks and contingencies to be completed each hour. Special activities were also provided, including plays and the writing of newspaper articles. The educational component was conducted by a teacher aide who had completed less than one full year of college. Space for the classroom was provided by a local community center.

Group sessions were held two afternoons per week, following the class, for approximately one hour. The sessions were conducted by one of the upper level Ss, on an alternating basis, who asked each member to respond to a number of questions including the following: S's positive accomplishments since the last meeting, personal problems for group solutions, each S's status in the program, suggested program changes desired by each S, things Ss would like to learn in the program, and open discussion. Specific contingencies were in effect for topic related responses.

The program included three hierarchial levels through which the Ss were required to move in order to graduate. When an S entered Kentfields, he was at the *June Bug* level. He was required to perform at an 80 percent level in all performance areas for two consecutive weeks. After accomplishing the above, the Ss progressed to the *Junior* level where two consecutive weeks of 90 percent performance were required. The final level, called *Ace* required 100 percent performance for two weeks. As an *Ace*, each S also chose a goal, i.e. what he was going to do after graduation. Essentially, the options open included return to school or employment. Following this decision, the program director assisted the S in accomplishing his chosen goal.

The contingency point system was parallel to programs generally described as token economies (Ayllon & Azrin, 1968) except that points were used. Table 15-I outlines the contingencies and backup reinforcers used in Kentfields. There were no restrictions on what points could be exchanged for within the system described. In general, the point system can be characterized as an open system (Phillips et al., 1971). The teacher and work supervisor informed each S of points earned immediately following each required performance, and current totals were reviewed on an hourly, daily, and weekly basis. Points could be exchanged on a daily and/or weekly basis.

TABLE 15-I

KENTFIELDS POINT SYSTEM

Performance		Points earned
A.	On time for bus, attend full day	100/day
B.	Assigned work task complete	50/hour
C.	Entire group assigned work task complete	15/hour (bonus)
D.	Extra work tasks complete	0 - 100/day (bonus)
E.	Turning in all work tools	20/day
F.	Lining up for lunch, washing hands	20/day
G.	Cleaning lunch table	40/day
H.	0-100% correct on class work	0 - 100/hour
I.	Attending group sessions	25/day
J.	Appropriate comments in group sessions	5/response
Privilege		**Cost**
A.	Money	$.01/point
B.	Merchandise	$.01/point
C.	Recreation Activities (Bowling, roller skating, etc.)	200 points
D.	Rock concert tickets	250 points
E.	Movie tickets	200 points
F.	Cigarettes	40 points
G.	Candy, potato chips, etc.	15 points

Design

Two kinds of data were necessary to evaluate the program in the context of both its community and behavior modification perspectives. The operant or behavior modification tradition requires observations of specific performances functionally related to the in-program contingency system. The community psychologist, in addition, must be interested in the follow-up effectiveness and institutional impact of the interventions utilized. Thus, pre- and postprogram data on all Ss were recorded.

It must be clearly stated at the outset that no comparison group was available for the outcome portion of this study. The Ss treated were the total population considered. This situation was demanded by the community served and indeed is one of the "real world" problems the community psychologist-researcher must face. Thus, we have a single group time series analysis (Campbell & Stanley, 1963). Quasi-control groups from other communities or earlier time periods, though considered, failed to provide any legitimate comparison due to differences in court practices, community characteristics, and excessive use of long-term institutional placement for similar populations. Thus, concomitant examination of any conjured control group was abandoned.

Pre- and Postmeasures

Preprogram data were gathered through structured interviews with Ss and their families, examination of juvenile court records, interviews with respective probation officers, and examination of Ss' school records. The information included (1) a global statement of S's activity for the year prior to entering Kentfields—enrolled in school, employed, excluded from school, in a correctional institution; (2) length of time on probation; (3) number of police referrals to court (arrests); (4) attendance rate in school (if in school); (5) academic grade level performance measured by the Wide Range Achievement Test (Jastak & Jastak, 1965).

Follow-up measures were taken an average of eighteen months (range 2 to 26 months) after Ss had completed Kentfields. The data, collected in a parallel fashion to the preprogram data, were gathered by the program director with the assistance of two Grand Valley State College students. The information was the same as the premeasures, with the exception of time on probation, which was omitted. At follow-up, arrest rates were gathered from both juvenile court and adult court records since most Ss had reached age seventeen and would have come under adult court jurisdiction if apprehended. In addition, a cost comparison of operating Kentfields, as opposed to institutional alternatives, was accomplished.

A comparison was also made, at follow-up, of program graduates (98) and nongraduates (27). The following were reasons for twenty-seven Ss being removed from the program before completion: (1) being placed in other local educational programs $(N = 11)$; (2) S's family moved from the community $(N = 10)$; (3) further law violations $(N = 6)$. Generally, the Ss were removed within the first four weeks. Premeasure comparison of the graduate and nongraduate found no significant differences on any of the measures utilized.

Measures of S's behavior while in the program consisted of the performance rates for each specified response set. These measures included (1) attendance—performance rates of all Ss on contingency A in Table 15-I; (2) work behavior—performance rates of all Ss on contingencies through G excluding bonuses; (3) classroom behavior—accuracy rates of all Ss on programmed instruction material; (4) group sessions behavior—rates on all Ss' appropriate verbal responses in group sessions of a criteria ten responses per meeting. The above data were drawn from the records of the contingency point system. In other words, the points earned were based on the observations concerning task completion and accuracy. The hourly point records then were the basis of in-program data. The program offered a senior level seminar in Applied Behavioral Science with the Psychology Department of Grand Valley State College. During ten school days in school year 1970-71, two of the college students independently kept hourly point records for all Ss in the program. Interjudge agreement between the two students and the program staff was 93 percent. Agreement was based on assignment of exactly the same number of similar point assignments divided by the total number of opportunities to assign points. More specific data were collected for a one-month period in order to examine the efficacy of the contingency point system utilized in the educational component. Selection of additional target educational behaviors to enable changes in contingencies resulted in examination of (1) time in seat—percent of time sitting at designated desk; (2) study behavior—percent of time looking at school work, talking to teacher, or writing; (3) percent of accuracy on written classwork; (4) rate of returning from five-minute hourly breaks on time. Nineteen Ss were involved in this subexperiment, representing the total program population during the four-week period.

Observation techniques involved having two observers (Grand Valley State College psychology students) and the teacher each independently record the above behaviors. The class lasted three hours each day. The 180 minutes were divided into 36 five-minute intervals, and 12 of the 36 were randomly selected each day as observation intervals. Also, an individual student was randomly selected for observation during each time interval. Interjudge agreement (agreements divided by total) was 93 percent. The observerers used an observation sheet with the designated time intervals and Ss's names. Time in seat was recorded by using a hand stopwatch. The observers were present in the classroom throughout each educational session included in the study. The experiment included five conditions:

BASELINE. Two weeks prior to initiation of the systematic observations, classroom points were put on a noncontingent basis. The third week of noncontingent reinforcement served as baseline.

MANIPULATION NUMBER ONE. After five days of baseline, the Ss were informed by the teacher that they would receive points each hour on the basis of the percent correct of their classwork. In addition, the Ss earned fifty points for returning from all breaks on time. This condition was in effect four days.

MANIPULATION NUMBER TWO. The second experimental condition involved changing the contingencies so that an individual S, by exhibiting study behavior, could earn points for the entire group. The teacher explained that each S would be observed for a five minute interval. If he was studying for the entire interval he would earn points for everyone. The Ss were not told when they were being observed. The observers signalled the teacher when the group had received points for studying. The returning from break contingency remained in effect. This condition lasted four days.

MANIPULATION NUMBER THREE. The third manipulation was a return to the baseline condition. This is the A-B-A paradigm prescribed for demonstration of behavioral control (Sidman, 1960). The reversal condition lasted two days.

MANIPULATION NUMBER FOUR. The fourth experimental manipulation was parallel to condition two and lasted four days.

RESULTS

Preprogram Data

The global measures of the Ss' activity for the year prior to Kentfields admission yielded the following: excluded from school—48 percent; enrolled in school—32 percent; in a correctional institution—20 percent; employed—0 percent. During the mean of 2.6 years on probation, each S had committed a mean of 2.95 offenses per year with larceny, breaking and entering, and auto theft the most common. Of those enrolled in school, records indicate they had attended at a 69 percent rate for the year prior to Kentfields admission. The Ss tested at a mean grade level of 5.3 on theWide Range Achievement Test.

In-Program Data

Program attendance demonstrated an overall mean of 87 percent, work behavior a mean of 89 percent, and group session behavior a mean of 71 percent.

Figure 15-1 indicates the pattern of in-program behavior demonstrated by all 125 Ss over the average length of treatment of nine weeks. The graph represents an average pattern and is divided into the three program levels according to the average time spent in each. The performance rates tend to increase with time in the program and progress through the three levels. However, since initial rates were high, it appears that existing behavior was strengthened rather than new performances initiated.

The results of a multiple baseline examination of the classroom contingencies, depicted in Figure 15-2, demonstrated the

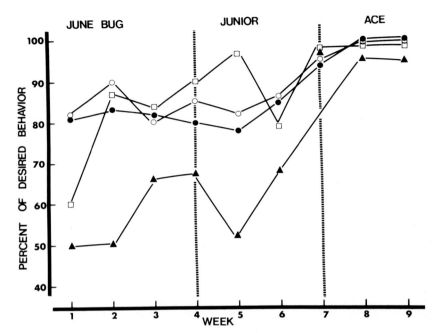

Figure 15-1.   Mean percent of performance in three program components by mean number of weeks to attain graduation.   Open circles are mean attendance rates.   Solid triangles are mean group session performance rates.   Open squares are mean accuracy rates in educational sessions.   Solid circles are mean work project performance rates.   Weeks are divided into the three hierarchical status levels according to mean length of time spent in each by all Ss.   N=125.

efficacy of the techniques utilized.   It is interesting to note that experimental conditions one, two, and four produced essentially the same behavior rates even though different behavior were targeted.

Postprogram Data

In examining follow-up measures, separate data are presented for program graduates and nongraduates.   At the time of follow-up, 117 of the total Ss were available to provide information other than arrest records.   Arrest rates, from court records, were available on all Ss.

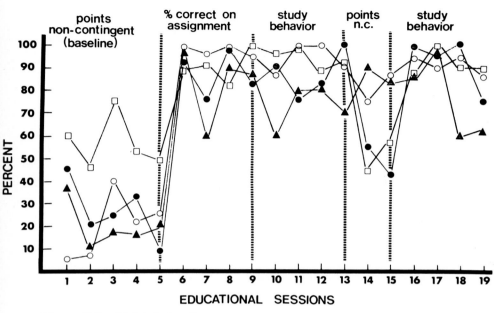

Figure 15-2. Multiple baseline examination of classroom contingency system. Figure represents performance in four classroom areas by educational sessions (three hours each). Solid circles are mean accuracy rates on in-class written work. Solid triangles are mean percents of time in seat. Often circles are mean percents of study behavior. Open squares are mean rates of returning from breaks on time $(N = 19)$.

Arrest rates for program graduates yield a mean of .46 per year. This represents a significant reduction from 2.95 per year $(t = 13.4;\ df = 96;\ p < .001)$. Arrest rates for nongraduates were .64 per year. However, this is a somewhat meaningless measure since more than half of them (55%) were in a correctional institution at the time postprogram data were gathered.

Follow-up global measures demonstrate that graduates, in comparison to nongraduates, tend to return to school, secure employment, if not in school, and stay out of penal institutions. Table 15-II demonstrates all graduate versus nongraduate comparisons to be significant in the desired direction using Yates's corrected chi-square method (Hayes & Winkler, 1971). More specifically, a greater proportion of graduates are employed and in school. Similarly, a smaller proportion are in a correctional institution or are unemployed. It should be added that the unemployed category includes only those Ss not in school, not employed, and not in an institution and therefore is not the reciprocal of the employed category.

TABLE 15-II

OUTCOME COMPARISON OF GRADUATES VS. NONGRADUATES

Outcome status	*Graduates* (95)	*Nongraduates* (22)	X^2	df
In school	28	0	6.971*	1
Employed	33	2	4.399**	1
In a correctional institution	16	12	8.918***	1
Unemployed	18	10	5.392****	1

*$p<.01$
**$p<.05$
***$p<.005$
****$p<.025$

Postprogram measures of school records indicate a mean attendance rate of 91 percent. No pre- postprogram statistical comparison is presented, however, since the postprogram Ss enrolled in school were not the same group as the Ss in school prior to the program.

Just prior to completing the program Ss were given the Wide Range Achievement Test a second time. The mean follow-up grade level was 6.3 as compared to a 5.3 level at admission, only nine weeks earlier. This represents a significant increase ($t = 2.18$; $df = 97$; $p < .05$).

The cost of operating Kentfields was $30,000, or $480 per S treated. This amount is compared to treatment costs of $8,000 (10-month average) for the state training school and $5,000 (12-month average) for private institutions per individual commitment. During the eighteen months prior to initiation of the Kentfields Program there was a mean of eighty-two males in residential institutions from the Kent County Juvenile Court. For the eighteen months following initiation of Kentfields the mean was reduced to fifty-six. This represents a significant decrease

$(t = 12.2; df = 34; p < .001)$. These data are presented graphically in Figure 15-3.

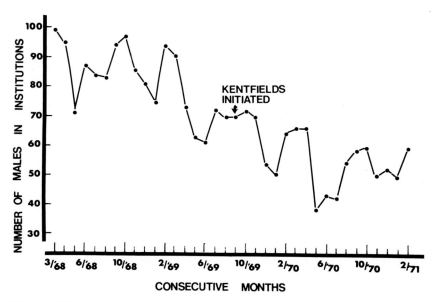

Figure 15-3. Figure represents the number of males institutionalized by the Kent County Juvenile Court from March, 1968 to February, 1971. Solid circles are mean numbers institutionalized per month. Arrow indicates the date Kentfields was initiated.

DISCUSSION

At the outset, it was stated that the goals of the Kentfields Program included establishment of a community-based treatment program as an alternative to institutionalization for hard-core juvenile offenders. Within this framework, specific program criteria were used to demonstrate the efficacy of behavioral techniques in affecting significant increases in prosocial perofrmances and significant reduction of delinquent behavior in the community. It was similarly proposed that such an approach would require minimal expenditures of funds in comparison to traditional institutional placement.

A high and stable rate of appropriate behavior in all program components was demonstrated. However, since initial rates were high in all areas, it is more appropriate to say that existing performances were strengthened rather than new ones initiated. Each program component—work projects, educational sessions, group sessions—involved performances crucial to community adjustment. The only legitimate means to desirable ends (Merton, 1957) for program graduates were return to school and employment. Thus, target behaviors were directly related to community adjustment.

A common issue raised concerning behavioral approaches is whether or not changes are a function of the contingencies utilized or the mere delivery of rewards. The multiple baseline evaluation of the classroom contingency system, reported in Figure 15-2, indicates the dependence of the classroom behavior on contingent reinforcement. To a marked extent, generalization is demonstrated between time in seat, study behavior, and performance on written work. Following experimental manipulations one, two, and four, though differential contingencies were in effect, each of the above response sets demonstrated a stable performance pattern.

Of primary interest to those responsible for juvenile corrections planning is the significant reduction in delinquent behavior. Not only is the decrease in reported offenses statistically significant, but the reduction in delinquent activity of 84 percent has practical significance as well. It is also apparent that completion of the full program sequence is related to socially desirable outcomes (Table 15-II).

The demonstrated increases in classroom target behavior appear related to academic achievement in general. An increase of one full grade level in an average of nine weeks adds substantial credibility to the approach utilized.

It has been demonstrated that large expenditures of monies were not necessary to produce desired changes in delinquent populations. Utilizing a community-based approach with nonprofessionals serving as treatment agents eliminates the need for large administrative bureaucracy, extensive facilities, and other complex organizational costs. Nearly half of the program's budgeted expenses involved provision of contingent reinforcers.

Although no hard data are available on the specific effects of the community relations strategy, described earlier, or on the relative potency of its various components, it should be pointed out that the program continued, and continues at this writing, to receive local governmental funding. In many ways this is the essence of what is frequently ignored in psychological descriptions of programs. However, in this program such efforts are of equal status with our use of behavioral technology in program success.

Many of the original local governmental officials who were the program's skeptics became its most adamant champions and recommended similar approaches in other areas. Where the initiation of the program had been a political issue, by the end of the time covered here it provided considerably less mass media material, was considered a success by local officials, and provided a technical and theoretical base for a halfway house for males and females currently in operation in the same community.

A number of conclusions result from the experimental program examined here. First, although quasi-experimental outcome design was utilized, a viable alternative to long-term institutionalization for hard-core delinquents has demonstrated promising results. Second, the techniques of behavior modification appear to be effective in increasing prosocial performances with hard-core delinquents. It should be kept in mind however, that reported findings, though encouraging, must necessarily be interpreted with some caution, due to possible confounding with Ss' history, maturation, and the interaction of observations and treatment inherent in the design (Campbell & Stanley, 1963; Underwood, 1957).

Despite the above cautions, the significant reduction in illegal behavior, coupled with the relative inexpensiveness of the described approach, enhances its appeal for program planners. While only systematic replication, utilizing control group and factorial research designs, will allow causal attribution to the techniques utilized (Paul, 1969), it appears that a firm basis for more sophisticated approaches to the evaluation of the proposed techniques has been established.

Again, although the results of the educational aspects of the program must be regarded with some caution since retest reliability statistics for the Wide Range Achievement Test are unavailable for parallel populations over similar time periods, the increase in academic achievement demonstrated is also promising and generally considered central to rehabilitative interventions (Cohen, 1968).

Given the design utilized and the social setting in which this program took place, it is not possible to definitely separate the active program ingredients. Kentfields included the use of a community-based intervention, behavior modification techniques, nonprofessionals, and college volunteers which have all produced desired outcomes in other situations. Causal attribution to any specific component or examination of the relative potency of each awaits further investigation. Thus, it is concluded that an alternative to institutionalization has established a level of efficacy warranting further investigation in applied settings. In addition, the combination of community psychology and behavior modification conceptions and approaches represents a successful model for the creation of alternative settings for delinquent youth.

REFERENCES

Text

Ayllon, T. & Azrin, T. *The token economy.* New York: Appleton-Century-Crofts, 1968.

Bednar, R.I., Zelhart, P.R., Greathouse, L., & Weinberg, S. Operant conditioning principles in the treatment of learning and behavioral problems with delinquent boys. *Journal of Counseling Psychology,* 1970, *17,* 492-497.

Buehler, R.E., Patterson, F.R., & Furness, J.M. The reinforcement of behavior in institutional settings. *Behavior Research and Therapy,* 1966, *4,* 157-167.

Burchard, J.D. Systematic socialization: A programmed environment for the habilitation of antisocial retardates. *Psychological Record,* 1967, *17,* 461-476.

Campbell, D.T. & Stanley, J.C.. *Experimental and quasi-experimental designs for research.* Chicago: Rand McNally, 1963.

Cohen, H.L. Educational therapy: The design of learning environments. *Research in Psychotherapy,* 1968, *3,* 21-33.

Empey, L.T. *Studies in delinquency: Alternatives to institutionalization.* Department of H.E.W., Washington, D.C., United States Government Printing Office, 1967.

Franks, C.L. *Behavior therapy: Appraisal and status.* New York: McGraw-Hill, 1969.

Goldenberg, I. *Build me a mountain.* Cambridge: M.I.T. Press, 1971.

Gruver, G.C. College students as therapeutic agents. *Psychological Bulletin,* 1971, *76,* 111-127.

Hayes, W.L. & Winkler, R.L. *Statistics.* New York: Holt, Rinehart and Winston, 1971.

Jastak, J.F. & Jastak, S.R. *Wide Range Achievement Test.* Manual, Los Angeles: Western Psychological Services, 1965.

James, H. *Children in trouble: A national scandal.* Boston: Christian Science Publishing Society, 1969.

Klein, W.L. The training of human service aides. In Cowen, E.L., Gardner, E.A., & Zax, M. (Eds.), *Emergent approaches to mental health problems.* New York: Appleton-Century-Crofts, 1967.

Meichenbaum, D.H., Bowers, K.S., & Ross, R.R. Modification of classroom behavior of institutionalized female offenders. *Behavior Research and Therapy,* 1968, *6,* 343-353.

Merton, R.K. *Social theory and social structure.* New York: Glencoe Press, 1957.

Patterson, G.R., Ray, R.S., & Shaw, D.A. Direct intervention in families of deviant children. Eugene, Oregon: Oregon Research Institute, Mimeo., 1969.

Paul, G.L. Behavior modification research: Design and tactics. In C.M. Franks (Ed.), *Behavior therapy: Appraisal and status.* New York: McGraw-Hill, 1969.

Petrock, F.A. & Elias, A. A summary of the readjustment unit program. Bordentown, New Jersey, Mimeo., 1969.

Phillips, E.L., Phillips, E.A., Fixsen, D., & Wolf, M.M. Achievement place: Modification of the behaviors of pre-delinquent boys within a token economy. *Journal of Applied Behavior Analysis,* 1971, *4,* 45-59.

Sarason, I.G. & Ganzer, V.J. Social influence techniques in clinical and community psychology. In C.D. Spielberger (Ed.), *Current topics in clinical and community psychology,* Vol. 1. New York: Academic Press, 1969.

Schwitzgebel, R.L. Preliminary socialization for psychotherapy of behavior disordered adolescents. *Journal of Consulting and Clinical Psychology,* 1969, *33,* 71-77.

Sidman, M. *Tactics of scientific research.* New York: Basic Books, 1960.

Tharp, R.G. & Wetzel, R.J. *Behavior modification in the natural environment.* New York: Academic Press, 1969.

Ullman, L.P. & Krasner, L. *A psychological approach to abnormal behavior.* Englewood Cliffs: Prentice-Hall, 1969.

Ullmann, L.P. & Krasner, L. *Case studies in behavior modification.* New York: Holt, Rinehart and Winston, 1965.

Ulrich, R., Stachnick, T., Mabry, J. Control of human behavior, Vol. 2. Glenville: Scott, Foresman, 1970.

Yates, A.J. *Behavior therapy.* New York: John Wiley, 1970.

CHAPTER 16

REDUCING JUVENILE DELINQUENCY: A BEHAVIORAL-EMPLOYMENT INTERVENTION PROGRAM*

CAROLYN M. MILLS AND TIMOTHY L. WALTER

EDITORIAL COMMENTS

Just as there is a general belief that schools can do something to prevent delinquency (see Chap. 13), so too it is believed that jobs can prevent delinquency. A strong behavioral case can be made for this notion. Not only can working be viewed as incompatible with delinquent behavior, but a job (hopefully) has natural **positive** consequences (pay, praise, satisfaction) which will act to maintain it. But employers are often reluctant to hire youths who have been in trouble, and up until the time of this study, there has been no clear behavioral demonstration that jobs per se reduce delinquency. The reader should note that work for wages was one aspect of the Kentfields Rehabilitation program as well (Chap. 15).

In this hallmark, original chapter, Mills and Walter provide a model that could be applied and evaluated in any number of communities. Delinquents were not simply placed on jobs. Indeed, if this were the case there would be good reason to expect yet another failure experience. The investigators helped insure success by **recruiting and training employers,** and by **shaping pro-employment behaviors** in these youths.

*This study was made possible by a grant from the Office of Criminal Justice Training Programs, Grant LEAA No. 01-0492-01 and No. 01-0492-02 through the State of Michigan. The study began Dec. 1, 1971 and ended Jan. 15, 1973. The authors gratefully acknowledge the cooperation of the Washtenaw County Vocational Center.

The project was successful on three major scores. Not only did these adjudicated delinquents successfully continue on their jobs, but school involvement was improved and arrests were reduced to a significant degree.

ABSTRACT

THE BEHAVIORAL-EMPLOYMENT INTERVENTION PROGRAM was a one-year study involving (1) recruitment and behavioral training of local employers, (2) establishment of contingency contracts between delinquents and experimenter, (3) shaping delinquents in pro-employment behaviors and (4) placing delinquents on jobs. There were three phases in the program: Phase I involved weekly meeting between the experimenter and subject and experimenter and employer, during which verbal reinforcement was used to increase or maintain subjects' job-appropriate behavior and employers' commitment; Phase II involved biweekly meetings and fading of verbal reinforcement; Phase III was a maintenance phase. Subjects were juvenile court wards from fourteen to seventeen years of age with a mean of 3.9 arrests. Arrests and institutionalization were substantially reduced in the experimental group and the intervention strategies were effective in keeping delinquents on the job and in school.

Behavior intervention studies designed to increase the frequency of prosocial behaviors of juvenile delinquents in noninstitutional environments have met with limited success (Tharp and Wetzel, 1969). These results contrast with those obtained by investigators working with juvenile delinquents in institutional environments wherein the usual problems of control and assessment are not as great (Phillips, Phillips, Fixsen, and Wolf, 1971). Nevertheless, the potential gains associated with developing an effective behavioral intervention program for delinquents residing in their "natural environments" are considerable. Hence the present investigation was initiated in order to develop a more effective way of using behavioral technology for delinquents in noninstitutional settings.

Four basic considerations guided the design and execution of Behavioral-Employment Intervention Program. First, as Fleisher's (1966) analysis of sociological data indicates a positive correlation between unemployment and delinquency, job placement had to be an essential ingredient of the program. Secondly, as employers were not likely to possess techniques for promoting effective task performance, they were given basic training in positive reinforcement philosophy.   Third, since the culturally deprived backgrounds of many juvenile delinquents (Nye, Short, and Olson, 1958) provide them with little in the way of basic job skills and positive job attitudes (attendance, performance, grooming), the subjects were given considerable training to help correct these deficiencies.   Finally, as contingency contracting has proven to be an effective way of insuring subject cooperation (Homme, Csanyi, Gonzales, and Rechs, 1969), contracts describing the obligations of the experimenter, subject, and employer were signed by the parties involved.

METHOD
Subjects
Subjects were convicted delinquents referred to the program by the Juvenile Courts' probation or intake caseworkers.   While arrest records varied, subjects had from one to eight convictions with a mean arrest rate of 3.85.   Subjects referred were the court's most serious offenders and such felonies as arson, armed robbery, rape, and larceny were commonly found in the records of the referrals.

Seventy-six subjects were referred to the program.   Out of the seventy-six, twenty-three were in the comparison group and fifty-three were in the experimental group.   More subjects were referred than could be placed on jobs; those referred when a job was not available were placed in the comparison group.   The comparison and experimental groups were similar in age and background.   The demographic data is shown in Table 16-I.

PROCEDURES
Employers
The forty-five employers who volunteered to hire a delinquent agreed to follow the procedures outlined by the experimenter (senior author) in order to maintain consistency in the treatment program.   The procedures were as follows:

1. Employers gave the subject's paycheck to the experimenter.
2. Employers filled out weekly feedback sheets describing the

TABLE 16-I

DEMOGRAPHIC DATA

Variable	Experimental Group	Comparison Group
Number of subjects	53	23
Age range	14 - 17	14-17
Mean age	15.7	15.7
Race		
White	34	16
Minority	19	7
Sex		
Male	44	16
Female	9	7
Social Class		
Low	33	20
Lower Middle	10	2
Middle Class	10	1
Lived with both parents	22	7
Parents and family members		
unemployed	19	3
Job history		
1 or more jobs held by subject	48	18
Average tenure on job	−2 weeks	−2 weeks
Attending school at time of referral	28	18

subject's performance.

3. Starting pay was at least $1.50 per hour.

4. Subject received, as a minimum raise, $.20 per hour at the end of Phase I and II.

5. Each day employers asked for and initialed subject's report form.

6. Employers met weekly with the experimenter to discuss the subject's progress.

7. Employers terminated a subject who did not meet his or her obligations to the experimenter.

8. Employers signed a contract agreeing to the above.

Employers were reimbursed for 50 percent of the subject's wages for the first three months the subject worked for them. The experimenter scheduled weekly appointments with employers to reinforce them for following the guidelines of the project. Shaping took place during the conversations the experimenter had with the employers. The employer's positive statements about the subject were consistently responded to positively. The experimenter praised the employer for providing positive feedback to his employee. Negative statements about "delinquents" or about the subject were ignored by the experimenter, unless there was a serious problem affecting the youth's performance on the job.

Interview

Prior to each subject's interview, the experimenter familiarized herself with the subject via the referral form from the court caseworker. Baseline data were gathered from the referral form, court records, and the interview. During the interview conducted with all subjects, the experimenter encouraged subjects to talk about their interests in order to put them at ease and to investigate possible types of job placement. Positive statements subjects made about their desire for working or how they might get a job were reinforced by smiles, head nods, or verbal encouragement as the statements were a first approximation toward acceptable job performance. If the subject's appearance promised to eliminate them from the job market, they were asked what they might be willing to do about it. Subjects were praised for any response indicative of positive change. The experimenter told subjects that since only a limited number of jobs were available, it might be months before they could be helped in job placement, hence subjects were offered job-finding suggestions. Subjects were praised for any statements they made as to how they would obtain employment. The experimental subjects were contacted from one day to three weeks later about possible placement. Controls were not contacted.

Contingency contracts had to be signed before a youth could be in the program and placed on a job. Major points of the contract were as follows:

1. The subject agreed to see the experimenter weekly during Phase I and biweekly during Phase II.
2. The employer gave the experimenter the subject's paycheck; she in turn presented it to the subject at the com-

pletion of the appointment.

3. To receive the paycheck, the subject had to bring in his or her report form each week. Failure to do so meant the check was held until the next appointment.

Orientation

When interests, location, and availability were matched to a job, the subject was asked to come to the experimenter's office to be taken to the job interview. The experimenter offered advice on grooming and appropriate dress for the interview, and the subject was praised for attempts to improve appearance. The experimenter and subject role-played the job interview and, if necessary, role reversal was used. To insure a realistic interview, the experimenter did not participate in the actual job interview.

One to three days before the subjects started work, they were required to attend a counseling session with the experimenter as a prerequisite to entering the job. The focus of the session was to begin shaping job-appropriate behavior. The subjects were asked to list on a weekly checklist report form eight behaviors they felt necessary to maintain their job. First responses were praised even if they were off target. Systematic shaping of on-target responses helped subjects complete the list of job-appropriate behaviors. If the subjects could not produce a list, they were given a list of Employer Expectations with twenty items from which they could choose. Selections were based on importance to the subject.

During orientation and throughout Phase I, subjects were required to list, on their report form, behaviors they felt to be important measures of success on the job. While working they earned one point per day for each behavior listed and completed. Subjects also earned one point for each listed behavior their employers indicated the subject had completed. In addition, while in orientation, Phase I, and Phase II, subjects earned two points a week for listing behaviors on the checklist sheet under the following headings:

"Things I need to improve on this week."

"Good things that happened at work this week."

"Things that happened at work that I did not like this week."

Subjects' points were plotted weekly on individual graphs which hung in the experimenter's office.

The subjects met with the experimenter two to three days after starting work. This final meeting, which ended the orientation phase, was devoted to further reinforcing appropriate job behaviors and attitudes. If at any time subjects lost their job due to failure to meet contracted obligations, no further attempt was made to place them.

Phase I

During Phase I, the subjects received a high level of verbal reinforcement from the experimenter in addition to the daily and weekly points earned for job-appropriate behavior. Employers verbally reinforced task accomplishment when signing the check list at the end of each day. Employers also filled out weekly feedback sheets for the subject's positive job behaviors and behaviors needing improvement. The experimenter collected these feedback sheets once each week. Employers were asked to emphasize positive aspects of subjects' performance. If the employer listed any negative feedback, the experimenter made use of "sandwiching" procedures in reporting this information to the subject during the weekly counseling sessions. The experimenter first drew attention to a positive point, discussed how well the subject had done on this, then mentioned a negative point and asked the subject what he felt could be done to improve, encouraged his responses, then returned to a positive statement from the employer. The criticism was thus "sandwiched" in between statements of praise.

The experimenter was often perceived to be an agent of the court, and thus weekly appointments were initially perceived unfavorably by many subjects. A high schedule of reinforcement was utilized in Phase I to overcome the negative reactions of subjects. As soon as the subjects came in the door, they were welcomed and praised for keeping their appointment. If on time, they received ten bonus points. Checklist forms were discussed at length; praise and immediate points were given for every item completed. Areas of performance identified by the subjects in writing as "Needing Improvement" were treated as insightful and relevant.   Shaping positive attitudes toward work was accomplished in discussing the second section of the form where the subjects listed "Things that happened at work that I liked."   In order to extinguish unwarranted complaints about work demands, negative comments listed were ignored.   On the other hand, legitimate problems were given serious attention and solutions were sought.

During Phase I, emphasis was on shaping the following behaviors:

1. Being at work every scheduled day
2. Being on time
3. Calling in ahead of time if ill or if going to be late
4. Following regulations of organization, including dress code, lunch time, and breaks
5. Good job performance (specified behaviorally according to subject's job)
6. Learning names of employees with whom the subject was in contact
7. Cooperation in following directions.

Subjects' statements as to what they wanted to do well were always listed on their report form.   Initially, subjects did not have a clear idea as to employer expectations, thus prompting was used to encourage listing the above items.   Once the desired work guidelines were behaviorally established, there was more flexibility in items subjects listed.

At the end of each session subjects were given their paycheck and praised for their monetary accomplishment.   Subjects added and recorded their points on a graph hanging on a large bulletin board where they and their peers could see each other's progress.

During the session, some subjects periodically elected to talk about personal problems external to the work situation.   Such conversations were not encouraged.   The experimenter's objective was to extinguish old behavior patterns and shape a repetoire of new behaviors centered around work rather than establishing a conventional "personal counseling" relationship.   If problems were work related, they were discussed to the extent that subjects had positive suggestions as to how the problem might be handled. If talking was reinforcing for the subjects, the experimenter let them talk. However, subjects' conversations were shaped so that positive statements were made about their work and how it affected their life. Conversations regarding topics such as school, further vocational training, and joining the armed forces were praised. If at any time a subject decided to quit a job in order to advance educationally, the subject was encouraged to do so.

The experimenter was in weekly contact with subjects' court caseworkers to inform them of the subjects' progress. Caseworkers generally had little contact with subjects while they were in the program unless a subject was involved in a legal violation. Throughout the program data were collected on contacts the subjects had with law enforcement agencies and also on work attendance and performance.

When subjects earned 240 points, they completed Phase I of their contract. Reinforcement for completion of Phase I consisted of reducing the counseling sessions from weekly to biweekly meetings and a raise from employers of twenty cents an hour or more.

Phase II

Fading of reinforcement from consistent high levels to decreasing levels began with Phase II and the bi-weekly sessions. Pro-employment behaviors necessary for satisfactory job performance were assumed to have been well established. Phase II's objective was to maintain vocationally appropriate behavior which competed with deviant behaviors previously in the subject's repetoire. Solutions for problematic behaviors were more stringently sought. Subjects were expected to generate solutions and were verbally reinforced for doing so. Reinforcement was frequently from job-related experiences rather than from the experimenter.

In Phase II, written feedback forms were no longer required from employers; reports on progress were verbal. Subjects now used a checklist prepared by the experimenter requiring weekly rather than daily completion. Five points per week were given for each listed item completed. Bonus points were awarded items added to the checklist by subjects when they deemed a particular behavior important for good job performance. Verbal reinforcement for good performance was intermittent; however, ten bonus points were still given for punctuality at counseling sessions. Points were charted by subjects on the Phase II graph and hung on a special Phase II bulletin board. Subjects still received paychecks at the end of each bi-weekly session; if the employer paid weekly, one check was received at work and one check from the experimenter.

When subjects earned 300 points, Phase II was completed. There were several rewards for completing Phase II. Subjects earned a second raise, at least twenty cents per hour, and no longer had counseling sessions with the experimenter. Moreover, the experimenter wrote a letter to the court (which the subjects were permitted to read) recommending the subjects' release from court jurisdiction. If the subjects had been getting school credit for their jobs, a letter was written to the school informing them of the subjects' successful completion of the program and continuing progress on the job.

Phase III

Phase III required minimal contact between the experimenter and subjects: fading was nearly completed. There were no formal contacts with subjects or employers, but the experimenter informally contacted subjects approximately once a month thus providing intermittent reinforcement for continued successful performance. If either subjects or employers had a problem, they were asked to call the experimenter, who volunteered to assist in a solution. By the time subjects were in Phase III, they generally had been working for six months and socially desirable behavior patterns were well established. This phase lasted for one year from the time subjects were initially placed on a job. The experimenter used the phase to continue data collection on subjects' attendance, job performance, promotions, arrests, schooling, and establishment of independence.

RESULTS

All comparisons between the experimental and comparison groups were done from the date a subject was initially interviewed. Results were recorded beginning the first day after the interview and thus, when outcomes are reported, the time reference is identical for comparison and experimental groups. Anything occurring prior to the interview was baseline data.

There were two criteria for overall success:

1. The subject should have no further arrests nor be institutionalized.
2. The subject should be on the job a minimum of three months or stay in school, and if a drop-out, go back to school or get further vocational training.

If the subject had an arrest and/or dropped out of school, he or she was termed unsuccessful. A Chi-square analysis of the success data is shown in the fourfold contingency Table 16-II, yielding a Chi square of 34.27, df $= 1$, p $< .001$.

TABLE 16-II

OVERALL SUCCESS

	Success	*Failure*
Experimental	45 (84.9%)	8 (15.1%)
Comparison	3 (13.6%)	20 (86.4%)

Subjects in the comparison group were compared to the experimental group for arrests during and after treatment. The Chi square fourfold contingency table lumps all classes of arrests together, with Chi square yielding 29.0, df $= 1$, p $< .001$. These data are shown in Table 16-III. The treatment was significant in prevention of further arrests.

In Table 16-IV, the number of temporary or permanent institutionalization of members of the comparison and experimental groups is compared. Chi square analysis yields 16.8, df $= 1$, p $<$

TABLE 16-III

ARRESTS AFTER TREATMENT

	No Further Arrests	*One Or More Arrests*
Experimental	48 (90.6%)	5 (9.4%)
Comparison	7 (30.4%)	16 (69.6%)

TABLE 16-IV

INSTITUTIONALIZED

	Yes	*No*
Experimental	5 (9.4%)	48 (90.6%)
Comparison	12 (52.2%)	11 (47.8%)

.001, showing that the treatment was effective in preventing institutionalization of delinquents.

Forty-six of the subjects were in school at the time they were interviewed; thirty stayed in school and sixteen dropped out. A comparison of the experimental and comparison group on the variable of school attendance indicates that the experimental group had fewer dropouts, as shown in Table 16-V. Chi square analysis yields 13.25, df = 1, p < .001.

Table 16-VI lists overall tenure of experimental versus control group for the period of the study following the initial interview.

TABLE 16-V

REMAINED IN SCHOOL

	Yes	*No*
Experimental	24 (85.7%)	4 (14.3%)
Comparison	6 (33.3%)	12 (66.7%)

TABLE 16-VI

	Obtained Jobs	Still On Jobs	Average Total # Weeks On Job
Experimental (from 53)	53	18	13.6
Comparison (from 23)	9	0	2.7

DISCUSSION

The present study indicates that the utilization of a broadly based behavioral intervention program involving job placement, the reinforcement of pro-employment behaviors and attitudes, employer education, and contingency contracting extended the job tenure and/or school attendance of juvenile delinquents. More importantly these procedures, coupled with the possibility of full release from court jurisdiction, effected a marked reduction in arrest frequency over the duration of the program, following initial job placement. Thus this program appears to deserve the same serious attention enjoyed by such other intervention procedures as contingent attention and the token economy in the handling of inappropriate social behaviors.

It should be apparent that without such a broadly based behavioral intervention program, the present results would have been quite unlikely. While it is possible that the success of the Behavioral-Employment Intervention Program might be especially attributed to a single intervention strategy, the following considerations suggest this approach to be fruitless and sterile. (1) Many of the subjects did not possess such basic skills as punctuality, good grooming, appropriate office manners, or performance behaviors so as to have been able to keep their jobs without training. (2) An additional complication resides in the employer-employee relationship. It is likely that without discussions on the utilization of positive reinforcers in effecting change, the employer could have easily aborted this relationship by a justified but negative comment. (3) Further complicating the question of major responsibility attribution was the role of the experimenter.

She served not only to recruit community employers but also provided them with some information on positive reinforcement, served as a trouble shooter, provided a sympathetic ear, and reinforced their own positive behaviors.   (4) To the subjects, the experimenter was an individual who had provided them with a job, was genuinely interested in their future and provided much in the way of day-to-day positive reinforcement. Possibly, a major weakness in any one of these facets might have served to completely override the beneficial effects of the others.

Another variable possibly affecting the success of the study was the subject's clear understanding that failure to complete Phase II of the program meant an automatic return to full court jurisdiction and possible institutionalization. While such a threatening alternative probably played some role in producing the desired results, the high arrest rate in the comparison group would suggest that the punishment value of this alternative was minor.

An unexpected and unassessed contribution may have resided in the attitude of the delinquent peer group. Initially subjects' peers were opposed to the program; early initiates were subjected to no small amount of verbal harrassment by their peers. But, as the economic circumstances of these initiates soon made possible the purchases of such highly valued items as radios, clothes, and cars, these initiates were seen bringing in their friends who specifically requested placement in the program.

It was originally anticipated that as the stay in the program increased, the arrest frequency would decrease. To our surprise, the data indicate that all subjects who completed the orientation phase were arrest free for the duration of the program. The early interviews, job placement, and a single interview three days after job placement seem to be adequate in significantly reducing arrest frequency. This relationship should make this program even more appealing to social agencies who might find the total intervention procedure employed here too expensive.

REFERENCES

Text

Fleisher, B.M., *The Economics of Delinquency,* Chicago, Quadrangel Books, 1966.

Homme, L., Csanyi, A., Gonzales, M., Rechs, J., *How to Use Contingency Contracts in the Classroom,* Champaign, Illinois, Research Press, 1969.

Nye, L., Short, J. and Olson, V., Socioeconomic status and delinquent behavior, *American Journal of Sociology,* 1958, 63, I.

Phillips, E.L., Phillips, E.A., Fixsen, D.L. and Wolf, M.M., Achievement Place: modification of the behaviors of pre-delinquent boys within a token economy, *Journal of Applied Behavior Analysis,* 1971, *4,* 45-59.

Tharp, R.G. and Wetzel, R.J., *Behavior Modification in the Natural Environment,* N.Y., Academic Press, 1969.

CHAPTER 17

THE BUDDY SYSTEM: RELATIONSHIP AND CONTINGENCY CONDITIONS IN A COMMUNITY INTERVENTION PROGRAM FOR YOUTH WITH NONPROFESSIONALS AS BEHAVIOR CHANGE AGENTS*†

WALTER S. O. FO AND CLIFFORD R. O'DONNELL

EDITORIAL COMMENTS

There are not enough professionals to go around. Even if there were, there is considerable reason to believe that they are inapproriate change

*This article was adapted from a thesis submitted to the University of Hawaii by the first author in partial fulfillment of the requirements for the MA degree in psychology. Support of the Buddy System was provided through Model Cities funds administered by the Department of Housing and Urban Development, and through demonstration Grants 69787 and 76-P-45109/9-01 from the Office of Juvenile Delinquency and Youth Development, U. S. Department of Health, Education, and Welfare to the Family Court, First Circuit, State of Hawaii.

The authors wish to express their gratitude to Jack Nagoshi and Robert Omura of the Social Welfare Development and Research Center for the excellent consultation they provided. Grateful acknowledgement is also extended to Bill Chambers and Mary Jane Lee of the Hawaii Family Court for their support of the study; Jules Greenberg, David Lam, and Dorothy Pluta, who served as behavior analysts along with the first author; Gilfred Tanabe and Roland Tharp, who served as members of the thesis committee with the second author; and Leonard Ullmann for his critical reading of the manuscript.

†Reprinted with permission from *Journal of Consulting and Clinical Psychology*, 1974, 42, 163-169. (American Psychological Association)

agents. Tharp and Wetzel (1969) and others make a convincing case for **natural mediators** — parents, peers, teachers, employers. In this chapter Fo and O'Donnell utilize another important group of natural mediators. **Volunteers** represent a virtually limitless yet, for the most part, untapped resource for working with problem youth.

The Buddy System in Hawaii demonstrates that volunteers who receive minimal training and guidance can help redirect youth with a variety of problems. As part of a Model Cities program, buddies were recruited in newspapers, received limited basic behavioral training, and then were assigned to be the buddy for up to three youths at a time. In this chapter a series of conditions was compared: (1) "warm and positive" relationship, (2) contingent social approval plus noncontingent money allotment, (3) contingent approval plus contingent money allotment, and (4) a control condition. Contingent reward conditions were most effective in improving school attendance and behaviors such as curfew and fighting.

In a further analysis of the Buddy System, Fo and O'Donnell (1975) investigated the frequency of **delinquent** offenses of 264 youths who participated in the program as compared to 178 controls, even though delinquent behaviors per se were not targeted for change in the program. In addition, they differentiated the effects of the program on delinquent offenses in youths who **had** committed prior offenses in comparison to youths who **had not.** The Buddy System was effective in reducing offenses among previous offenders, but one in six of those who had not previously committed offenses did so in the project year (significantly more frequently than controls). Why this apparent iatrogenic effect? The authors suggest that this may have resulted from contact with other youth in the program who **were** offenders.

In a third analysis, O'Donnell and Fo (1976) investigated locus of control as measured in the buddies and youths and correlated this with success in the program. Results suggest important relationships in the **relative** locus of control of the buddy/youth pairs; e.g. the greater the externality of the Buddy relative to the assigned youth the less the improvement (see also Chap. 8).

ABSTRACT

THE APPLICATION of the triadic model of therapeutic intervention was tested within a community-based program that trained indigenous nonprofessionals as behavior change agents. Forty-two youngsters, aged 11-17, referred for behavior and academic problems participated in the study. Each of these youths received the friendship and companionship of an adult resident in the community. These adult buddies attempted to influence their youngsters through their relationship and through the contingent use of social and material reinforcement. The results indicate that school attendance increased when placed on social or social-material contingency, while no change occurred in noncontingent relationship and control conditions. Social-material contingency also was effective in decreasing assorted problem behaviors, such as fighting, returning home late, and not doing home chores. However, there were no effects across conditions when academic achievement (i.e., improved grades) was the target behavior.

The Buddy System is a community-based program for youth using indigenous nonprofessionals as change agents. In this program operated by the Family Court, adult residents in two Model Cities communities served as "buddies" of youth referred for behavior and academic problems. These buddies met regularly with youngsters in their natural environment and attempted to guide and influence them to engage in socially appropriate behavior.

Such intervention with youth is in keeping with the current trend in the helping professions toward establishing in-community treatment programs and tapping the manpower resources of the target community. It is becoming widely acknowledged that the greatest potential for fostering behavioral change resides in the community (Smith & Hobbs, 1966). The traditional mode of treatment (removal of the deviant individual from his home environment to large institutional settings such as correctional facilities and psychiatric hospitals) has not been widely successful (Berelson & Steiner, 1964; Bloch & Flynn, 1966; Harlow, 1970). In the wake of the failure of institutional environments to provide therapeutic amelioration, treatment of behaviorally disordered youth in community-based settings has become increasingly evident (Patterson, 1969; Phillips, 1968; Rose, Sundel, DeLange, Corwin, & Palumbo, 1970; Stuart, 1971. In addition, in recent years the use of indigenous nonprofessionals in the human services has gained increased impetus (Cowen, Gardner, & Zax, 1967; Grosser, Henry, & Kelly, 1969; Guerney, 1969).

The successful application of a model of community intervention with youth in which nontraditional community workers functioned as change agents has been demonstrated by Tharp and Wetzel (1969). These investigators developed an organizational plan, which they termed the triadic model of therapeutic intervention, for escalating professional help in the delivery of social and mental health services. In this operational schema, behavioral modification is effected in the natural environment through a person (mediator) who occupies some normal role relationship with the deviant individual (target). The professional (consultant) or subprofessional (behavior analyst) does not deal directly with the target but instead advises the mediator in ways of intervening with the target.

The triadic model of intervention served as the operational basis of the Buddy System. The professionals, graduate students (behavior analysts) and their supervisors (consultants), provided training and consultation to indigenous nonprofessionals (mediators). These buddies intervened directly in altering the deviant behaviors of referred youths (targets) through the establishment of buddy relationships.

The primary aim of the Buddy System was to change behavior, with priority given to increasing school attendance. A second major objective of the project was to demonstrate the use of nonprofessional residents as effective change agents. The aim was to equip nonprofessionals with the requisite skills and techniques for successful behavioral intervention with youth, thereby increasing the number of skilled and experienced helpers in the community.

During the first year of operation, evaluation of the project included investigating the efficacy of various treatment techniques employed in the program. The focus of this paper is on this investigation.

METHOD

Personnel

YOUTH. The target population served by the Buddy System consisted of youngsters presenting behavior management problems in the home, school, and the community at large. Youths referred to the project displayed a wide range of problems, including truancy, poor academic achievement, classroom disruption, curfew violation, and fighting. The vast majority of youths participating in the project were referred by the public schools in the

Model Cities neighborhoods, although referrals were also received from the police, Family Court, various social welfare agencies, concerned community residents, and parents.

Youngsters of both sexes were invited to participate in the Buddy System if they were residents of the Model Cities neighborhoods and between 11 and 17 years of age ($\overline{\chi} = 14$). The large majority of these youths were in the seventh and eighth grades. Their ethnic backgrounds included Hawaiian, Filipino, Japanese, Chinese, and Caucasian.

BUDDIES. Buddies were recruited through advertisements in newspapers in the Model Cities communities. They ranged in age from 17 to 65, included both sexes, and represented a diversity of ethnic and occupational groups. They ranged in education from the fourth grade to completion of master's degrees, with a median educational attainment of the twelfth grade.

Each youngster participating in the project received the friendship and companionship of an adult resident in the community. Each adult buddy worked with three youths and extended to them a relationship of mutual affection, respect, and trust. The buddy met with his youngsters individually and at the appropriate times, as a group; they engaged in such activities as arts and crafts, going to rock concerts, camping, surfing, fishing, and simply rapping.

Buddies were paid up to $144 per month by earning points for engaging in the following specific behaviors: *(a)* making a weekly contact with each of their assigned youngsters, *(b)* submitting weekly behavioral data and completing weekly assignments on each youngster, *(c)* submitting weekly log sheets, and *(d)* attending biweekly training sessions.

Training of buddies consisted of six initial three-hour weekly sessions followed by biweekly sessions for the duration of the project year. Buddies received ongoing training and supervision in developing the necessary skills and techniques for effective behavioral intervention with target youths. The emphasis of the training program was in equipping buddies with the knowledge, skills, and techniques of contingency management—for developing a warm and meaningful relationship with their youths, as well as for fostering behavior change. Through such training, buddies learned to influence their youngsters through their relationship and through the application of contingent rewards. As in the case of youths participating in the project, specific behaviors of adult buddies were targeted, and their occurrence was programmed to meet with reinforcing consequences in the form of the social approval of the trainer as well as greater point earnings. Modeling and role-playing procedures were also used extensively in teaching buddies the requisite human relations skills and intervention techniques for helping their youngsters.

Specifically, buddies were trained to engage in the following role behaviors: (a) meet weekly with each of their target youths and participate in social and recreational activities with them; (b) establish a warm, positive, and trusting relationship with their youngsters; (c) identify problem areas and specify them in behavioral terms; (d) count the frequency of occurrence of the targeted behaviors and submit weekly behavioral data to the behavior analyst; (e) draw up and carry out intervention programs aimed at ameliorating the youngsters' target behaviors; and (f) serve as an advocate for the youngsters in their dealings with persons in their environment.

BEHAVIOR ANALYSTS. Four first– and second-year graduate students—two males from psychology, and one male and one female from social work—served as behavior analysts. They earned internship credit for their year of participation in the project.

Each behavior analyst was responsible for the training and supervision of eight buddies assigned to him. The behavior analyst continuously sought to shape through systematic rewards those behaviors of the buddies that enhanced their functioning as change agents. In addition to the material rewards embedded within the point system, instructions, prompts, and socially reinforcing consequences were systematically employed by the behavior analyst as a means of fostering the acquisition and maintenance of desired buddy behaviors.

The following specific behaviors characterized the role of the behavior analysts: (a) maintain responsibility for the day-to-day details of managing the behaviors of the buddies; (b) provide the buddies with intensive, ongoing training in behavioral principles and techniques; *(c)* provide the buddies with continuous consultation and supervision in case management both by telephone and in the field; *(d)* design intervention plans for ameliorating behavior problems of the target youths; *(e)* collect and graph weekly behavioral data submitted by the buddies; *(f)* trouble shoot difficulties as they arose in the buddy–youngster relationship and in the intervention program; and *(g)* monitor the behaviors of the buddies and supervise the administration of the point system.

CONSULTANTS. The professionals were three staff members of the Social Welfare Development and Research Center of the University of Hawaii. Their collective expertise was in the fields of education, social work, and clinical/community psychology. The use of consultants was necessitated by the academic training requirements of the behavior analysts. In other circumstances both roles might be incorporated into one and served by the same people.

The role of the consultants encompassed the following task behaviors: *(a)* maintain overall administrative responsibility for training, reesarch, and evaluation of the project; *(b)* conduct ongoing program planning and development; *(c)* provide the behavior analysts with expertise and training in behavioral technology; *(d)* provide ongoing consultation and supervision to the behavior analysts in designing and implementing intervention programs for the target youths; *(e)* monitor the record-keeping functions of the behavior analysts to ensure decision making consistent with the data; *(f)* collect and analyze the data for research and evaluative purposes; *(g)* oversee the behaviors of the behavior analysts and provide necessary feedback to maximize their success in working with the buddies; and *(h)* monitor the operations of the project at every organizational level so as to ensure efficient and effective functioning consistent with the goals of the program.

Design and Procedure

Within a 4 × 3 research design, the effects of four conditions —three experimental and one control—were compared across three time periods: baseline, first intervention, and second intervention.

Youngsters eligible for participation in the Buddy System

were randomly assigned to one of four conditions:

1. Relationship. Buddies were instructed that a warm and positive buddy–youngster relationship that is always present (i.e., noncontingent) is most effective in producing behavior change. In addition, the youth's monthly allotment of $10 was to be spent in a noncontingent manner.

2. Social approval. Buddies were instructed that a warm, positive relationship, contingent on the performance of desired behavior, is effective in obtaining the greatest amount of behavior change. As in the relationship condition, the $10 monthly allotment was to be spent on the youngster in a noncontingent fashion.

3. Social and material reinforcement. This condition was similar to social approval except that the $10 monthly allotment was to be spent contingent on performance of the desired behavior.

4. Control. This condition consisted of youngsters who were referred to the Buddy System, met all criteria of acceptability, but were not invited to participate in the project.

Each buddy was assigned three youngsters and instructed to respond differently to each youngster in accordance with the three treatment conditions. Behavioral frequency data were collected on a total of 42 youngsters: 26 with school attendance as the target behavior ($n = 5, 7, 7,$ and 7 for the relationship, social approval, social and material reinforcement, and control conditions, respectively) ; 6 with assorted target behaviors, all in the social and material reinforcement condition; and 10 with academic achievement as the target behavior ($n = 6, 2,$ and 2 for the relationship, social approval, and social and material reinforcement conditions, respectively.*

Stable baseline frequency recordings were first obtained for each youth. The treatment conditions were then instituted, comprising the first intervention. Upon stabilization of the target behavior, all treatment youngsters were switched to the social and

---

*Originally 15 of the 32 buddies were assigned a youngster from each of the three treatment conditions. For various reasons, such as youngsters moving, frequency counts of target behavior not being taken, and baseline data indicating no problems, 10 youngsters were not included in the study. Only school attendance data were collected on control youth as this could be done unobtrusively.

material reinforcement condition, constituting the second intervention. Each time period averaged 6 weeks.*

Frequency counts of the target behavior of youths placed on intervention were continuously collected by the buddies. For example, in the case of intervention on truancy, buddies visited the school at least once weekly and obtained frequency counts of their youngsters' school-attending and class-attending behaviors. School personnel routinely opened their records to the buddies. In some cases, buddies met with the school counselors or went directly to the teachers involved to determine whether or not a youngster was in class on a given day of the week. In other cases, buddies arranged with the youngsters themselves to keep daily records of their class attendance. In all cases, buddies confirmed the reliability of these data by continuing to monitor on a weekly basis the school's official daily attendance tallies.

For those youths placed on contingency intervention, buddies responded to them on the basis of the behavioral data collected. That is, buddies dispensed social and material reinforcers to these youngsters on a weekly basis contingent on the performance of the target behaviors to criterion. The degree of reinforcement depended on the intervention plan and the discretion of each buddy. Buddies were instructed to make it clear to these youngsters that the rewards were contingent on the occurrence of the desired behavior.

RESULTS

The behavioral data were collected from the buddies and recorded in frequency of occurrence per week. In the case of the school attendance data, an additional check of the official school records was made. A reliability correlation with the school attendance records of the buddies was computed $(r = .97)$. The minor discrepancies in the data were then averaged out. Since the behavioral frequency data were readily and conveniently put into the form of proportions, all data were analyzed by means of a test of the equality of two proportions (Freund, Livermore, & Miller, 1960). In this procedure, a proportion was computed for

---

*A more detailed description of procedures is available in Fo (1972).

each group as a unit. For example, the number of school absences per group was expressed as a proportion of the number of school days times the number of youngsters in each group.

The mean truancy rate (unexcused absences) for time periods and conditions is presented in Table 17-I. Implementation of the social approval and social and material reinforcement conditions during Intervention 1 resulted in substantial reductions in truancy rate from baseline ($p < .001$). There was correspondingly little change from baseline for the relationship and control conditions. In addition, both the social approval and social and material reinforcement groups had lower truancy rates during Intervention 1 than the relationship and control group ($p < .001$). While both contingency conditions (social approval and social and material reinforcement) were effective in increasing school attendance from baseline, there were no reliable differences between them in their truancy rates during Intervention 1.

TABLE 17-I

EFFECT OF INTERVENTION ON TRUANCY RATE

Condition	Baseline	Intervention 1	Intervention 2
Relationship	52.1	57.0	25.0
Social approval	49.3	19.8	19.5
Social and material reinforcement	44.3	21.4	14.3
Control	54.1	52.2	56.1

Note. The data are expressed in mean percentage of days per time period that the youngster was truant from school.

During Intervention 2, the truancy rate of the social and material reinforcement group was again reduced ($p < .05$). More importantly, the truancy rate for the relationship group, which received social and material reinforcement treatment during Intervention 2, decreased ($p < .001$). The truancy rate for the control group showed no reliable change throughout the three time periods. As a result, the truancy rates at the conclusion of Intervention 2 were lower for youth in each treatment condition than for those in the control group ($p < .001$).

In addition, each youngster was classified with respect to absolute improvement exhibited during each intervention period. Improvement was defined as a decline in truancy of 10 percentage points or more. With one exception, all of the youngsters in the contingency conditions improved from baseline to Intervention 2, with improvement ranging from 13 to 92 percentage points, while only two youngsters in the control group and one in the relationship group improved.

To determine whether the group changes could be attributable to large changes by only a few youngsters, each youth was ranked by his amount of improvement. The greater the degree of improvement, the higher was the assigned rank. The following mean rankings were obtained for improvement from baseline to Intervention 1: control = 9.8, relationship = 8.6, social approval = 18.2, social and material reinforcement = 16.0. These data were analyzed by means of the Kruskal-Wallis one-way analysis of variance by ranks (Siegal, 1956; $H = 14.14$, $df = 3$, $p < .01$). A similar analysis was also computed for improvement from Intervention 1 to Intervention 2 (control = 9.4, social and material reinforcement = 13.8; $H = 5.56$, $df = 1$, $p < .02$). The source of these differences is the greater improvement of youngsters under contingency conditions compared with those in the relationship and control conditions.

Data were also collected on six additional youngsters who received social and material reinforcement treatment for assorted problem behaviors, such as fighting, not doing home chores, staying out late, and not completing homework assignments. The treatment was the same for both intervention periods; the mean percentage of days that the problem behavior occurred was as follows for each time period: baseline = 58, Intervention 1 = 17, and Intervention 2 = 8.

The frequency of these behaviors during Intervention 1 changed markedly from baseline ($p < .001$). These changes continued during Intervention 2 ($p < .001$). Improvement from baseline to Intervention 2 ranged from 28 to 60 percentage points for all six youngsters.

The effects of the contingency conditions, social approval and social and material reinforcement $(n = 4)$, on academic achievement as measured by quarterly grades were also compared with the relationship group $(n = 6)$ for 10 additional youngsters. The letter grades were converted to percentages as follows: A = 90, B = 80, C = 70, D = 60, F = 50. The mean percentage was 64, with a range from 61 to 65 and did not vary reliably across treatment or time periods.

DISCUSSION

These results suggest the successful application of the triadic model of intervention within the Buddy System. Training of mediators (buddies) resulted in behavior changes in targets (youths) as compared to control youngsters. In addition, instructing buddies in the use of contingency conditions (social approval and social and material reinforcement) resulted in greater increase in school attendance than the use of a noncontingent relationship. Furthermore, the relationship group did not differ from the control group during Intervention 1; however, when these same youngsters were switched to a contingency condition (social and material reinforcement) during Intervention 2, a large increase in school attendance occurred. The results of the analysis using the Kruskal-Wallis test further support these findings by indicating more reliable improvement for youths in the contingency conditions than for youngsters in the noncontingency groups. Moreover, the results of the social and material reinforcement condition on assorted target behaviors indicate that the effects of contingency may not be limited to school attendance.

Changes occurred in the actual target behaviors rather than merely in the youngsters' verbal reports of such changes since the youngsters knew that the buddies had routine access to school records and teacher/parent reports. The effectiveness of this intervention procedure is supported in particular by the lack of major discrepancies between attendance data based on the youngsters' reports and school records.

These results support the importance and feasibility of promoting socially desirable behaviors in youth through the systematic application of contingent rewards. Through judicious use of social and material reinforcers, behaviors such as attending school, returning home on time, doing chores around the house, and interacting constructively with others can be reliably fostered.

Although the relationship alone did not appear to be sufficient to produce the desired behavior change, it was of course a necessary part of both contingency conditions. Within this system, the buddy–youngster relationship is inseparable from the implementation of the contingencies. It is possible that the findings of this study are a result of a Relationship × Contingency interaction.

The failure to find differences between the social approval and social and material reinforcement conditions may be attributable to *(a)* the effects of contingency being stronger than social–material differences, *(b)* the amount of material reward ($10 per month in purchasable items) being insufficient, or *(c)* the youngsters not perceiving that the $10 per month was in fact noncontingent in the social approval condition.

No reliable differences in academic achievement occurred among treatment conditions. This may be, as suggested by Tharp and Wetzel (1969), because quarterly grades are insensitive and unreliable measures. It may also be necessary to develop intervention programs that target specific academic behaviors such as increased studying and enhanced performance on weekly tests. Changes on these measures may be more likely to translate into correspondingly improved quarterly grades if the teacher is also a part of the contingency system. At the very least the teacher should be aware of the intervention program and its results.

Overall, these findings indicate that the use of contingency procedures within the triadic model may be highly effective when the contingencies can be used with those who influence the target behavior. Thus, reinforcement contingencies effectively applied to both buddies and youngsters increased school attendance. However, when others who are not within the contingency system have influence on the target behaviors, change may be less likely to occur. For example, the Buddy System found that failure to include the teacher in the contingency system may have contributed to the failure to effect positive changes in academic achievement, a target behavior under the functional control of teachers. It is apparent, then, that those who employ this model of intervention must carefully assess to whom they can effectively apply contingencies and whether to also direct change efforts at intermediary targets, such as parents and teachers.

Indeed, an alternative model of intervention may be derived by conceptualizing the role of the buddy as that of training natural mediators—parents, teachers, and significant others in the target youngster's immediate environment—to behave in ways that produce and maintain desired behavioral changes in the target. The implications of this view point to the use of artificial (buddy) relationships more as adjunctive, rather than as primary, mediating vehicles. In terms of the consultative triad, the role of the buddy may thus be construed as a dual one—that of mediator with target youth as well as that of behavior analyst vis-à-vis significant persons in the youth's natural environment.

Finally, it is essential that attempts be made to discern the functional relationship between behavior analyst contingencies and mediator behaviors, and between consultant contingencies and behavior analyst behaviors when these roles are separated. In this regard, the success of training and consultation is usually assessed by the twice-removed indices of the changes in the target's behaviors. Such indices are often too indirect to serve as precise and valid data for evaluating the process and outcome of training and consultation. Accordingly, a methodology for the systematic variation of aspects of consultant, behavior analyst, and mediator behaviors—both across and within cases—needs to be developed. In particular, reliable measures of behavior change for each link in the consultative chain need to be devised and related to behavior changes with target youth.

REFERENCES

Editorial Comments

Fo. W.S.O., & O'Donnell, C.R. The buddy system: effect of community intervention on delinquent offenses. *Behavior Therapy*, 1975, *6*, 522-524.

O'Donnell, C.R., & Fo, W.S.O. The buddy system: Mediator-target locus of control and behavioral outcome. *American Journal of Community Psychology,* 1976, *4,* 161-166.

Tharp, R.G., & Wetzel, R.J. *Behavior modification in the natural environment.* New York: Academic Press, 1969.

Text

Berelson, B., & Steiner, G.A. *Human behavior: An inventory of scientific findings.* New York: Harcourt, Brace & World, 1964.

Bloch, H.A., & Flynn, F.T. *Delinquency: The juvenile offender in America today.* New York: Random House, 1966.

Cowen, E.L., Gardner, E.A., & Zax, M. (Eds.) *Emergent approaches to mental health problems.* New York: Appleton-Century-Crofts, 1967.

Fo, W.S.O. *The Buddy System model: Community-based delinquency prevention utilizing indigenous nonprofessionals as behavior change agents.* Unpublished master's thesis, University of Hawaii, 1972.

Freund, J.E., Livermore, P.E., & Miller, I. *Manual of experimental statistics.* Englewood Cliffs, N.J.: Prentice-Hall, 1960.

Grosser, C., Henry, W.E., & Kelly, J.G. (Eds.) *Nonprofessionals in the human services.* San Francisco: Jossey-Bass, 1969.

Guerney, B.G., Jr. (Ed.) *Psychotherapeutic agents: New roles for nonprofessionals, parents, and teachers.* New York: Holt, Rinehart & Winston, 1969.

Harlow, E. Intensive intervention: An alternative to institutionalization. *Crime and Delinquency Literature,* 1970, *2,* 3-46.

Patterson, G.R. A community mental health program for children. In L.A. Hamerlynck, P.O. Davidson, & L.E. Acker (Eds.), *Behavior modification and ideal mental health services.* Calgary: University of Calgary Press, 1969.

Phillips, E.L. Achievement place: Token reinforcement procedures in a home-style rehabilitation setting for "pre-delinquent" boys. *Journal of Applied Behavior Analysis,* 1968, *1,* 213-223.

Rose, S.D., Sundel, M., DeLange, J., Corwin, L., & Palumbo, A. The Hartwig project: A behavioral approach to the treatment of juvenile offenders. In R. Ulrich, T. Stacknik, & J. Mabry (Eds.), *Control of human behavior: From cure to prevention.* Glenview, Ill.: Scott, Foresman, 1970.

Siegal, S. *Nonparametric statistics for the behavioral sciences.* New York: McGraw-Hill, 1956.

Smith, M.B., & Hobbs, H. The community and the community mental health center. *American Psychologist,* 1966, *21,* 499-509.

Stuart, R.B. Behavioral contracting with families of delinquents. *Journal of Behavior Therapy and Experimental Psychiatry,* 1971, *2,* 1-11.

Tharp, R.G., & Wetzel, R.J. *Behavior modification in the natural environment.* New York: Academic Press, 1969.

CHAPTER 18

THE TOKEN ECONOMY COMMUNITY YOUTH CENTER: A MODEL FOR PROGRAMMING PEER REINFORCEMENT*

J. R. STAHL, ELOISE J. FULLER, MARK F. LEFEBVRE, AND JOHN BURCHARD

EDITORIAL COMMENTS

If a youth center is opened in a community, will youth voluntarily attend and can the center be utilized to prevent the development of problem behaviors? The concept of **Youth Service Bureaus** (YSB) is a relatively new one (National Council on Crime and Delinquency, 1970). YSBs may take several forms, depending on the needs and resources of a given community. Some may be primarily used for juvenile justice diversion in which first-time offenders are referred to the YSB rather than arrested. Others are open community activity centers with more general aims. In this original chapter Stahl, Fuller, Lefebvre, and Burchard present one such center in Burlington, Vermont.

The Hunt Youth Center developed in three stages: (1) an experimental analysis of the Youth Center, (2) a focus on those youths who were having social or academic problems in school, and (3) expansion of the scope of the Center with youth and adults from the community taking over the operation of the program.

This chapter contains many fertile ideas which could be implemented by other communities as well. Especially noteworthy is the use of the behavioral approach with existing facilities and volunteers directly in the community in an **open** social system in which participation is voluntary

*The authors would like to express their appreciation to Karen Olio, Richard Lates, Jim Bickford, and Chris Gomberg for their valuable assistance throughout the duration of this project.

(Buehler, 1973).   In **Behavior Therapy With Delinquents,** Burchard
(1973) expressed concern about generalization of effects from token
economies in institutions to behavior in the community.   Together with
colleagues, Burchard has, in this chapter and elsewhere (Burchard et al.,
1976), gone on to develop alternative programs directly **in** that natural
environment.

ABSTRACT

THIS PAPER DESCRIBES a three-stage project to investigate the systematic employment of activities with peers as reinforcers in a program to modify
the behavior of problem youth. The project took the form of a token
economy based youth center. Data are presented which demonstrate that
youth with adjustment difficulties would voluntarily attend the youth center.
The preferences of youth for the various activities available were assessed,
and it was demonstrated that access to preferred activities could be employed
as reinforcers in programs aimed at modifying the classroom behavior of the
problem youth. In the final stage of development, attempts were made to
establish the youth center as a community-operated institution. Data relevant to the enlistment training and performance of three levels of staff
(junior high school, high school students, and adults) drawn from the community are presented. The program achieved community impact both by
providing effective reinforcers for programs designed to improve the school
performance of problem youth and by providing recreational/educational
resources for all youth in the community.

The last twenty years have witnessed the successful application of behavioral technology to an increasingly large number of
social problems. Difficulties of adjustment among youth, however, continue to pose a challenge to behavior modifiers. The
crux of the problem, from a behavioral viewpoint, inheres in the
reinforcement contingencies of the natural environment. The
most powerful reinforcers for adolescents are often mediated not
by parents, police, or school officials, but by other youth. Maintenance of deviant behavior by the social approval of peers has been
observed by a number of investigators (e.g. Buehler, Patterson, and
Furness, 1966; Solomon and Walher, 1973; Wahler, 1967). Participation with peers in certain activities and peer praise for
achievements may be of great importance to adolescents, and in
the natural environment these reinforcers are often arranged so
as to maintain rather than eliminate such problems as vandalism,

social aggression, truancy, and academic misbehavior.

An intervention program designed to effect positive and lasting change in youth behavior would seem to require a realignment of peer reinforcement contingencies within the youth's social environment. The Youth Service Bureau of Burlington, Vermont initiated in 1972 a long-term project to investigate the employment of peer activities as reinforcers in behavior modification programs. The project took the form of a token economy based youth center wherein access to a variety of recreational activities was contingent upon the emission of desirable behaviors.

The program was implemented in three phases. In Phase I the youth center was established and the model tested to determine whether the available activities would serve as reinforcers. In Phase II behavior of clinical relevance were targeted; Youth Center activities were employed as reinforcers in behavioral contracts aimed at the modification of school behaviors. In Phase II efforts were initiated to establish the youth center as a community-operated institution, independent of the Youth Service Bureau. Behavioral techniques were employed during this phase to train youth and adult volunteers in the administration of the program. The following sections of this paper describe the implementation of these phases and the ongoing evaluation of the program.

PHASE I: EXPERIMENTAL ANALYSIS
OF THE YOUTH CENTER MODEL

In September 1972 a Youth Center was established at the Lyman C. Hunt Junior High School in Burlington, Vermont. The three objectives of the program during its first phase of operation were as follows: (1) to determine whether a target population of youth with school or community adjustment problems would attend the Youth Center; (2) to assess the preferences of these youth toward the different components of the Youth Center program by measuring participation in various activities; and (3) to determine whether preferred aspects of the program would serve as reinforcers in increasing the youths' performance of low frequency behaviors. The procedures employed in establishing

HUNT YOUTH CENTER

	PHASE I	PHASE II	PHASE III			
			SESSIONS 1-3	SESSIONS 4-7	SESSIONS 8-11	SESSIONS 12-15
GOALS	Analysis of the reinforcing properties of the Youth Center activities	Classroom intervention: 5 Procedures	Development of a Hunt Student Staff: Selection of jobs and training	Performance of jobs by Hunt student staff while attendance of non-staff students increased	Phasing in of Adult staff	Replace college students with adult volunteers
STAFF	Youth Service Bureau 20 college students	Youth Service Bureau 20 college students	Youth Service Bureau 15 college students	Youth Service Bureau 15 college students 30 Hunt students	Youth Service Bureau 15 college students 5 high school students 30 Hunt students	Youth Service Bureau 5 adult volunteers (per session) 5 high school students 30 Hunt students
TARGET YOUTH	91 youth with school or community adjustment problems	65 youth with school or community adjustment problems	36 randomly selected youth 10 "problem youth"	Gradually increase from 30 to 52 the number of non-staff Hunt students admitted	Youth Center open to all Hunt students: Average attendance 81 per session	Youth Center open to all Hunt students: Average attendance 129 per session

Figure 18-1. Phases of Hunt Youth Center.

the program will be merely outlined here; a more complete description of this phase of the Youth Center is provided in Burchard, Harig, Miller, and Amour (1975).

Burlington is a city of approximately 43,000 people. The Hunt Junior High School is located in Burlington's North End, a geographically distinct section of the city which has high rates of juvenile offenses and few recreational/educational facilities for youth. During its first phase of operation the Youth Center was open two nights per week, Monday and Wednesday, from seven o'clock to ten o'clock. The Youth Center utilized a wing of the school which included the main lobby, the library, the gymnasium, the home economics room, and the cafeteria. The gymnasium was partitioned into two halves; basketball or street hockey occurred on one side while volleyball and trampoline activities were available on the other. The cafeteria was decorated as a coffee house on Youth Center evenings. The school's large tables were replaced by small café tables; drapes were hung; candles were used to provide lighting; and live or recorded music was presented. A snack bar was located within the coffee house area. The home economics room was utilized for a variety of arts and crafts activities. The library was employed as a study area, though in later phases of the program it served as a game room and was referred to as the "den."

The program's target population was junior high school students who were experiencing adjustment difficulties. Five students whose behavior was considered by school personnel to be the most problematic were each asked to elect ten to twelve of their friends to the program. Their friends were then asked to elect additional friends until a student membership of ninety-one youth was assembled. Data were collected which demonstrated that this group had had significantly more police contacts than a control group and were much more likely to be truant from school and to have grade point averages below C.

The Youth Center was staffed by approximately twenty college students who earned course credit by working on the project. The staff was responsible for organizing activities within the areas and for managing the token economy point system. The point system required each youth to carry a "bank book" on which points were entered. Youths could earn points between 7:00 and 8:30 by remaining in certain activity areas. For every fifteen minutes that a youth spent in a particular area he would earn a specified number of points—twenty points per fifteen-minute interval spent in the gym or coffee house, thirty points in arts and crafts, and forty points in the library. Points could be exchanged between 8:30 and 10:00 for admission to the coffee house or gym, for snack bar commodities (candy, soft drinks, sandwiches) and for items such as books, records, and model cars that were variously auctioned, raffled, or sold.

During the project's first phase of operation it was demonstrated that the programs established at the Youth Center were attractive to the target youth. Attendance at the Youth Center ranged between forty-three and sixty-seven and averaged fifty-five members per evening. Among sixteen of the youth with the greatest number of police contacts, attendance was somewhat more frequent than that of an equal group of members with no police contacts. An attitude survey which required all regular members to rate the various components of the Youth Center further suggested their satisfaction with the program. All aspects of the Youth Center were rated positively, and the Youth Center as a whole was rated slightly more preferable to "Christmas vacation."

The reinforcement value of the various activities at the Youth Center was determined empirically according to the "Probability of Behavior Rule" (Ayllon and Azrin, 1968). The rule states that those activities in which an individual is very likely to engage when the opportunity exists will serve as reinforcers for activities which occur at a lesser frequency. To assess the natural reinforcing properties of the Youth Center activity areas, points were administered noncontingently during every third session of the youth center. It was found that on noncontingent nights youth spent the majority of available time in the gym (43%), the coffee house (25%), and the arts and crafts area (22%). Only 7 percent of the time was spent in the library.

Contingent nights provided a test of whether the preferred activities at the Youth Center could function as reinforcers to increase low-probability behaviors. As described above, points could be earned most readily (between 7:00 and 8:30) by remaining in the library. The percentage of time spent in the library during contingent nights increased from 7 percent to 26 percent, exceeding the time spent in all other areas except the gymnasium. The level was maintained even when the criteria for point earning in the library required subjects to perform a writing task.

A comparison of contingent versus noncontingent nights also revealed that the point contingency contributed substantially to the maintenance of a constructive atmosphere within the Youth Center. Data collected over the course of Phase I indicated that the average amount of time spent in the semistructured activity areas on contingent nights was double the amount of time spent in these areas on noncontingent nights. In other words, on noncontingent nights much more time was spent in the hallways, lavatories, and outside the building. In addition, staff reported that on noncontingent nights there was much more restlessness and commotion among the youth. These findings demonstrated the efficacy of the point system as a means of structuring activity among large numbers of youth, while retaining a positive atmosphere. Consequently, a token economy point system was incorporated into the organization of the Youth Center when its membership and aims were expanded in Phase III.

The results of the first phase of research at the Hunt Youth Center established that the target youth would attend the program and that the reinforcers available within the setting could be mediated through a point system. The data demonstrated that the participation of youth in nonpreferred activities at the Youth Center could be increased through the contingent application of the center's reinforcers. The next step in the analysis of the Youth Center as a form of community intervention was to determine whether the same reinforcers could be employed in the modification of behaviors occurring outside the Youth Center. The second phase of research then focused on academic behaviors and student/teacher relationships.

PHASE II: CLASSROOM INTERVENTION PROGRAMS

As part of the Youth Center's overall commitment to community service, Phase I provided new, much-needed recreational opportunities for a large segment of youth.   While maintaining these recreational opportunities, Phase II focused on particular youths having social or academic problems in school.   In the context of evaluative research, a number of intervention techniques were examined in terms of feasibility and comparative effectiveness.

During the initial stages of the program, close contact with the school administration and Guidance Department made the Youth Center personnel aware of a number of students having extraordinary school adjustment problems manifested by academic failure and classroom disruptions.   During the third semester of Phase II (spring and fall, 1973 and spring, 1974) research programs were conducted to examine the feasibility of using access to Youth Center activities as reinforcement for improvement in specific classroom behaviors.   In addition, the relative effectiveness of a number of different intervention procedures was compared.

A number of programs have focused on the improvement of classroom behavior through the use of behavior contracting procedures with contingent home-based reinforcers (Bailey, Wolf, and Phillips, 1970; Cohen, Keyworth, Kleiner and Brown, 1974; Mac-Donald, Gallimore, and MacDonald, 1970; Patterson, Cobb, and Ray, 1972; Stuart, 1971).   Integral to all programs of this sort is a means of recording and reporting the youth's behavior to the mediator of the contract.   A number of experimenters (Bailey, Wolf, and Phillips, 1970; Cohen et al., 1974; Stuart, 1971) have employed a daily behavior card system to achieve this end.   In such a system, the youth typically carries a card to school on which various in-school behaviors are recorded.   The youth will usually receive reinforcement later at home according to the specifications of the behavioral contract.   The Youth Service Bureau sought to determine whether Youth Center reinforcement could be used in place of home-based reinforcement in a behavioral contracting, daily behavior-card paradigm.

Miller & Burchard (1974) conducted one study to assess the effects of teacher ratings (daily feedback) on on-task and disruptive behavior. The study utilized a within-subject, *A-B-A* design with eight subjects.

During Phase A of this study each subject carried attendance cards to two classes for a period of four weeks. The teacher merely signed the card indicating that the student attended class, and in so doing the card became worth fifteen points exchangeable at the Youth Center. During Phase B the attendance card was replaced with a behavior rating card on which the teacher rated the student's on-task and disruptive behaviors (see Fig. 18-2). During this phase the Youth Center points were contingent upon the teacher's ratings. Following Phase B the students were again given the attendance cards (Phase A). The second and third phases also lasted a period of four weeks. Throughout the three phases, trained observers utilized a time-sampling procedure to obtain systematic data on on-task and disruptive behavior.

Student_____	Date_____				
Points	4	3	2	1	0
On Time to Class	yes				no
Prepared for Class	yes				no
Participation in Classroom Activity	90–100%	80–90%	70–80%	60–70%	Less than 60%
Failed to Follow Instructions	none	once	twice	three	four or more
Classroom Disruptions	none		once	twice	three or more
Disrespectful to you or other teacher	no				yes

Total Points Earned on this card_____ Teacher's Signature_____

Comments: Class_____

Figure 18-2. Daily behavior rating card.

Unfortunately, results could be obtained only for three of the eight subjects. Three subjects were dropped because of excessive absences, and two others were dropped because of large decreases in the number of cards they carried during Phase B. For the remaining subjects, on-task behavior increased and disruptive behavior decreased during the behavior-card phase. Although the behaviors did not return to baseline rates in the third phase, all three subjects showed increased disruptive behavior and decreased on-task behavior in this phase. Miller and Burchard (1974) suggested that the positive effects of the daily behavior card may be a result of the frequent feedback, especially that of a positive nature, provided by the behavior card. Low ratings may have functioned as an aversive stimulus, for fewer behavior cards than attendance cards were turned in.

In the fall of 1973, Stahl (1975) employed a modified daily behavior card in an experiment that compared the effectiveness of three different intervention procedures for the Youth Center model. Negatively phrased categories were minimized on this card, and a rating category on attitude was added. All subjects were reinforced for carrying daily behavior cards in order to encourage youth to turn in cards even with poor ratings.

The three intervention procedures employed were conventional behavioral contracting (BC), behavior rehearsal (BR), and self-evaluation training (SE). In the BC condition, points were contingent upon teachers' ratings of classroom performance. The BR condition was designed to develop desirable behaviors that were lacking. Subjects in this group practiced appropriate classroom behaviors at the Youth Center. The practiced behaviors included attending to the teacher, asking questions in class, and approaching the teacher for individual help. Self-evaluation procedures seek to establish self-control of inappropriate behavior (Broden, Hall, and Mitts, 1971; Glynn, 1970; Drabman, Spitalnik, and O'Leary, 1974). Subjects assigned to the SE condition were reinforced for monitoring their behavior and matching teachers' ratings.

The subjects were forty youth attending the Youth Center. During the four weeks of baseline, all subjects were reinforced for carrying cards to two classes each day, five days a week. At the fourth week, the subjects were randomly assigned to one of the three groups. During intervention the BC group received greater reinforcement in the form of more points for higher ratings on the behavior card. The BR group was reinforced for engaging in sessions during which appropriate social and academic behaviors were rehearsed. The behavioral rehearsal sessions were conducted in a one-to-one fashion by college student trainers for a thirty-minute period at the Youth Center. The SE group evaluated their own behavior by filling out a behavior card prior to the teacher's doing so. These youth were reinforced for matching the teacher's evaluation of their behavior. The dependent variables consisted of the teacher's ratings of attitude and participation and grades.

Improvement in teacher ratings was observed in all three groups during intervention. Considering only those students who were functioning relatively poorly during baseline, more improvement was found in the BC group than in the other groups. Analyses of grades also favored the BC procedure over the other treatments. Of primary interest, however, was the demonstration that Youth Center reinforcers could be employed in the modification of clinically relevant behaviors occurring outside the Center.

Discussion with school personnel indicated that a need for individualized behavioral counseling existed. A program was developed for counseling troubled youth on a one-to-one basis within the context of the Youth Center. The goals were to (1) identify youth in need of counseling, (2) bring these youth in contact with relatively untrained undergraduates, and (3) provide supervision and guidance to the undergraduates as they designed and implemented individual intervention programs for the youths.

Sixteen college students with limited training in behavior modification (usually no more than 6 credit hours) were paired with sixteen youth referred by the Guidance Department. These youth had a variety of academic and social problems including learning disabilities, social adjustment problems such as extreme shyness or unmanageability, and physical handicaps such as obesity, resulting in personal conflict.

The procedure involved four stages. In the first stage, the sixteen youths were contacted in school by the undergraduate students and invited to join the Youth Center Staff. All sixteen agreed to participate as Staff. In Stage 2 the college students had two objectives. The most important objective was to build a comfortable social relationship with each referral, both in the context of the Youth Center and in relaxed social settings unrelated to the school or the Center. During this period the college students explored through informal conversation the personal problems which concerned the youth. The second objective during this stage was to establish contact with teachers and parents of the youth and to gather pertinent information about the student's environment.

During the third stage, specific target behaviors and potential reinforcers were identified through discussions with guidance counselors, teachers, and the selected students. Target behaviors were identified in four ways: (1) by direct systematic observations in school or at the Youth Center, (2) by examining school attendance records, (3) by obtaining daily or weekly reports from teachers, or (4) by recommendation from the students themselves. After specifying target behaviors, the college students devised individual intervention programs. In the fourth stage they implemented their intervention programs, collected data, and prepared reports detailing the intervention program and their relationship with the students.

Several basic types of behavioral intervention programs were designed. These included (1) traditional behavioral contracting employing positive reinforcement and point-cost contingencies, (2) self-control procedures, (3) immediate and delayed reinforcement in time-sampled observations and (4) reinforced role-playing. Target behaviors included (a) inappropriate behaviors such as talking in class, unexcused absence from class, fighting, swearing, and criticizing others and (b) appropriate behaviors such as completing homework, participating in class, carrying daily behavior cards to class, or engaging in specific social behaviors.

Several behavior managers succeeded in demonstrating the

effects of the procedures experimentally through the employment of multiple-baseline or reversal (A-B-A) designs. Due to the variety of behaviors targeted and the relative inexperience of the college students who served as behavior analysts, it was not possible to provide systematic empirical evaluation of the total intervention program. However, the subjective reports of teachers and guidance personnel suggested that improvements in social and classroom behaviors were made in many cases.

PHASE III: INSTITUTIONALIZATION OF THE HUNT YOUTH CENTER

The first two phases in the development of the Hunt Youth Center demonstrated that a voluntary token economy youth program could be established and that its reinforcers could be employed in the modification of classroom behaviors. Literature suggests that community recreational programs are not only of benefit to the youth who attend them but also contribute to the well-being of the community (President's Commission on Law Enforcement and Administration of Justice, 1967; White House Conference on Children and Youth, 1960). Phase III sought (1) to expand the scope of the Youth Center to provide recreational/ educational services to all local youth and (2) to transfer responsibility for the operation and control of the program to the youth and adults of that community.

The aims and procedures of Phase III are outlined and compared with those of Phases I and II in Figure 18-I. The specific objectives of Phase III were to phase the college students out of the Youth Center's administration and to enlist and train three levels of staff from the Youth Center community: (1) junior high school students, (2) adult volunteers, and (3) high school student assistants. This transfer of Youth Center staff was accomplished during Phase III in the four-part sequence described in Figure 18-I. The graduated increase in the nonstaff membership of the Youth Center is also described in the table. Procedures employed in the enlistment and training of the community-housed staff are detailed below.

TABLE 18-I

STAFF ATTENDANCE DATA

Session	1	2	3	4	5	6	7	8	9	10	11	12	13	14	15	$\overline{X}$
Date	2/6	2/13	2/20	2/27	3/6	3/13	3/20	4/3	4/17	4/56	5/3	5/10	5/17	5/24	6/7	
A. Total Staff Employed	37	40	39	38	39	38	40	39	36	36	37	36	37	37	36	37.7
Number Added		3	4	1	1	0	2	0	0	0	6	0	1	0	0	
Number Released		0	5	2	0	1	0	1	3	0	5	1	0	0	1	
Net Change in Staff		+3	−1	−1	+1	−1	+2	−1	−3	0	+1	−1	+1	0	−1	
B. Number Back-up Workers	0	1	2	3	5	5	5	5	8	8	4	5	6	5	5	
C. Attendance	27	31	28	35	30	29	37	35	26	21	32	28	26	33	25	29.5
Percent of Total Staff	73	78	72	92	77	76	93	90	72	58	86	78	70	89	69	78.2

Structure of the Youth Center Program

The Youth Center was based on a token economy for all youth who attended. The selection and training of those youth who served as staff are described below. The token economy system for nonstaff students was designed to foster a constructive atmosphere in the Youth Center. Prior research at the center (Burchard et al., 1976) as well as the general literature on recreational programs (Danford, 1964; Kiaus, 1966; Shivers, 1963) suggested that the participation of youth in organized activities was crucial to the effectiveness of a program. The point system of the Phase III program was designed specifically to channel youth into activity areas. Youth could earn points exchangeable for food and other items by remaining in the various areas. Every ten minutes in an activity area was reinforced with five points. In order to operate this system all youth (other than staff) carried cards which were marked in ten-minute intervals, and these intervals were punched upon entering or leaving an activity area. Those ten-minute intervals which were not punched because a youth spent the entire time in an activity area were converted to points which could be spent at the store.

Enlistment and Training of the Junior High School Student Staff

The utilization of junior high school students as staff in their own Youth Center was designed to serve several important functions: (1) it would help fill the need for manpower; (2) it would provide a learning experience for student staff members, allowing them to acquire organizational skills and to exercise responsibility; (3) it would foster a constructive atmosphere at the center, the behavior of the student staff serving as a model of appropriate behavior for other students; and (4) it would help the students of the school develop a sense of identity with the Youth Center and a sense of control over its programs.

Students were randomly selected from the 650 students in the school and invited to join the program until thirty-six Hunt students (hereafter referred to as Hunt Staff) were "hired." These students were assigned to jobs necessary to the operation of the

Youth Center. The thirty-six jobs fall into three main types: area support (15 jobs), door workers (15 jobs), and administration (six jobs). The Hunt Staff were assigned to teams (A, B and C) and each team worked a one-hour shift each night. The specific jobs in each category were are follows:

Area Support. Six youths worked in the coffee house and store, two on each shift. Their job was to handle all transactions. Nine youths worked in the gym, three per shift. They assisted the adult staff in supervising activities and maintaining order.

Door Workers. The job of the door workers was to punch the card of each youth who entered or left an area. Three Hunt Staff (one per shift) were assigned to each of the five areas.

Administration. Three Hunt Staff (one per shift) worked at the front door of the Center and helped to collect fees and distribute point cards. The other three Hunt Staff were used to notify the door personnel of each area when the intervals changed and to provide general assistance.

The Hunt Staff was "paid" with points exchangeable for a variety of reinforcers. They could earn ten points for being on time to the Youth Center and helping to set up the activity areas, fifteen points for being on time for their job shift, and up to fifty points for performing their job correctly (10 points for appropriate behavior in each of five ten-minute intervals).

Training

The first three weeks of the program were devoted to training the Hunt Staff in their jobs. The objective of the training program was to make the students proficient in the required skills without destroying their interest in the Youth Center. To introduce the students to the job tasks, a program was designed that utilized the behavioral techniques of behavioral contracting, modeling, role-playing, immediate feedback and positive reinforcement, and shaping. Undergraduate college students and Youth Service Bureau employees trained the students and supervised their performance throughout training.

At the first training session the Hunt Staff met individually with college supervisors who described the Youth Center, the various jobs, and the point system. They were informed that each week they would sign a contract which stipulated that they could earn points by engaging in certain behaviors. The first week's contract stated that points could be earned by remaining at the Youth Center until 9:30. The students were also asked to indicate three jobs they would be interested in performing. The staff was then encouraged to explore the various areas and become acquainted with the activities available, while the supervisors performed the jobs which the students would be doing in the future.

At the second training session, the staff members were assigned to specific jobs according to preference and contracted to participate in a forty-five-minute mock training session conducted by the college student supervisors and a half hour discussion of the issues and problems relevant to each area. During the training session the staff was taught how to setup, operate, and cleanup each area. After the training and discussion groups, the staff was free to participate in any of the Youth Center's activities.

During the third training session the staff contracted to practice performing their specific jobs for one-half hour. College supervisors acted as guests and also guided the staff in their jobs, giving feedback in the form of correction or praise. Staff members were assigned permanently to teams (A, B or C), and each team "practiced" its job for a half hour while the other two teams participated in activities.

From the fourth through seventh sessions the Hunt Staff was allowed to invite an increasing number of guests in order to give the staff more realistic practice in operating the Youth Center. The contract stipulated that staff members could earn points by being on time to the Youth Center, helping to set up activity areas, and working at their jobs for one hour. As before, college supervisors provided constant feedback to the staff as they performed their jobs.

The number of guests was increased gradually over the next three weeks as the staff members became more proficient at their jobs. Guests were required to pay twenty-five cents admission to help defer the costs of the program. By the seventh week the training procedure was completed, and the Youth Center was opened to all youth enrolled at Hunt School.

Enlistment and Training of the Adult Volunteer Staff

A crucial factor in efforts to institutionalize the Hunt Youth Center was the enlistment of adult volunteers from the community. Supportive citizenry is not only a source of manpower to operate the center and raise funds, but their involvement insures that the program is responsive to the needs of their community and so provides for the program's long-term maintenance.

In order to assess community opinion toward youth problems and the youth center approach, a survey was conducted by the Youth Service Bureau in 1974. The parents of sixty Hunt School students were randomly selected from the total school population and interviewed by telephone. Forty percent of those contacted expressed interest in working in a youth center program. Attempts to enlist staff via letters were unsuccessful, however. Efforts to tap the pool of citizens willing to volunteer were then directed toward (1) establishing support for the Youth Center within the community at large and (2) making personal contact with interested persons.

The services of local media were obtained to establish the legitimacy of the Youth Center in the community . A local newspaper with community-wide circulation cooperated by printing several articles describing the procedures and goals of the project. The aid of a local civic organization was solicited in attempts to meet the second objective. A community group titled the North End Community Youth Center (NECYC) had been responsible for the administration of a less structured youth center program. In several meetings with representatives from this group, the programs of the Hunt Youth Center were explained. In view of the overlapping purposes of the two youth centers and of administrative problems encountered in the operation of the NECYC program, a plan was accepted whereby the latter youth center would be discontinued and its staff would be trained to operate the Hunt program.

In three pretraining meetings with NECYC, volunteers were oriented to the procedures and aims of the Hunt Youth Center, and the details of institutionalization were drafted. Written descriptions of staffing requirements and the program's point system were distributed. Two training sessions were held at the Youth Center. More than twenty volunteers attended each session, during which the administration of the Youth Center was discussed in detail. Volunteers were assigned to activity areas on the basis of interests. The operation of the program required one adult in each of the following five areas: the front door, the gymnasium, arts and crafts, the coffee house door, and the coffee house store. During the training sessions the performance of administrative and supervisory jobs was modeled by college student staff and Youth Service Bureau personnel. The adult volunteers were encouraged to practice the performance of the tasks during the training sessions.

Enlistment and Training of the High School Student Staff

During the first two phases in the development of the Hunt Youth Center, the college student staff fulfilled several functions. They not only administered the point system and supervised the operation of the areas, but they organized and participated in the scheduled activities. While adult volunteers were trained to exercise each of these functions, their primary responsibility was the overall supervision of the areas. High school students were recruited to serve as assistants to the adult volunteers in organizing and maintaining the activities in the gym, arts and crafts, and coffee house areas.

High school students were recruited through the cooperation of the guidance department and administrative personnel of Burlington High School. The student body was informed that a number of part-time jobs were available at the Youth Center. Interested students were briefed on the responsibilities of the job by high school personnel and were instructed to contact the Youth Service Bureau. The prospective high school student employee was then interviewed by a representative of the Youth Service Bureau. The history and aims of the Youth Center were described, and the jobs were explained in detail. Students were required to work one night per week for three hours; the salary was four dollars per night. (Arrangements for students to earn course credit in lieu of money had been made, but the recruitment of students occurred too late in the semester for this option to be viable.)

The training of each high school student staff member occurred at the Youth Center in two parts. On the first night the student was provided with printed material describing the responsibilities attached to each job. Issues and questions were discussed, and the student spent the remainder of the session familiarizing himself with the Youth Center and its activities. On the second training session the student selected a particular job and worked that night with a Youth Service Bureau staff member who coached his performance of the job and provided feedback. Two high school students were employed in the gymnasium, two in the coffee house and one in arts and crafts.

Evaluation of the Performance of Enlisted Staff

Integral to the goal of developing a youth-operated center was a system to evaluate the effectiveness of the Hunt Staff, e.g. the thirty-six junior high school students. The performance of the Hunt Staff was monitored in three ways: (1) through attendance figures recorded each evening, (2) through job performance ratings by supervisors, and (3) through recordings of participation in clean-up.

Attendance was taken at the main door as the staff arrived. Two unexcused absences resulted in dismissal from the staff. A student dismissed from the staff was either placed on the waiting list or in the group of back-up workers. New staff members were added from either the waiting list or from back-up workers. The staff attendance data appear in Table 18-II. A total of eighteen staff members were added and nineteen dismissed (approximately 47% turnover) during the fifteen weeks of the program. Staff attendance varied from 58 percent to 93 percent across weeks, with a mean of 78.2 percent.

Starting with the sixth week of the program, performance of the workers on their jobs was rated by the job supervisors at ten-minute intervals throughout each work shift. The job supervisor noted on the work evaluation form whether or not the youth was observed doing the job correctly during that interval. After re-

TABLE 18-II

SUMMARY OF JOB PERFORMANCE DATA

Session	1	2	3	4	5	6	7	8	9	10	11	12	13	14	15	$\overline{X}$
A. Number of Staff with Work Data reported						26	31	27	23	12	19	20	19	22	16	21.5
Percent of Staff in Attendance						90	84	77	88	57	59	71	73	67	64	73
B. Correct Job Performance During Each Interval of Work Shift																
Interval 1						92%	93%	92%	96%	100%	94%	90%	95%	100%	92%	94.4%
2						96	97	96	96	100	100	95	100	95	86	96.1
3						88	97	96	100	100	100	100	100	86	85	95.2
4						96	100	88	100	92	100	95	94	90	83	93.8
5						88	100	91	95	100	100	100	88	90	83	93.5
6						100	96	95	95	100	—	—	—	—	—	97.2

cording, the supervisor gave the youth feedback either in the form of correction or praise. From session eleven on, job performance was rated only five times during the work shifts to accommodate a change in the point system. At this time, workers were awarded ten points for each time they were observed doing their job correctly. The summary of job performance data appears in Table 18-III. Staff were not observed on all occasions either because the supervisors were absent from their jobs or because they failed to report their data. Over the ten sessions that job performance was observed and recorded, the percentage of staff observed by the supervisors ranged from 57 percent to 90 percent with a mean of 73 percent. During any interval, the percentage of students observed working correctly ranged from 83 percent to 100 percent.

In each area, clean-up jobs were clearly specified and were staffed according to the difficulty of the job on any given night. Area supervisors recorded who completed each specific clean-up job, i.e. Hunt Staff, high school supervisor, or clean-up worker— a nonstaff, stand-by Hunt student who was hired if the Hunt Staff did not show up and was rewarded with an admission ticket (25¢) for the next session if he or she did the job. Table 18-III summarizes the percentage of jobs performed by each category of Youth Center personnel starting with the sixth week of the program. Over the ten weeks that clean-up data were collected, the number of jobs averaged 25.2. The mean percentage of jobs performed by Hunt Staff was 11.1 percent, clean-up workers, 38.8 percent, supervisors, 31.8 percent, and high school students, 7.3 percent.

It is clear from the job performance data in Table 18-III that the training program was successful in making the students proficient in their evening jobs. Students also performed the majority of clean-up jobs. While staff attendance averaged only 78.2 percent and staff turnover was about 47 percent for the fifteen weeks of the program (average 3% per week), the Youth Center continued to operate efficiently. It is possible that the high standards of job performance were maintained because of the reinforcing qualities of the Youth Center and the prestige associated with being a staff member. It was possible to keep a small group of stu-

TABLE 18-III

SUMMARY OF THE PERCENTAGE OF JOBS PERFORMED BY PERSONNEL

Session	1	2	3	4	5	6	7	8	9	10	11	12	13	14	15	$\overline{X}$
A. Number of Clean-up Jobs						32	24	24	24	24	28	27	24	24	21	25.2
B. Percent of Jobs Performed by Staff																
Hunt Staff						22%	24%	29%	25%	21%	18%	26%	17%	15%	24%	22.1%
Clean-up Workers						31	38	46	46	46	46	37	37	28	33	38.8
Supervisors						47	38	25	29	20	36	33	29	42	19	31.8
High School						—	—	—	—	13	0	4	17	15	24	7.3

dents as back-up workers. These students substituted for absent staff members, thereby becoming proficient in a variety of jobs. Replacement staff was drawn largely from this group, helping to maintain a highly motivated and skilled staff.

Adult volunteers were employed at the Hunt Youth Center during its final four weeks of operation in spring, 1974. Fourteen different volunteers worked at the center; five worked on two occasions on any particular evening, one volunteer was assigned to each of five jobs, replacing the college student supervisors (refer to Table 18-I).

The performance of the volunteers was assessed by Youth Service Bureau staff who completed work evaluation forms for each activity area. Volunteers were rated by Youth Service Bureau personnel with respect to their familiarity with their jobs, their supervision of the Hunt Student Staff and the high school student employees, their effectiveness in the general administration of the area, their interaction with nonstaff students, and their completion of data forms.

The performance of the adult volunteers was rated as more than adequate with respect to all the tasks required of them. Upon arrival at the Youth Center, volunteers were sufficiently familiar with the tasks associated with their jobs in 68 percent of the cases. Volunteers were rated as quite successful (a rating of "1" or "2" on a 7-point scale) in their supervision of the Hunt Student Staff in 69 percent of the cases; they were rated as quite successful in their supervision of high school students in 53 percent of the cases. In 84 percent of the cases, activity areas were judged to operate effectively under the volunteers' direction. With regard to nonstaff students, volunteers were encouraged to participate in activities with youth. Volunteers interacted effectively with youth 89 percent of the time.

Volunteers were required to gather data on two types of forms. A work evaluation form was to be completed for each Hunt Student Staff member in his area. The form divided each work shift into ten-minute intervals. At the end of each interval the volunteer was to determine whether each student staff member was working, provide verbal feedback to the student, and record the finding on the data form.　Volunteers successfully completed these forms 56 percent of the time.　(This figure includes the results of Session 1 when no volunteers turned-in data due to confusion over the completion of these forms.)　A second data form required volunteers to rate the way in which their area functioned during that session.　These forms were completed 95 percent of the time.

Overall, volunteers were successful in carrying out administrative duties (supervising staff, directing activity within their areas, etc.) and interacting appropriately with nonstaff students.　The performance of only two volunteers was found to be inadequate. The findings in general indicated that adults with little prior experience in structured youth programs could be trained in a short time to assume many of the administrative tasks required in the operation of a youth center program.

Nine different high school students were employed at the Youth Center during Phase III.　The first five students who were enlisted withdrew from the project within six weeks.　Two of these youth reported finding higher paying jobs; one reported losing interest in the project and two terminated without explanation.　Four students ranging in age from fifteen to seventeen were hired as replacements.　One position, arts and crafts assistant, remained vacant.　Each of the four new staff members worked at the Youth Center up to its closing in June.

Objective data on the performance of the high school student staff were not obtained.　The adult volunteers and Youth Service Bureau Staff who supervised the high school students reported subjectively that the performance of the students improved over sessions.　Initially, the students appeared to experience difficulty in assuming a supervisory role over the junior high school youth who were but a few years younger than themselves.　All members of the high school student staff became proficient within three sessions, however, and executed all responsibilities competently. The four students who were enlisted later in the semester required little supervision.　Over the course of the semester they came to assume all the responsibilities of Youth Service Bureau and adult volunteer supervisors, i.e. they supervised individual

Hunt student staff members, completed work evaluation forms and awarded points contingent upon performance.

The results of this phase of the project indicate that the Hunt Youth Center can operate with trained adults and youth in the roles described. The budget for the operation of the Hunt Youth Center during Phase III was close to two thousand dollars. A sizable proportion of this amount, though, was spent for materials or services employed in researching and developing the Youth Center programs. By eliminating these costs and by acquiring supplies and materials through wholesale purchase and through donation, it would be possible to operate a community youth center without extensive outside funding.

CONCLUSIONS

The project at the Hunt Junior High School represents an attempt to establish a model for community-based intervention with youth. The Youth Center model is designed to achieve impact on several levels: (1) effective reinforcers are provided for classroom intervention programs with problem youth, (2) recreational/educational resources are provided for all youth in the community, and (3) youth and residents of the community are trained to operate the youth center program. During phase III of the Hunt Project, progress was made toward transfer of control of the Youth Center to the community while efforts were made to maximize the participation of the school's guidance department in the administration of the classroom intervention component of the Project. Behavioral technology has been integral to the Hunt Youth Center program at each stage in its development—in the identification of reinforcers important in maintaining the attendance of target youth at the Youth Center, in the contingent application of Youth Center reinforcers to modify classroom behaviors, in the training of a student and an adult-volunteer staff, and in the maintenance of an ordered and constructive atmosphere within the Youth Center. Research conducted thus far by the Youth Service Bureau has suggested that the concept of a youth center as a form of behavioral intervention is viable. The aim of further research will be to fully institutionalize the Hunt Youth Center, to apply the the model in other communities, and to assess the long-term effects of such programs on the social adjustment of youth.

REFERENCES

Editorial Comments

Buehler, R.E. Social reinforcement experimentation in open social systems. In J.S. Stumphauzer (Ed.) *Behavior therapy with delinquents.* Springfield, IL: Thomas, 1973, 250-262.

Burchard, J.D. Behavior modification with delinquents: Some unforseen contingencies. In J.S. Stumphauzer (Ed.) *Behavior therapy with delinquents.* Springfield, IL: Thomas, 1973, 66-74.

Burchard, J.D., Harig, P.T., Miller, R.B., & Amour, J. New strategies in community based intervention. In E. Ribes-Inesta & A. Bandura (Eds.) *Analysis of delinquency and aggression.* New York: Lawrence Erlbaum, 1976, 95-122.

National Council on Crime & Delinquency. *The youth service bureau: A brief description of five current programs.* Paramus, NJ: NCCD, 1970.

Text

Bailey, J.S., Wolf, M.M., and Phillips, E.L. Home-based reinforcement and the modification of pre-delinquents' classroom behavior. *Journal of Applied Behavior Analysis,* 1970, *3,* 223-233.

Broden, M.R., Hall, R.V., and Mitts, B. The effect of self-recording on the classroom behavior of two eighth grade students. *Journal of Applied Behavior Analysis,* 1971, *4,* 191-199.

Buehler, R.E., Patterson, G.R., and Furness, R.M. The reinforcement of behavior in institutional settings. *Behavior Research and Therapy,* 1966, *4,* 157-167.

Burchard, J.D., Harrig, P.T., Miller, R.B., and Amour, J. New strategies in community based intervention. In E. Ribes-Inseta and A. Bandura (Eds.) *Analysis of delinquency and aggresion.* New Jersey: Lawrence Erlbaum Associates, 1976.

Cohen, S.I., Keyworth, M.J., Klein, R.I., and Libert, J.M. The support of school behaviors by home based reinforcement in a parent-child contingency contract. In E.A. Rany and B.L. Hopkins (Eds.), *A new direction for education: Behavior analysis.* Lawrence, Kansas: University of Kansas Press, 1971.

Danford, H.G. Creative leadership in recreation. Boston: Allyn and Bacon, 1964.

Drabman, R.S., Spitalnik, R., and O'Leary, K.D.   Teaching self-control to disrupt children, *Journal of Abnormal Psychology,* 1974, in press.

Glynn, E.L.   Classroom applications of self-determined reinforcement. *Journal of Applied Behavior Analysis,* 1970, *3,* 123-132.

Kraus, R. *Recreation and leisure in modern society.*   New York: Appleton-Century-Crofts, 1971.

MacDonald, W.S., Gallimire, R., and MacDonald, G.   Contingency counseling by school personnel: A commercial model of intervention. *Journal of Applied Behavior Analysis,* 1973, *3,* 175-182.

Miller, R.B. and Burchard, J.D.   The daily behavior card system: An experimental analysis of the effects of monitoring classroom behaviors.   In preparation, 1974.

Patterson, G.R., Cobb, J.A., and Ray, R.S.   Direct intervention in the classroom: A set of procedures for the aggressive child.   In F.W. Clark, D.R. Evans, and L.P. Hamesbynt (Eds.), *Implementing behavior in educatioal and clinical settings.*   Champaign Research Press, 1972.

President's Commission on Law Enforcement and Administration of Justice, 1967.

Shivers, J.S. *Leadership in recreational service.*   New York: Macmillan, 1963.

Solomon, R.W. and Walker, R.G.   Peer reinforcement control of classroom problem behavior. *Journal of Applied Behavior Analysis,* 1973, *6,* 49-54.

Stahl, J.R. *The comparative effects of behavioral contracting, behavior rehearsal and self-evaluation training on the classroom behavior of problem youth.*   Doctoral dissertation, University of Vermont, 1975.

Stuart, R.B.   Behavioral contracting within the families of delinquents. *Journal of Behavior Therapy and Experimental Psychiatry,* 1971, *2,* 1-11.

Wahler, R.G.   Setting generality: Some specific and general effects of child behavior therapy. *Journal of Applied Behavior Analysis,* 1969, *2,* 239-246.

White House Conference on Children and Youth.   Washington, D.C.: Superintendent of Documents, U.S. Government Printing Office, 1960.

CHAPTER 19

EAST SIDE STORY: BEHAVIORAL ANALYSIS OF A HIGH JUVENILE CRIME COMMUNITY*†

Jerome S. Stumphauzer, Thomas W. Aiken, and Esteban V. Veloz

EDITORIAL COMMENTS

There is no doubt that the behavioral analysis model (Kanfer & Saslow, 1969) can be utilized to understand the variables maintaining problem behaviors in individuals. Behavioral treatment plans then logically draw from these conclusions. While there are times when such an individualized analysis is useful in treating delinquent behavior (see Chap. 14), all too often the conclusion reached is that the delinquent behavior is being maintained, in large part, by the extended peer group or even by the entire subculture in which the youth lives. The (then) logical treatment plan leaves the therapist with three equally untenable propositions: (1) to remove the youth from that environment and place him or her elsewhere; (2) change the peer group's influence; or (3) change the whole community. These are ambitious goals for the treatment of one person!

In Chapter 19, Stumphauzer, Aiken, and Veloz begin applying a different approach. Here they report a preliminary attempt to expand the

*The authors are indebted to Federick Kanfer and George Saslow for their suggestions and encouragement in developing this program. We would also like to give credit to the Chicano Studies Department of the California State University at Los Angeles for this Work-Study support of the third author in the early development of this program.

†Reprinted with permission from *Behavioral Disorders,* 1977, 2, 76-84. (Council for Children with Behavioral Disorders)

behavioral analysis model to understand delinquent behavior where it occurs, directly in the open community, by behaviorally analyzing a particular high juvenile crime community, and by doing a behavioral analysis of the violent youth gang which dominates that community.   There are many indications that the violent youth gangs that many thought were disappearing in the 1960s are now increasing in number, are more violent, more organized, and better armed than their predecessors (Bayh, 1977; Miller, 1977).   This chapter presents an analysis of one such violent Mexican-American youth gang in Los Angeles.   Individual treatment — if indicated, and if they would participate — would not be able to keep up with the apparent recruitment and "teaching" program these authors observed.

In Chapter 20 a dyad behavioral analysis of two nondelinquent brothers is presented by Aiken, Stumphauzer, and Veloz as an extension of the community program.   Naturally occurring self-control and trouble avoidance, as well as other adaptive behaviors are documented. Since these behaviors **are** being acquired and maintained in this high juvenile crime community, there is encouragement for extending this learning to others in a prevention program.

Rather than treating a few individuals after they are in trouble (even though the behavior may be adaptive or even desirable in their own community!), the community/gang/nondelinquent analysis approach will likely conclude with plans for wide-scale community change and prevention utilizing natural mediators of behavior change: parents, teachers, local businessmen, and nondelinquent or exdelinquent peers.   This is no small task.   However, this may be the **only** logical approach for improving life in high juvenile crime communities.

L os ANGELES IS TYPICAL of many major cities in that not only is there a high rate of juvenile crime, but there is a severe youth gang problem as well.   It has been estimated that there are 200 such gangs in Los Angeles with about 100 of them being Chicano, reflecting the large Mexican-American population in Southern California.   Many of them are violent gangs (Yablonsky, 1962) in which territoriality and gang violence (shootings, beatings, extortion, etc.) have become a daily way of life to the point where it is no longer "news."   The Los Angeles County-University of Southern California Medical Center is located in East Los Angeles in the midst of a predominently Chicano population and certainly in "gang territory."

When we began to look at the problem it was obvious that traditional psychotherapeutic and law enforcement approaches had not (and could not) change all this; indeed there are indications that the gang problem is increasing. Some ten years ago Klein (1969, 1971) did a series of studies of juvenile gangs in Los Angeles utilizing a detached-worker program. He concluded that such a program inadvertently increases gang cohesiveness and defeats its own purpose. Stumphauzer (1973, 1974, 1976, in press) has reviewed the many contributions of behavior therapy to the treatment of delinquents from token economies to group homes, outpatient treatment, and community programs. While behavior therapy results are promising, it has largely been treatment after the fact, or very limited "demonstration projects" with a few delinquents or "predelinquents." What we believe is being missed, and what we hope to focus on is the whole *behavior ecology* of a high juvenile crime community. We find it necessary, after attempting to work in one such area, to first understand how delinquent behavior is being *taught* and **learned** throughout a community so that more global, preventative strategies can be implemented to encourage the learning of incompatible, *non*-delinquent behavior. We selected a particular East Los Angeles community and gang, Eastside Loma (a pseudonym), to develop the approach as a preliminary to seeking funding for a more thorough project. We were told repeatedly that "this is no *West Side Story*," and we had to agree that the East side of Los Angeles has its own story.

BEHAVIORAL ANALYSIS MODEL

Until recently the behavioral approach has utilized its functional method of understanding people (behavioral analysis) and its methods of treatment (behavior therapy) to focus on one person at a time or, in some cases, to small groups of individuals (e.g. token economies). What we are suggesting is the utilization and expansion of the behavioral analysis concept first to understand broad community problems and then to directly apply this information to community change and prevention programs. The authors see this as a necessary step if behaviorism is to make a meaningful contribution both in understanding and preventing delinquency.

Kanfer and Saslow (1965, 1969) can be credited with the clearest presentation of the behavioral analysis model for individual treatment. The following is a brief outline of the seven major points covered in their behavioral analyses for individual patients. We hope to expand each concept in analyzing a particular high juvenile crime community, a particular youth gang, and nondelinquents in that same community.

1. *Initial analysis of the problem situation.* Problem behaviors are objectified and then classified into *behavioral excesses* (those behaviors that occur too much), *behavioral deficits* (those that do not occur enough), and *behavioral assets* (good or non-problematic behaviors).

2. *Clarification of problem situation.* Who objects to the problem behaviors and who supports them? Under exactly what circumstances do they occur and what are their consequences?

3. *Motivational analysis.* How does this person rank his or her incentives and what has the specific experience with those reinforcers been? What are the major aversive stimuli or punishers for this person? Who currently has control over these reinforcements and punishments?

4. *Developmental analysis.* What are the biological limitations of this person? When and how did they develop? What are the most characteristic features of the person's sociocultural milieu? Were there deviations in behavioral development in comparison to social and developmental norms and under what circumstances did they occur?

5. *Analysis of self-control.* Under exactly what circumstances does the person control problem behaviors? What situations or persons change this self-controlling behavior? In treatment, can self-control be expanded?

6. *Analysis of social relationships.* Who are the most significant and influential people and how do they exercise their influence on this person?

7. *Analysis of the social-cultural-physical environment.* What are the norms in the person's social milieu for the problem be-

haviors? Would there be support in this environment for changing or improving these problem behaviors?

ANALYSIS OF A COMMUNITY: EAST SIDE STORY

One approach we are taking in our attempt to formulate a behavioral understanding of how delinquent behavior is learned and maintained in a particular community is to take a broad look at the *entire* community. We are doing this by examining the physical, sociocultural, and economic environment of these youths as well as studying their behavior as viewed by various factions of their social environment (parents, teachers, law enforcement, etc.).

The first task is to define and describe the community (Kanfer, personal communication, July 1, 1976). There is a psychological identity in that residents say that they are *from* Eastside Loma. It also has a physical identity: the community is a series of hills three miles square bounded by fenced freeways to the North and East and by major streets on the South and West side. Fortunately, Eastside Loma comprises two census tracts and therefore a fund of demographics is available. The following information was gathered from the U.S. Census Bureau and from the Los Angeles County Sheriff and Probation Departments.

Eastside Loma is a densely populated area with 15,310 residents of which over 90 percent are of Mexican descent. The median per family income of the community is $8,705 with most of the residents employed in unskilled labor and clerical jobs. The percentage of high school graduates is 21 percent with only 1 percent having obtained any post-secondary education.

The community is made up of small, single-dwelling living units with many rear add-on houses. It is primarily a residential neighborhood with no industry in close proximity. The homes are mostly 50 years old or older with a mean market value of between $16,000 to $17,000. Most of the inhabitants are renters.

The community has three elementary schools for its 3,324 children between the ages of 6-13, with no high school within the two census tracts for its 1,479 adolescents between the ages of 13-18. There is a small clinic, one park, no major businesses, and several "mom-and-pop" grocery stores. Buses, the only rapid transit available, serve the major streets, but provide no direct service to the "hill" area.

Behavioral Analysis of the Community

An initial behavioral analysis, stressing assets, deficits, excesses, and controlling variables of the youth population was conducted with the law enforcement agency patrolling the area. Veteran peace officers were interviewed and a structure survey constructed for this study was utilized.

BEHAVIOR EXCESSES. All officers interviewed (ten thus far) stated unequivocally that the use of firearms by youths was the number one problem in the community. Reporting district statistics of the Sheriff's Department for 1975 reveal that out of 14 reported homicides in the 10 census tracts comprising East Los Angeles, the gang within the census tract under investigation herein is suspected in at least six of them.

The first two authors, while gathering data from officers assigned to a "Gang Suppression" Unit, were on a "ride along" in a patrol car when a call came in that a young male Chicano was shooting at passing cars. Upon arriving at the scene, two youths with rifles opened fire on the responding units. After a brief skirmish, one youth was dead and another wounded by returned police fire. Some alarm was expressed that this had been a "set up" with the Sheriff a direct target of shooting rather than the more usual gang vs. gang episode. Other problematic behaviors listed in succeeding order include felonious assault, robbery, burglary, car theft, and rape.

BEHAVIOR DEFICITS. Behavior deficits listed by those interviewed stressed truancy, not working, and poor community relations. Deficits seen in the general community included lack of vocational programs and jobs; lack of highly structured programs for 15 to 18 year olds, lack of early identification and gang prevention programs, lack of programs designed to help parents learn how to control their children's behavior, and lack of adequate family planning facilities in the community.

BEHAVIORAL ASSETS. Behavioral assets listed by those interviewed were strong family relationships, competitive skills, artistic ability (murals and graffitti some of which have been acclaimed locally as art forms) , and "smooth talking" ability.

Those objecting to the problem behaviors can be put into three distinct groups: (1) the parent who has lost control of the child's behavior, (2) community residents and neighbors who are continually confronted with the problem behavior and are often directly involved in it, and (3) the law enforcement agencies that have, as their express duty, the upholding of the "spirit" of the law.

Parents who have lost control over their child will often enlist the aid of community agencies, the church, or even the police in order to reestablish control, using fear of punishment as the means whereby the child's behavior is brought under control. However, contact with the police, especially if there is no punishment associated with contact, may prove to be a valuable source of reinforcement from the peer group. For parents, loss of control, if not followed by intensive family intervention, usually leads to the parents' development of fear of their own child and, at this point, the refocus of control becomes more difficult, if not impossible, to establish.

Community residents report many of the incidents that they observe provided that their anonymity is guaranteed. Intimidation of the local citizenry has provided the delinquent culture with an immunity from prosecution which doubly serves the learning process by enhancing the prestige of the individual who can exercise such intimidation and, likewise, by the almost complete removal of the possibility of aversive consequences. Many residents who have attempted to stand up to the gang have been threatened and beaten; some killed.

Whereas the residents maintain the behavior by ignoring it, other groups maintain the behavior by attending to it. This is accomplished by the peer group who reinforce inappropriate or *loco* behavior by praising or otherwise rewarding it. Another example might be when the media (television, newspapers, etc.) reinforce gang activity by sensationalizing gang exploits and cliques in the news.

Another source of community support for delinquent behavior

comes from the family who teaches it directly because it has been, and still is a part of their own history and lifestyle. It is not unusual to see three generations of the same family bearing similar tattoos depicting their gang affiliation, and this serves as a reminder of the historical pervasiveness of the preoccupation with this life-style.

The police are clearly the strongest objectors to the community's problem behaviors. It has been mentioned that stepped-up patrols, more police saturation in the area, and more arrests serve only to attend to, and thus reinforce, the very problem behaviors that are trying to be eliminated. Those officers interviewed did not see themselves as having a "punishing" effect on the delinquent culture in the hill area. At best they concede that they may be occasionally instrumental in stopping potentially explosive situations by "keeping a lid on," but admit to not putting the slightest dent in the problem.

Supposedly, it is up to the Juvenile Court to punish wrongdoers. However, a review of the arrest records of several gang members in the census tracts revealed that even though convicted many times (as many as 9 offenses) these individuals had not received any punishment whatsoever. For every one of these individual cases, adjudication resulted in continuation of probation only.

It is also possible that the police department may be reinforcing inappropriate behaviors because of the sheer excitement that some aspects of police gang work brings. It had been stated by more than a few of the officers that busy nights are more desirable than slow, quiet nights when there is no "action."

What stands out in this analysis thus far is the fact that delinquent gang behavior is reinforced overtly by peers and often indirectly by many parents and/or family members, police, community members, and agencies. We are just beginning to piece together what appears to be quite a comprehensive system for teaching and maintaining gang violence. Very little evidence has been found thus far to suggest that behavior incompatible with gang delinquent behavior is being supported on any scale that would begin to turn the process around. One encouraging development has been the formation of a Parents' Coalition by concerned parents and the Sheriff, they are beginning to meet together to see what can be done.

Much work remains in this community analysis. The Sheriffs interviewed have one important point of view and, as seen, play an integral part in understanding and eventually changing gang violence in Eastside Loma. We have just recently begun interviewing parents, community social service workers, probation, business people, clergy, and teachers who all have important data to report on the learning and maintenance of gang related delinquent behavior. Not everyone sees gangs as bad. They have many positive social aspects which need to be analyzed behaviorally and explored as assets to build on as one possible intervention.

A CHICANO YOUTH GANG: LA VIDA LOCA

In order to best understand how gang related delinquent behavior is being taught and learned in this particular *barrio,* the behavioral analysis model is being employed to focus on the youth gang, called "Eastside Loma" with the gang "placa" or insignia "E/L," that dominates this particular community. Extensive community work has been done by the third author in the E/L area over the last three years. Further interviewing of gang members with a structured behavioral analysis questionnaire especially prepared for this study was used in order to acquire behavioral data on this particular gang. The interviews were conducted individually with several gang members "street-corner" style in various neighborhood hang-out locations. The following are our preliminary findings.

The E/L gang has been in existence for well over 50 years, dating back to the early 1920's. It began as a social group wherein Chicanos and Mexican Nationals congregated on a particular street in this community. This early banding together has been attributed to the lack of recreational facilities in the area and for self-protection purposes from external groups (i.e., immigration, police), and it has grown steadily ever since.

The current *barrio* gang member is easily identified by the proud and "cool" manner of walk and uniform: khaki pants, camp or prison jacket, plaid wool shirt, and head bandana or brim hat. Moreover, many of the gang members *(vatos)* are decorated with tattoos such as a teardrop beside the eye, an insignia representing the *barrio* they belong to, or something dramatically announcing their life style as with *Mi Vida Loca* (my crazy life, see Fig. 19-1).

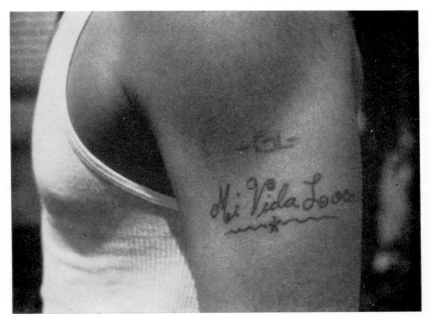

Figure 19-1. "What is *Mi Vida Loca?* That's my crazy life. I will do anything today because there might not be any tomorrow. And I'll do it because I am a *loco.*

Estimates ranging from 300 to 400 gang members have been reported by residents, community agencies and gang members themselves; with no one gang leader and cluster or cliques of young people making up the various ranks. The ranks are divided into groups roughly by age, what Cartwright (1975) calls a "vertical" gang:

Varrio Trece (daring ones)	ages 9-13
Chicos (little ones)	ages 14-17
Balazos (bullets)	ages 18-22
Disciples	ages 22-25

The Disciples, and some Bullets, comprise what is commonly referred to as the *Veteranos* (gang veterans). The Veteranos are, in a sense, retired soldiers holding administrative positions. They do not usually get involved in gang warfare unless they are personally attacked or their family is endangered.

In addition, approximately 150 girls, ranging in age from 12 to 18, associate with the boys of the E/L gang. Although they live in the area, they no longer have a special girls' clique.

There was such a girls' clique called *Las Primas* (The Cousins) but the clique was abolished by the males because of, among other reasons, an excess of gang violence which was attributable indirectly to them. In a curious application of self-control, the males reportedly realized that the girls' clique was intensifying their problems with rival gangs, as well as causing fights among E/L members, and they disbanded them. Now the girls are, as one gang member states, "our silent partners."

Behavioral Analysis of the Gang

BEHAVIORAL EXCESSES. In considering behavior excesses with Chicano gang members the rather unique and pervasive gang concept must be identified. Literally translated, as with many words and phrases, *Mi Vida Loca* loses much of its intrinsic cultural meaning but, in short, refers to the belief of the individual that he is living his life fatalistically, dangerously, and with the greatest amount of excitement/enjoyment. *Mi Vida Loca* usually has a violent connotation, meaning that the individual conducting his life accordingly is willing to put himself in maximum risk situations such as risks of personal freedom (as with conflict with the police), or those stuations in which the risk may involve the potential loss of his life (drug abuse gang violence, etc.). As one gang member put it "What is *Mi Vida Loca?* That's my crazy life. I will do *anything* and everything *today* because there might not be any tomorrow. And I'll do it because I am a *loco.*"

Problem behaviors occurring most frequently include shootings, getting loaded (drugs or alcohol), extortion of money from residents, street fighting, and vandalism. All of these behaviors are considered to be acts of risk by the gang members interviewed, acts that were supported by a considerable amount of peer group social reinforcement. The more *loco* the act, the greater the reinforcement. In light of this concept, the very presence of the police in the *barrio* serves as a challenge to the *locos* to act out, to take even greater risks with their lives. This puts the law enforcement agency in a difficult situation, as they become the very stimulus controlling much of the delinquent behavior acted out by the gang member.

TERRITORIALITY. This is a key concept in understanding E/L and other Chicano youth gangs. Community territories are often firmly held lines, and much of the violence between gangs is stimulated by a breach of territoriality. Another stimulus fairly certain to touch off violence is a threat or act against any gang member or his family by a rival gang. Much of the problem behavior is maintained through social reinforcement by peer gang members and the significant models in the community, such as the Veterano. The Veterano is a well-respected gang veteran who has shown that he could survive life in the *barrio* as well as in the penitentiary, as is often the case.

BEHAVIORAL DEFICITS. It has become evident throughout this study that a large proportion of gang members do not attend school and have no incentive to do so in the future. None of the high schools servicing the community are in the E/L "turf." Thus, school attendance would involve going into another rival gang's territory. A second deficit is not working which seems to be due to the fact that there is almost no vocational training and very few jobs. This lack of jobs serves as an additional stimuli in maintaining delinquent behavior as those without work will seek other means of obtaining money (robbery, burglary, and extortion).

BEHAVIORAL ASSETS. The data thus far collected seem to indicate that, among many of the gang members, there is a certain amount of self-control given certain stimuli conditions. Many of the existing conditions (gang beatings, shootings, extortion) will not occur, or will be lessened in their probability of occurrence if an older adult, particularly a woman, is present. Among most gang members there seems to be an almost mystical, reverential adoration for the mother figure. Of the many gang members interviewed, more than three fourths of them wore tatoos reading "Mom," "Madre," or "Madre Querida" (beloved mother) despite the fact that many reported they were constantly at odds with their mothers. There is some evidence that the "code" of never harming a mother, a young child, or an old man is breaking down, especially in the recent practice of opening fire on houses without knowing (or caring) who is inside.

This preliminary analysis of the E/L gang in Eastside Loma provided some evidence of the extent and magnitude of the problem and the many-faceted "learning program" operating to teach and maintain gang related delinquent behavior. A much more thorough analysis is indicated before firm, data-based conclusions can be reached and logical interventions offered. A wider sample of gang members and leaders is needed; perhaps behavioral analyses of Veteranos and certainly behavior studies of young members who are now in the process of learning their role in the gang. Also needed is a behavioral analysis of non-gang members in this same community to determine how behavior incompatible to gang violence is learned.

BEHAVIORAL ANALYSIS OF NON-DELINQUENTS

In this third preliminary behavioral analysis we are taking an unusual yet what we see as an obvious fact. Within the Eastside Loma community there is a fairly high probability that any given youngster will become a gang member. However, some do not. Some manage to live in this community without being a gang member or delinquent in any traditional sense. By conducting behavioral analyses of several of these non-delinquents we hope to determine precisely how and from whom they learned alternate, incompatible, non-criminal behaviors. This study is consistent with a behavioristic position: determine how these youths avoid gang delinquency and perhaps this information can be utilized in helping others stay out of trouble.

By non-delinquent we mean a youth who is not in trouble with the police, family or school because of gang related behavior and at the same time is engaged in *productive,* non-criminal behavior. At present, several youths in the target community are being interviewed and observed following fairly traditional behavioral analysis techniques. Youths who were troublemakers and somehow stopped, as well as young men who grew up in this area and are presently involved in productive, non-criminal lives (even anti-criminal in the case of some police officers) are likewise being interviewed. Findings are only tentative at this point. By definition, there are no notable excessive or deficient behaviors. We expect to focus on *asset* behaviors. In these youths too, social attention is apparently the critical reinforcer but it does not come from gang members. Rather reinforcement comes from a strong family, from peers who are also not in the midst of gang life, and from other influential adults in the community: occasionally teachers, community workers, even older brothers who are in a gang but are intent on keeping their younger brother out of it! One of the adult "non-delinquents" interviewed, a sheriff in the East Los Angeles area who is himself a Chicano, and was raised in the target community, states "I was more afraid of my father than of the gangs. Also, I learned that to stay out of the gangs I had to do a lot of fighting with them. I had to be 'badder' than the gangs."

A promising finding, based on a research program which trained paraprofessionals in this community to do behavioral contracting in the families of alcohol abusing adolescents, was that once these youths can be engaged in helping other, younger children stay out of trouble they become less delinquent themselves (Teicher, Sinay & Stumphauzer, 1976). In other words, these individuals found it reinforcing *to help* other youngsters in their own community, especially when they had an enthusiastic community worker who served as a model. This finding lends support to the concept of utilizing young people from a community to help their own people. This concept seems fairly well represented in drug abuse, but less so in delinquency prevention programs.

In a sense, this study centers on self-control and our analysis will specifically focus on this aspect to a large degree. Nondelinquents either have external reinforcers that are stronger than those controlled by the gangs or they have self-control in a behavioral sense. We will include at least two systems of behavioral self-control which are currently gaining wide attention. In one, Kanfer and Karoly (1972) suggest study of three aspects of self-control which seem relevant here, too: how do these non-delinquents learn to *measure* their own behavior, to *evaluate* it, and finally how do they *reinforce themselves?* As one youth put it, "I tell myself that I'm not going over there (where the trouble is), I go in the other direction."

Actually, these kinds of "internal dialogues" are the focus of a second system of self-control study exemplified by the work of Meichenbaum (1974) whose cognitive behavior modification, or assessing and improving internal dialogues, may well become an important focus of this study. What do gang members say to themselves in this community and what do *non*-delinquents say to themselves that is different? How is this self-controlling language being learned and can it be taught to others?

This study of non-delinquents is still in its early stages, but already we can suggest that non-delinquent behavior *is* being learned in this high probability juvenile crime community. Analysis of non-delinquent and successful self-controlling behavior does look like a meaningful path to follow—if we could only get it into the newspapers!

PRELIMINARY CONCLUSIONS

It should be readily apparent that a multigenerational phenomenon like the gang structure we found in Eastside Loma can only be changed through a unified community approach. We believe that behavioral analyses, necessarily more thorough than those accomplished here thus far, would provide a solid basis for understanding problem behavior and its maintaining variables in this and similar high juvenile crime communities. Only then can a behavioral, community intervention be logically planned, carried out, and assessed. This is the first attempt at such a community analysis.

Incarceration and/or removal of individual youths from the community has been and will be ineffective in most cases because the same stimuli conditions for delinquent gang behavior exist in the community when they return. Likewise, psychotherapy or individual behavior therapy is no answer. Other attempts to reduce juvenile crime and gang violence in this community have been small, isolated, community based programs with little in the way of funding and interagency support.   Perhaps what is indicated is a banding together of a group of agencies and residents under a common analysis and intervention methodology with the express purpose of solving problems directly where they occur, in the natural environment.

East Side Story is unfinished.   The efforts reported here are just a beginning.   Our three analyses are in various stages of development.   Each is adding important perspectives for understanding this community, its people, and how gang-delinquent and non-delinquent behavior is being taught and learned   Most sobering is consideration of the tremendous effort and funding that would be required to give communities like this one new and more productive directions, while at the same time preserving their rich cultural heritage and identity.

REFERENCES

Editorial Comments

Bayh, Senator B.   Report of the subcommittee to investigate juvenile delinquency. Washington: U.S. Senate, 1977.

Kanfer, F.H., & Saslow, G.   Behavioral diagnosis.   In C.M. Franks (Ed.) *Behavior therapy: Appraisal and status.* New York: McGraw-Hill, 1969, 417-444.

Miller, W.   The rumble this time. *Psychology Today,* 1977, *10,* 52-54.

Text

Cartwright, D.S.   The nature of gangs.   In D.S. Cartwright, B. Tomson, & H. Schwartz (Eds.) *Gang delinquency.*   Monterey CA: Brooks/Cole, 1975, 1-22.

Kanfer, F.H., & Karoly, P. Self-control: A behavioristic excursion into the lion's den. *Behavior Therapy,* 1972, *3,* 398-416.

Kanfer, F.H., & Saslow, G.   Behavioral diagnosis.   *Archives of General Psychiatry,* 1965, *12,* 529-538.

Kanfer, F.H., & Saslow, G.   Behavioral diagnosis.   In C.M. Franks (Ed.) *Behavior therapy: Appraisal and status.* New York: McGraw-Hill, 1969, 417-444.

Klein, M.W.   Gang cohesiveness, delinquency, and a street-work program. *Journal of Research in Crime and Delinquency,* 1969, *7,* 135-166.

Klein, M.W. *Street gangs and street workers.* Englewood Cliffs, N.J.: Prentice-Hall, 1971.

Meichenbaum, D.H. *Cognitive behavior modification.* Morristown, NJ: General Learning Press, 1974.

Stumphauzer, J.S. (Ed.) *Behavior therapy with delinquents.* Springfield, IL: Charles C Thomas, 1973.

Stumphauzer, J.S. *Six techniques of modifying delinquent behavior.* Leonia, NJ: Behavioral Sciences Tape Library, 1974.

Stumphauzer, J.S. Modifying delinquent behavior: Beginning and current practices. *Adolescence, 1976, 11,* 1-28.

Stumphauzer, J.S. (Ed.) *Progress in behavior therapy with delinquents.* Springfield, IL: Charles C Thomas, in press.

Teicher, J.D., Sinay, R.D., & Stumphauzer, J.S. Training community based paraprofessionals as behavior therapists with families of alcohol abusing adolescents. *American Journal of Psychiatry,* 1976, *133,* 847-850.

Yablonsky, L. *The violent gang.* New York: Macmillan, 1962.

CHAPTER 20

BEHAVIORAL ANALYSIS OF NON-DE-LINQUENT BROTHERS IN A HIGH JUVENILE CRIME COMMUNITY*†

THOMAS W. AIKEN, JEROME S. STUMPHAUZER, AND ESTEBAN V. VELOZ

Los ANGELES has the most serious gang problem in the nation. From January 1, 1974 to October 30 of the same year its over 140 active gangs with as many as 15,000 adolescents were responsible for over 1,600 reported violent crimes including 51 deaths, 885 assaults with a deadly weapon, 294 assaults with intent to commit murder, 279 kidnappings, 19 reported rapes, 8 firebombings, and 99 cases of shooting into an inhabited building, (Bayh, 1977) ; and these are only *reported* figures.

Two particularly high juvenile crime census tracts are currently the object of investigation in an ongoing behavior analysis attempting to determine the variables constituting the teaching, learning, and maintenance of delinquent and violent gang behavior in this community (Stumphauzer, Aiken, & Veloz, 1977).

During the data collection process of these analyses, an interesting phenomenon was observed. Within these high juvenile crime census tracts it was noted that there were youths who were not delinquent, i.e. not in trouble with the police, their family, or

*The authors are indebted to Frederick Kanfer and George Saslow for their suggestions and encouragement in developing this program. We would also like to give credit to the Chicano Studies Department of the California State University at Los Angeles for their Work-Study support of the third author in the early development of this program.

†Reprinted with permission from *Behavioral Disorders*, 1977, 2, 212-222. (Council for Children with Behavioral Disorders)

school because of any delinquent or gang-related behavior. A review of the literature reveals that the nondelinquent *per se* has been studied but primarily as a control group with the focal point of such studies being to delineate and clarify some aspect of *delinquent* behavior. The nondelinquent, particularly one from a high juvenile crime community, has received little attention (Reckless, Dinitz, & Murray, 1956, 1957; Scarpitti, Murray, Dinitz, & Reckless, 1960). It is surprising that relatively few studies have been devoted to nondelinquents. Speculatively, it may be that our medical model heritage has tended to focus on the deviate, pathological, or abnormal. It may be that the disease model severely limits our understanding of *naturally occurring adaptive behavior*. Current theoreticians are stressing the obsolescence of the medical "disease" model because it seems to fit neither "problems of living" (Szasz, 1967), drug abuse (Stumphauzer, 1974), nor delinquency (Stumphauzer, 1973, in press).

By conducting several behavioral analyses of these nondelinquents, it is hoped that the way in which they learn, teach, and utilize alternate, incompatible, noncriminal behavior can be determined. Such analyses have direct application: determine how these youths stay out of trouble and perhaps this knowledge can be applied directly in community-wide delinquency prevention.

Kanfer and Saslow (1965, 1969) can be credited with the clearest explication of the behavior analysis model for individual treatment. They critically explored the shortcomings of traditional diagnostic processes and the futility of labeling, offering behavior analysis as a more parsimonious alternative for understanding people. The intention here is to utilize the behavior analysis model to examine the behavior of nondelinquents in a high juvenile crime community. The seven major points covered in Kanfer and Saslow's behavior analysis model include (1) Initial Analysis of the Problem Situation, (2) Clarification of the Problem Situation, (3) Motivational Analysis, (4) Developmental Analysis, (5) Analysis of Self-Control, (6) Analysis of Social Relationships, and (7) Analysis of the Social-Cultural-Physical Environment. (See Stumphauzer, Aiken, & Veloz (1977) for a more detailed outline of this model.)

According to Zifferblatt and Hendricks (1974), applied behavior analysis methodology is particularly suited to results-oriented research and interventions and, because the procedure used is designed to analyze behaviors in their *natural* context, this process is generally culture free. This is an asset when dealing with a subculture, especially when the nature of the study is evaluating nondelinquent and/or nonpathological behavior in a community which may well have different norms for such behavior.

METHOD

Video and audiotape interviews are being conducted with members of a *barrio** clique within the census tracts being investigated in a comprehensive study by the present authors (Stumphauzer Aiken, & Veloz 1977). These interviews are being held both in street and office settings to determine how delinquent behavior is being taught and learned in a high juvenile crime community and in a violent youth gang. During one such session the investigators became aware of three brothers (ages 23, 19, and 14; see Fig. 20-1) who live in this *barrio* and who, although they visit with this clique in their "alley" and are accepted by them, openly disavow any participation in delinquent behavior generally, and violent gang behavior in particular. Arrangements were made to conduct a behavior analysis in-depth interview with these brothers directly in their *barrio,* and a structured, open-ended interview and observation following Kanfer and Saslow's behavior analysis model was tape-recorded. To evaluate the motivational analysis aspect of the interview, a Reinforcement Survey patterned after Cautela and Kastenbaum (1967) was utilized. Caesar and Richard, the oldest and youngest brothers, were interviewed as the middle brother was unable to participate because of full-time work commitments.

---

*Although the literal translation of this word is *neighborhood,* it is also construed to mean *gang* by law enforcement agencies and the mass media in Los Angeles.

RESULTS

Initial Analysis of the Problem Situation

ASSETS. Definite asset behaviors reported and observed in Caesar during the interview and observation period included restoring old cars, dressing plainly (no outstanding *barrio* insignia), knowing as many *vatos* ("bad dudes") from as many *barrio* cliques as possible, being able to communicate with the various clique members in their particular jargon about current events relevant to the gangs in the local area, having cultural and ethnic pride, being a particularly articulate speaker, having an established reputation in the *barrio* for not "snitching" or "ratting," and being persistent in his attempts to meet goals that he has set for himself, e.g. has applied for and interviewed several times for a particular

Figure 20-1. Videotaped interview in the "alley." Note the contrasting dress of Caesar (center, in white T-shirt and jeans) and the more typical attire of clique members "Nasty" and "Fox" on his left. Richard, dressed identically to Caesar, is observed to closely listen to what his older brother is saying.

job that he wants. Caesar is currently unemployed due to company economic problems (high gasoline prices); he was a short-haul truck driver.

Asset behaviors listed by the younger brother, Richard, included: fixing up bicycles for himself and neighbor children, dressing like his older brother (blue jeans, white T-shirt and tennis shoes—no gang-affiliation clothing), and being considered a dependable and seldom-absent student at Belvedere Junior High School.

EXCESSES. Excesses are not necessarily a focal point of this study as, by definition, one would not expect them in nonproblematic adolescents. Observational data reveal, however, that excessive behavior might be applicable in that both Caesar and Richard were observed to and express that they often hang around the "alley", which is the meeting place of the clique, during the times various members are engaging in illegal activities (drinking, smoking marijuana, sniffing glue etc.). Such behavior might be construed as excessive in that the activities therein are definite discriminative stimuli for negative police contact.

DEFICITS. What *they* thought that they should be doing but were not doing now was explained by Caesar as not attending school, although he had graduated from high school and had gone to junior college for one year. It was necessary to quit school and work to support his family (the father had left some 12 years earlier). Other deficits listed by Caesar included not working, finding a new job, lack of marketable job skills, and also the fact that helping his "homeboys" stay out of trouble was an activity that he should be more deeply involved with although it is carried out to some extent.

Richard saw his deficits in the area of school work. He states that he wants to be smart like his older brother, but admits to being a slow learner who doesn't read well. He reports that in his math class he just sits quietly to avoid being called on.

Clarification of the Problem Situation

A discussion of the assets, deficits, and excesses revealed that, for Caesar, restoration of old cars into customized "low-riders" was seen as positively reinforcing because of the monetary gains received on resale and highly reinforcing because of the social praise received for his efforts. Social praise was received formally, in that he had won many trophies as prizes for entering his cars in custom car shows, and informally through the praise and bragging of his mother to her friends and from the "homeboys" who see his care as *firme* (cool, together). This activity was self-reinforcing in terms of Caesar's pride in his accomplishments. Interestingly, Caesar's mother initially disapproved of the time and money spent on restoring cars but stopped all nagging when the trophies were won and the cars were sold at a substantially higher rate than when originally purchased.

For Richard, repairing bicycles is a highly reinforcing activity in that many neighborhood peers rely on his ability to strip down, repaint, repair, and rebuild their bicycles and value him highly.

Whereas Richard reports that he fixes bicycles as a way to relieve boredom, Caesar actively spends his spare time restoring cars. According to Caesar, his hobby provides a "high" that no drug could possibly give. It is of some interest to note that the bicycle repairing of Richard may be viewed as generalized imitation of his brother/model's car restoration.

According to Caesar, the only groups that object to these assets are the police, who see low-rider automobiles as fraught with motor vehicle equipment violations, and neighborhood peers who are sometimes envious of someone else's automobile. He likewise mentioned that he thought that some police take offense that someone from a poor community might drive a better automobile than they do.

Richard reports that sometimes his bicycle repairing skills are exploited by neighbors who expect him to "fix their bikes all of the time for free," and if he does not, he is called names.

Motivation Analysis

A Reinforcement Survey patterned after Cautela and Kastenbaum (1967) was adopted for this study and centered on the people, places, things, activities, and social situations that an individual finds most and least rewarding. Results of the Survey are summarized in Table 20-I.

TABLE 20-I

INITIAL ANALYSIS OF BEHAVIOR AND MOTIVATION

CAESAR	*RICHARD*
A. *BEHAVIORAL ASSETS*	
1. staying out of trouble	1. staying out of trouble
a. dress differently from *vatos*	a. dressing like older brother
b. know as many *vatos* as possible	b. know as many *vatos* as possible
c. self-control strategies	c. self-control strategies
d. model after *barrio counselor* ("Hood")	d. model after older brother (Caesar)
2. strong family relationships	2. strong family relationships
3. restores old cars	3. fixes bicycles
4. good work record	4. regular school attendance
5. articulate speaker	5. cultural and ethnic pride
6. cultural and ethnic pride	
B. *BEHAVIORAL EXCESSES*	
1. hangs around cliques' "alley"	1. hangs around cliques' "alley"
C. *BEHAVIORAL DEFICITS* (by own report)	
1. out of work	1. slow learner (reading and math)
2. not attending college	
3. not helping "homeboys" enough	
D. *MOST REINFORCING*	
1. *People:*	1. *People:*
immediate family	immediate family
barrio counselor ("Hood")	older brother (Caesar)
girl friend	"homeboys"
2. *Places:*	2. *Places:*
home	home
school	movie theatre
movie theatre	school
3. *Activities:*	3. *Activities:*
working on cars	working on bicycles
listening to music	reading comics
dating	going to dances
4. *Items:*	4. *Items:*
cars	bicycles
books	cars
sports equipment	camping equipment
5. *Social:*	5. *Social:*
being praised for a job well done	being praised for hobbies

CAESAR	RICHARD

being seen as warm and friendly
being asked for advice
	making others happy
	being told that he is right
	having others see him as
	    a nice guy being asked for
	    advice

E. *LEAST REINFORCING*

CAESAR	RICHARD
1. *People:* police store owners some neighbors	1. *People:* school teachers some neighbors
2. *Places:* police station relatives' homes	2. *Places:* school library police station
3. *Activities:* drinking getting high and talking about "bad dudes"	3. *Activities:* drinking getting high and gambling school sports
4. *Items:* rifles hats knives liquor tobacco pistols	4. *Items:* liquor tobacco firearms knives uniforms some sports equipment

5. *Social:*
being famous and rich
being seen as hard and tough
being seen as a daredevil, *loco,* or
  as a guy who can hold his liquor
	5. *Social*
	having others see him as
	  cold and indifferent, crazy
	  (loco), or as a guy who
	  can hold his liquor

F. *PUNISHERS*

CAESAR	RICHARD

1. being in the wrong place
  at the wrong time
	1. harrassment at school by
	  cliques

2. fear of being shot, killed	2. harrassment by the police
3. harrassment by the police	

Both Richard and Caesar see their success with positive reinforcement as being contingent solely on themselves and their behavior and not as by-products of fate, luck, or the whim of powerful others.

Caesar states, however, that although an individual is responsible for what becomes of him, he notes that it is not too infrequent an occurrence in his community for an individual to receive negative police contact. In some cases, such police contact can and does lead to mistaken imprisonment. For this reason, Caesar is unequivocally opposed to the death penalty and states that law enforcement agencies possess and exert a tremendous amount of control over his *barrio*.

Both Caesar and Richard currently perceive themselves as being helpers in and of the *barrio*. Getting rich and famous and moving out of their *barrio* is seen as "ranking out" by Caesar who states, "How can you leave life-long friends, *familia* (family), just because you've made some money—only our politicians do that."

Richard has entertained the future goal of community service work and cites a television hero, "Baretta," an undercover cop, as a model. The reinforcing characteristics that make Baretta an attractive model for Richard are the fact that Baretta is from the community that he is trying to help, and that he tries to be pleasant with everybody.

Major aversive stimuli noted by Caesar include fearing that he could find himself in the wrong place at the wrong time, catching a bullet from some gang member who mistakes him for someone else, dying, and having his family victimized by some crosstown *vatos* or by the police. Future fears include getting old and wondering who will take care of him should he become sick or disabled; and getting arrested, put into jail, and completely forgotten and left there.

Major aversive stimuli reported by Richard include fears of being harrassed by the strong cliques at school, which is more of an occasional actuality than an imagined fear. They also include the possibility of not being happily married someday and also of being harrassed by the police.

Developmental Analysis

BIOLOGICAL CHANGES: Caesar and Richard have no biological limitations that are currently affecting their behavior; both appear physically healthy, although Richard does have a reading disability according to the school and, in reporting on such disability, refers to himself as being "not very smart" and a "slow learner."

SOCIOLOGICAL CHANGES: According to Caesar and Richard there have been no sociological changes of which they have been aware, and they have lived in their *barrio* since they were children. They have moved only once, and that move was two blocks. Both brothers agree that they feel comfortable in their *barrio*, have a great deal of affection for it and most of its members, many of whom they have known for most of their lives. Each states, however, that he would feel uncomfortable going into a strange *barrio* without being invited there and without being well protected. (See Stumphauzer, Aiken, & Veloz, 1977) for a more complete physical description of this *barrio*.)

BEHAVIORAL CHANGES: Caesar and Richard attribute a good deal of their nondelinquent behavior to specific models in their environment. Caesar states that an older *veterano* (retired gang member) named "Hood" was instrumental in helping him to formulate a code of conduct within which to live in the *barrio*. Caesar comments on the factors that make "Hood" a successful model: "Hood's been through it all. He's lived here all his life —he's done time—he's been a user but now he's clean. He is harrassed by the cops so much that he had to get a letter from a judge saying that he was clean and that he should be left alone. He helps all of us in the *barrio*. He tells it like it really is, takes us to the ball game, helps raise money for bail, whatever. He does it all for nothing. Not even teachers and counselors work for nothing."

Richard states that it was his older brother, Caesar, who was instrumental in providing the appropriate modeling experience for the development of prosocial behavior. According to Richard, "My mother told my brother when my father left that he was responsible for me, she wasn't. My brother counseled me, looked out for me and told me what to do. He told me never to steal— that if I wanted something to come to him and he'd try to get it for me or see if I could earn it. If my brother thought that I was getting into any trouble, he would probably kick my butt."

Analysis of Self-Control

Both brothers agree that they can control their own behavior relative to avoiding getting into trouble. Caesar states that self-control entails having the "guts" to say no to friends when saying yes would spell trouble. Richard imitates his brother's recipe for self-control and states that not getting into trouble is more reinforcing than peer approval for not being a "sissy." Caesar and Richard state that they do not drink, smoke, or use any drugs, and further state that they have never been arrested. Subsequent interviews with *barrio* members have corroborated their statements, and there is some videotaped and observational evidence that they do not engage in these behaviors. Loss of self-control is related by Caesar to the real or imagined threat of someone bothering his family. Richard reports that he sometimes loses self-control when he gets caught up in the excitement of something that may have a negative attraction, e.g. watching two tough guys "slug it out" after school. However, if weapons are brandished (knives, guns, or tire irons), Richard states that he will immediately leave the scene.

Trouble Situations. An interesting pattern of self-control emerged when it came to defining trouble situations and the way in which each of the brothers identified and avoided them. A convenient way of conceptualizing the process of trouble avoidance can be seen in D'Zurilla's and Goldfried's (1971) five-stage, problem-solving model which includes (a) general orientation, (b) problem definition, (c) generation of alternatives, (d) decision making, and (e) verification.

For this discussion of trouble avoidance, general orientation can be viewed as the desire to stay out of trouble. For both brothers, situations that are seen as potentially dangerous include any group of five or more adolescents gathering on a street (rated as more dangerous if they are strangers); parties, weddings, or any get together where liquor, marijuana, or pills are being passed around. A car full of "cruisers" is seen as potentially dangerous and so is the mere presence of the police. Other potentially trouble-filled areas include owning a "low-rider" automobile because of negative police attention, and proclaiming a particular *barrio* by word or by manner of dress because of the high probability of being challenged by someone from another *barrio*.

Both brothers use past experience and observational learning in evaluating present environmental circumstances. Whenever Caesar goes to a wedding or party he checks over all of the guys present to see who looks like a potential troublemaker. After the party has been going for awhile he again analyzes any changes in the way that the party is progressing (is anyone getting drunk and belligerent, have any party-crashers from another *barrio* come in, is there a group of guys sitting in the corner and whispering, etc.) and picks up on any negative cues that may indicate that it is better to leave than to stay. Caesar states that he usually leaves parties and get-togethers early because most of the trouble starts when they are over.

Caesar and Richard generally look at other factors in evaluating the potentiality of trouble. A brief behavior analysis of the prevailing environment is generally involved. Such factors as how some strangers are dressed, which *barrio* they come from, what their numbers are, how they are behaving, combined with a knowledge of the current news on inter*barrio* confrontations (who is at war with whom and over what) are helpful in avoiding trouble situations. Caesar states that he makes it his business to get to know every *vato* from every *barrio* and for them to know him. Familiarity, according to Caesar, is a stepping-stone to security.

With major problem areas defined, both brothers use different strategies to avoid trouble. Whereas Richard generally uses more problem-avoidance strategies (looking as if he forgot something and turning around when a group of tough guys are in front of the store where he planned to spend his quarter for ice cream), Caesar generally relies more on his ability to manipulate the environment when the potential source of trouble is his peers, but uses avoidance strategies when the potential source of trouble is the police. According to Caesar: "If a Mexican dude challenges me to a fight, I tell him to give me a good reason why the two of us from the same *raza* (race, background) should fight when we should be uniting against outside oppressions. I can usually talk a guy out of a fight without either of us losing face. When I see a cop following my car, I casually turn off into the parking lot of a nearby store, as if I had to go there, and let him pass."

Caesar also gets to know as many of the patrolling officers as possible so as to know who is out to help him and who is out to "get" him. He will also pull over to the side of the road when the police are field interrogating an isolated subject and watch them, ensuring that they know they are being watched, and looking for any unnecessary harrassment. Caesar states, "I watch them, I look at them as if to say, 'Someone is watching you, so don't try anything funny.' "

Another strategy employed by Caesar and Richard to avoid negative contact with the police and other *barrio* members is the manner in which they dress. Whereas *vatos* generally wear a uniform (tatoo, pleated pants, brim and knit hats, bandanas, plaid wool shirts, khaki's (see Fig. 1) ; these brothers dress plainly and make it a point *not* to include anything in their personal appearance that can be taken for a *barrio* uniform. Caesar has even taken to driving a more nondescript car around town because it calls less attention to itself.

The decision on what to do, or how to act, after the problem situation has been defined and evaluated depends primarily on the situation. Some trouble situations may call for avoidance behaviors while others may call for the utmost in tact, diplomacy, and, as Richard puts it, "bluff." Being a successful nondelinquent in a high-crime community may depend on the ability to exhibit the "best" behavior, at the right time, and in the appropriate setting. This is no small task.

Verification of whether the most appropriate trouble-avoiding behavior has been used depends on whether or not it has been followed by punishing or reinforcing consequences. Both brothers report that they have had continued success with their trouble-avoidance strategies. They have never been arrested, and they have had few negative contacts with other *barrio* cliques which turned out badly for them.

Both brothers make use of *inner dialogues* to define, evaluate, decide, and reinforce their own behavior in trouble-avoidance situations (see Meichenbaum, 1977). An example of such a dialogue might be: "There are Boom-Boom and Loco from East Side Loma, and it's too late for me to do something to avoid them. Let me lay a rap on them about what's happening with their clique and the clique that they are getting it on (warring) with . . . . All right, the're going for it, now I can relax and not have to worry about getting into it with them. Now I know two more dudes from the Loma and they know me, and that may come in handy someday. *Firme!*"

Caesar states that he feels pretty comfortable in most social settings because he has more than one way of evaluating a situation and plotting a course of action. Caesar helps other "homeboys" to stay out of trouble by trying to increase their "awareness" of what is going on around them in the *barrio*—quite a natural behaviorist. He models appropriate, nondelinquent behavior for his younger brothers, sets general guidelines for them, and usually enforces those guidelines with some consistency. Richard states that he admires his older brother because he knows that he is being told the truth by him, and that his best interests are being kept in mind. Caesar has demonstrated this on numerous occasions by actively looking out for and taking necessary action in situations that might prove to be harmful to his younger brother.

Analysis of Social Relationships

Both brothers stated that the most important people in their environment are their immediate family and then the *barrio familia,* or close neighbors and peers with whom they have grown up. Particular emphasis was placed on "Hood," the ex-offender adult who has served time and is now serving as *barrio* counselor and prosocial model. Caesar states that, without a father, he naturally found himself looking up to "Hood." Richard, on the other hand, emphasized the strong prosocial modeling of his brother as a major influence on his behavior.

It is interesting to note here that much research and theory on delinquent behavior has addressed itself to father absence as a major causal influence (see Nye, 1955). In this case, however, Caesar and Richard show that strong, naturally occurring, prosocial modeling effects can steer a child away from delinquent and/or gang affiliations and behavior, and that broken homes, per se, need not necessarily be the scapegoat for explanations of delinquency.

Both brothers go on to state that the models thus described facilitate positive, constructive, and prosocial behavior. Both "Hood" and the brothers' mother are seen as positively responsive individuals in that they are able to (1) listen attentively and without interruption, hear you out open-mindedly, (2) have a better understanding of problems because of their own life experiences, (3) refrain from passing value judgments or statements that put the advisee down, (4) set rules, guidelines for appropriate behavior, (5) help others in the *barrio familia* without expectation of reward or repayment (seen by both brothers as the most admirable trait), and (6) have the ability to express the "truth," that is, "tell it like it really is."

Antagonistic and problematic behaviors are seen to originate from members of other *barrios,* some *barrio familia* members with a heavy clique orientation, the police, and the news media that portray East Los Angeles in an exaggerated, negative light.

According to both brothers, it is difficult to remain nondelinquent because of police harrassment by deputies who "can't tell a *vato* from a straight dude, and that's what they're getting paid for."

Incentives for being a nondelinquent in a high-crime community seem to be rare. Caesar and Richard express some concern about the "payoffs" for being good. Caesar has a cogent complaint that there are job opportunities and programs for ex-offenders, and gang members are always getting publicity in the media. He graduated from high school and stayed out of trouble, and there is no program for him or others like him. Richard also stated that his easygoing manner and politeness are often thought of as being insincere (by some teachers) and as a sign of weakness, or being a sissy, by peers.

Both brothers agree that if a *vato* suddenly decided to "go straight," it would be extremely difficult, if not impossible, for him to do. Old connections—police, neighbors, "homeboys," and rival *barrio* cliques—would not support the change in behavior. Previous behavior in the *barrio* will tend to follow him, making change difficult to accomplish. Caesar cites the case of "Hood," mentioned earlier, who still experiences negative associations with old contacts despite the fact that he has led an exemplary life over the past five years.

According to Caesar and Richard, if you are a "straight dude," often the gang members will take it upon themselves to keep you straight. If an individual is seen by the gang as *firme,* yet straight, they may reinforce appropriate and constructive behavior in that individual, e.g. Caesar's car restoration, Richard's bicycle repairing. The gang may likewise actively keep straight individuals out of trouble by directly counseling them. ("Do you want to end up like us, you're together, you can go someplace, don't screw up like we do.")

Both brothers choose their friends based on shared activities and similarity of interests rather than pure neighborhood association. Caesar finds friends at work (when employed), car shows, and at school when he attended. Richard makes friends with peers of similar interests at school. Caesar reports that their mother has no influence over their choice of friends and that she does not mind their associating with members of a gang as long as they "hang around the fire without getting burned."

Analysis of Social-Cultural-Physical Environment

Both brothers agree that their *barrio* is a nice place to live, despite the kinds of problems that it has. Caesar states that media portrayal of East Los Angeles has created an exaggerated sense of fear in outsiders, but that he has found it a help to his personal development rather than a hindrance. Caesar states that he has learned how to survive in East Los Angeles and that his training has better equipped him for life's difficulties than, for example, children from safer, middle-class neighborhoods. Richard expressed concern that too many neighbors are fearful for themselves and their children, afraid of being robbed, vandalized, or hurt.

The brothers see their *barrio* as adequate in terms of its

social, intellectual, and religious life. Both agree that it is lacking in appropriate recreational facilities (teen posts, youth centers, parks, swimming pools, etc.) and vocational opportunities.

Caesar states that the activities of the *barrio* cliques and the police have helped to create an atmosphere of restricted movement due primarily to the cliques' indiscriminate assaultive behavior and also to police patrolling practices, especially in the latter part of the evening when anyone on foot is suspicious and a cue for police contact.

Caesar reports that he does not feel the loss of personal freedom because he is always trying to learn how to move more smoothly among the different *barrios* and is teaching his brother how to do likewise. He keeps as good an eye on the police as he does on the community, the rationale being that if you know where the police are, and which deputies are to be approached and which are to be avoided, you can usually avoid the possibility of negative contacts with them. He states that many of the non-Chicano police (and some Chicano police too) often insult the Mexican's intelligence by stereotyping them all as stupid and lazy. By successfully avoiding contact with the police Caesar asserts that he gets the last laugh and makes *them* out to be the idiots.

School is seen by both the brothers as valuable because of work skills and trades that can be learned but they stress that many "good" kids do not attend because (1) they would have to cross into a rival *barrio* clique's territory and (2) they are often ashamed of their own learning weaknesses. Good teachers were seen by Caesar as being qualified, that is, being properly educated and having the appropriate credentials and mental attitudes to work in primarily Mexican-American schools. Caesar remembers that some of the teachers he experienced did not have the necessary qualifications to do their job appropriately, were unconcerned or indifferent to the fact that many children were coming to school daily without having had anything to eat, and perpetuated the myth of the stupid, lazy Mexican. Richard reports that one of his teachers seems to be very upset all of the time and is continually taking pills to calm down. He also states that it is easier to stay out of trouble by going to school than by staying home, with the exception of gang-related violence at school. Richard also states that, although he does not think that school is offering him very much, it does make him feel good to know that he is at least not getting into trouble there.

CONCLUSIONS

The behavior analysis case study presented here has attempted to delineate the factors that contribute to the teaching, learning, and maintenance of behaviors incompatible with delinquency. Basically, we are looking at community problems from the point of view of those who live in the community but display none of the problems themselves, e.g. delinquent and violent gang behavior. Knowledge about nondelinquents and how they function in a high juvenile crime community is relatively untapped. It does appear that some individuals *are* learning to be nondelinquent, however, and that many factors influence that development. These behavioral analyses did discover a remarkable series of effective trouble-avoiding behaviors in these two brothers. The older brother learned these behaviors both by trial and error and by the shaping of an adult model in the community. He, in turn, then taught his younger brother these and other adaptive behaviors through modeling and reinforcement. The nondelinquent behaviors are maintained by successful experience and a good deal of social and self-reinforcement. Results suggest that nondelinquent, adaptive behavior *is* being taught and learned in this high juvenile crime community, and that natural mediators such as these two brothers could go on to teach this behavior to other young people in a community-based delinquency prevention program. Indeed, they have both expressed interest in doing so. Perhaps if the prosocial behavior discovered in nondelinquents were taught to delinquents as well, incarceration and/or removal from the community would become an obsolete treatment strategy.

Additional research can be done to determine more specifically the behaviors and their controlling variables that constitute nondelinquency. The current study is limited in that it is one case study of two brothers who may be rare exceptions in that they

Progress in Behavior Therapy with Delinquents

were both extremely articulate (one had gone to college for a year, making him highly unrepresentative of the community, i.e. top 1%). Participant observation, street-corner research approaches such as this one would add more definitive data if conducted on nondelinquents in a *variety* of settings, including, for example, *in vivo* observation of asset behaviors and controlling variables in school, home, work, and neighborhood. The research model, behaviorally analyzing *naturally occurring* adaptive and self-controlling behavior in high-risk populations, may well prove useful for other problems as well. In addition, behavioral analyses of *dyads,* or two persons in important social relationships, shows promise in understanding their reciprocal behavior.

In closing, it must be mentioned that the authors have been receiving a good deal of unexpected reinforcement from numerous community members and agencies for focusing on "something good about East Los Angeles for a change." Thus, studying nondelinquents does appear to be a meaningful path to follow. If only we could get this into the newspapers.

REFERENCES

Text

Bayh, B. Report of the Subcommittee to Investigate Juvenile Delinquency. Challenge for the Third Century: Education in a Safe Environment-Final Report on the Nature and Prevention of School Violence and Vandalism. Washington, D.C., U.S. Government Printing Office, 1977.

Cautela, J.R. and Kastenbaum, R.A. A reinforcement survey schedule for use in therapy, training and research. *Psychological Reports.* 1967, *20,* 1115-1130.

D'Zurilla, T.J. and Goldfried, M.R. Problem solving and behavior modification. *Journal of Abnormal Psychology.* 1971, *78,* 107-126.

Kanfer, F.H. and Saslow, G. Behavior diagnosis. *Archives of General Psychiatry.* 1965, *12,* 529-538.

Kanfer, F.H., and Saslow, G. Behavior diagnosis. In C.M. Frank's (Ed.) *Behavior Therapy: Appraisal and Status,* New York, McGraw-Hill, 1969, 417-444.

Meichenbaum, D.M. *Cognitive Behavior Modification,* New York, Plenum, 1977.

Nye, F.I. *Family Relationships and Delinquent Behavior,* New York, Wiley, 1955.

Reckless, W.C., Dinitz, S., and Murray, E.   Self-concept as an insulator against delinquency. *American Sociological Review* 1956, *21*, 740-746.

Reckless, W.C., Dinitz, S., and Murray, E.   The good boy in a high delinquency area. *Journal of Criminal Law, Criminology and Police Science,* 1957, *48, 1*, 18-25.

Reckless, W.C., Dinitz, S. and Kay, B.   The self-component in potential delinquency and potential non-delinquency. *American Sociological Review.* 1957, *22*, 566-570.

Scarpitti, F.R., Murray, E., Dinitz, S. and Reckless.   The good boy in a high delinquency area—four years later. *American Sociological Review.* 1960, *25*, 555-558.

Stumphauzer, J.S. (Ed.)   *Behavior Therapy with Delinquents.*   Springfield, Il.: Charles C Thomas, 1973.

Stumphauzer, J.S.   Social learning analysis of teenage alcohol and drug use. *Los Angeles County Medical Association Bulletin.* 1976, *106*, 12-13.

Stumphauzer, J.S. (Ed.)   *Progress in Behavior Therapy with Delinquents.* Springfield, Il.: Charles C Thomas, in press.

Stumphauzer, J.S., Aiken, T.W., and Veloz, E.   East side story: behavioral analysis of a high juvenile crime community. *Behavioral Disorders.* 1977, *2*, 76-84.

Szasz, T.   The myth of mental illness.   *American Psychologist.*   1960, *15*, 113-118.

Zifferblatt, S.M., and Hendricks, C.G.   Applied behavior analysis of societal problems, *American Psychologist.* 1974, *29*, 750-761.

AUTHOR INDEX

A

Abelson, P. H., 187, 218
Abuddabeh, N., 101, 115
Achenbach, T. M., 35, 42, 54
Ackoff, R. L., 188, 218
Agras, W. S., 94, 115
Aiken, T. W., 345-381
Alberti, R. E., 91, 93, 115-116
Alper, B. S., 119, 144
Allen, J. D., 16, 18
Allison, T. S., 73-90
Alvord, J. R., 11, 18
Amour, J., 321, 343
Arnkoff, D. B., 31, 33
Arnoff, D., 157, 185
Arrill, M. B., 191, 219
Atrops, M., 35, 54
Austin, N., 91, 115
Ayala, H. E., 126, 143
Ayllon, T., 8, 18, 273, 284, 322
Azrin, N., 8, 18, 273, 284, 322

B

Baer, D. M., 10, 18
Baily, J., 77-78, 90, 126, 143, 149, 154, 324, 343
Balcerzak, W. S., 187, 218
Bandura, A., 4, 19, 22-26, 32, 54, 58, 71, 157, 184, 218, 265, 343
Bartels, A., 119
Bayh, B., 346, 360, 362, 380
Becker, W. C., 227, 232
Becker-Haven, J. F., 156-185, 221
Bedner, R. I., 269, 284
Behles, M. W., 3, 15, 19, 146, 223-233, 235
Bem, S. L., 36, 54
Bennis, W., 187, 218
Berlson, B., 304, 316
Berne, E., 57, 72
Birtles, C. J., 12, 20

Bis, J. S., 239, 257
Bishop, B. R., 264-265
Boren, J., 256-257
Bloch, H. A., 304, 316
Blom, G. E., 34-55
Bolstad, O. D., 193, 219
Booraem, C. D., 93, 101, 115
Born, D. G., 191, 218
Bornstein, P. H., 40, 54
Bowers, K. S., 269, 285
Breiling, J., 242, 257
Broden, M. R., 326, 343
Bronfenbrenner, U., 150, 154
Braukmann, C. J., 4, 18, 118-145
Buehler, R. E., 8, 13, 19, 269, 284, 318, 343
Burchard, J. D., 4, 7, 18-19, 238, 257, 269, 284, 317-344
Burkhart, B. R., 3, 15, 19, 146, 223-233, 235
Burns, V. M., 238, 257

C

Cain, G. G., 187, 219
Candelora, K., 224, 233-235
Camp, B. W., 22, 34-55
Campbell, D. T., 128, 144, 226, 232, 274, 283-284
Cardarelle, J., 101, 117
Carter, D, E., 188, 219
Cartwright, D. S., 354, 360
Cautela, J. R., 12, 19, 364, 380
Chapman, J., 196, 221
Christie, R., 152, 154
Clement, P., 101-102, 115
Coates, T. J., 157, 166, 185, 197, 219
Cobb, J. A., 324, 344
Cohen, A. K., 152, 154
Cohen, H. L., 7-8, 19, 236, 239, 256-257, 269, 284
Cohen, J. E., 19

Cohen, S. I., 324, 343
Congers, R. E., 35, 54, 193, 220
Conley, R. W., 191, 219
Conners, C. K., 52, 54
Conwell, M., 191, 219
Cook, S. L., 187, 219
Corwin, J., 304, 316
Costello, C. G., 55
Cowen, E. L., 304, 316
Cronbach, L. J., 197, 219
Csanyi, A., 289, 301

D

Dahlem, N. W., 41, 54
Danford, H. G., 331, 343
Davidsen, W. S. II, 4, 18, 224-225, 232, 260, 265, 266-286
Davis, M. L., 191, 218
Davison, G. C., 28, 33, 157, 184
Deibert, A. N., 225-226, 232
DeLange, J., 304, 316
Denison, R. A., 188, 220
DeRisi, W. J., 9, 19, 56, 63, 71-72, 77, 89
Diament, C., 197, 220
Dinitz, S., 363, 381
Drabman, R. S., 326, 344
D'Zurilla, T. J., 372, 380

E

Eisler, R. M., 18, 94, 101, 115, 185
Eitzen, D. S., 146-155
Elashoff, J. D., 214, 219
Elias, A., 285
Elkin, R., 187, 219
Elliott, D. S., 238, 257
Emmons, M. L., 91, 93, 115
Empey, L. T., 119, 144, 285
Evans, J. W., 190, 221
Ewart, C. K., 166, 185

F

Fanshel, D., 192, 219
Farina, A., 26, 33
Fazzone, R., 102, 115
Ferris, C., 143
Figlio, R. M., 133, 145, 238, 258
Filipczak, J. A., 19, 236-258
Fixen, D. L., 4, 18, 20, 118-145, 154-155, 269, 285, 288, 301

Fleisher, B. M., 288, 301
Flowers, J. V., 93, 101, 115
Flynn, F. T., 304, 316
Fo, W. S. O., 13, 19, 302-316
Fox, P. D., 188, 219
Franks, C. M., 268, 285
Frease, D. E., 238, 257
Freund, J. E., 310, 316
Friedman, R. M., 236-258
Fuller, E., 317-344
Furniss, J. M., 8, 19, 269, 284, 318, 343

G

Gallimore, R., 324, 344
Ganzer, V. J., 96, 116, 267, 285
Gardner, E. A., 304, 316
Geis, F. L., 154
Gelder, M., 5, 19
Gelfand, D. M., 196, 220
Gittleman, M., 102, 115
Glesser, G. C., 197, 219
Glynn, E. L., 326, 344
Goffman, E., 26, 33
Gold, M., 238, 257
Golden, F., 225-226, 232
Goldenberg, I., 269, 285
Goldfried, M. R., 157, 184, 372, 380
Goldman, T. A., 188, 219
Goldstein, A. P., 102, 115
Goldstein, B., 102, 115
Gonzales, M., 289, 301
Goodman, J., 36, 39-42, 51, 55, 262
Graubard, A., 238, 257
Greathouse, L., 269, 284
Grosser, C., 304, 316
Gruver, G. C., 285
Guerney, B. G., Jr., 304, 316

H

Haggard, E. A., 196, 219
Hall, R. V., 326, 343
Hammerlynck, L. A., 33, 116, 219-221
Handy, L. C., 116, 219
Handy, L. D., 33, 220-221
Harig, P. T., 4, 18, 238, 257, 343
Harlow, E., 304, 316
Harper, T. M., 126, 144
Hartmann, D. P., 196, 220
Hauserman, N., 101, 115-116

Haven, W. G., 156-222
Hays, W. L., 202, 219, 279, 285
Hedquist, F. J., 101, 116
Heller, K., 102, 115
Hendricks, C. G., 364, 381
Henry, W. E., 304, 316
Herbert, F., 34-55
Hersen, M., 18, 94, 101, 115, 185
Hiebert, S., 190, 219
Hiken, J. R., 196, 219
Hirschi, T., 238, 257
Hobbs, H., 304, 316
Holden, H. M., 5-6, 19
Holland, J. G., 62, 72
Hollister, R. G., 187, 219
Homme, L., 289, 301

I

Isaac, K. S., 196, 219

J

Jakubowski, P., 95, 116
James, H., 119, 144, 285
Jastak, J. F., 274, 285
Jastak, S. R., 274, 285
Jeffery, R. W., 214, 222
Jensen, D. E., 101, 115
Jesness, C. F., 3, 9, 19, 56-72, 73, 77, 89
Johnson, S. M., 193, 219
Johnston, J. M., 221
Jones, H. G., 5, 19
Jones, R. R., 35, 54, 193, 220

K

Kagan, J., 35, 38, 42, 55
Kahana, B., 36, 55
Kahn, R. L., 189, 219
Kanfer, F. H., 157, 185, 261-263, 265,
  345, 348-349, 358, 360, 362-363, 380
Kanowitz, J., 197, 220
Karacki, L., 8, 19
Karoly, P., 157, 185, 262-263, 265, 359-
  360
Kastenbaum, R. A., 364, 367, 380
Katz, D., 189, 219
Keller, O. J., 119, 144
Kelly, J. G., 304, 316
Kendall, S., 73-90

Kennedy, R. E., 28, 33
Kenney, D. A., 55
Kent, R. N., 187, 197, 220
Keyworth, M. J., 324, 343
Kirigin, K. A., 118-145
Klein, M. J., 324, 343
Klein, M. W., 347, 360-361
Klein, S. B., 156-185, 194, 221
Klein, W. L., 269, 285
Koenig, C. H., 188-189, 220
Krapfl, J. E., 188, 219
Krasner, L., 4, 6, 19, 27, 33, 58, 72, 268,
  286
Kraus, R., 331, 344
Krumboltz, J. D., 116, 188, 191, 220-221
Kuldau, J. M., 188, 219

L

Landau, P., 93, 95, 116
Lange, A. J., 95, 116
Lawrence, J. R., 219
Lazarus, A., 92, 95, 102, 116-117
Lefebvre, M. F., 317-344
Leitenberg, H., 18
Lerman, P., 133, 144
Levin, H. M., 188, 192, 217, 220
Levinson, R. B., 8, 19
Liberman, R. P., 12, 19, 119, 143
Lipsitt, L. P., 55
Livermore, P. E., 310, 316
London, P., 6, 19

Mc

MacCulloch, M. J., 12, 20
MacDonald, G., 324, 344
MacDonald, W. S., 324, 344
McCall, R. B., 45, 55
McCormick, P. M., 77, 89
McFall, R. M., 102, 116

M

Mabry, J., 268, 286
Mahoney, F. E., 27, 33
Mahoney, M. J., 22-33, 34, 157, 184-185
Maloney, D. M., 126, 144
Martin, M. F., 196, 220
Martin, M. J., 188, 220
Mash, E. J., 33, 116, 219-221
Meichenbaum, D. M., 22-23, 32-33, 36,

39-42, 51, 55, 262, 269, 285, 359, 361, 375, 380
Merbitz, C., 188, 221
Merton, R. K., 282, 285
Miller, I., 310, 316
Miller, L. C., 37, 39, 55
Miller, P. M., 18, 185
Miller, R. B., 321, 325, 343-344
Miller, R. M., 101, 115
Miller, W., 346, 360
Mills, C. M., 287-301
Milne, P., 101-102, 115
Minkin, B. L., 126, 144-145
Minkin, N., 126, 144-145
Mischel, W., 25, 33, 192, 220
Mitts, B., 326, 343
Moos, R., 69, 72
Murray, E., 363, 381
Mussen, P. H., 55

N

Nanda, H., 197, 219
Neufeldt, A. H., 189, 220
Newman, F. L., 188, 219
Nowicki, S., 151, 154
Nye, F. I., 375, 380
Nye, L., 289, 301

O

O'Dell, S., 187, 220
O'Donnell, C. R., 13, 19, 302-316
O'Leary K. D., 9, 20, 187, 220, 326, 344
O'Leary, S. G., 9, 20
Olson, V., 289, 301
Osgood, C. E., 140, 145

P

Palkes, H., 36, 55
Palmer, T., 127, 133, 145
Palumbo, A., 304, 316
Patterson, G. R., 5, 8, 11, 19, 20, 35, 54, 193, 220, 260, 265, 269, 284, 304, 316, 318, 324, 343-344
Paul, G. L., 283, 285
Paulson, T. L., 93, 95, 101, 116
Pearson, L., 42, 55
Pennypacker, H. S., 188-189, 220-221
Peterson, T. L., 101, 117

Petrock, F. A., 269, 285
Phelps, S., 91, 115
Phillips, E. A., 18, 20, 122, 126, 145, 154, 269, 285, 288, 301
Phillips, E. L., 16, 18, 20, 77-78, 90, 118-145, 148-149, 154-155, 269, 273, 285, 288, 301, 304, 316, 324, 343
Platt, J., 30-31, 33
Plotkin, A., 101, 115-116
Polk, K., 237-238, 258
Predoni, J. R., 101, 115

Q

Quay, H. C., 54, 96, 116
Quevillon, R. P., 40, 54

R

Rajaratnam, N., 197, 219
Rathus, S. A., 101, 116
Ray, R. S., 269, 285, 324, 344
Rechs, J., 289, 301
Reckless, W. C., 363, 381
Reese, S. C., 236-258
Reid, J. B., 35, 54, 193, 220, 260, 265
Ribes, E., 265, 343
Risley, T., 17, 20
Rivett, P., 188, 218
Robin, G., 133, 145
Robins, L. N., 133, 145
Robinson, M. J., 266-286
Rogers, C. M., 6, 20
Romanezyk, R. G., 197, 220
Rose, S. D., 304, 316
Rosenhan, D. L., 26, 33
Rosenthal, R., 197, 220-221
Ross, R. R., 269, 285
Rossi, P. H., 219
Rotter, J. B., 151, 154-155
Russell, M. L., 194, 221
Ryan, B. A., 235

S

Salgado, P., 143
Salgado, J., 143
Salkind, N. J., 45, 55
Salter, A., 92, 116
Sarason, I. G., 96, 116, 267, 285
Sasieni, N. W., 188, 218
Saslow, G., 261, 265, 345, 348, 360, 362-

363, 380
Satterfield, D. O., 92, 94, 116
Scarpitti, F. R., 363, 381
Schafer, W. E., 237-238, 258
Scheff, T. J., 26-27, 33
Schwitzgebel, R. K., 6, 20
Schwitzgebel, R. L., 6, 20, 269, 285
Seaver, W. H., 188-189, 220
Sechrest, L. B., 102, 115
Seidman, E., 4, 18, 224-225, 232, 260, 265
Sellin, T., 133, 145, 238, 258
Serber, M., 94, 116
Sexton, J. W., 188, 221
Shakow, D., 196, 221
Shaw, D. A., 269, 285
Sheridan, W. H., 119, 145
Shinn, E. B., 192, 219
Shivers, J. S., 331, 344
Shoemaker, M. E., 3, 13, 20, 91-117
Short, J., 289, 301
Shure, E. M., 30-31, 33, 39-43, 55
Siddall, J. W., 187, 218
Sidman, M., 277, 285
Siegal, S., 140, 145, 312, 316
Sinay, R. D., 12, 15, 21, 358, 361
Skindrud, K., 197, 221
Skinner, B. F., 6, 20, 62, 72
Slack, C. W., 6
Slavin, J., 256-257
Sloane, D., 73-90
Smith, M. B., 304, 316
Smith, M. J., 93, 106, 117
Snibbe, H., 17, 20
Snibbe, J. 17, 20
Solomon, R W., 318, 344
Spiker, C. C., 55
Spitalnik, R., 326, 344
Spivack, G., 30-31, 33, 39-43, 55
Sprague, R. L., 52, 55
Stachnik, T., 268, 286
Stahl, J. R., 317-344
Stanley, J. C., 128, 144, 226, 232, 274, 283-284
Stedman, J. M., 101, 117
Stein, T. J., 233, 235
Steiner, G. A., 304, 316
Stephens, T. M., 4, 18
Stern, L. W., 238, 257

Sternberg, R. S., 196, 221
Stewart, M., 36, 55
Storm, R., 242, 257
Strickland, B. R., 151, 154
Strodtbeck, F., 150, 155
Stuart, R. B., 11, 20, 25-26, 33, 77, 79, 90, 262-263, 304, 316, 324, 344
Stumphauzer, J. S., 3-21, 71-74, 77, 90-92, 96, 115, 118-119, 146-147, 156-157, 186-187, 221, 223-235, 259-265, 266-267, 287-288, 302-303, 317-318, 343, 345-381
Suci, G. J., 145
Sundel, M., 304, 316
Swartz, M., 152, 155
Szasz, T., 363, 381

T

Tangri, S. S., 152, 155
Tannenbaum, P. H., 145
Tavormina, J. B., 187, 221
Teicher, J. D., 12, 15, 21, 358, 361
Temerlin, M. K., 26, 33
Tharp, R. G., 13, 21, 77, 79, 90, 225, 232, 267, 269, 285, 288, 301, 303-304, 314, 316
Thomas, J. A., 188, 191, 214, 221
Thoresen, C. E., 116, 156-222
Thoresen, K. E., 156-185, 221
Timbers, B. J., 126, 144
Timbers, G. D., 126, 144, 149, 155
Tobey, T. S., 194, 221
Trotter, S., 191, 221
Twentyman, C. T., 102, 116
Tyler, V. O., 5-6, 21

U

Ullmann, L. P., 27, 33, 58, 72, 268, 286
Ulrich, R., 268, 286

V

VanDoorninck, W. J., 34-55
Veloz, E. V., 345-381
Venema, H. B., 224, 233-235
Voss, H. L., 238, 257

W

Wahler, R. G., 318, 344
Walker, R. A., 193, 221
Walter, T. L., 287-301

Weathers, L., 19
Wedge, R. F., 77, 89
Weinberg, S., 269, 284
Weiner, B. J., 44-45, 50, 55
Weinhold, B. K., 101, 116
Welch, L., 42, 55
Wenk, E. A., 237, 258
Werner, J. S., 126, 145
Werry, J. S., 52, 54-55
Wetzel, R. J., 5, 13, 21, 77, 79, 90, 225, 232, 260, 265, 267, 269, 285, 288, 301, 303-304, 314, 316
White, S. H., 55
Wilbur, C. S., 156-185, 194, 221
Williams, C., 12, 20
Williams, W., 187, 190, 219, 221
Winkler, R. L., 279, 285
Wolf, M. M., 18, 20, 78, 90, 118-145, 154-155, 269, 285, 288, 301, 324, 343
Wolfensberger, W., 119, 145
Wolfgang, M. E., 133, 145, 238, 258
Wolins, M., 192, 221
Wolpe, J., 92-94, 117
Wortman, P. M., 217, 221
Wotkiewicz, H., 9, 21

Y

Yablonsky, L., 346, 361
Yates, B. T., 186-222
Yates, A. J., 268, 286

Z

Zax, M., 304, 316
Zelhart, P. R., 269, 284
Zifferblatt, S. M., 364, 381
Zimet, S. G., 37, 39, 41, 53-54
Zweback, S., 101, 115-116

SUBJECT INDEX

A

Achievement orientation, 150-154
Aggression, 24, 89, 91, 94, 101, 108, 110, 112-114, 124 (*see also* Fighting and Gang violence)
developing self-control of, 34-55
Alcohol abuse, 12, 15, 358 (*see also* Drug abuse)
Arguing, 164-166
Assertion training, 13, 91-114, 259, 264
Attitudes,
changes in, 7, 68-69, 71, 139-141, 143, 146-154, 223-232
Aversion therapy, 12

B

Behavioral analysis, 261-262, 345-360, 362-380
Behavioral psychodrama, 12
Behavior modification (*see* Behavior therapy)
Behavior therapy,
abuses of, 10, 225
criticisms of, 6
definition of, 4
knowledge of, 226-232
principles of, ix, 14, 17, 76, 223, 227, 268
reviews of, 4
Bibliotherapy, behavioral, 259-264
Big brothers, 15 (*see also* Volunteers)

C

California Youth Authority, 9-10, 56-71
Clinic treatment, 11-13
Cognitive behavior modification, 22-33, 36, 95, 166-169, 175-176, 259-260, 262-264, 359, 374-375
Consultation, 14
Contracting, contingency 11-12, 64-65, 78-79, 163-166, 181, 259-264, 267, 271-

284, 289-300, 324-329
Cost effectiveness, 74-75, 88-89, 119, 139, 143, 182, 186-218, 242, 267, 280-283, 300, 342
Counter control, 27-29
Courts, juvenile, 73, 124-125, 132-136, 138, 142-143, 184, 269-284, 289-300, 304-305, 352

D

Diagnosis, psychiatric, 26, 126, 182, 194
Discipline, 7, 75, 244, 252-253
Diversion, 17, 119, 317
Drug abuse, 15, 59, 75, 81, 124, 355, 363 (*see also* Alcohol abuse)

E

Employers, training of, 287-300
Exhibitionism, 12
Extortion, 355-356

F

Family therapy, 11-13, 259-269 (*see also* Parents)
Family training, 248-256 (*see also* Parents)
Father absence, 375-376
Fighting, 80-81, 110, 158, 305, 328, 373-374 (*see also* Aggression)

G

Gang violence, 153, 345-360, 362-380
Generalization, 6, 10, 13, 42, 113, 157, 235, 254-256, 318
Grooming, 83, 86, 365-366, 374
Group homes, 15-17, 118-143, 156-184

H

Hyperactivity, 36-37

I

Iatrogenic labeling, 26-27
Imitative learning (*see* Modeling)
Impulsivity, 35, 42
Intelligence, 123, 125
    changes in, 7

J

Job programs, 271-284, 287-300, 332 (*see also* Unemployment)
Juvenile hall, 73-89

K

Kung-fu, mental, 91, 103-105, 109, 111

L

Locus of control, 147, 151-154, 303

M

Machiavellianism, 149-154
Medical model, 18, 268, 363
Modeling, 7, 12, 41, 201, 224, 375-377, 379
Murder, 59, 124, 350, 355, 362

N

Nondelinquents, 18, 347, 357-360, 362-380

P

Parents,
    counseling, 176-178
    teaching-parents, 16, 120, 159
Parole, 9, 66-68, 70
Peer reinforcement, 12, 318-319, 351
Police, 17, 132-136, 138, 142-143, 223, 274, 350-353, 362, 369-370, 374, 376, 378
Prevention, 18, 223, 236-256, 267, 297, 347-348, 359-360, 363
Probation, 14, 92, 97, 119, 125, 184, 259, 274
    officers, training of, 14-15, 223-235
Problem-solving, personal, 30-31
Psychotherapy, 11, 359
Punishment, 8, 12, 17, 28, 91, 159, 182, 224, 234, 260, 352

R

Recidivism, 67, 70 (*see also* Courts)
    cost of non-, 215-217

Reinforcement survey, 364, 367-369
Recreation programs, 324-343
    lack of, 378
Running away, 75, 81

S

School,
    achievement in, 7, 9, 16, 68, 83-84, 170-175, 236-274, 305, 314
    attendance, 134, 137-138, 142, 244, 274, 298, 328
    truancy from, 75, 158, 305, 311-312, 350
Self-control, 104, 156-157, 259-264, 348, 356-359, 372-375, 380
    training of, 166-169, 175, 178, 180
Self-esteem, 149-154, 250
Social skills,
    training in, 237-256
Stealing, 5, 75, 81, 158, 259-264, 350
Stimulus control, 24-26
Subject-experimenter psychotherapy, 6-7

T

Teachers,
    ratings by, 39-40, 325-329
    training of, 245-246
Television, 351
Territoriality, 356
Tests, psychological, 25, 38-39, 41
    (*see also* Intelligence)
Theft (*see* Stealing)
Token economy, 5, 7-11, 56-71, 77-89, 121, 126, 159-163, 239-240, 271-273, 331-343
Transactional analysis, 9, 56-71
Truancy (*see* School)

U

Unemployment, 350, 356, 366, 376

V

Vandalism, 17, 355
Vocational training (*see* Job programs)
Volunteers,
    utilization of, 302-315, 317, 329, 343

Y

Youth service bureau, 317-343